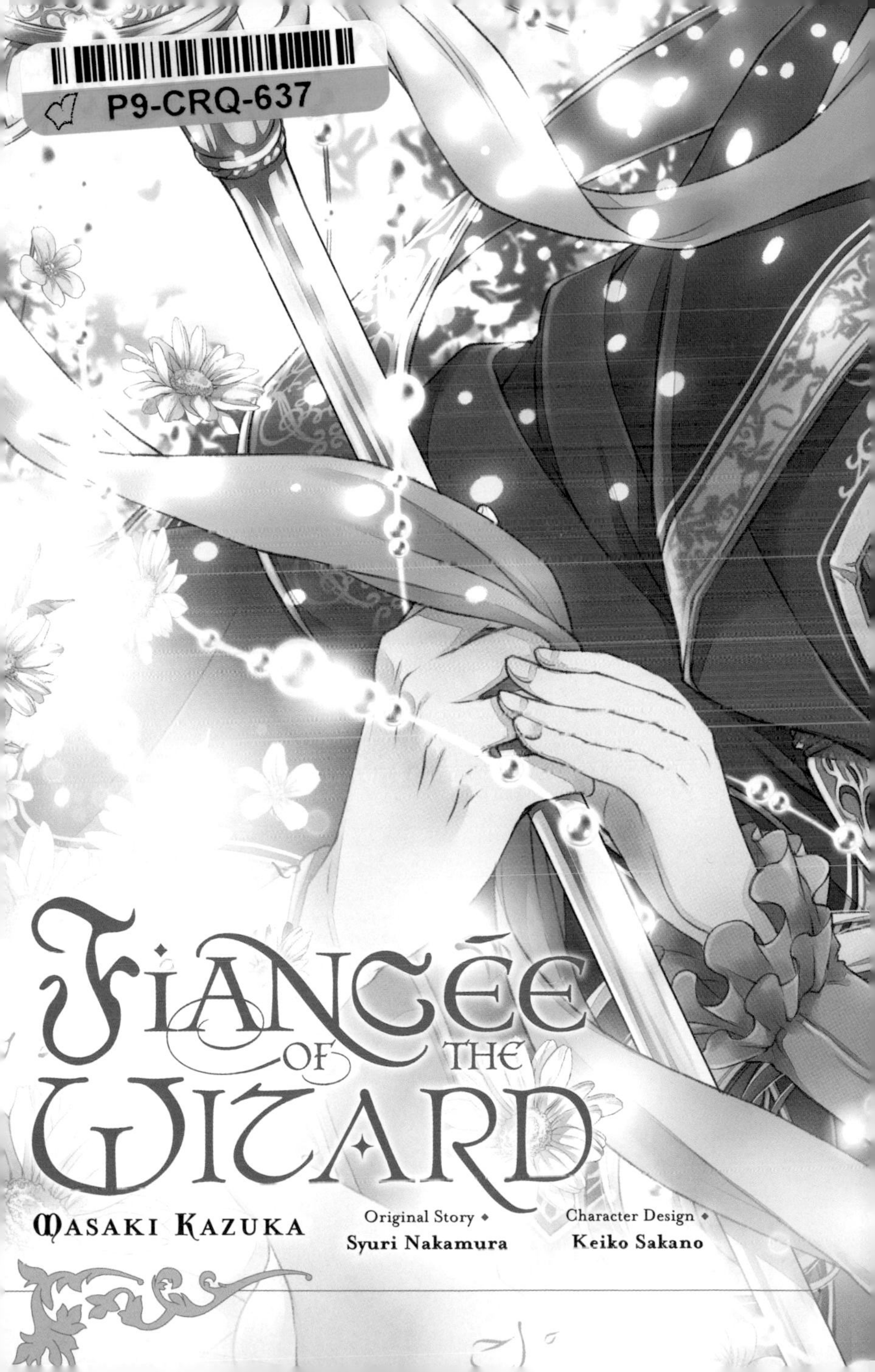

Fiancée of the Wizard

Masaki Kazuka

Original Story ◆
Syuri Nakamura

Character Design ◆
Keiko Sakano

CONTENTS

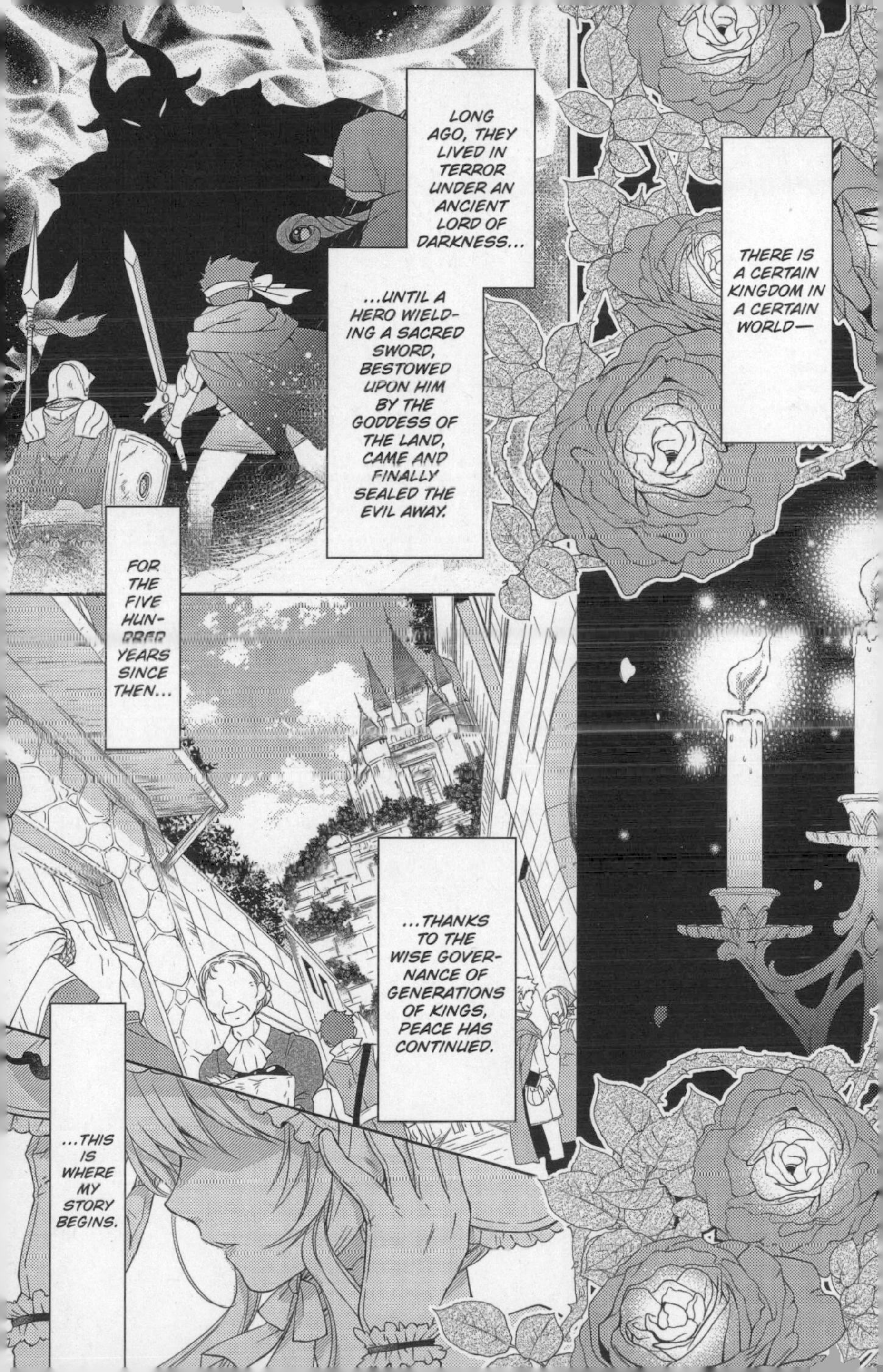
THERE IS A CERTAIN KINGDOM IN A CERTAIN WORLD—
LONG AGO, THEY LIVED IN TERROR UNDER AN ANCIENT LORD OF DARKNESS...
...UNTIL A HERO WIELDING A SACRED SWORD, BESTOWED UPON HIM BY THE GODDESS OF THE LAND, CAME AND FINALLY SEALED THE EVIL AWAY.
FOR THE FIVE HUNDRED YEARS SINCE THEN...
...THANKS TO THE WISE GOVERNANCE OF GENERATIONS OF KINGS, PEACE HAS CONTINUED.
...THIS IS WHERE MY STORY BEGINS.

I WAS REINCAR-NATED... REBORN HERE, IN THIS LIFE.

I WAS THREE YEARS OLD WHEN I REALIZED IT.

I FELL GRAVELY ILL, AND WHILE I HOVERED BETWEEN LIFE AND DEATH FOR MORE THAN A WEEK...

...I REMEM-BERED WHO I USED TO BE—A PERFECTLY ORDINARY CITIZEN IN A COUNTRY CALLED JAPAN, ON A PLANET CALLED EARTH.

WHEN MY THREE-YEAR-OLD SELF MADE A MIRACULOUS RECOVERY...

THE ECONOMY WAS BAD FOR A WHILE, AND I GOT LAID OFF. AS I WALKED HOME ON A DARK STREET, CURSING SOCIETY, I WAS STRUCK BY A CAR.

I PASSED AWAY JUST SHY OF MY THIRTIETH BIRTHDAY.

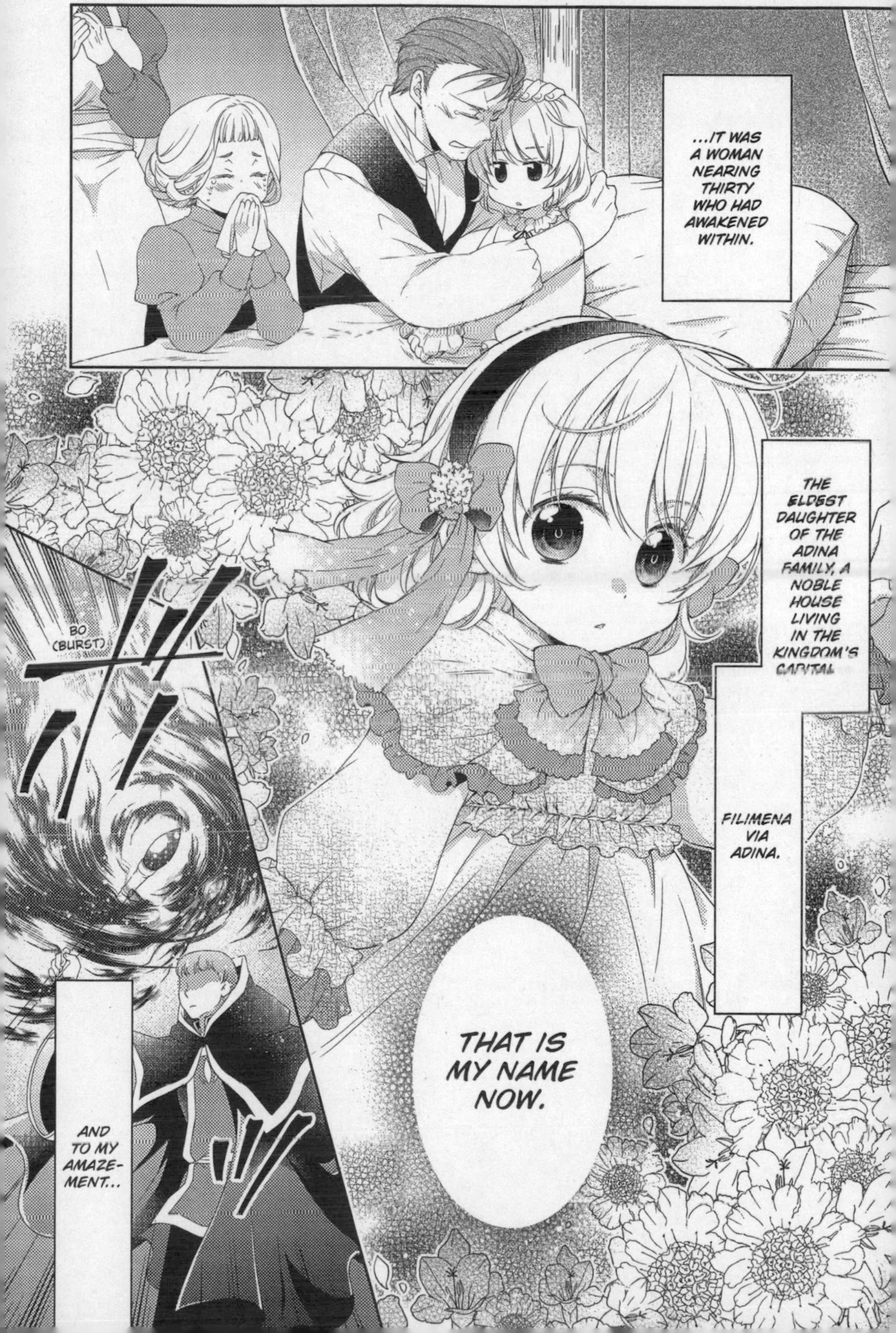
...IT WAS A WOMAN NEARING THIRTY WHO HAD AWAKENED WITHIN.
THE ELDEST DAUGHTER OF THE ADINA FAMILY, A NOBLE HOUSE LIVING IN THE KINGDOM'S CAPITAL
FILIMENA VIA ADINA.
THAT IS MY NAME NOW.
BO (BURST)
AND TO MY AMAZEMENT...

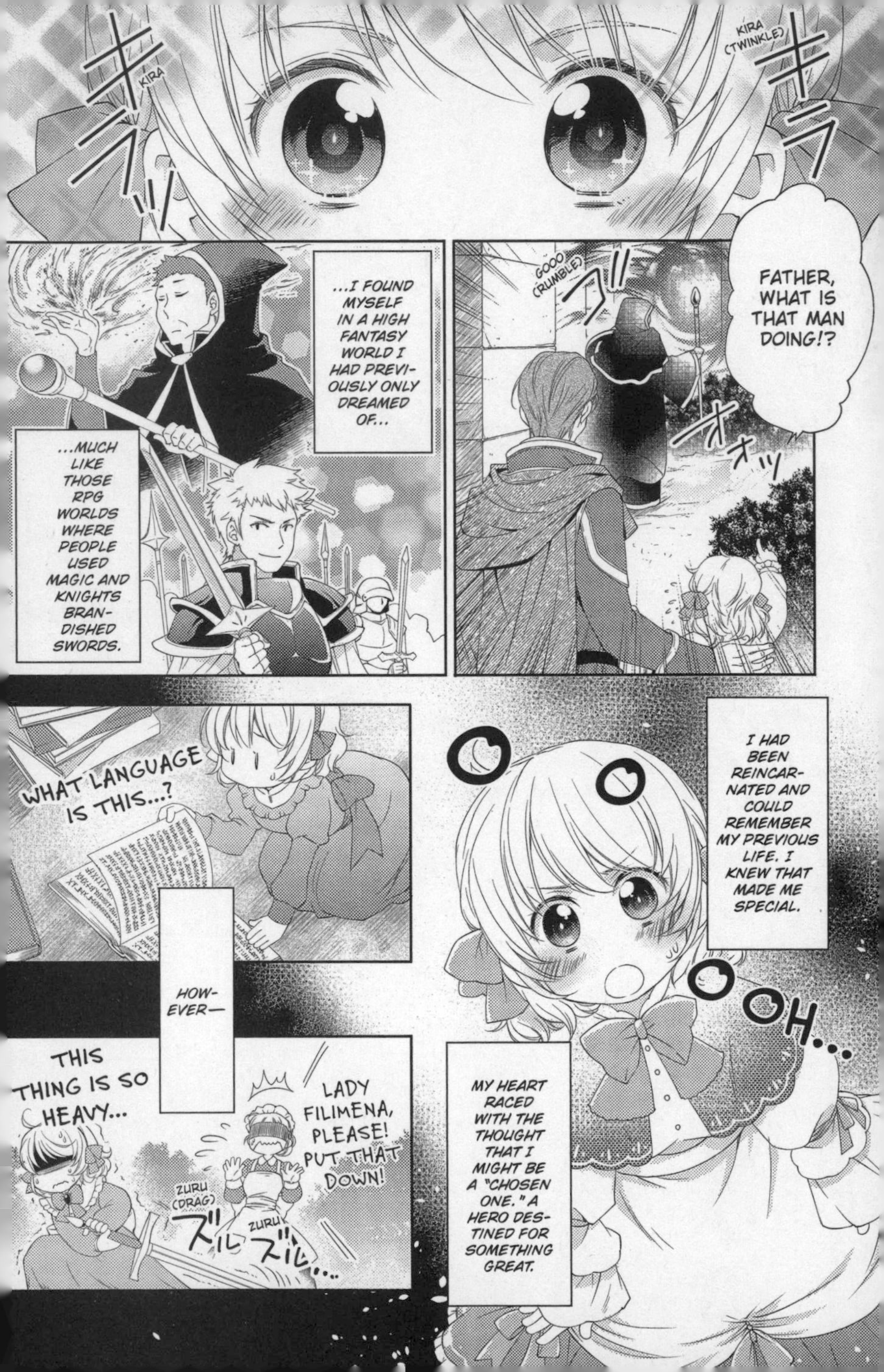
KIRA (TWINKLE)
KIRA
GOOO (RUMBLE)
FATHER, WHAT IS THAT MAN DOING!?
...I FOUND MYSELF IN A HIGH FANTASY WORLD I HAD PREVIOUSLY ONLY DREAMED OF...
...MUCH LIKE THOSE RPG WORLDS WHERE PEOPLE USED MAGIC AND KNIGHTS BRANDISHED SWORDS.
I HAD BEEN REINCARNATED AND COULD REMEMBER MY PREVIOUS LIFE. I KNEW THAT MADE ME SPECIAL.
OOOOH...
MY HEART RACED WITH THE THOUGHT THAT I MIGHT BE A "CHOSEN ONE." A HERO DESTINED FOR SOMETHING GREAT.
WHAT LANGUAGE IS THIS...?
HOW-EVER—
LADY FILIMENA, PLEASE! PUT THAT DOWN!
THIS THING IS SO HEAVY...
ZURU (DRAG)
ZURU

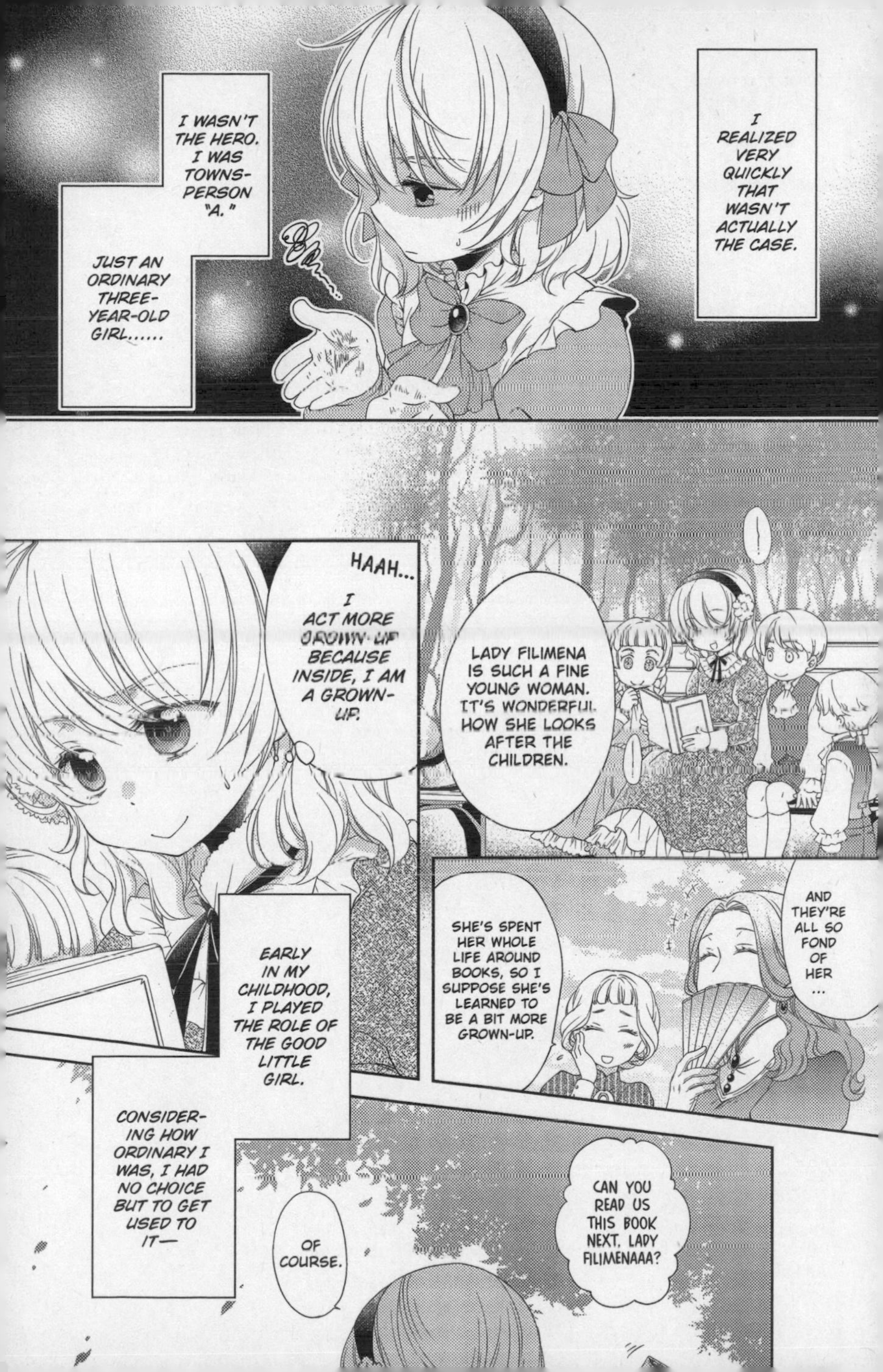
I REALIZED VERY QUICKLY THAT WASN'T ACTUALLY THE CASE.
I WASN'T THE HERO. I WAS TOWNS-PERSON "A."
JUST AN ORDINARY THREE-YEAR-OLD GIRL......
!
LADY FILIMENA IS SUCH A FINE YOUNG WOMAN. IT'S WONDERFUL HOW SHE LOOKS AFTER THE CHILDREN.
!
AND THEY'RE ALL SO FOND OF HER...
SHE'S SPENT HER WHOLE LIFE AROUND BOOKS, SO I SUPPOSE SHE'S LEARNED TO BE A BIT MORE GROWN-UP.
HAAH...
I ACT MORE GROWN-UP BECAUSE INSIDE, I AM A GROWN-UP.
EARLY IN MY CHILDHOOD, I PLAYED THE ROLE OF THE GOOD LITTLE GIRL.
CAN YOU READ US THIS BOOK NEXT, LADY FILIMENAAA?
OF COURSE.
CONSIDER-ING HOW ORDINARY I WAS, I HAD NO CHOICE BUT TO GET USED TO IT—

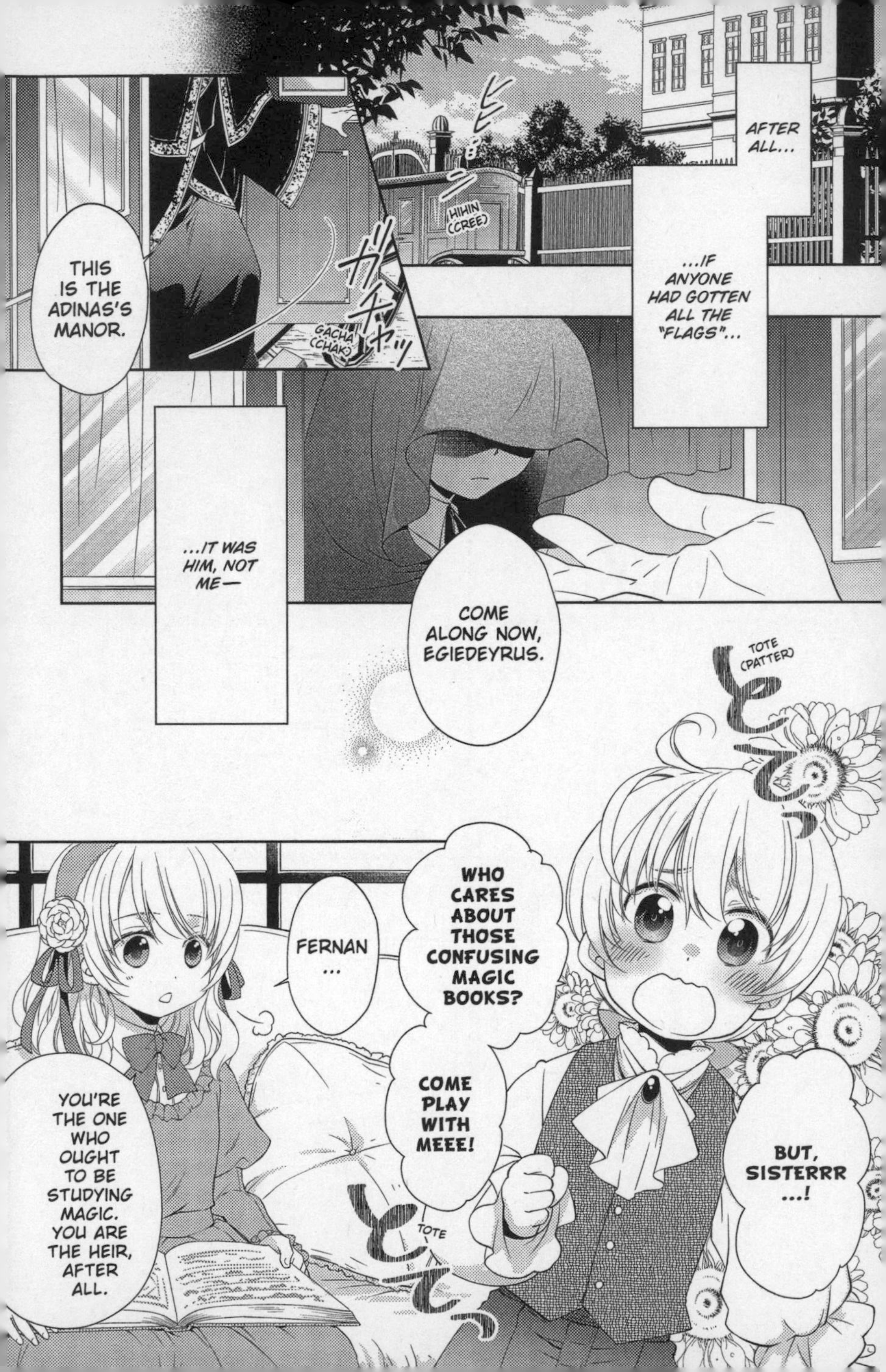
AFTER ALL...
HIHIN (CREE)
GACHA (CHAK)
THIS IS THE ADINAS'S MANOR.
...IF ANYONE HAD GOTTEN ALL THE "FLAGS"...
COME ALONG NOW, EGIEDEYRUS.
...IT WAS HIM, NOT ME—
TOTE (PATTER)
BUT, SISTERRR...!
WHO CARES ABOUT THOSE CONFUSING MAGIC BOOKS?
COME PLAY WITH MEEE!
TOTE
FERNAN...
YOU'RE THE ONE WHO OUGHT TO BE STUDYING MAGIC. YOU ARE THE HEIR, AFTER ALL.

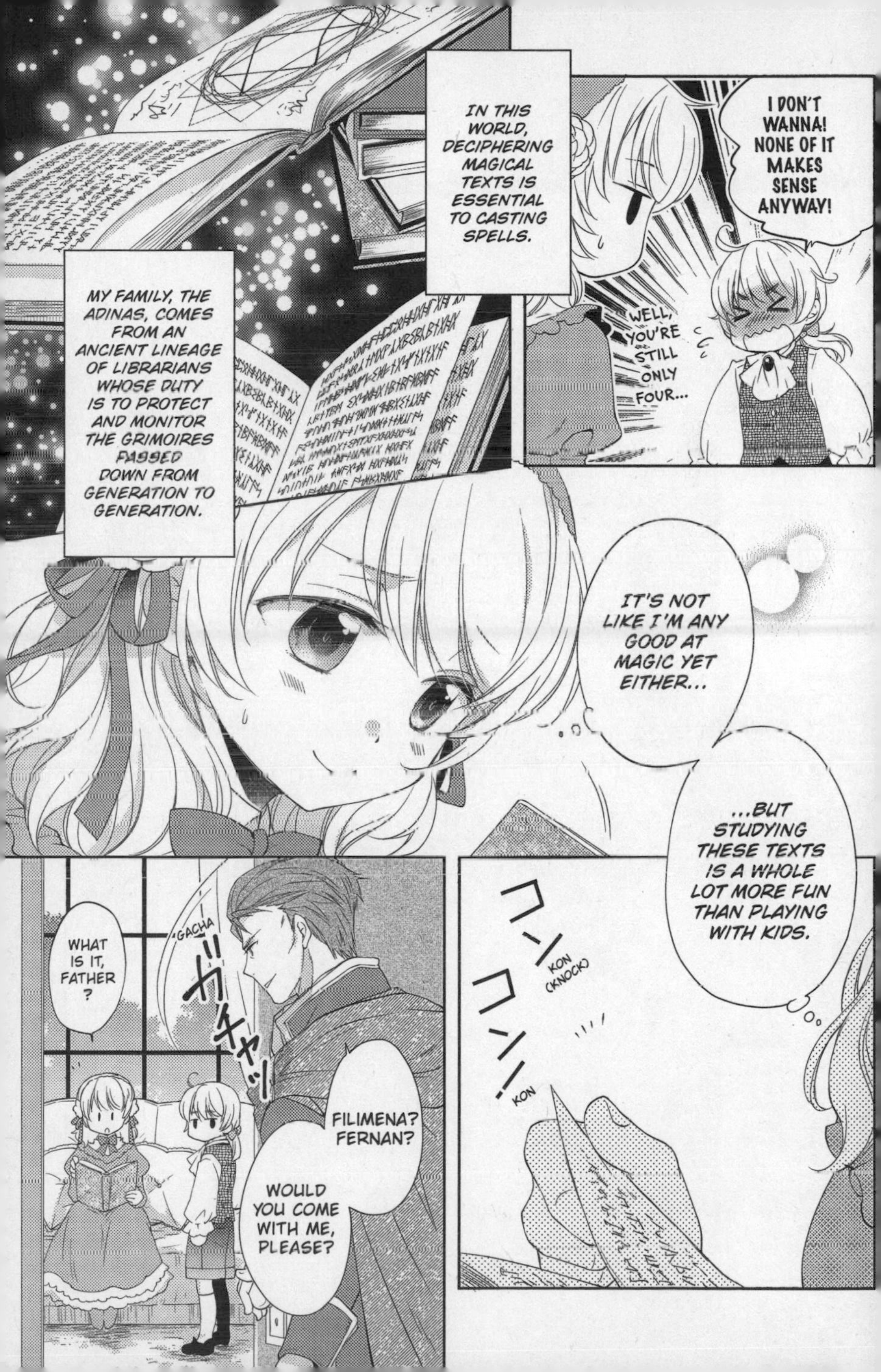

I DON'T WANNA! NONE OF IT MAKES SENSE ANYWAY!
WELL, YOU'RE STILL ONLY FOUR...
IN THIS WORLD, DECIPHERING MAGICAL TEXTS IS ESSENTIAL TO CASTING SPELLS.
MY FAMILY, THE ADINAS, COMES FROM AN ANCIENT LINEAGE OF LIBRARIANS WHOSE DUTY IS TO PROTECT AND MONITOR THE GRIMOIRES PASSED DOWN FROM GENERATION TO GENERATION.
IT'S NOT LIKE I'M ANY GOOD AT MAGIC YET EITHER...
...BUT STUDYING THESE TEXTS IS A WHOLE LOT MORE FUN THAN PLAYING WITH KIDS.
KON (KNOCK)
KON
GACHA
FILIMENA? FERNAN?
WOULD YOU COME WITH ME, PLEASE?
WHAT IS IT, FATHER?

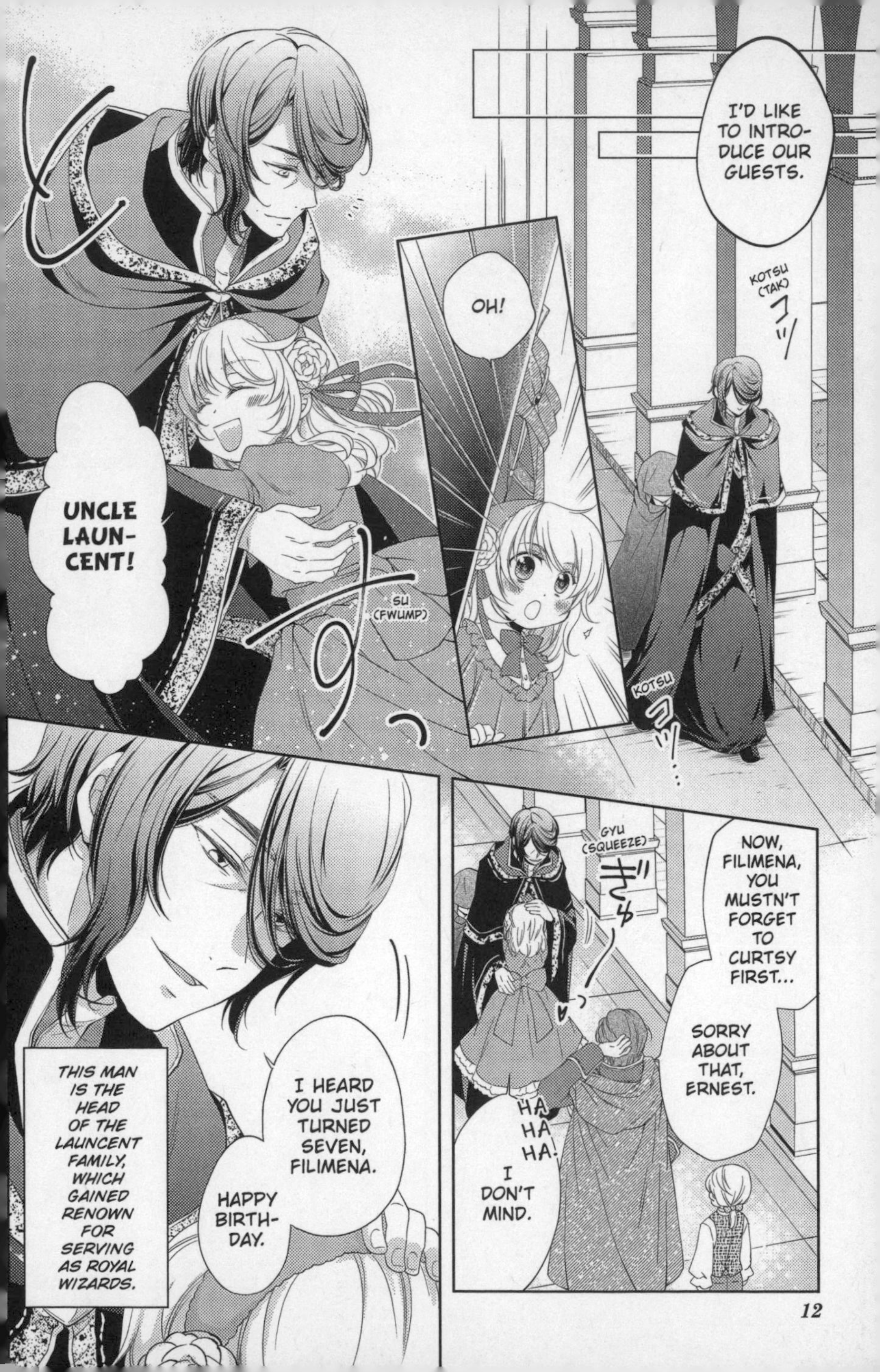

I'D LIKE TO INTRODUCE OUR GUESTS.
KOTSU (TAK)
KOTSU
OH!
UNCLE LAUNCENT!
SU (FWUMP)
NOW, FILIMENA, YOU MUSTN'T FORGET TO CURTSY FIRST...
GYU (SQUEEZE)
SORRY ABOUT THAT, ERNEST.
HA HA HA!
I DON'T MIND.
I HEARD YOU JUST TURNED SEVEN, FILIMENA.
HAPPY BIRTHDAY.
THIS MAN IS THE HEAD OF THE LAUNCENT FAMILY, WHICH GAINED RENOWN FOR SERVING AS ROYAL WIZARDS.

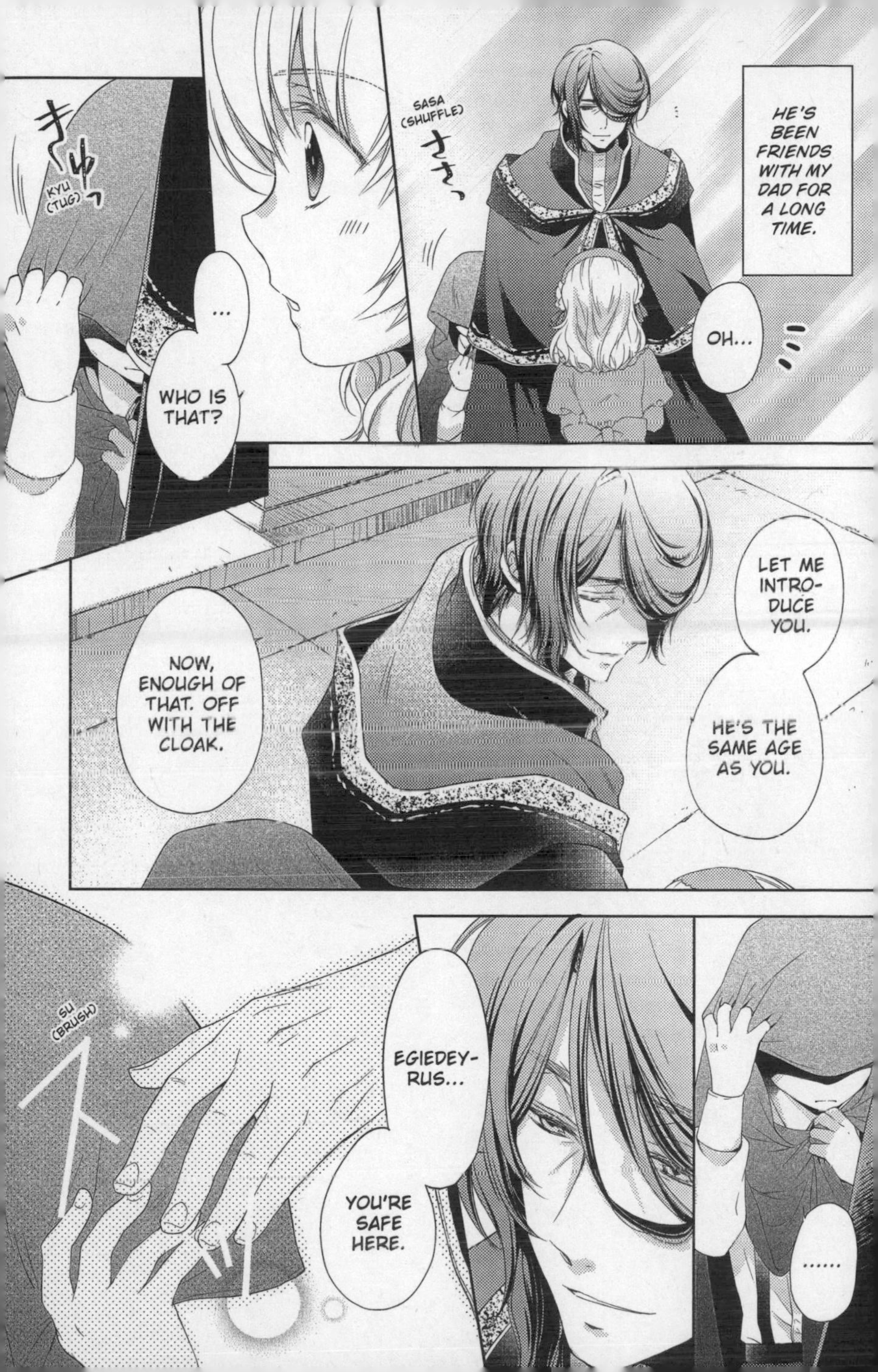
HE'S BEEN FRIENDS WITH MY DAD FOR A LONG TIME.
SASA (SHUFFLE)
OH...
KYU (TUG)
... WHO IS THAT?
LET ME INTRODUCE YOU.
HE'S THE SAME AGE AS YOU.
NOW, ENOUGH OF THAT. OFF WITH THE CLOAK.
......
EGIEDEYRUS...
YOU'RE SAFE HERE.
SU (BRUSH)

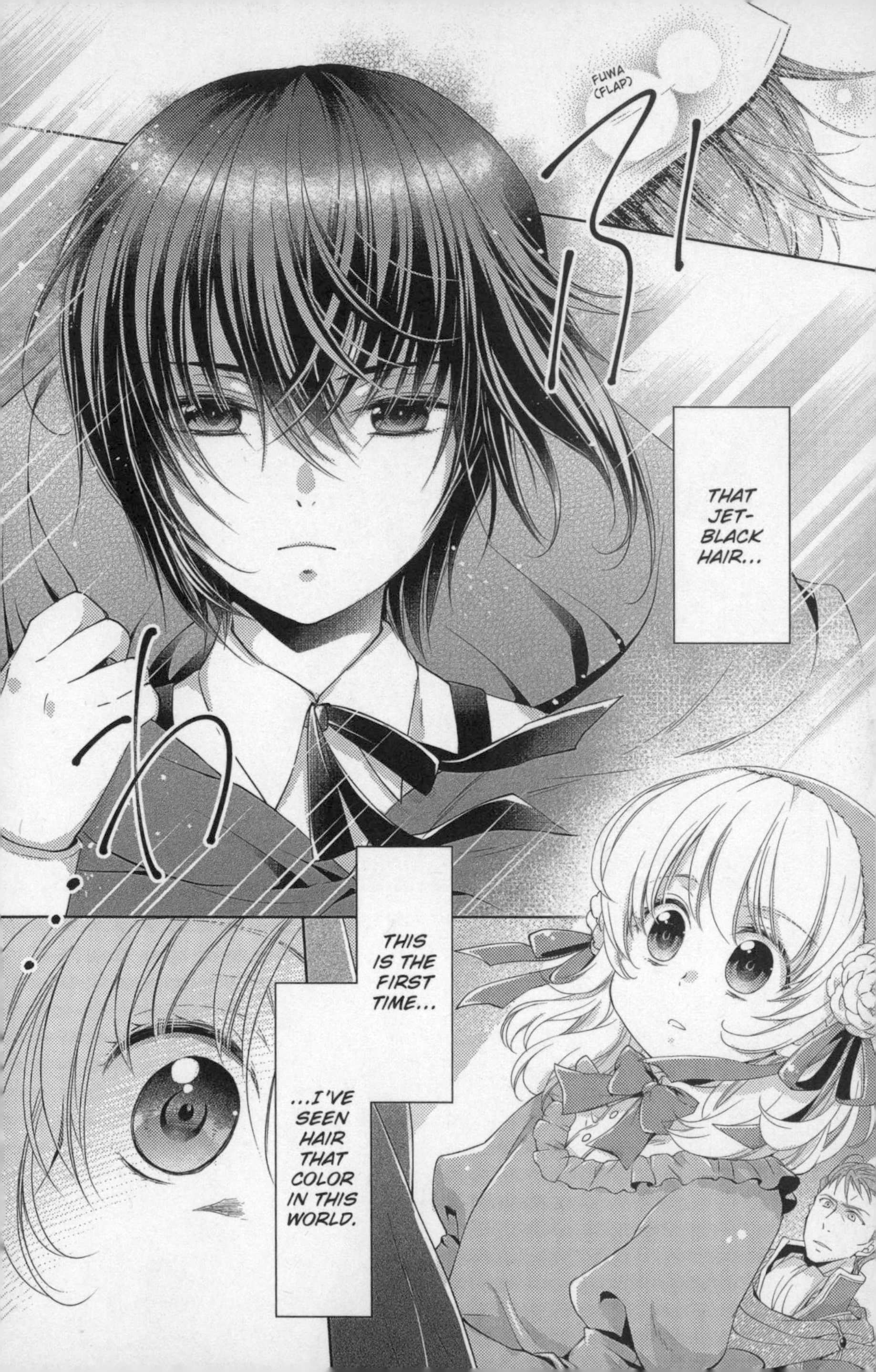
FUWA (FLAP)
THAT JET-BLACK HAIR...
THIS IS THE FIRST TIME...
...I'VE SEEN HAIR THAT COLOR IN THIS WORLD.

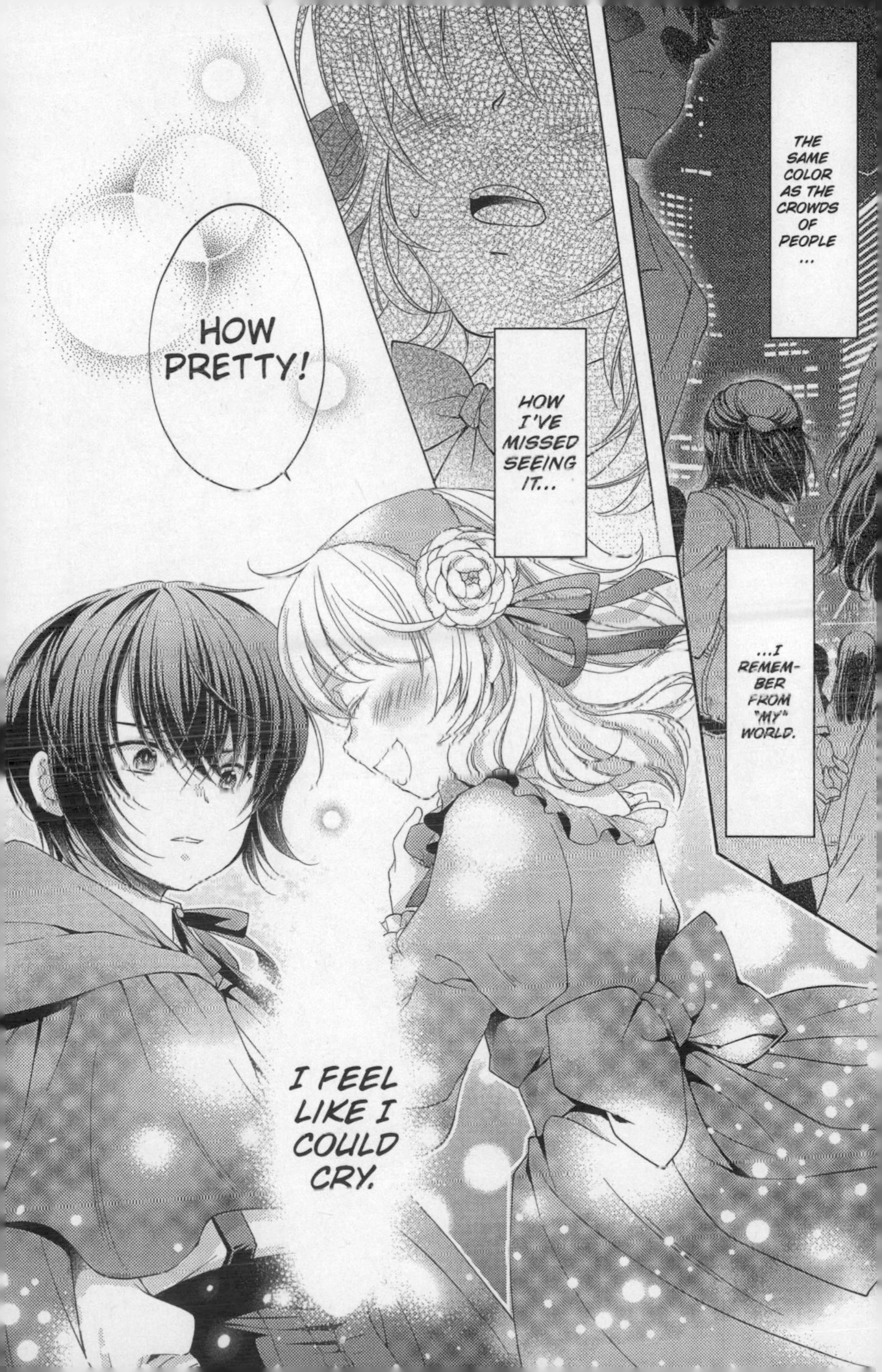
THE SAME COLOR AS THE CROWDS OF PEOPLE ...
...I REMEMBER FROM "MY" WORLD.
HOW I'VE MISSED SEEING IT...
HOW PRETTY!
I FEEL LIKE I COULD CRY.

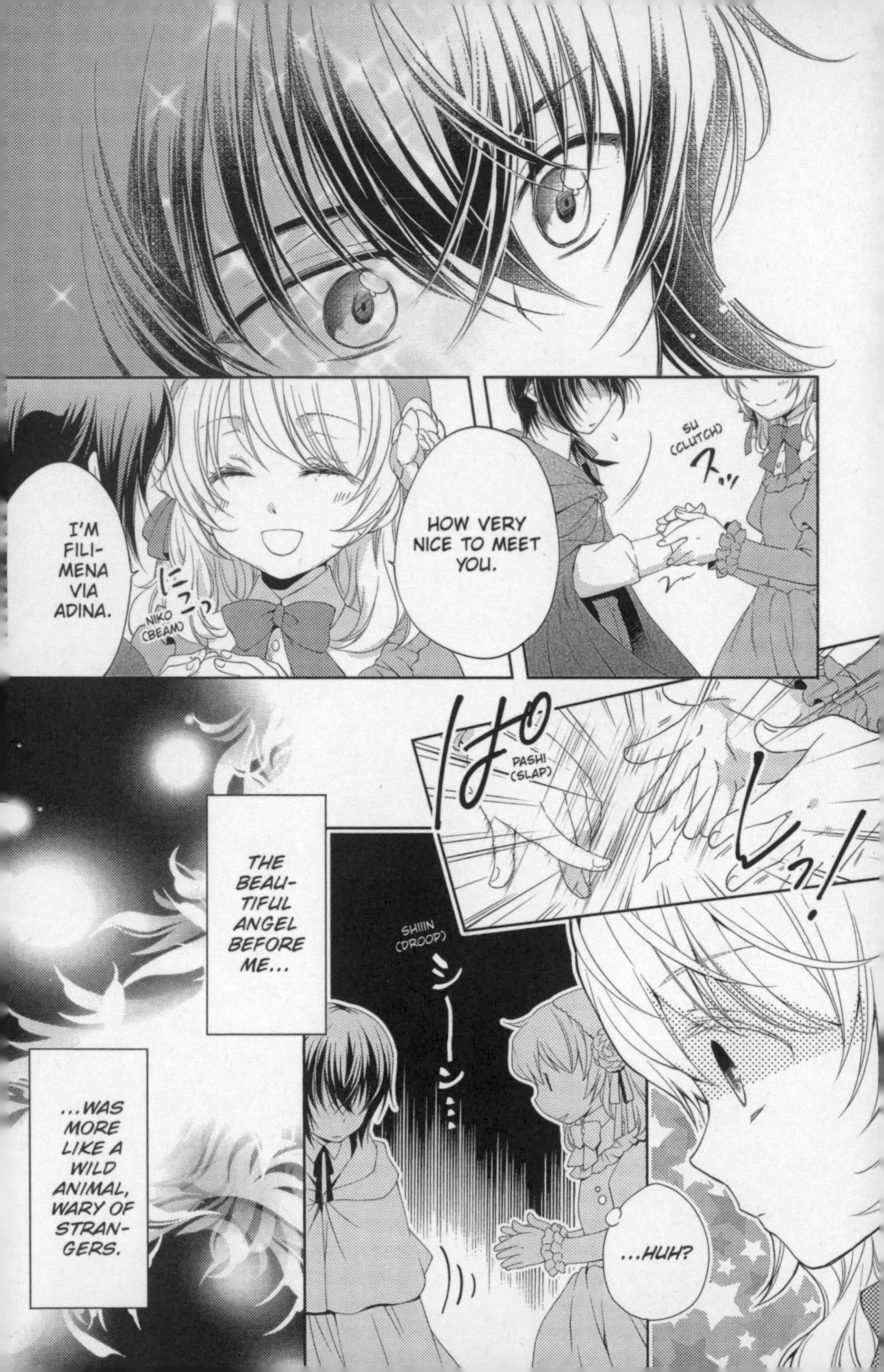
SU (CLUTCH)
スッ
HOW VERY NICE TO MEET YOU.
I'M FILI-MENA VIA ADINA.
NIKO (BEAM)
にこっ
ぱしっ
PASHI (SLAP)
THE BEAU-TIFUL ANGEL BEFORE ME...
SHIIIN (DROOP)
シーン…
...WAS MORE LIKE A WILD ANIMAL, WARY OF STRAN-GERS.
...HUH?

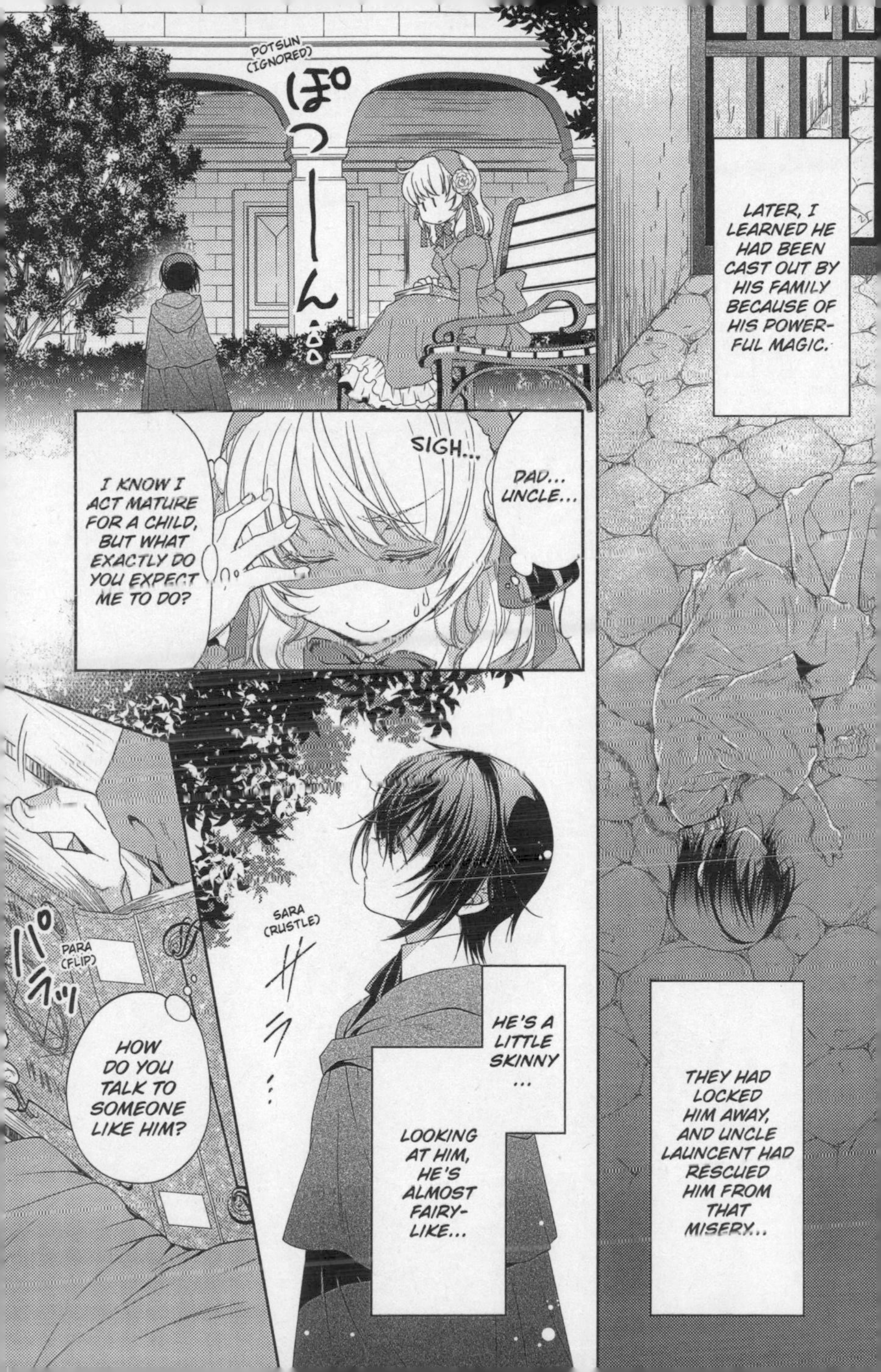
LATER, I LEARNED HE HAD BEEN CAST OUT BY HIS FAMILY BECAUSE OF HIS POWERFUL MAGIC.
THEY HAD LOCKED HIM AWAY, AND UNCLE LAUNCENT HAD RESCUED HIM FROM THAT MISERY...
ぽつーん
POTSUN (IGNORED)
SIGH...
DAD... UNCLE...
I KNOW I ACT MATURE FOR A CHILD, BUT WHAT EXACTLY DO YOU EXPECT ME TO DO?
HE'S A LITTLE SKINNY...
LOOKING AT HIM, HE'S ALMOST FAIRY-LIKE...
SARA (RUSTLE)
パラッ
PARA (FLIP)
HOW DO YOU TALK TO SOMEONE LIKE HIM?

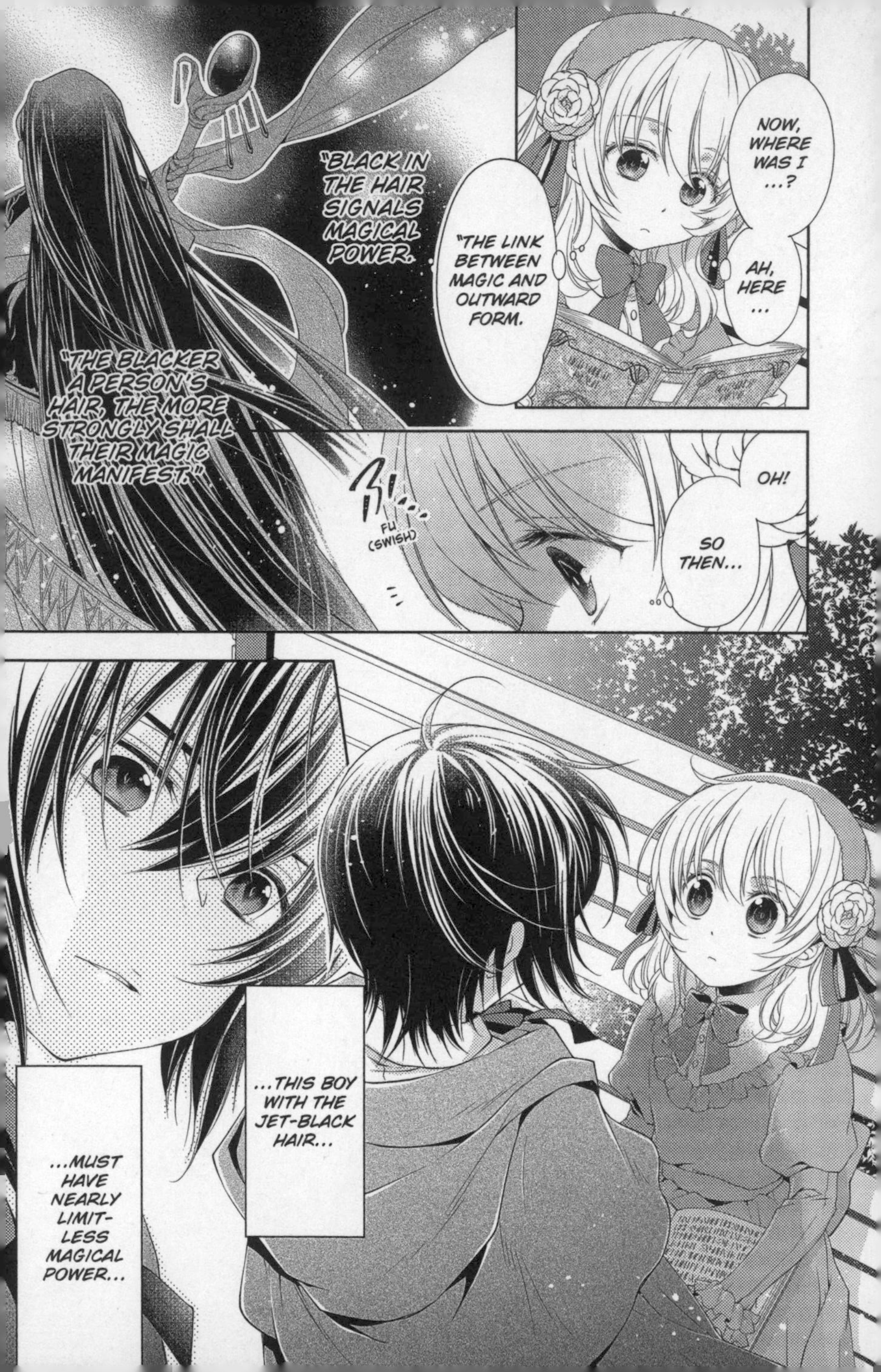
NOW, WHERE WAS I ...?
AH, HERE ...
"THE LINK BETWEEN MAGIC AND OUTWARD FORM.
"BLACK IN THE HAIR SIGNALS MAGICAL POWER.
"THE BLACKER A PERSON'S HAIR, THE MORE STRONGLY SHALL THEIR MAGIC MANIFEST."
FU (SWISH)
OH!
SO THEN...
...THIS BOY WITH THE JET-BLACK HAIR...
...MUST HAVE NEARLY LIMIT-LESS MAGICAL POWER...

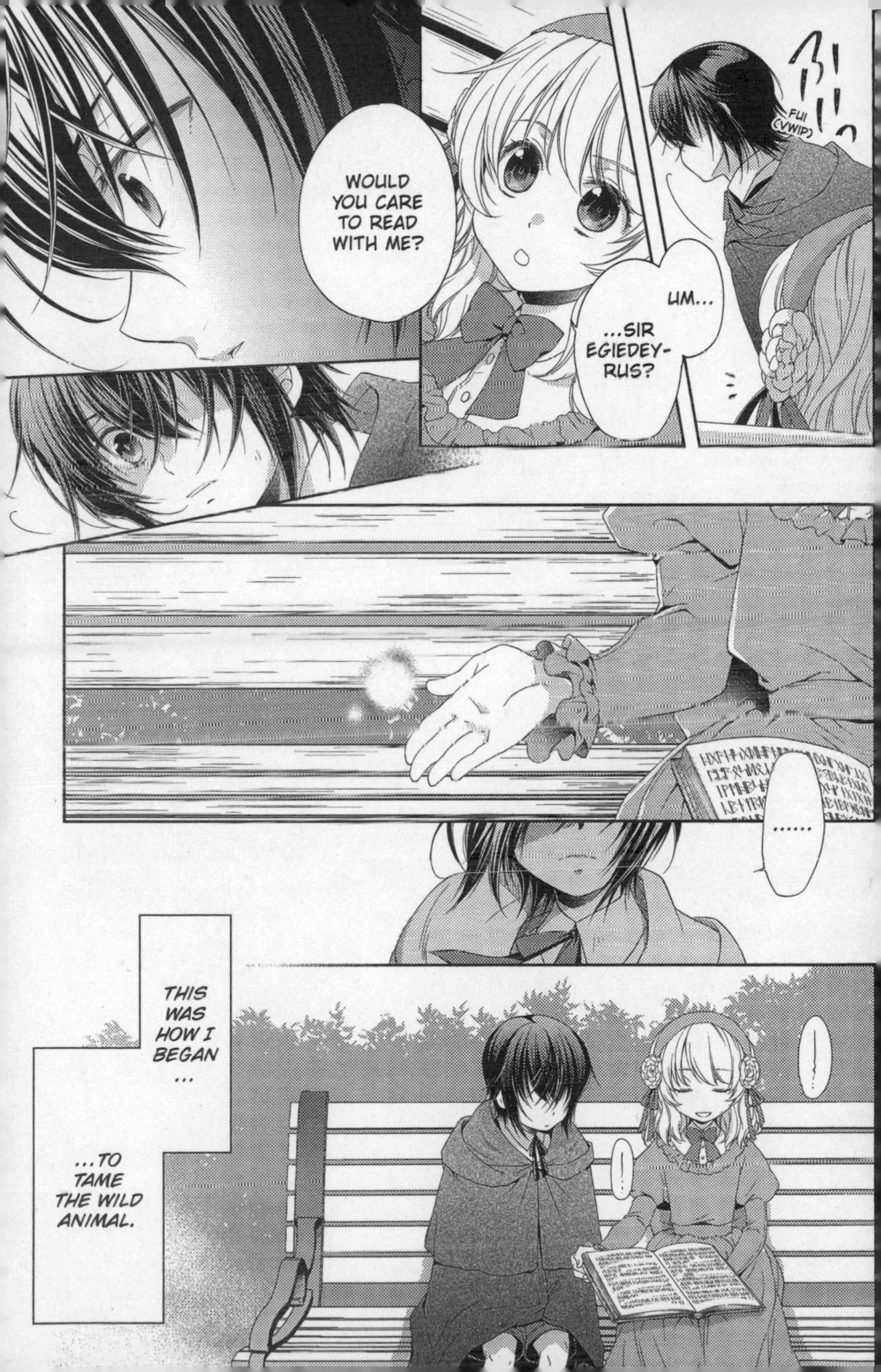
FUI (VWIP)
WOULD YOU CARE TO READ WITH ME?
UM...
...SIR EGIEDEY-RUS?
......
!
!
THIS WAS HOW I BEGAN ...
...TO TAME THE WILD ANIMAL.

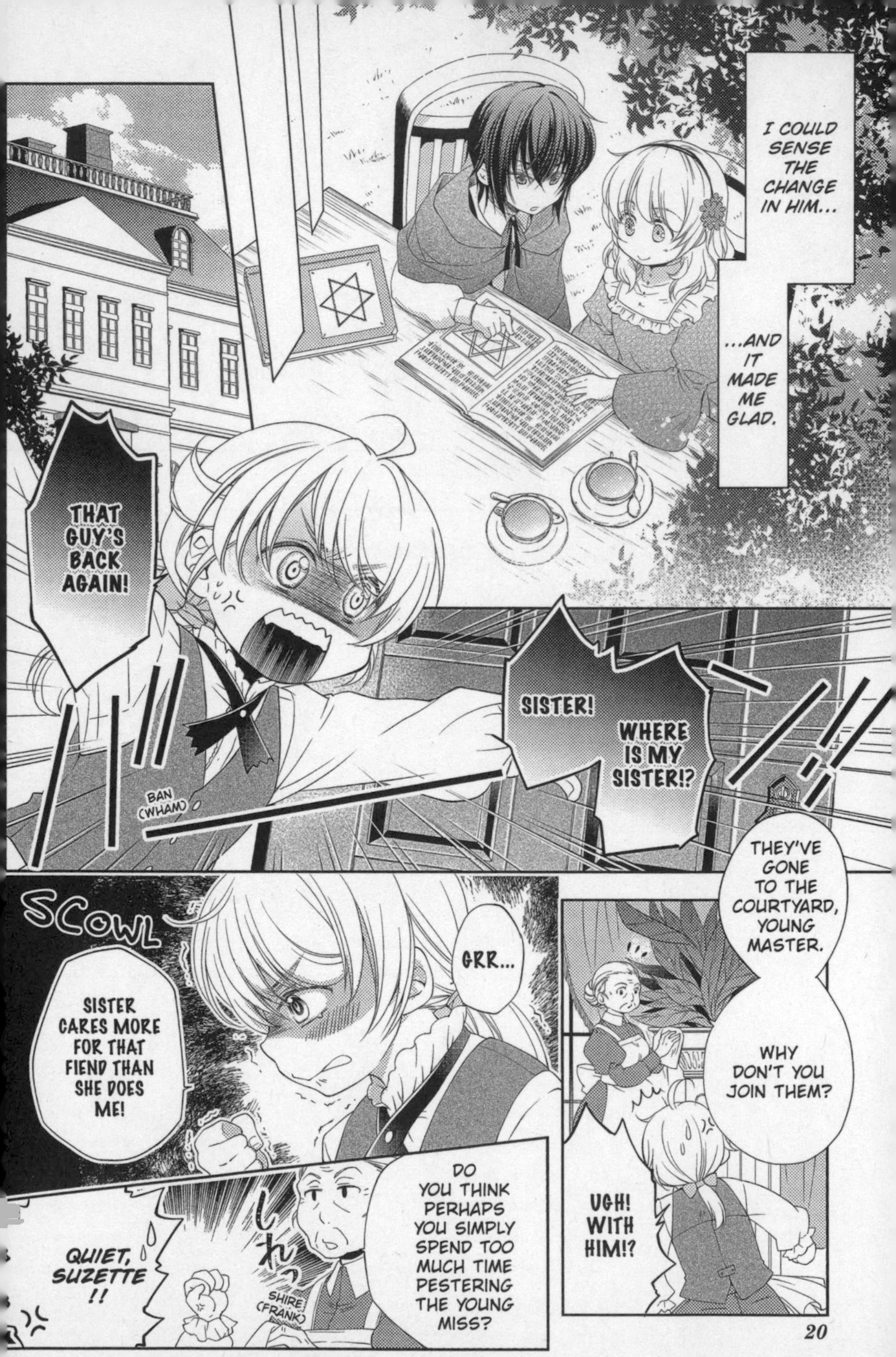
I COULD SENSE THE CHANGE IN HIM...
...AND IT MADE ME GLAD.
THAT GUY'S BACK AGAIN!
SISTER!
WHERE IS MY SISTER!?
BAN (WHAM)
THEY'VE GONE TO THE COURTYARD, YOUNG MASTER.
WHY DON'T YOU JOIN THEM?
UGH! WITH HIM!?
GRR...
SCOWL
SISTER CARES MORE FOR THAT FIEND THAN SHE DOES ME!
DO YOU THINK PERHAPS YOU SIMPLY SPEND TOO MUCH TIME PESTERING THE YOUNG MISS?
SHIRE (FRANK)
QUIET, SUZETTE!!

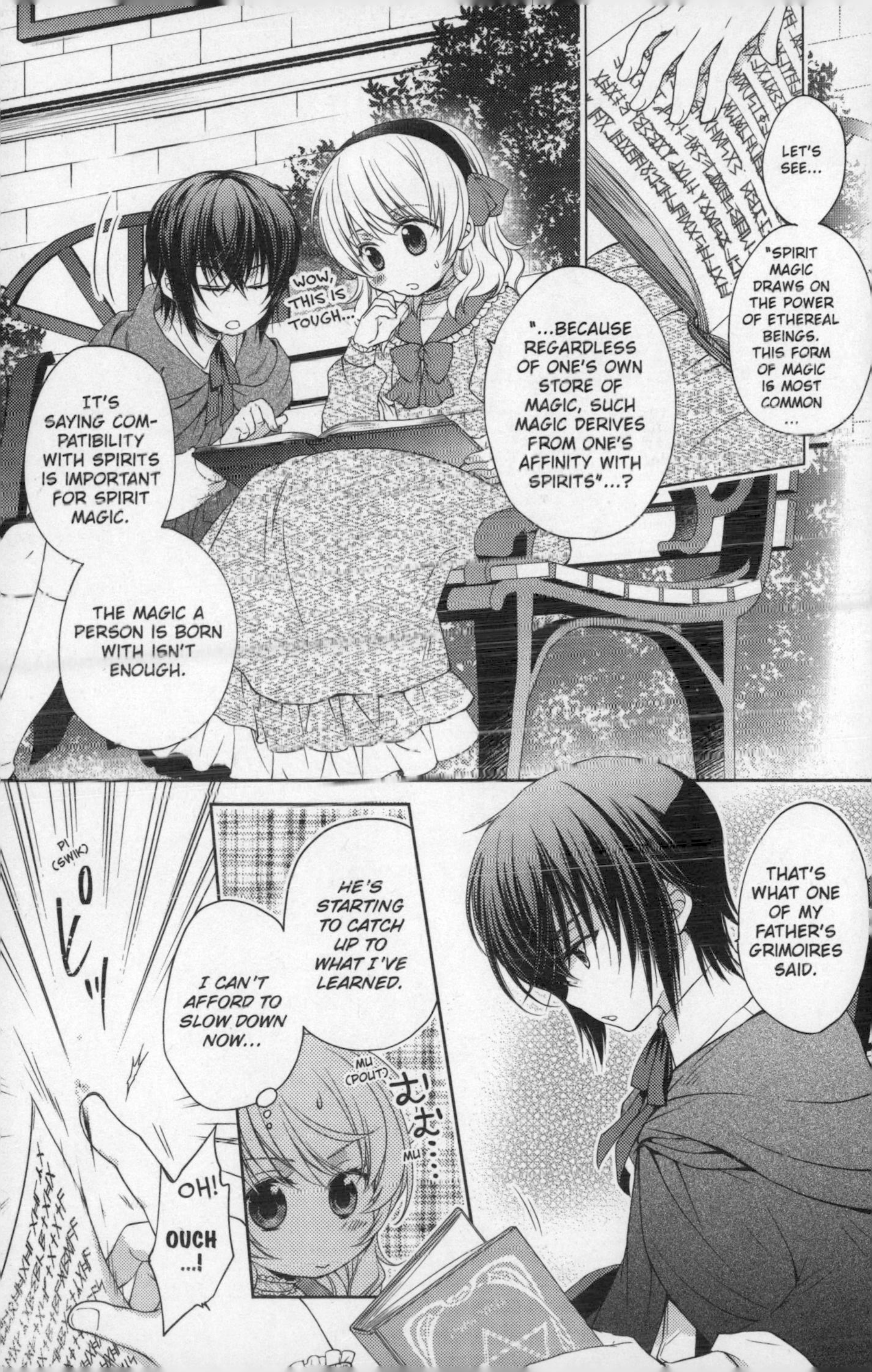
LET'S SEE...
"SPIRIT MAGIC DRAWS ON THE POWER OF ETHEREAL BEINGS. THIS FORM OF MAGIC IS MOST COMMON ...
"...BECAUSE REGARDLESS OF ONE'S OWN STORE OF MAGIC, SUCH MAGIC DERIVES FROM ONE'S AFFINITY WITH SPIRITS"...?
WOW, THIS IS TOUGH...
IT'S SAYING COMPATIBILITY WITH SPIRITS IS IMPORTANT FOR SPIRIT MAGIC.
THE MAGIC A PERSON IS BORN WITH ISN'T ENOUGH.
THAT'S WHAT ONE OF MY FATHER'S GRIMOIRES SAID.
HE'S STARTING TO CATCH UP TO WHAT I'VE LEARNED.
I CAN'T AFFORD TO SLOW DOWN NOW...
MU (POUT)
むむ…
MU
PI (SWIK)
ぴりッ
OH!
OUCH ...!

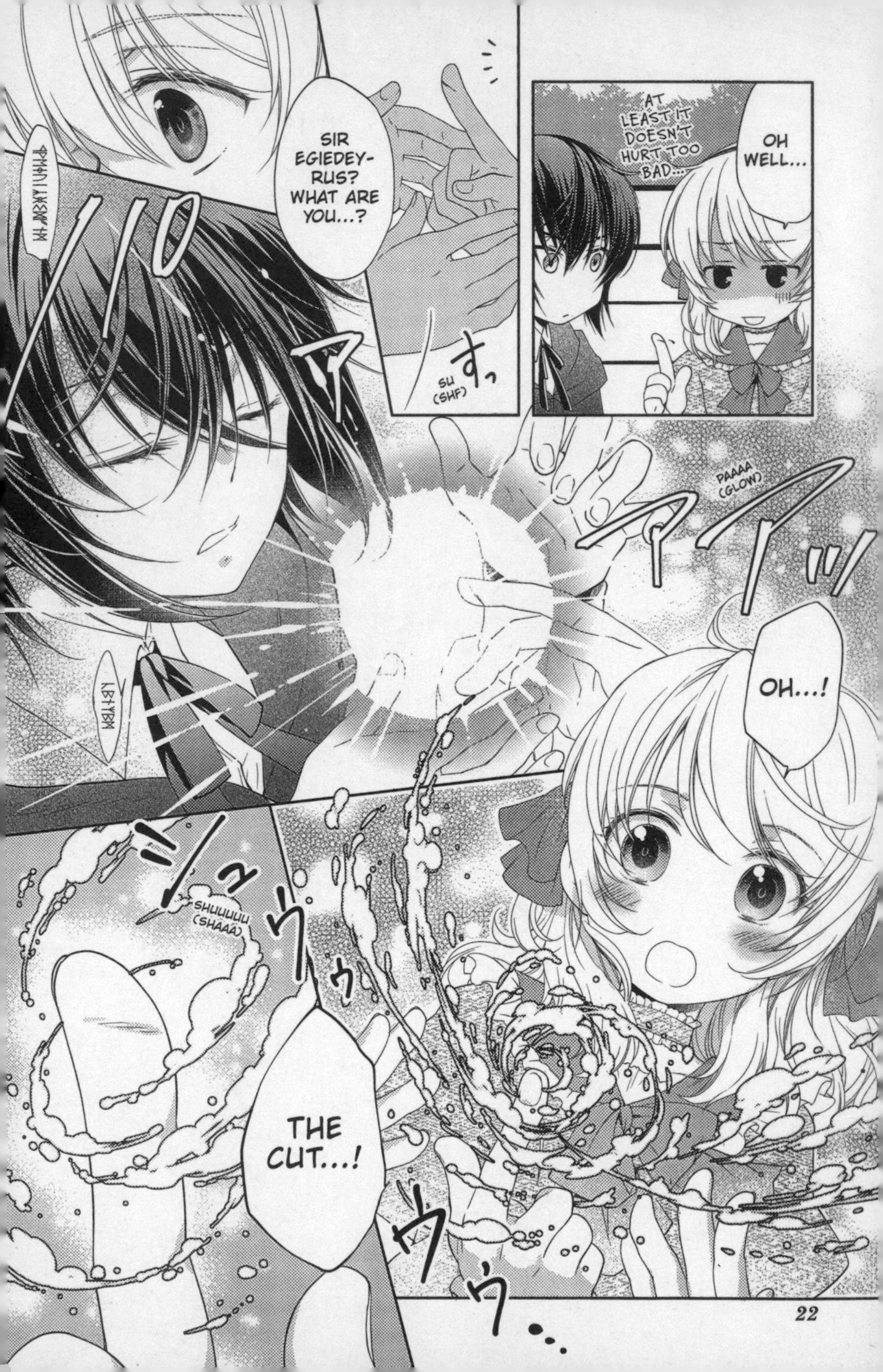
OH WELL...
AT LEAST IT DOESN'T HURT TOO BAD...
SIR EGIEDEY-RUS? WHAT ARE YOU...?
SU (SHF)
PAAAA (GLOW)
OH...!
SHUUUUUU (SHAAA)
THE CUT...!

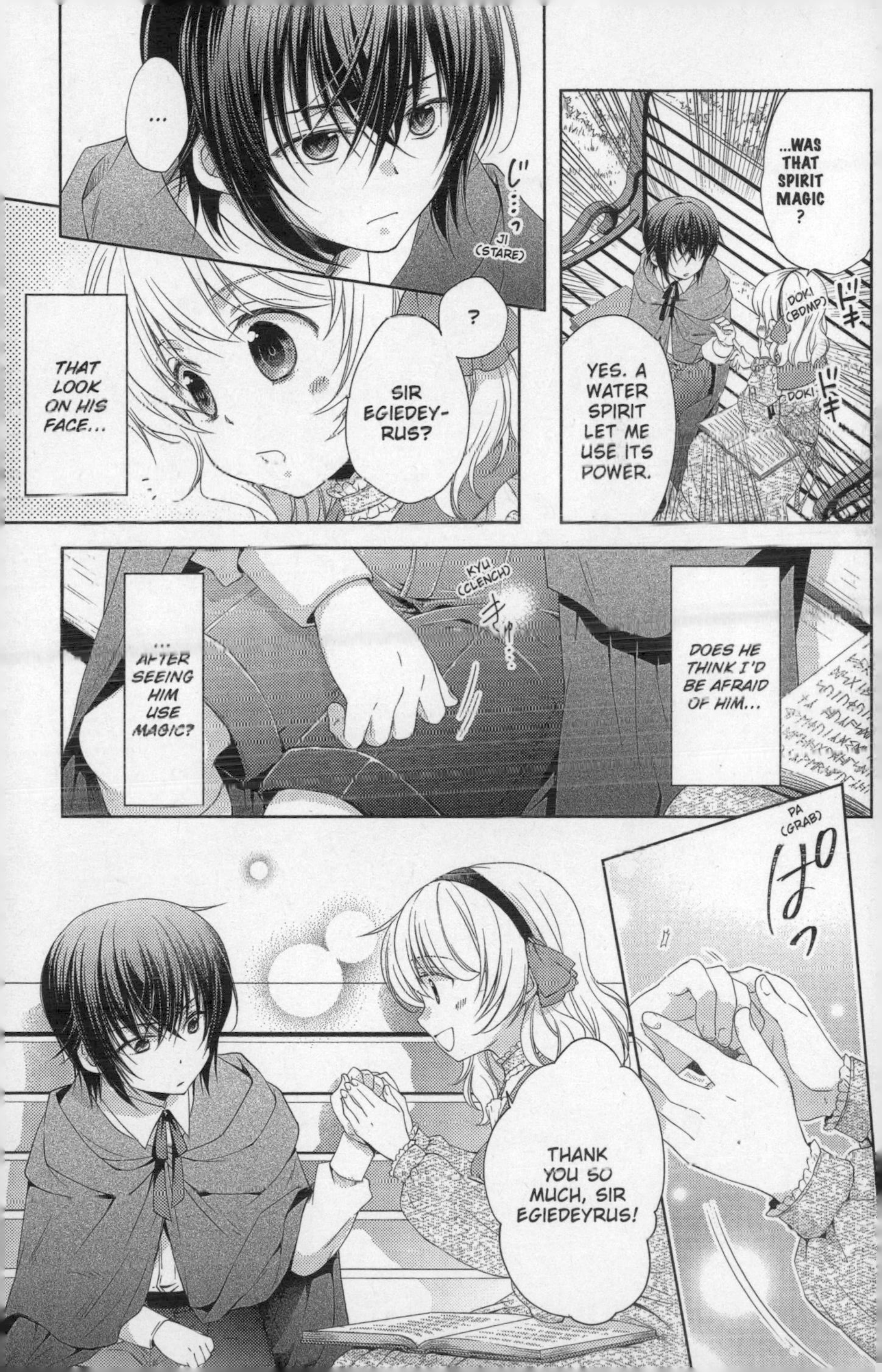
...WAS THAT SPIRIT MAGIC?
YES. A WATER SPIRIT LET ME USE ITS POWER.
DOKI (BDMP)
DOKI
...
JI (STARE)
?
SIR EGIEDEY-RUS?
THAT LOOK ON HIS FACE...
DOES HE THINK I'D BE AFRAID OF HIM...
KYU (CLENCH)
...AFTER SEEING HIM USE MAGIC?
PA (GRAB)
THANK YOU SO MUCH, SIR EGIEDEYRUS!

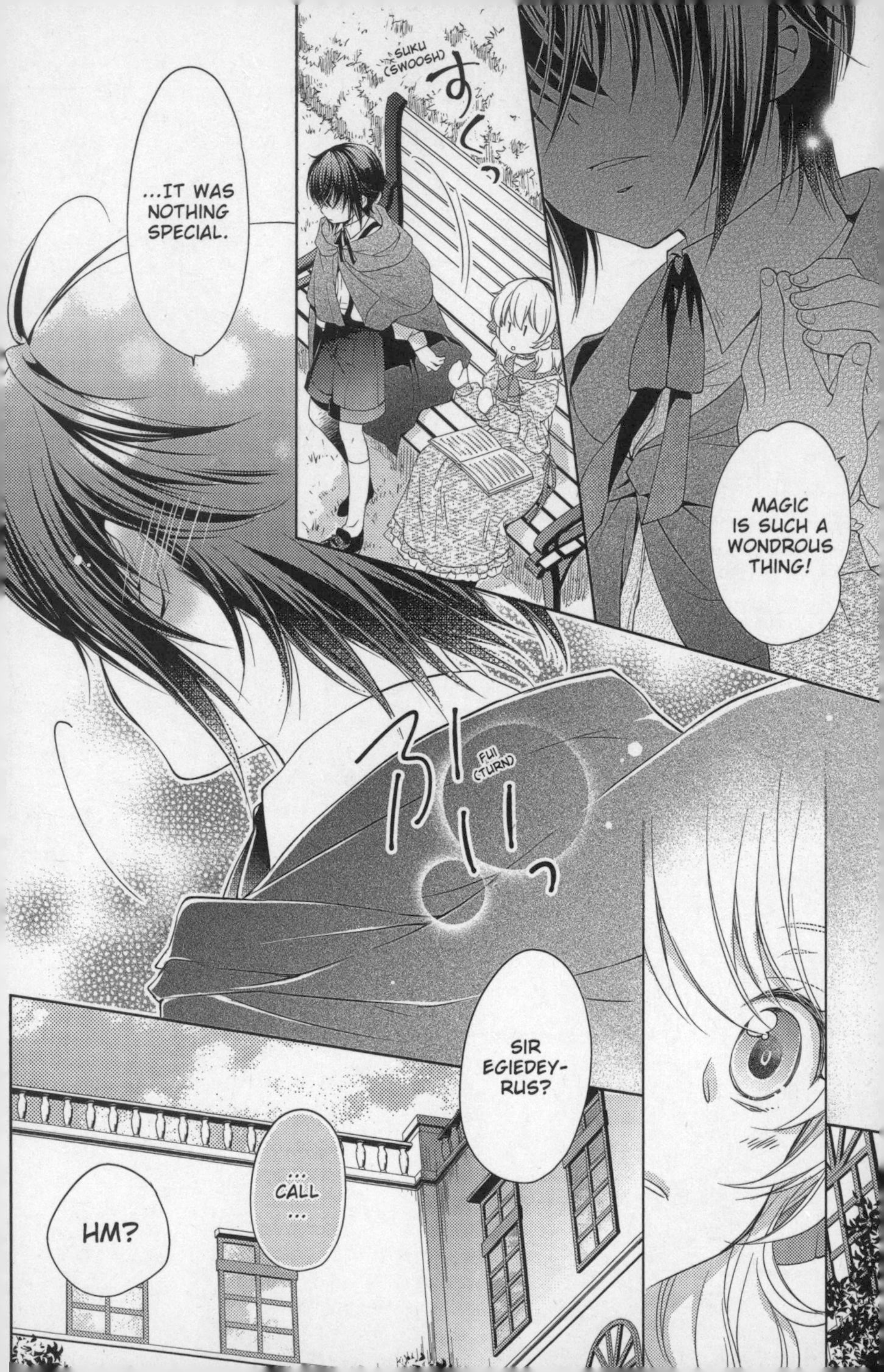
MAGIC IS SUCH A WONDROUS THING!
SUKU (SWOOSH)
...IT WAS NOTHING SPECIAL.
FUI (TURN)
SIR EGIEDEY-RUS?
... CALL ...
HM?

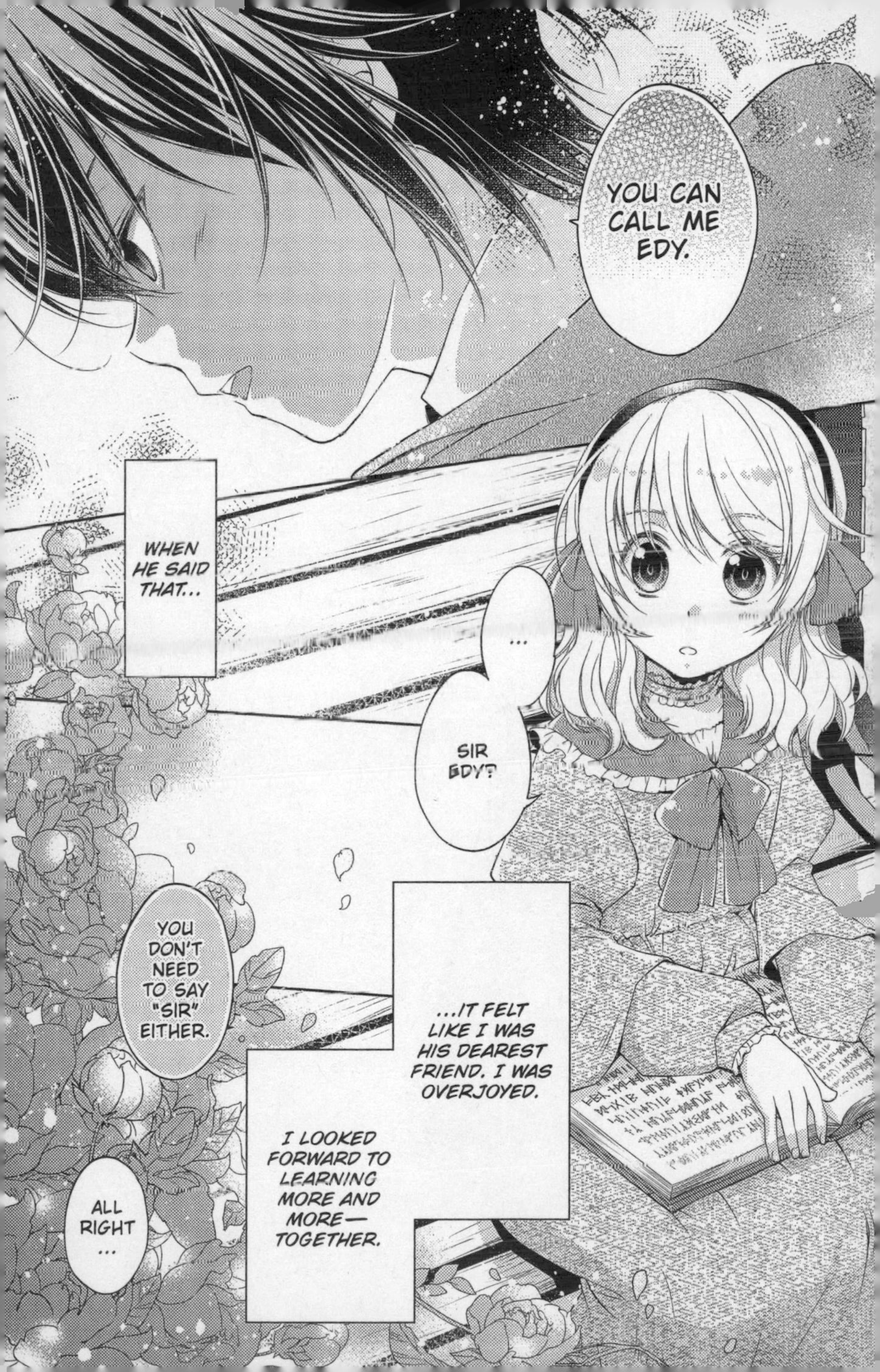
YOU CAN CALL ME EDY.
...
SIR EDY?
WHEN HE SAID THAT...
...IT FELT LIKE I WAS HIS DEAREST FRIEND. I WAS OVERJOYED.
YOU DON'T NEED TO SAY "SIR" EITHER.
I LOOKED FORWARD TO LEARNING MORE AND MORE—TOGETHER.
ALL RIGHT...

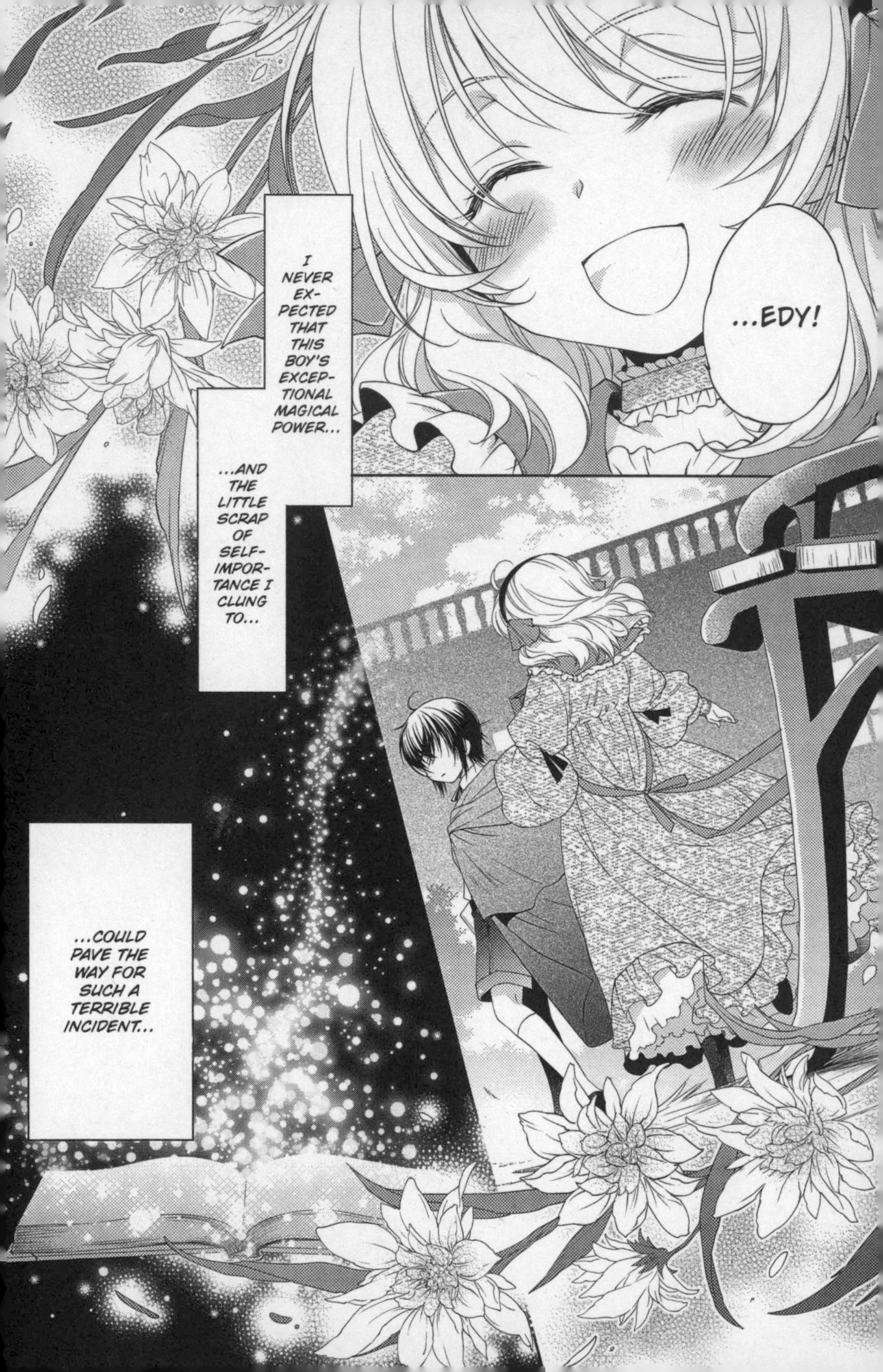
...EDY!
I NEVER EX-PECTED THAT THIS BOY'S EXCEP-TIONAL MAGICAL POWER...
...AND THE LITTLE SCRAP OF SELF-IMPORTANCE I CLUNG TO...
...COULD PAVE THE WAY FOR SUCH A TERRIBLE INCIDENT...

FIANCÉE OF THE WIZARD

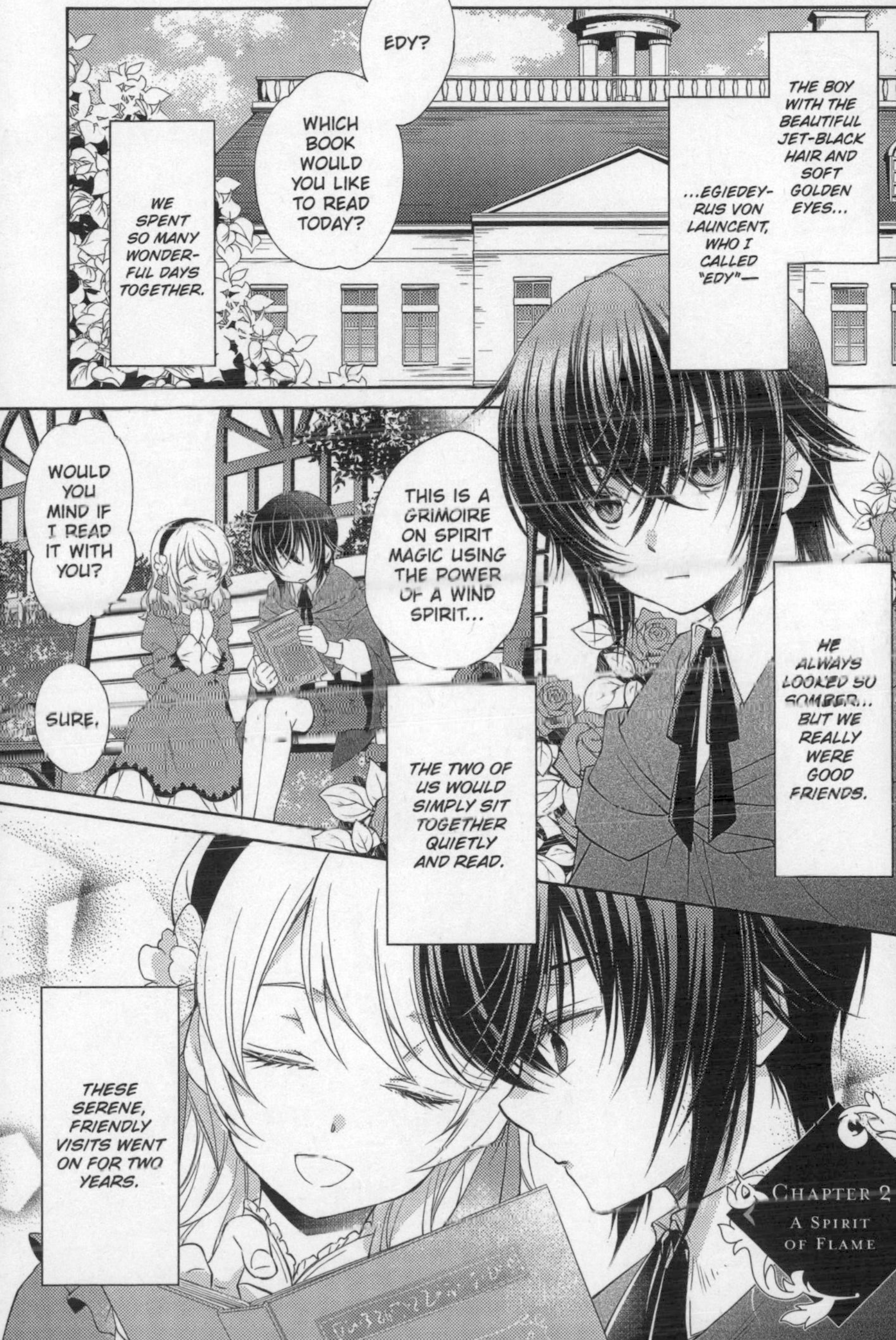
THE BOY WITH THE BEAUTIFUL JET-BLACK HAIR AND SOFT GOLDEN EYES…
…EGIEDEYRUS VON LAUNCENT, WHO I CALLED "EDY"—
EDY?
WHICH BOOK WOULD YOU LIKE TO READ TODAY?
WE SPENT SO MANY WONDERFUL DAYS TOGETHER.
HE ALWAYS LOOKED SO SOMBER… BUT WE REALLY WERE GOOD FRIENDS.
THIS IS A GRIMOIRE ON SPIRIT MAGIC USING THE POWER OF A WIND SPIRIT…
WOULD YOU MIND IF I READ IT WITH YOU?
SURE.
THE TWO OF US WOULD SIMPLY SIT TOGETHER QUIETLY AND READ.
CHAPTER 2
A SPIRIT OF FLAME
THESE SERENE, FRIENDLY VISITS WENT ON FOR TWO YEARS.

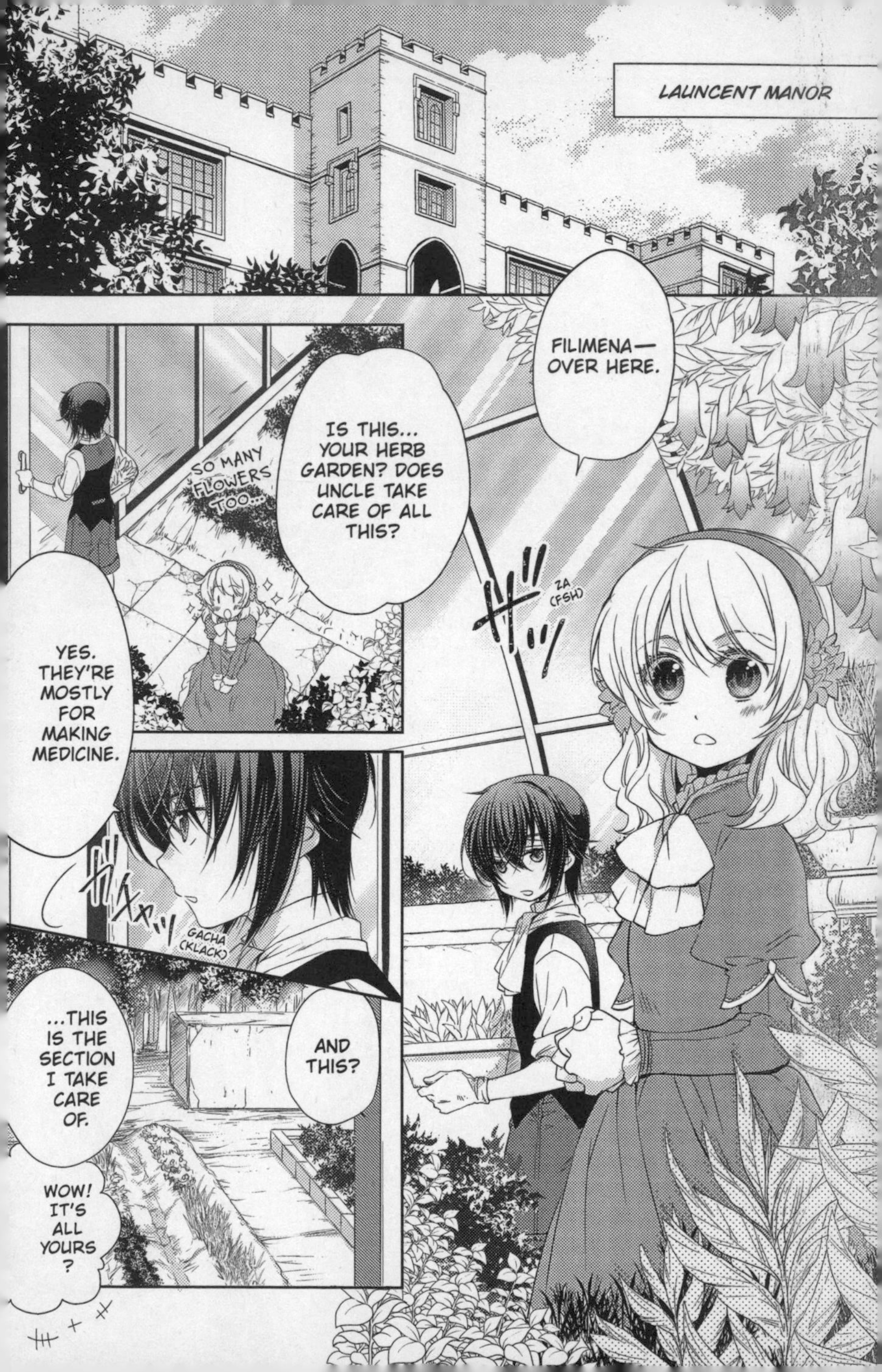
LAUNCENT MANOR
FILIMENA—OVER HERE.
ZA (FSH)
IS THIS... YOUR HERB GARDEN? DOES UNCLE TAKE CARE OF ALL THIS?
SO MANY FLOWERS TOO...
YES. THEY'RE MOSTLY FOR MAKING MEDICINE.
GACHA (KLACK)
AND THIS?
...THIS IS THE SECTION I TAKE CARE OF.
WOW! IT'S ALL YOURS?

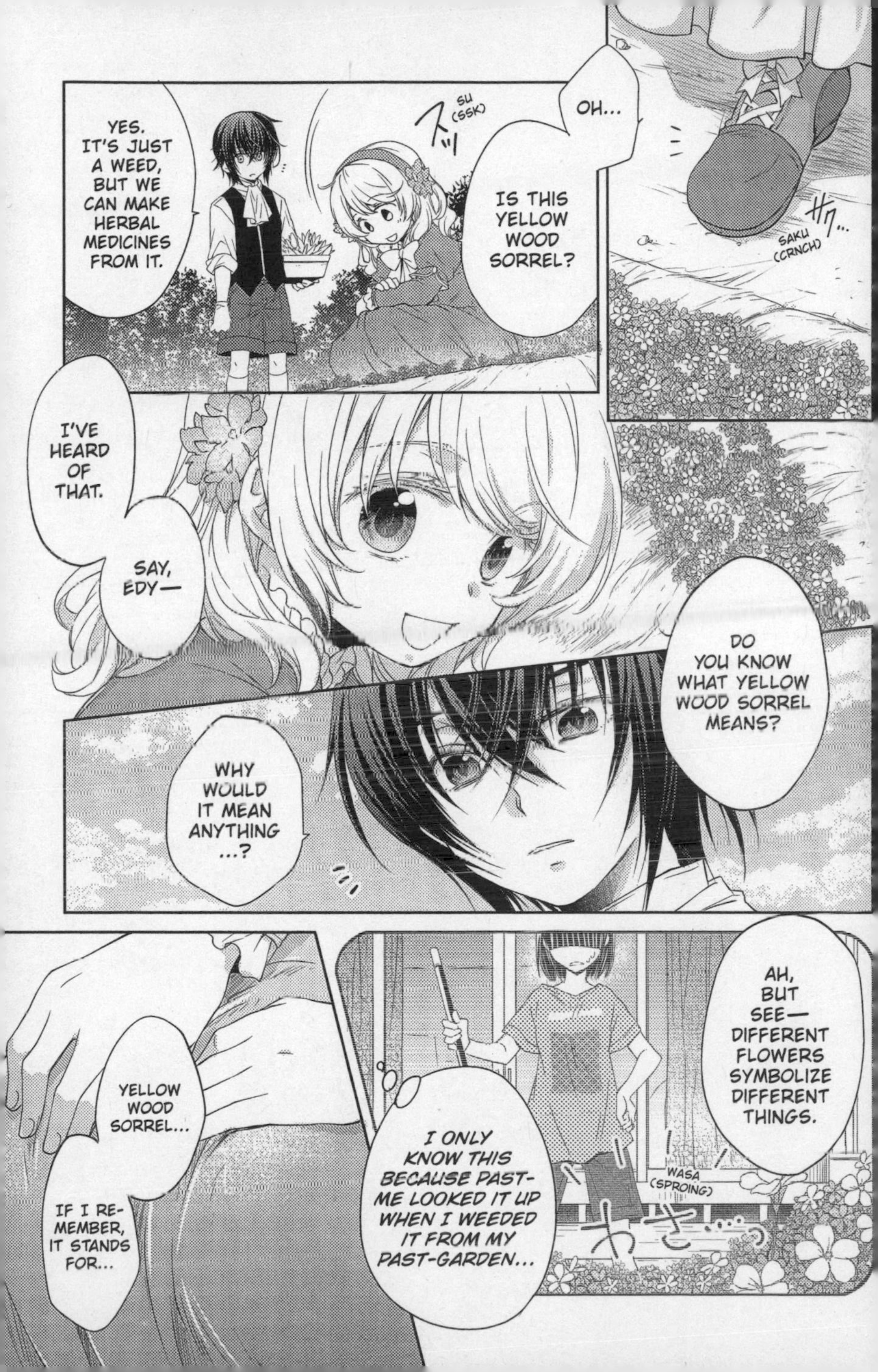
サク…
SAKU (CRNCH)
OH...
IS THIS YELLOW WOOD SORREL?
スッ
SU (SSK)
YES. IT'S JUST A WEED, BUT WE CAN MAKE HERBAL MEDICINES FROM IT.
I'VE HEARD OF THAT.
SAY, EDY—
DO YOU KNOW WHAT YELLOW WOOD SORREL MEANS?
WHY WOULD IT MEAN ANYTHING ...?
AH, BUT SEE— DIFFERENT FLOWERS SYMBOLIZE DIFFERENT THINGS.
WASA (SPROING)
I ONLY KNOW THIS BECAUSE PAST-ME LOOKED IT UP WHEN I WEEDED IT FROM MY PAST-GARDEN...
YELLOW WOOD SORREL...
IF I RE-MEMBER, IT STANDS FOR...

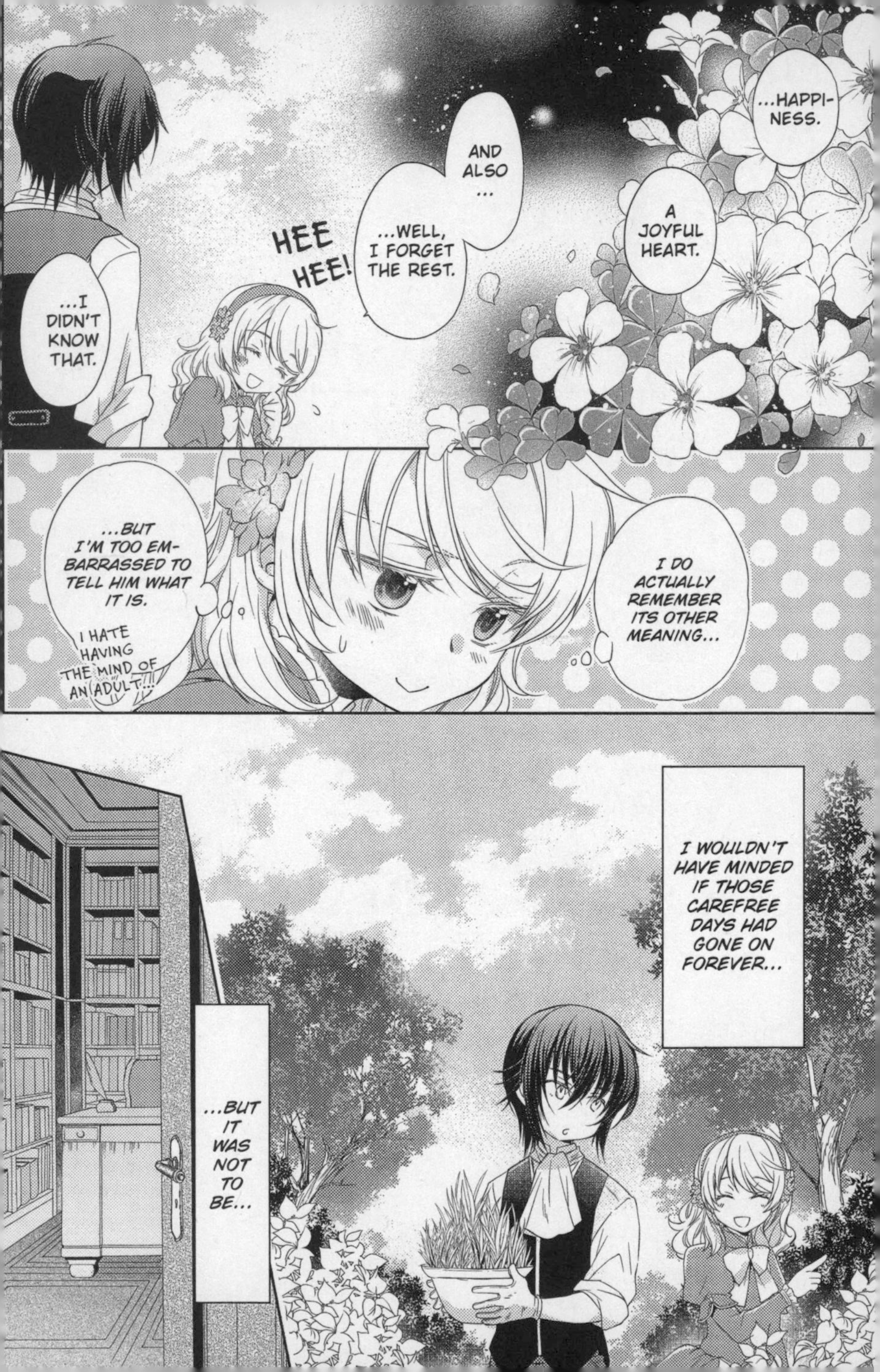
...HAPPI-NESS.
A JOYFUL HEART.
AND ALSO ...
...WELL, I FORGET THE REST.
HEE HEE!
...I DIDN'T KNOW THAT.
I DO ACTUALLY REMEMBER ITS OTHER MEANING...
...BUT I'M TOO EM-BARRASSED TO TELL HIM WHAT IT IS.
I HATE HAVING THE MIND OF AN ADULT...!!
I WOULDN'T HAVE MINDED IF THOSE CAREFREE DAYS HAD GONE ON FOREVER...
...BUT IT WAS NOT TO BE...

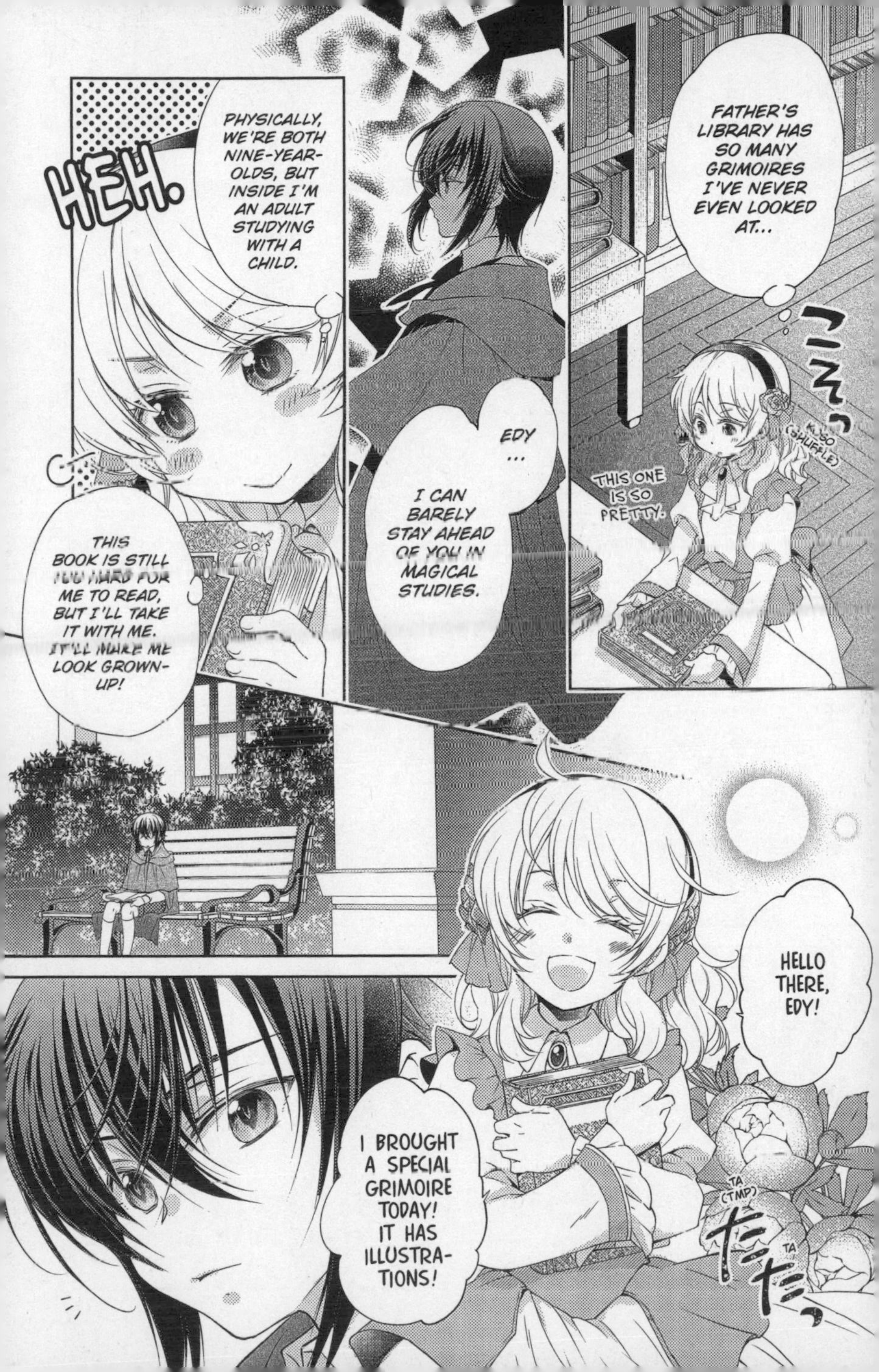
FATHER'S LIBRARY HAS SO MANY GRIMOIRES I'VE NEVER EVEN LOOKED AT...
KOSO (SHUFFLE)
THIS ONE IS SO PRETTY.
EDY ...
I CAN BARELY STAY AHEAD OF YOU IN MAGICAL STUDIES.
PHYSICALLY, WE'RE BOTH NINE-YEAR-OLDS, BUT INSIDE I'M AN ADULT STUDYING WITH A CHILD.
HEH.
THIS BOOK IS STILL TOO HARD FOR ME TO READ, BUT I'LL TAKE IT WITH ME. IT'LL MAKE ME LOOK GROWN-UP!
HELLO THERE, EDY!
TA (TMP) TA
I BROUGHT A SPECIAL GRIMOIRE TODAY! IT HAS ILLUSTRATIONS!

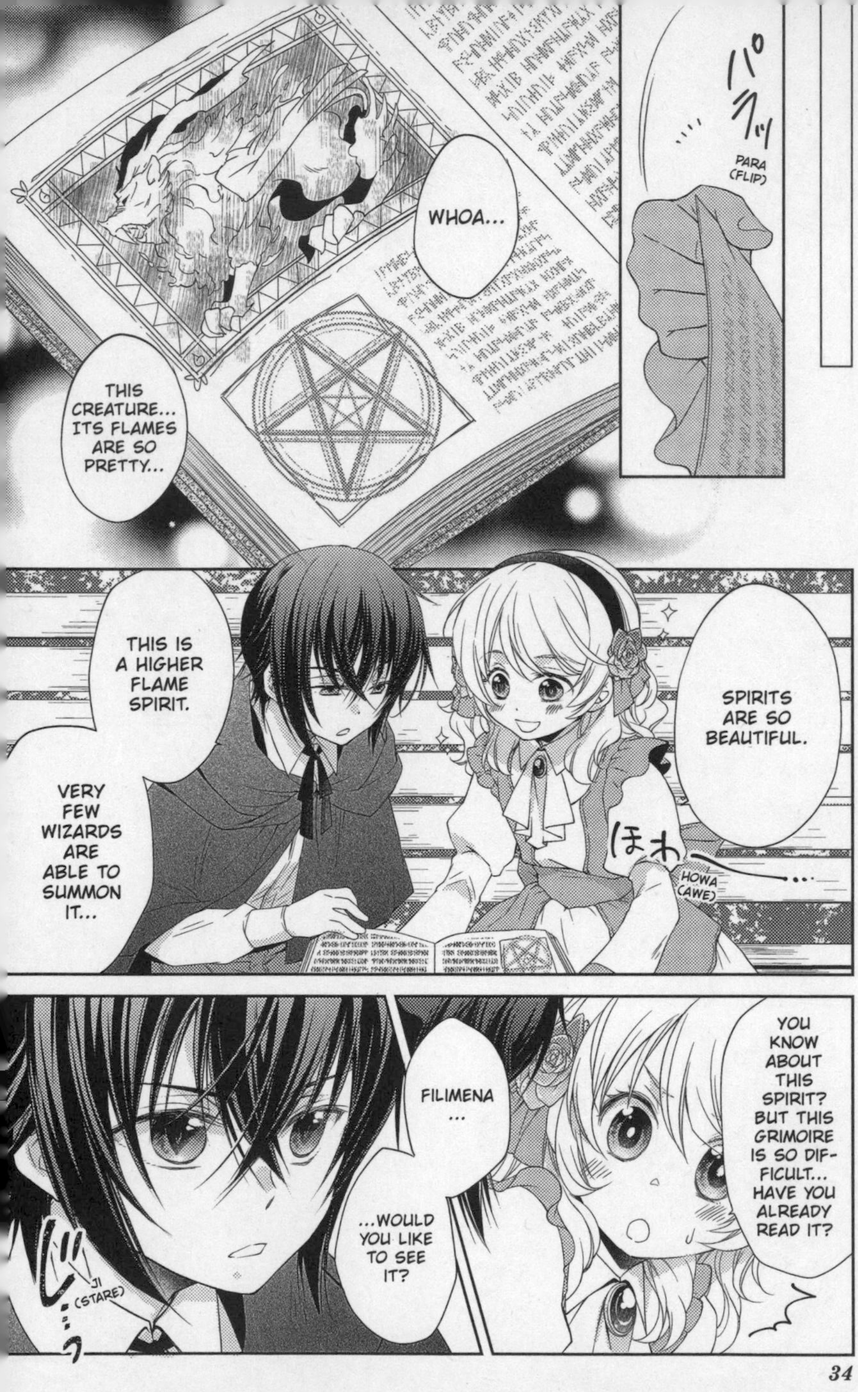
パラッ
PARA (FLIP)
WHOA...
THIS CREATURE... ITS FLAMES ARE SO PRETTY...
SPIRITS ARE SO BEAUTIFUL.
ほわ
HOWA (AWE)
THIS IS A HIGHER FLAME SPIRIT.
VERY FEW WIZARDS ARE ABLE TO SUMMON IT...
YOU KNOW ABOUT THIS SPIRIT? BUT THIS GRIMOIRE IS SO DIF-FICULT... HAVE YOU ALREADY READ IT?
FILIMENA...
...WOULD YOU LIKE TO SEE IT?
じーっ
JI (STARE)

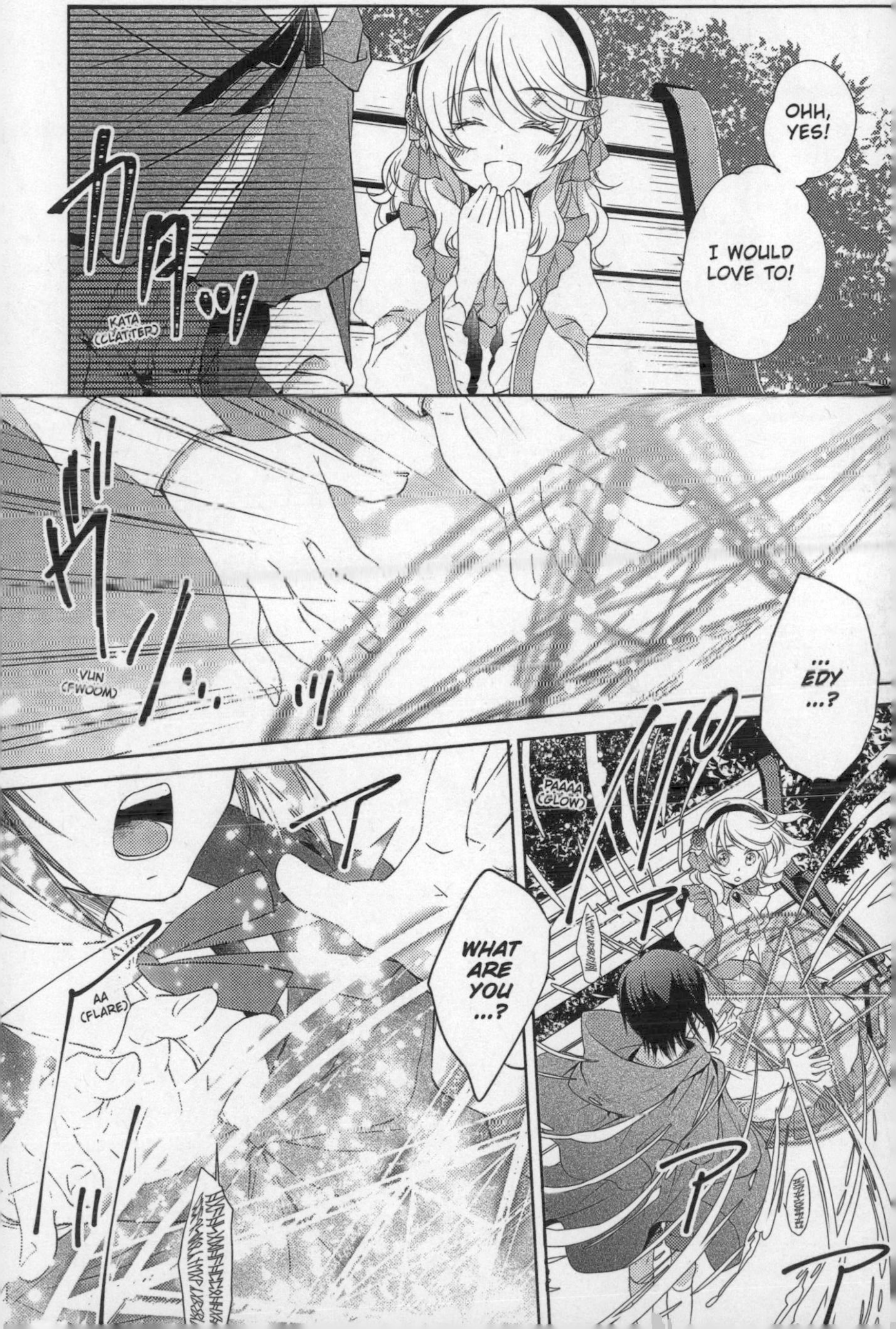
OHH, YES!
I WOULD LOVE TO!
KATA (CLATTER)
VUN (FWOOM)
... EDY ...?
PAAAA (GLOW)
WHAT ARE YOU ...?
AA (FLARE)

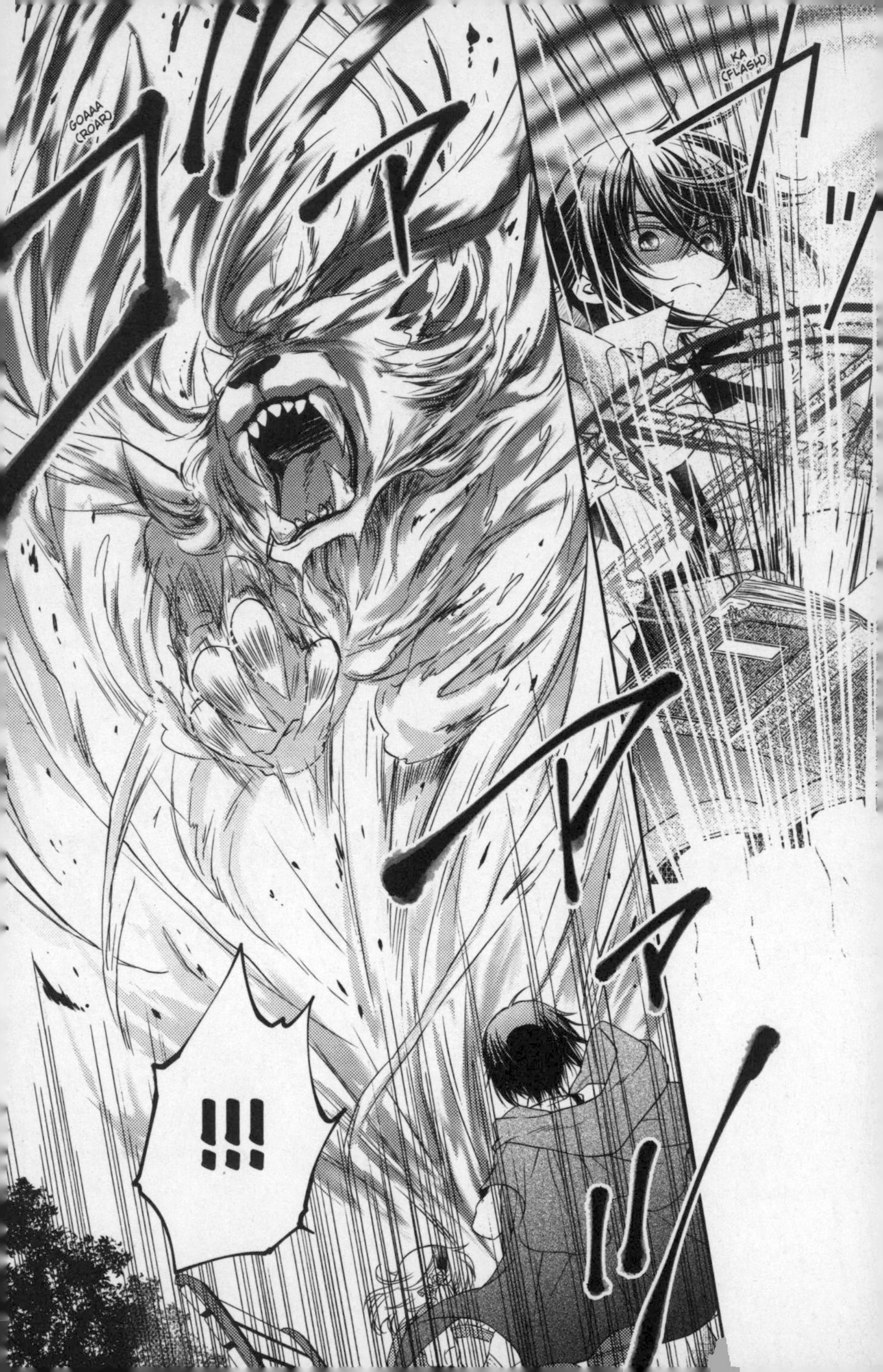
KA (FLASH)
GOAAA (ROAR)
!!!

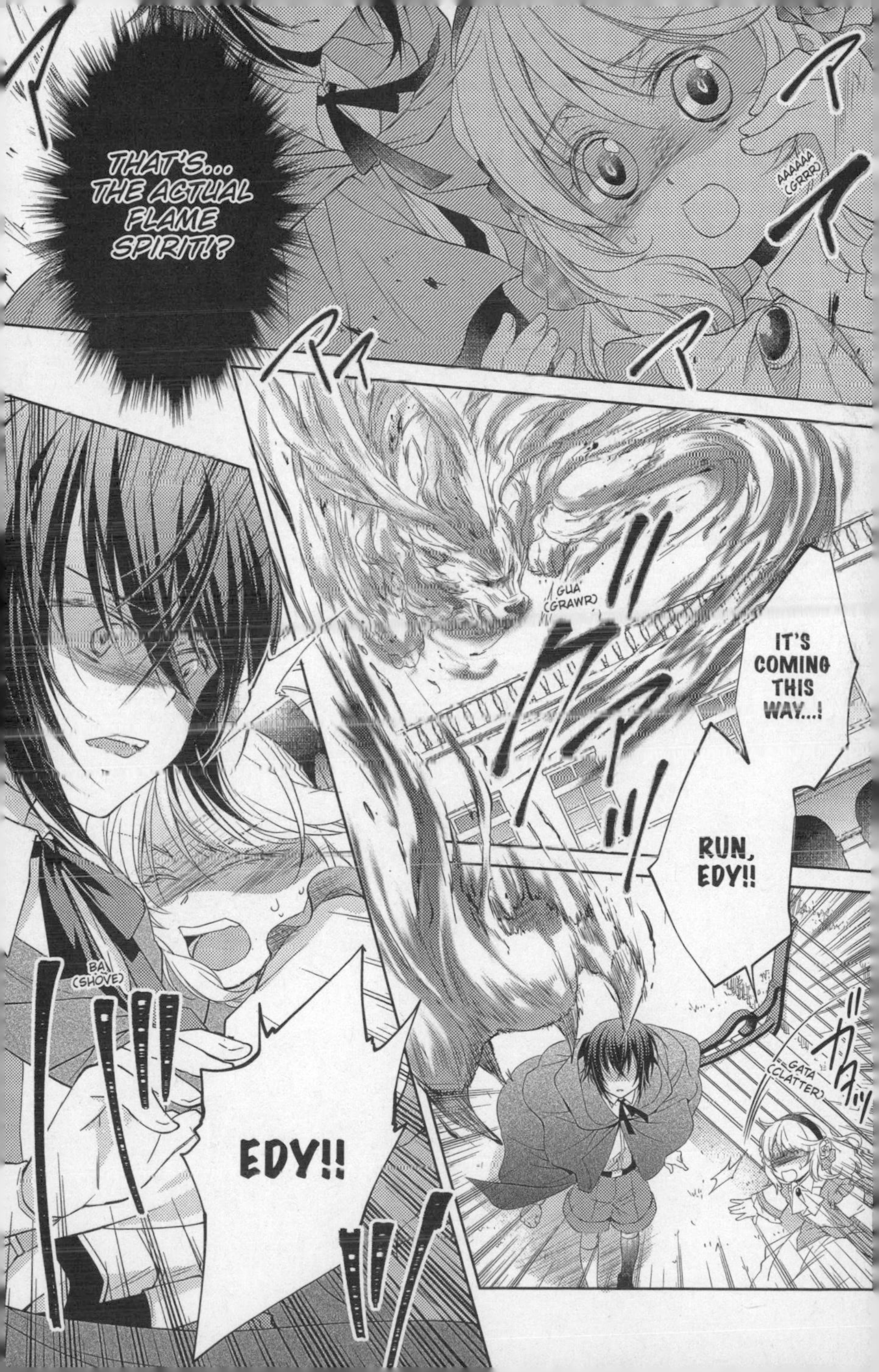
AAAAAA (GRRR)
THAT'S... THE ACTUAL FLAME SPIRIT!?
GUA (GRAWR)
IT'S COMING THIS WAY...!
RUN, EDY!!
GATA (CLATTER)
BA (SHOVE)
EDY!!

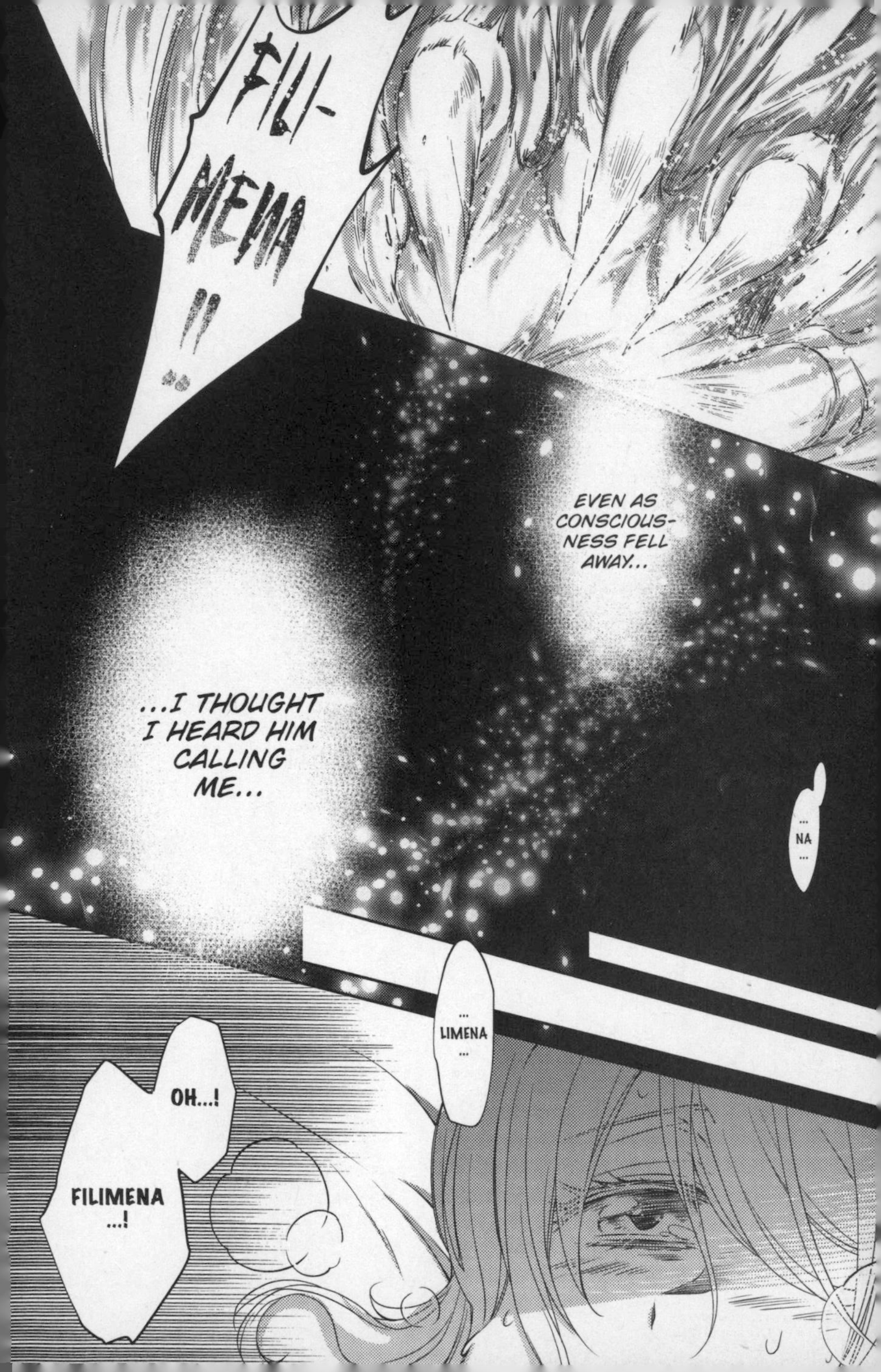
FILI-MENA!!
EVEN AS CONSCIOUS-NESS FELL AWAY...
...I THOUGHT I HEARD HIM CALLING ME...
...NA...
...LIMENA...
OH...!
FILIMENA...!

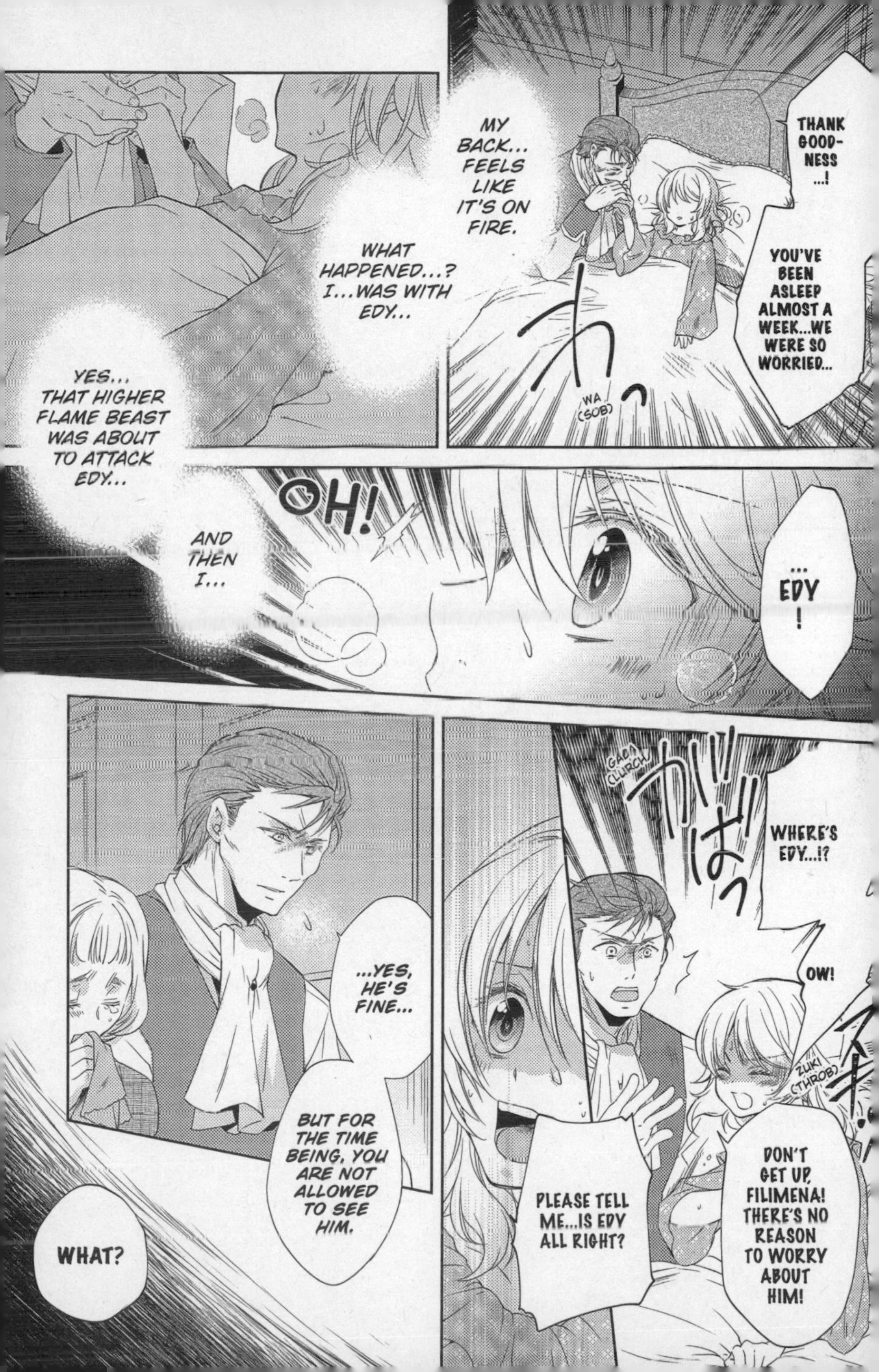
THANK GOODNESS...!
YOU'VE BEEN ASLEEP ALMOST A WEEK...WE WERE SO WORRIED...
WA (SOB)
MY BACK... FEELS LIKE IT'S ON FIRE.
WHAT HAPPENED...? I...WAS WITH EDY...
YES... THAT HIGHER FLAME BEAST WAS ABOUT TO ATTACK EDY...
...EDY!
OH!
AND THEN I...
GABA (LURCH)
WHERE'S EDY...!?
OW!
ZUKI (THROB)
DON'T GET UP, FILIMENA! THERE'S NO REASON TO WORRY ABOUT HIM!
PLEASE TELL ME...IS EDY ALL RIGHT?
...YES, HE'S FINE...
BUT FOR THE TIME BEING, YOU ARE NOT ALLOWED TO SEE HIM.
WHAT?

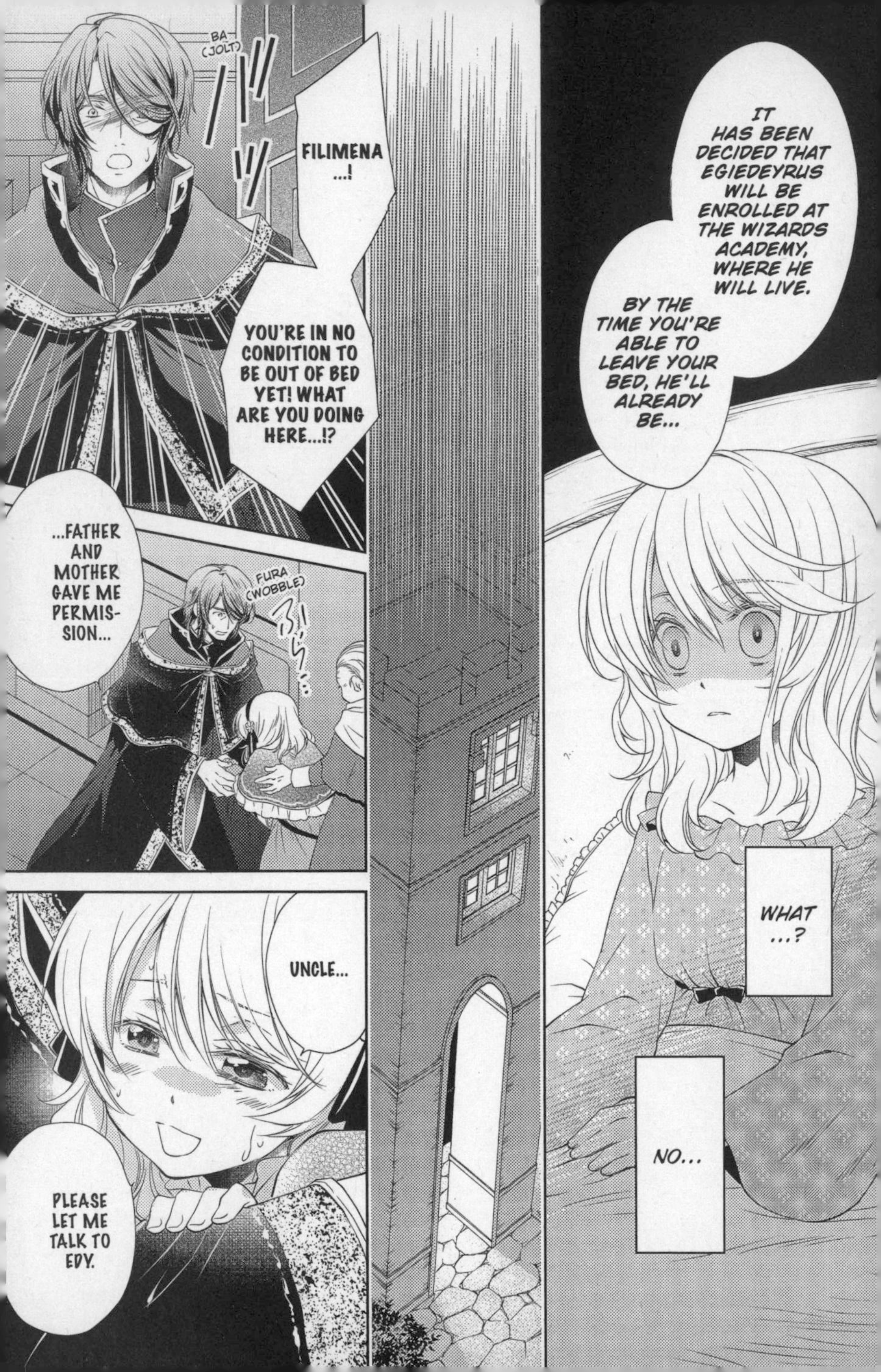
IT HAS BEEN DECIDED THAT EGIEDEYRUS WILL BE ENROLLED AT THE WIZARDS ACADEMY, WHERE HE WILL LIVE.
BY THE TIME YOU'RE ABLE TO LEAVE YOUR BED, HE'LL ALREADY BE...
WHAT ...?
NO...
BA— (JOLT)
FILIMENA ...!
YOU'RE IN NO CONDITION TO BE OUT OF BED YET! WHAT ARE YOU DOING HERE...!?
...FATHER AND MOTHER GAVE ME PERMIS-SION...
FURA (WOBBLE)
UNCLE...
PLEASE LET ME TALK TO EDY.

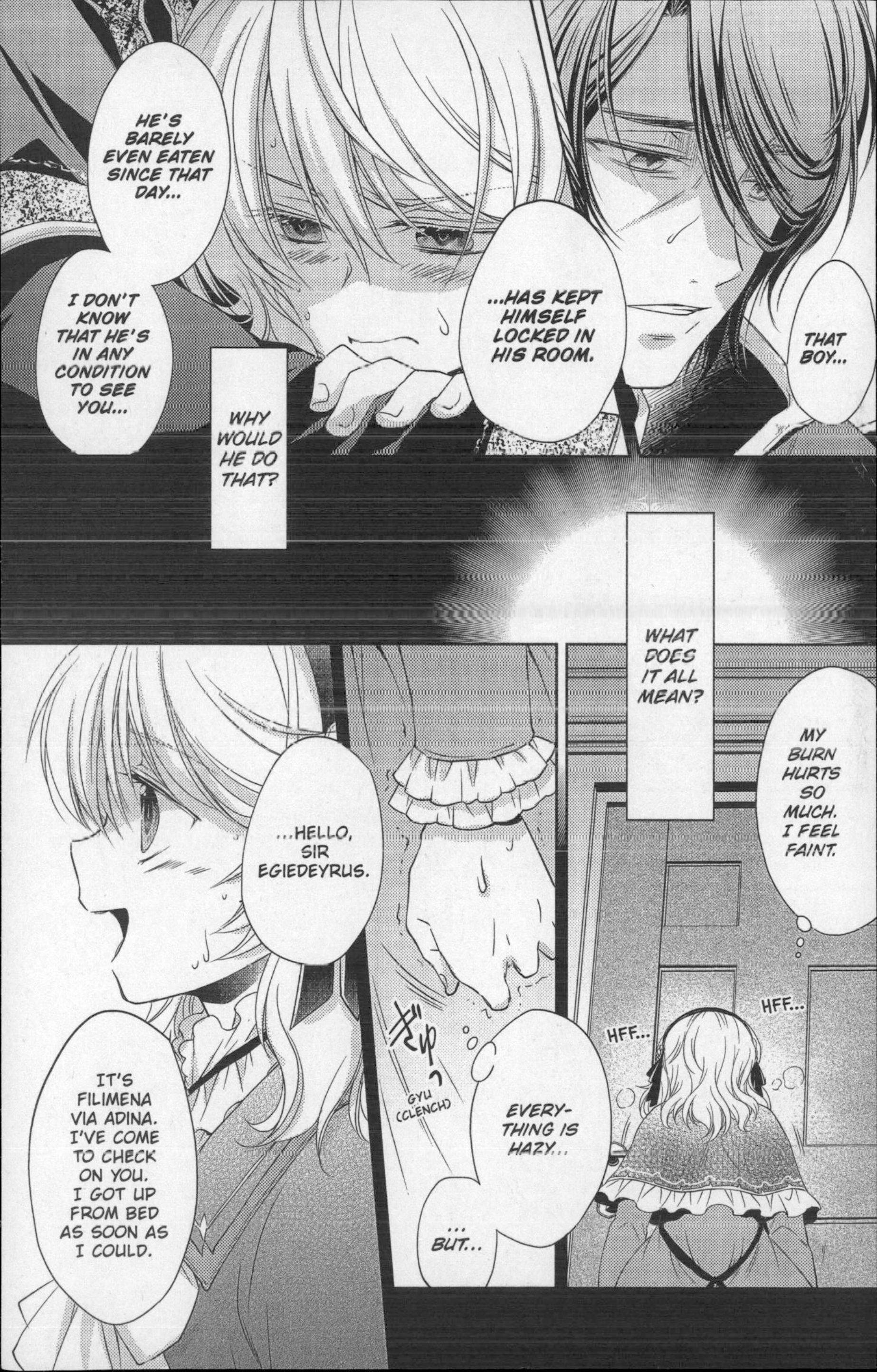
THAT BOY...
...HAS KEPT HIMSELF LOCKED IN HIS ROOM.
HE'S BARELY EVEN EATEN SINCE THAT DAY...
I DON'T KNOW THAT HE'S IN ANY CONDITION TO SEE YOU...
WHY WOULD HE DO THAT?
WHAT DOES IT ALL MEAN?
MY BURN HURTS SO MUCH. I FEEL FAINT.
HFF...
HFF...
EVERY-THING IS HAZY...
...BUT...
ぎゅっ
GYU (CLENCH)
...HELLO, SIR EGIEDEYRUS.
IT'S FILIMENA VIA ADINA. I'VE COME TO CHECK ON YOU. I GOT UP FROM BED AS SOON AS I COULD.

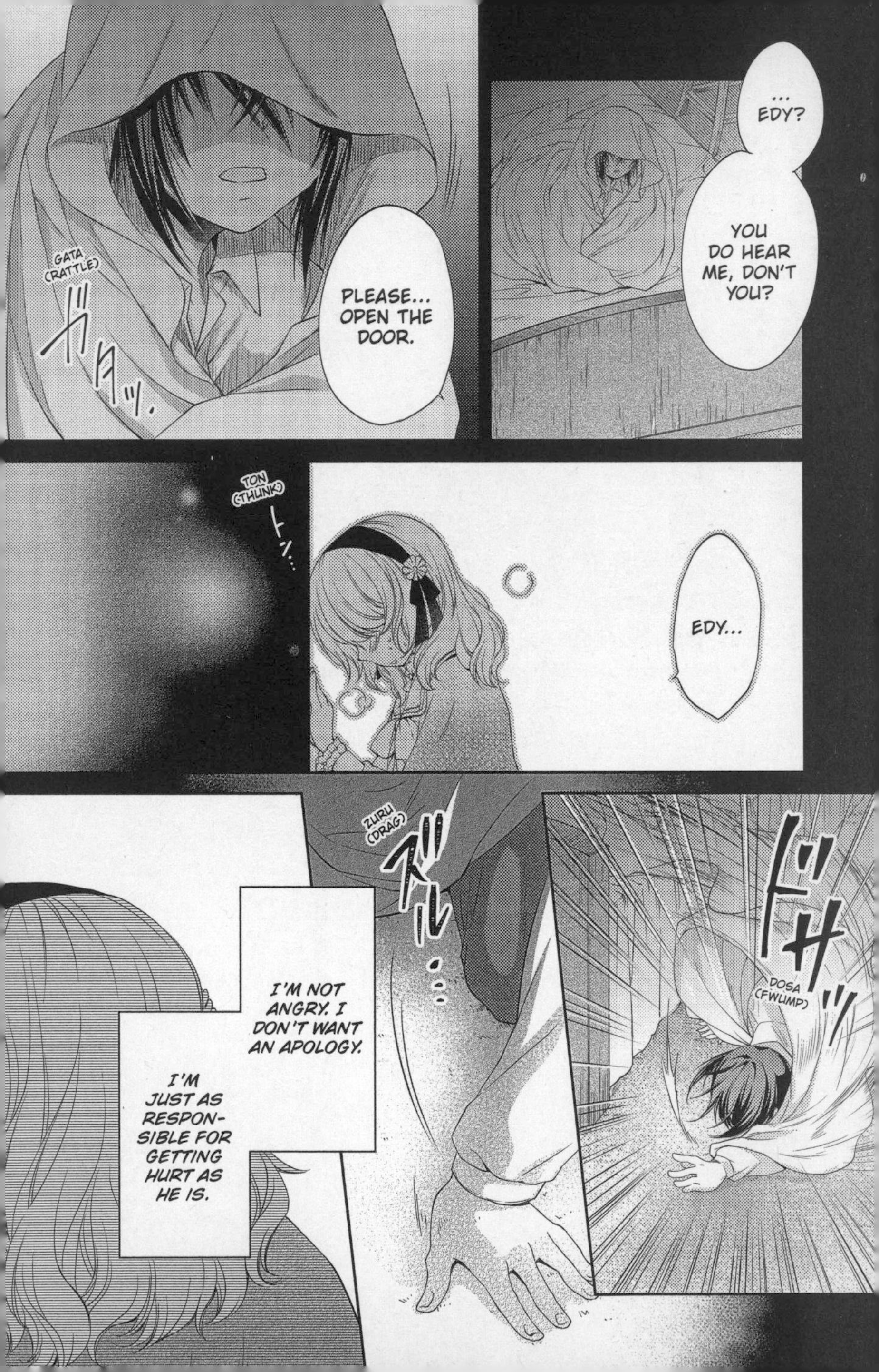
... EDY?
YOU DO HEAR ME, DON'T YOU?
GATA (RATTLE)
PLEASE... OPEN THE DOOR.
EDY...
TON (THUNK)
DOSA (FWUMP)
ZURU (DRAG)
I'M NOT ANGRY. I DON'T WANT AN APOLOGY.
I'M JUST AS RESPON-SIBLE FOR GETTING HURT AS HE IS.

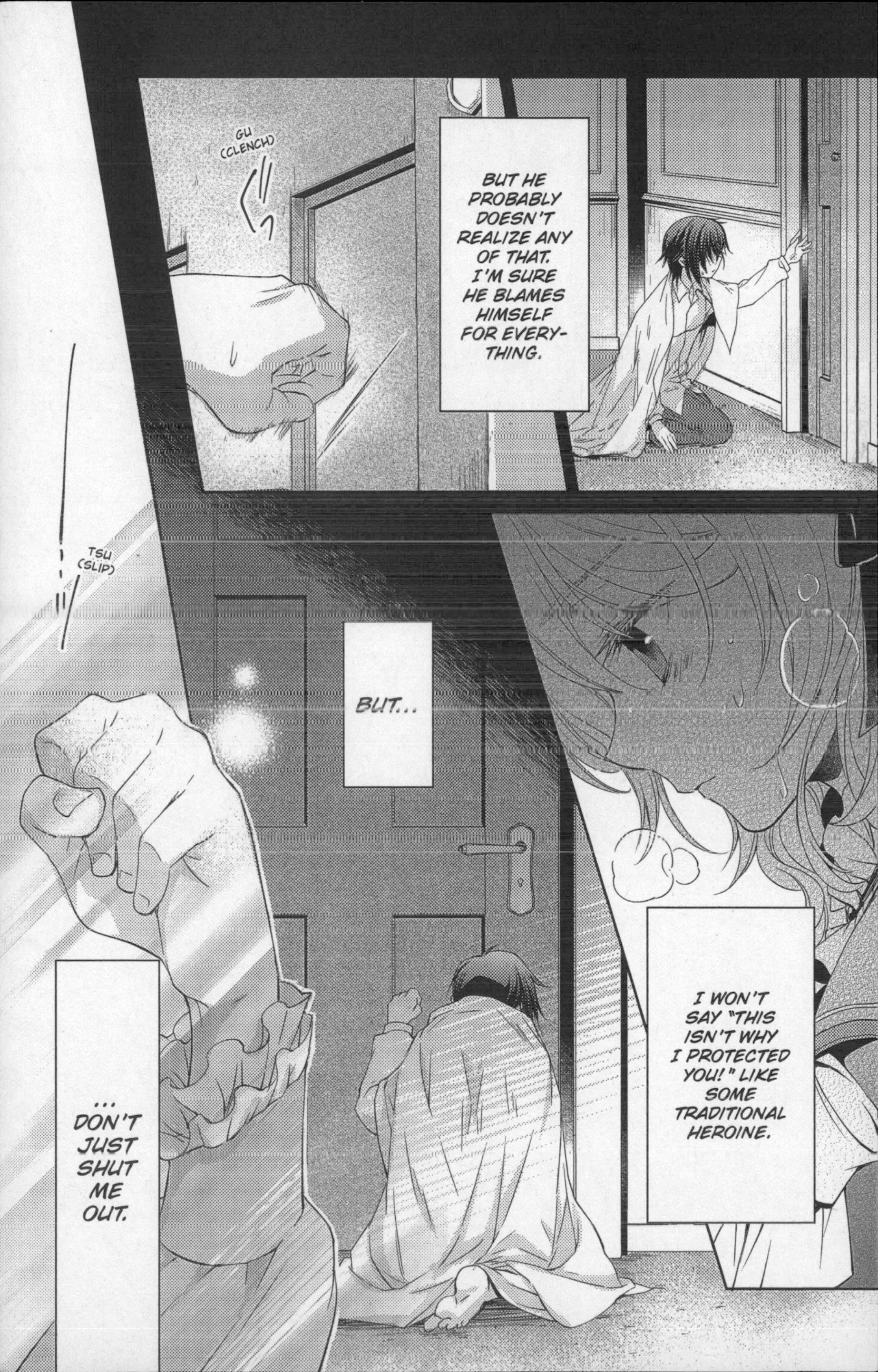
BUT HE PROBABLY DOESN'T REALIZE ANY OF THAT. I'M SURE HE BLAMES HIMSELF FOR EVERY-THING.
GU (CLENCH)
I WON'T SAY "THIS ISN'T WHY I PROTECTED YOU!" LIKE SOME TRADITIONAL HEROINE.
BUT...
TSU (SLIP)
...DON'T JUST SHUT ME OUT.

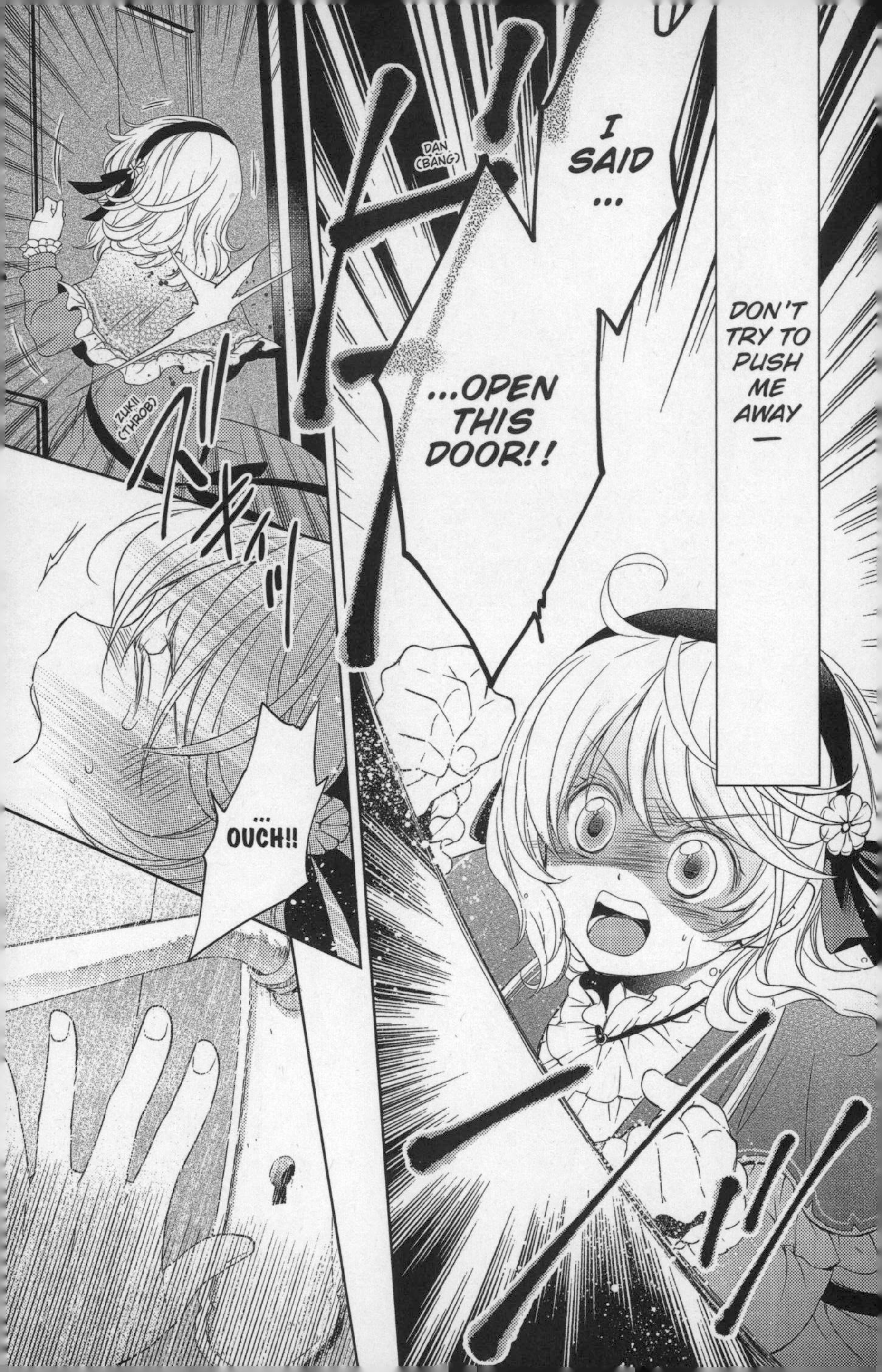
DON'T TRY TO PUSH ME AWAY—
I SAID...
...OPEN THIS DOOR!!
DAN (BANG)
ZUKI!! (THROB)
...OUCH!!

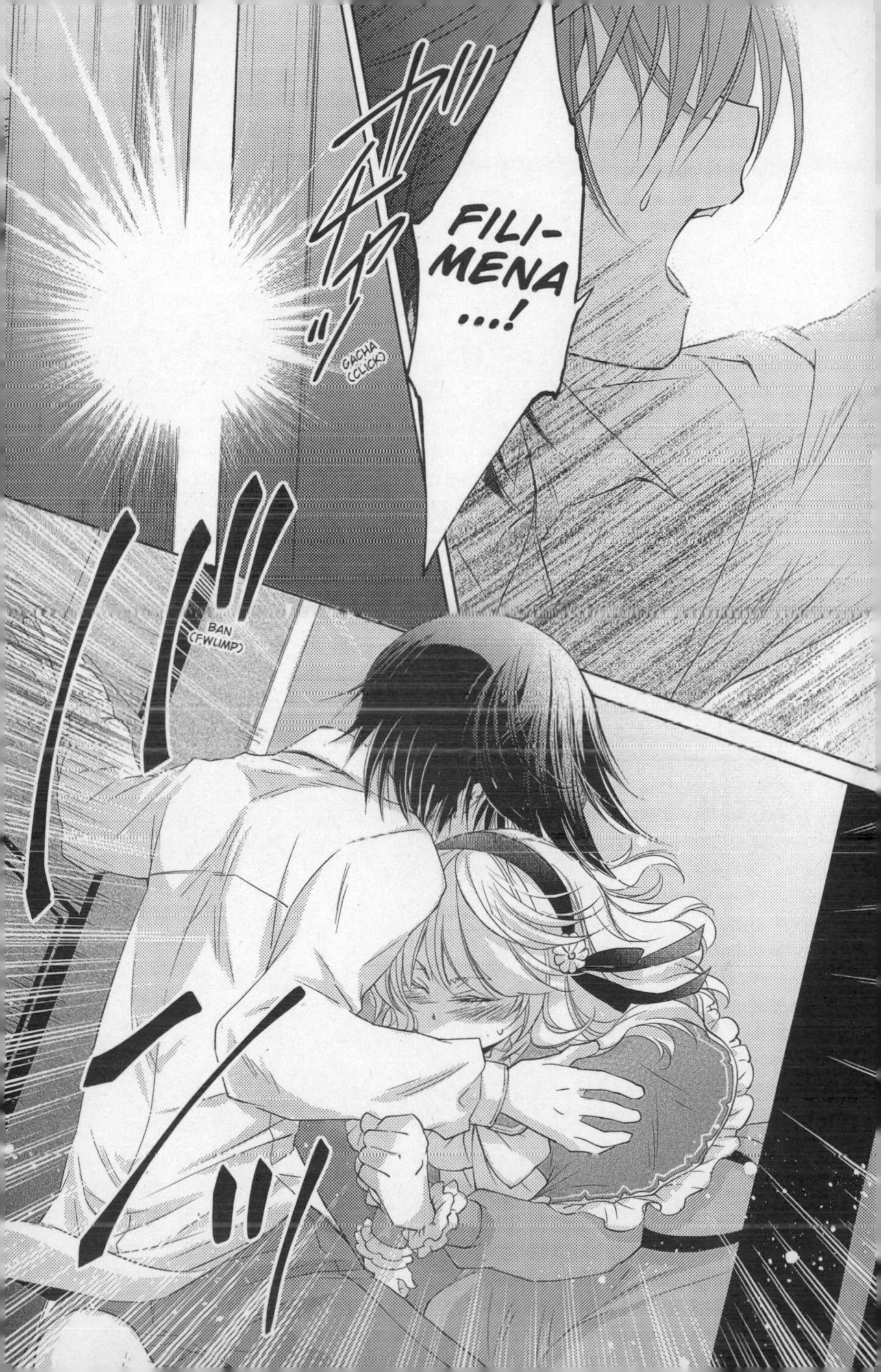
FILI-MENA ...!
GACHA (CLICK)
BAN (FWUMP)

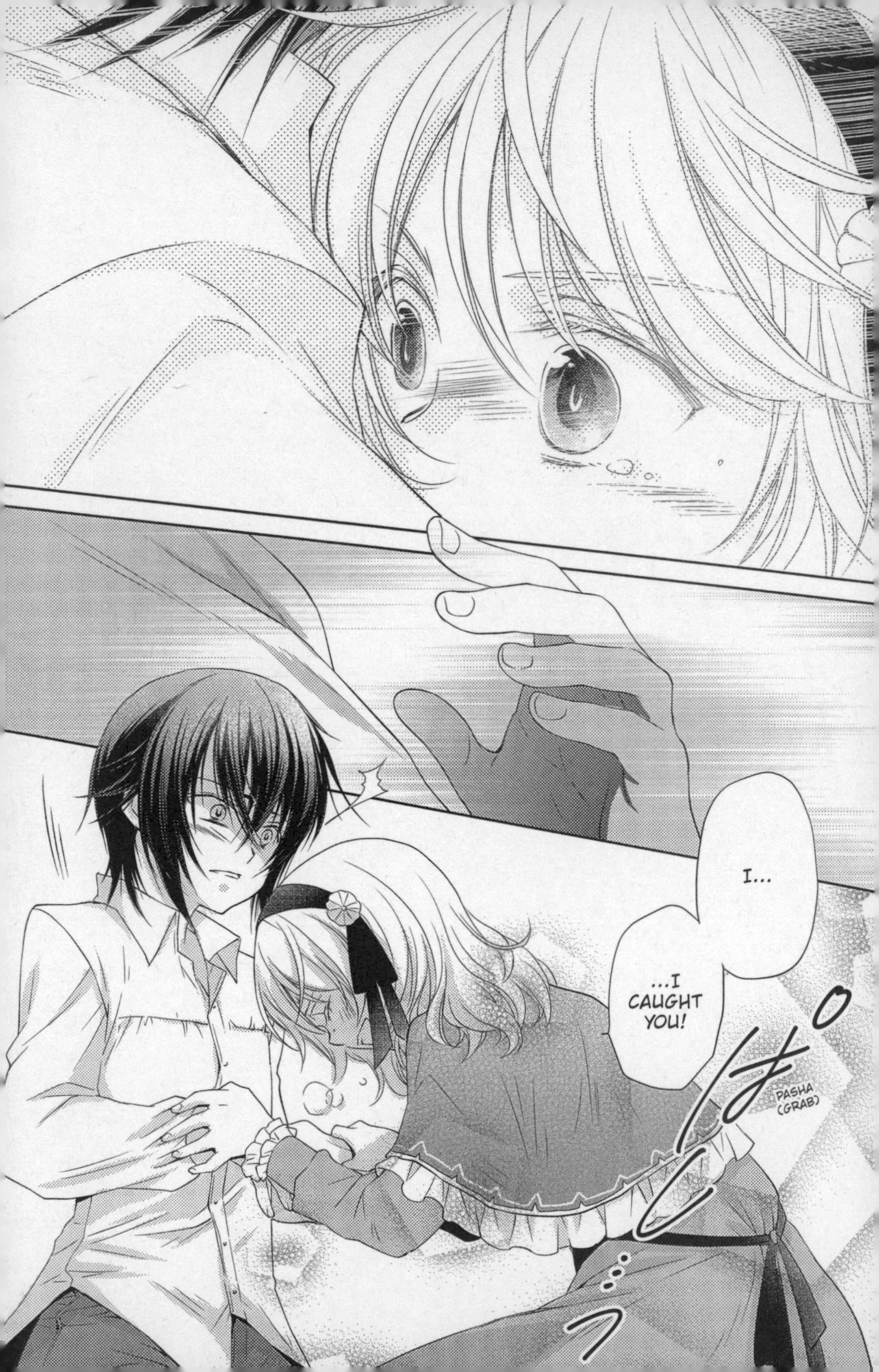
I...
...I CAUGHT YOU!
PASHA (GRAB)

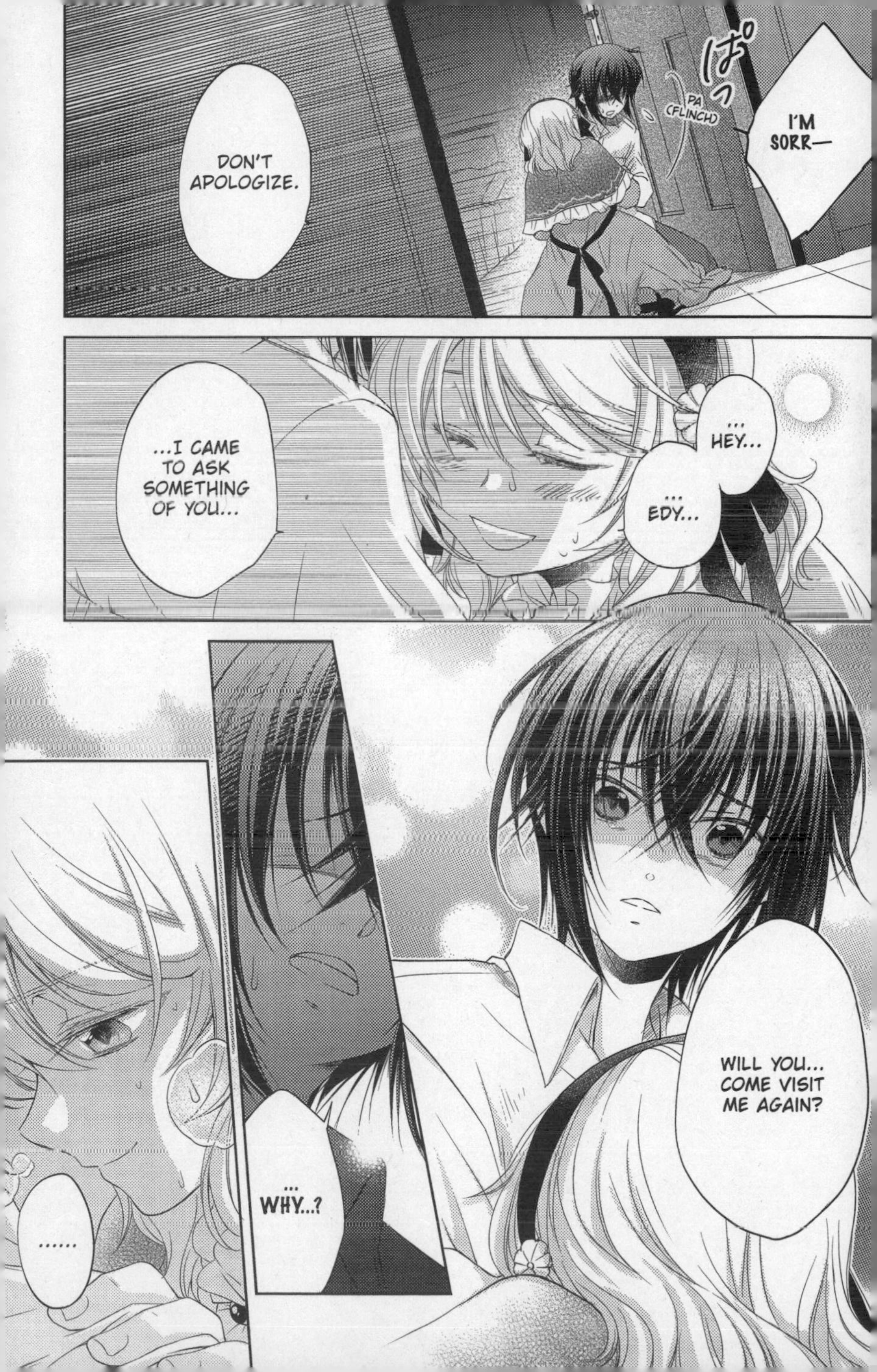
I'M SORR—
ぱっ
PA (FLINCH)
DON'T APOLOGIZE.
... HEY...
... EDY...
...I CAME TO ASK SOMETHING OF YOU...
WILL YOU... COME VISIT ME AGAIN?
... WHY...?
......

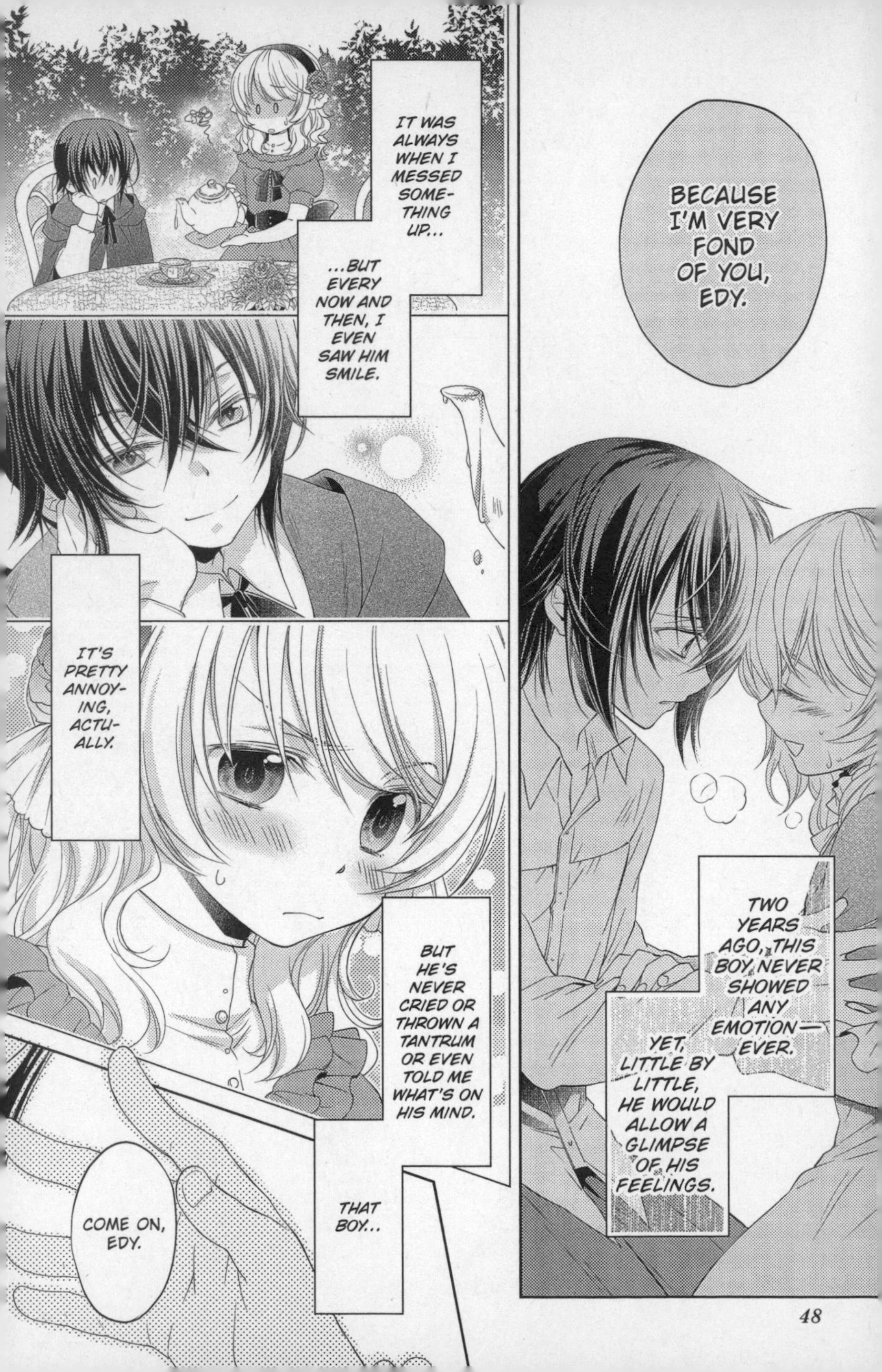
BECAUSE I'M VERY FOND OF YOU, EDY.
TWO YEARS AGO, THIS BOY NEVER SHOWED ANY EMOTION—EVER.
YET, LITTLE BY LITTLE, HE WOULD ALLOW A GLIMPSE OF HIS FEELINGS.
IT WAS ALWAYS WHEN I MESSED SOME-THING UP...
...BUT EVERY NOW AND THEN, I EVEN SAW HIM SMILE.
IT'S PRETTY ANNOY-ING, ACTU-ALLY.
BUT HE'S NEVER CRIED OR THROWN A TANTRUM OR EVEN TOLD ME WHAT'S ON HIS MIND.
THAT BOY...
COME ON, EDY.

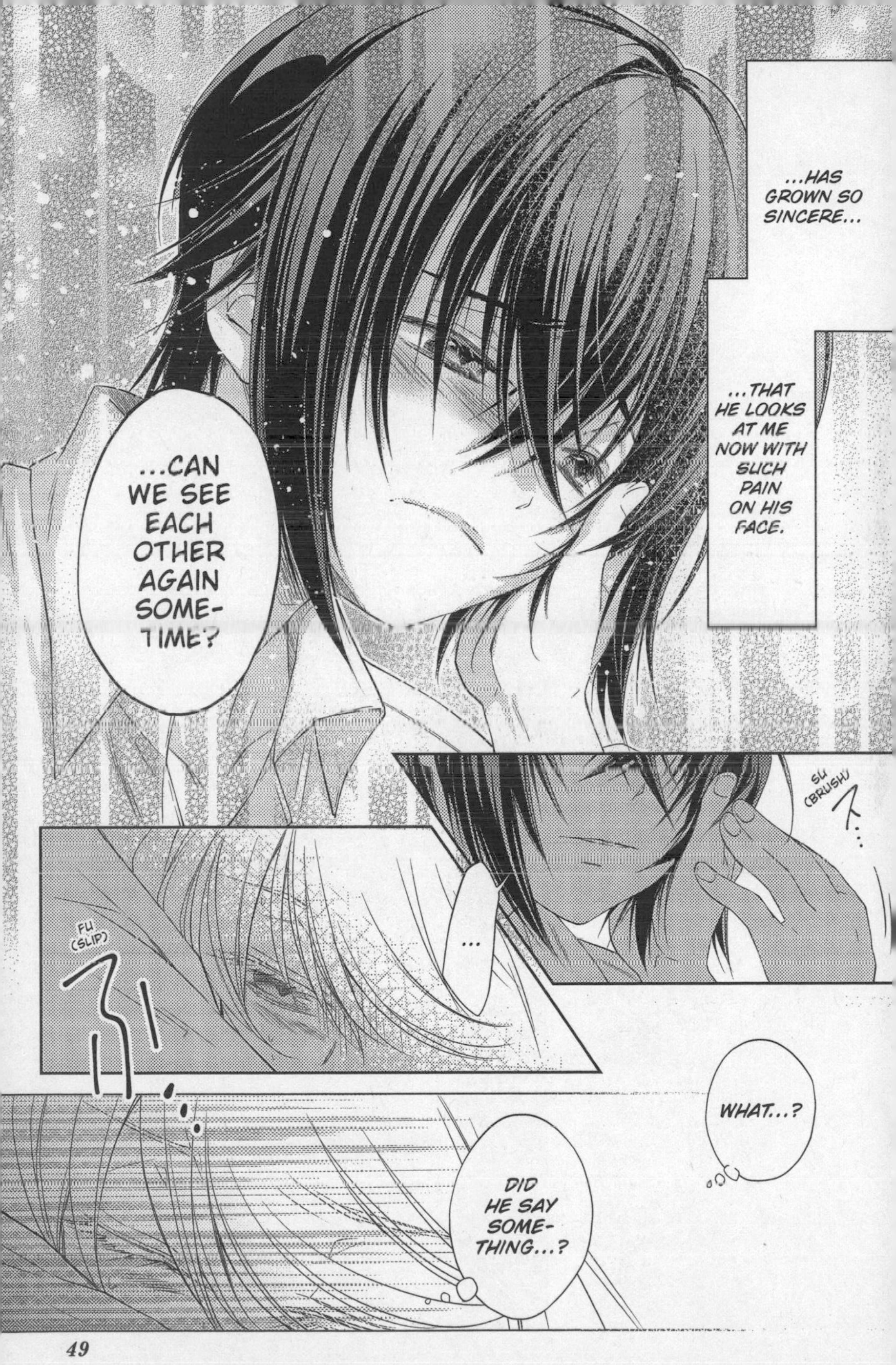
...HAS GROWN SO SINCERE...
...THAT HE LOOKS AT ME NOW WITH SUCH PAIN ON HIS FACE.
...CAN WE SEE EACH OTHER AGAIN SOME-TIME?
SU (BRUSH)
...
FU (SLIP)
WHAT...?
DID HE SAY SOME-THING...?

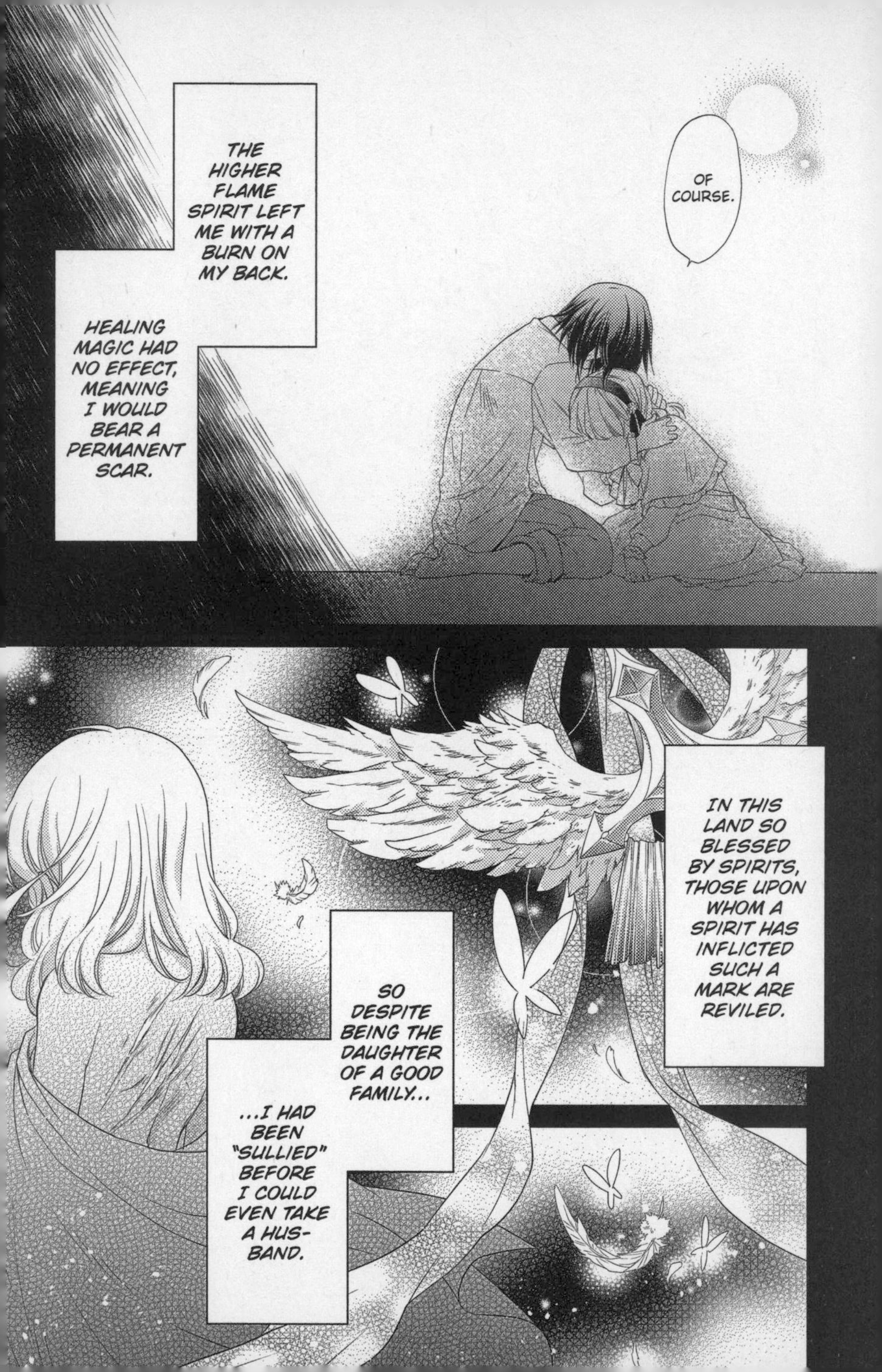
OF COURSE.
THE HIGHER FLAME SPIRIT LEFT ME WITH A BURN ON MY BACK.
HEALING MAGIC HAD NO EFFECT, MEANING I WOULD BEAR A PERMANENT SCAR.
IN THIS LAND SO BLESSED BY SPIRITS, THOSE UPON WHOM A SPIRIT HAS INFLICTED SUCH A MARK ARE REVILED.
SO DESPITE BEING THE DAUGHTER OF A GOOD FAMILY...
...I HAD BEEN "SULLIED" BEFORE I COULD EVEN TAKE A HUS-BAND.

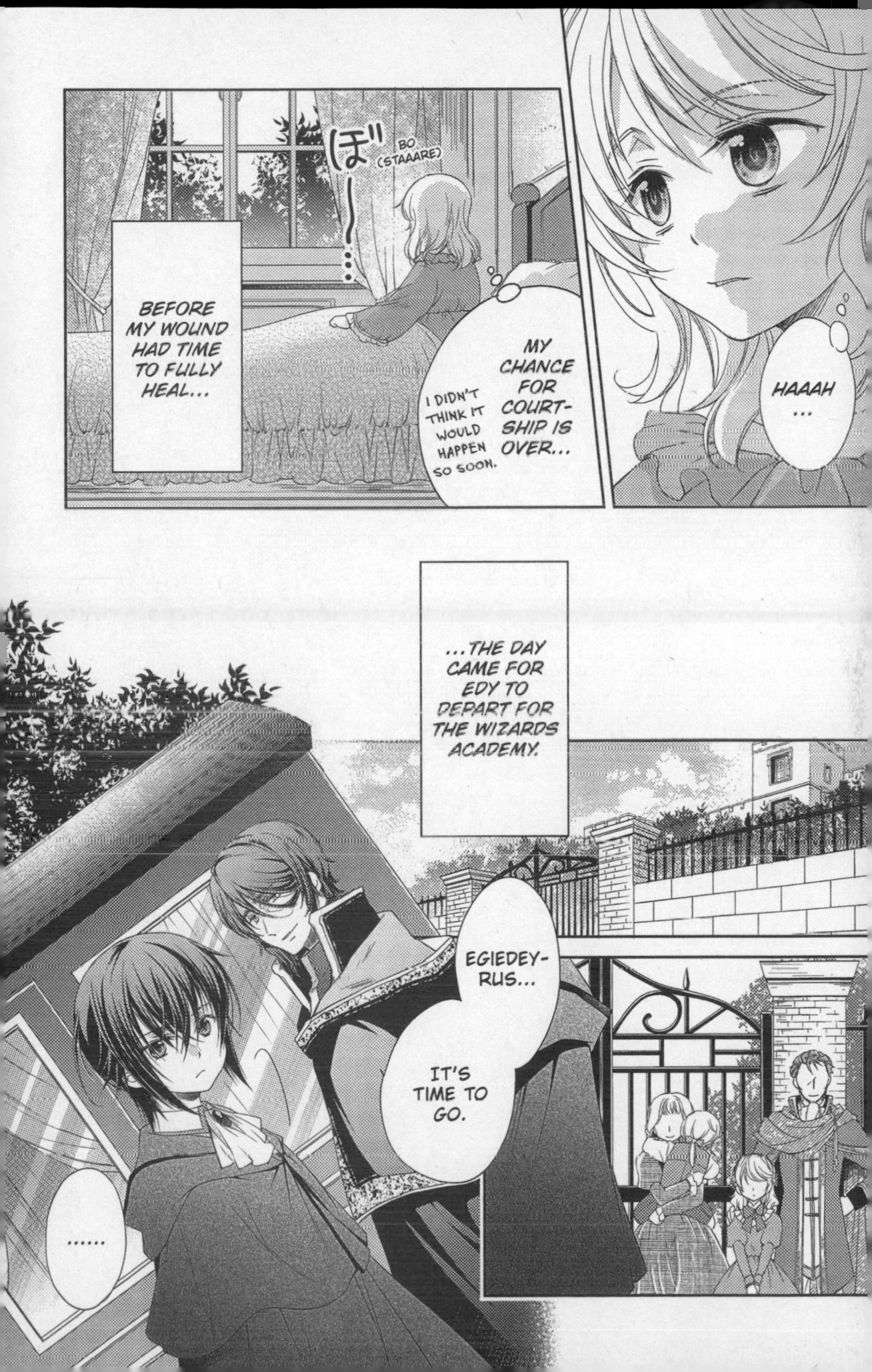
HAAAH…
ぼ
BO (STAAARE)
MY CHANCE FOR COURTSHIP IS OVER…
I DIDN'T THINK IT WOULD HAPPEN SO SOON.
BEFORE MY WOUND HAD TIME TO FULLY HEAL…
…THE DAY CAME FOR EDY TO DEPART FOR THE WIZARDS ACADEMY.
EGIEDEYRUS…
IT'S TIME TO GO.
……

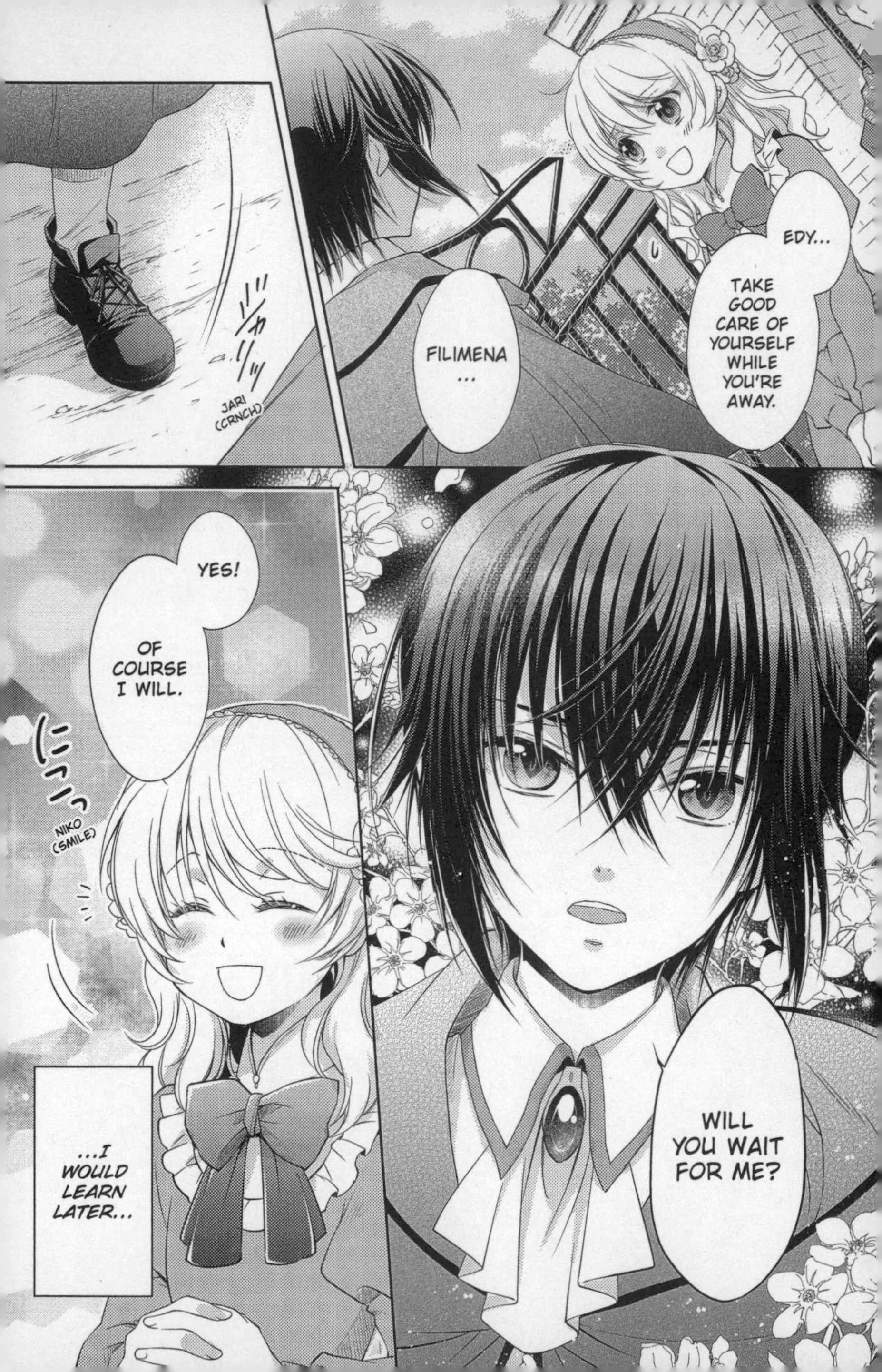
EDY...
TAKE GOOD CARE OF YOURSELF WHILE YOU'RE AWAY.
FILIMENA ...
JARI (CRNCH)
WILL YOU WAIT FOR ME?
YES!
OF COURSE I WILL.
NIKO (SMILE)
...I WOULD LEARN LATER...

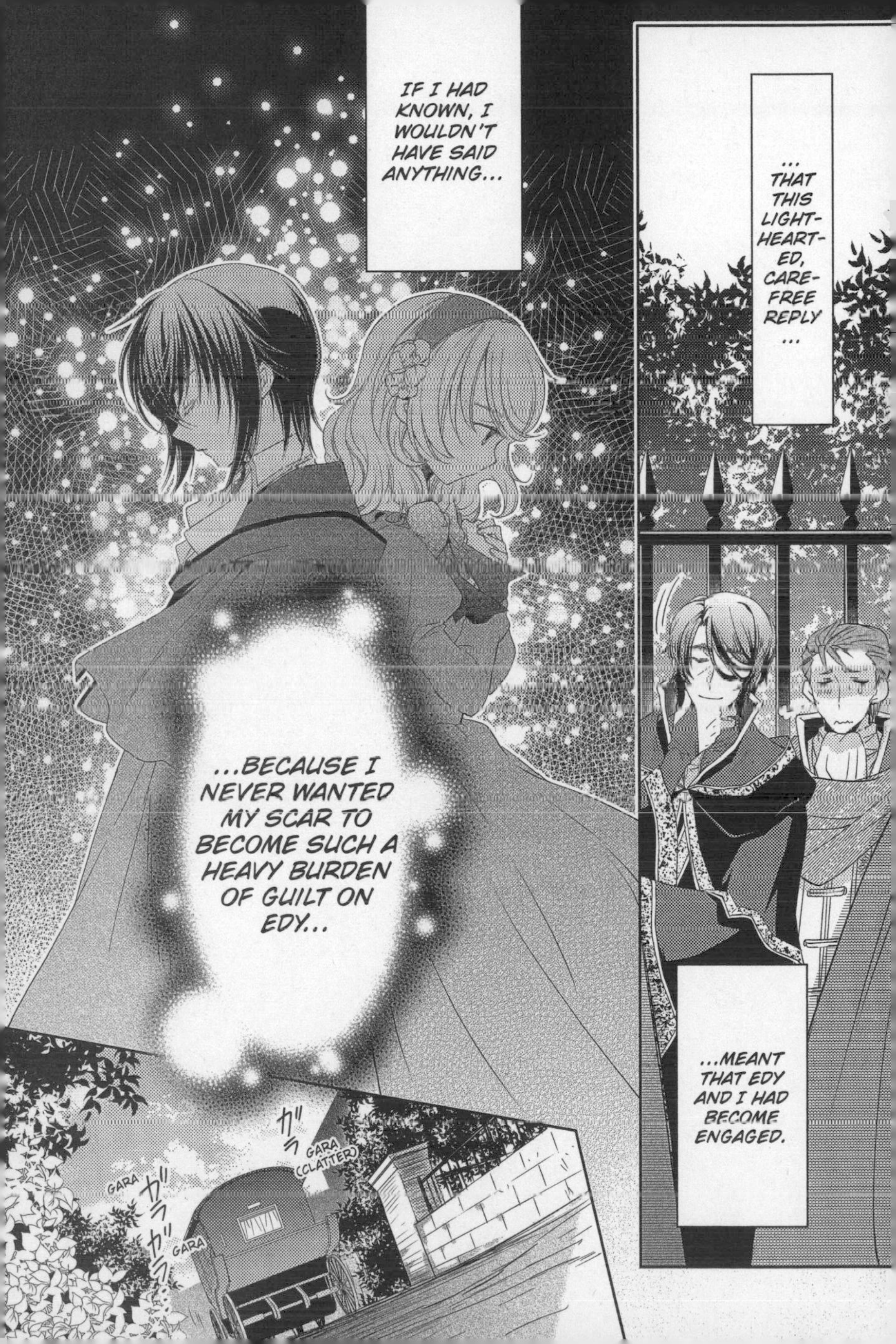
...THAT THIS LIGHT-HEARTED, CAREFREE REPLY...
...MEANT THAT EDY AND I HAD BECOME ENGAGED.
IF I HAD KNOWN, I WOULDN'T HAVE SAID ANYTHING...
...BECAUSE I NEVER WANTED MY SCAR TO BECOME SUCH A HEAVY BURDEN OF GUILT ON EDY...
GARA (CLATTER)
GARA
GARA

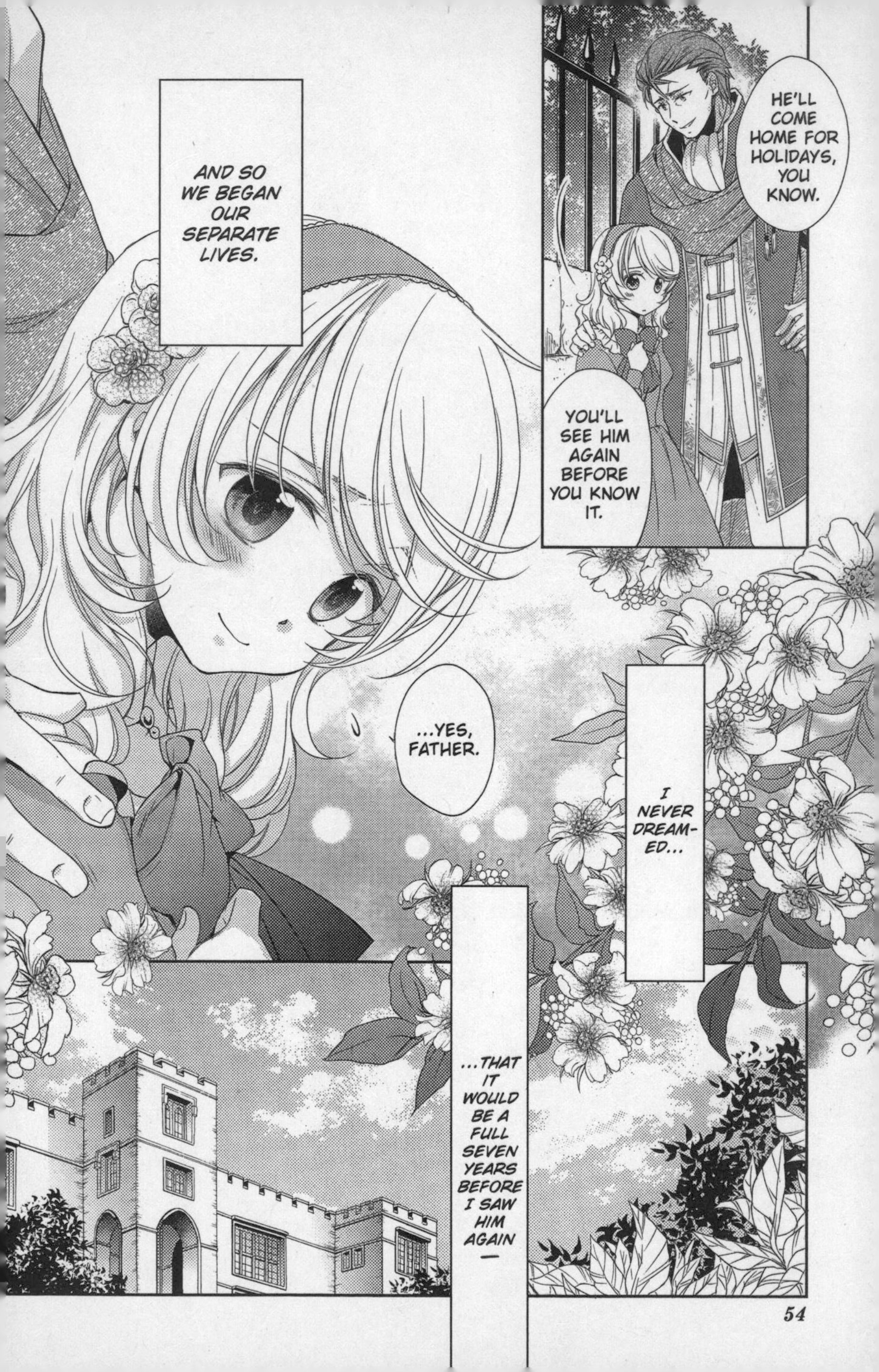
HE'LL COME HOME FOR HOLIDAYS, YOU KNOW.
YOU'LL SEE HIM AGAIN BEFORE YOU KNOW IT.
AND SO WE BEGAN OUR SEPARATE LIVES.
...YES, FATHER.
I NEVER DREAM-ED...
...THAT IT WOULD BE A FULL SEVEN YEARS BEFORE I SAW HIM AGAIN —

FIANCÉE OF THE WIZARD

Chapter 3
Egiedeyrus's Hope

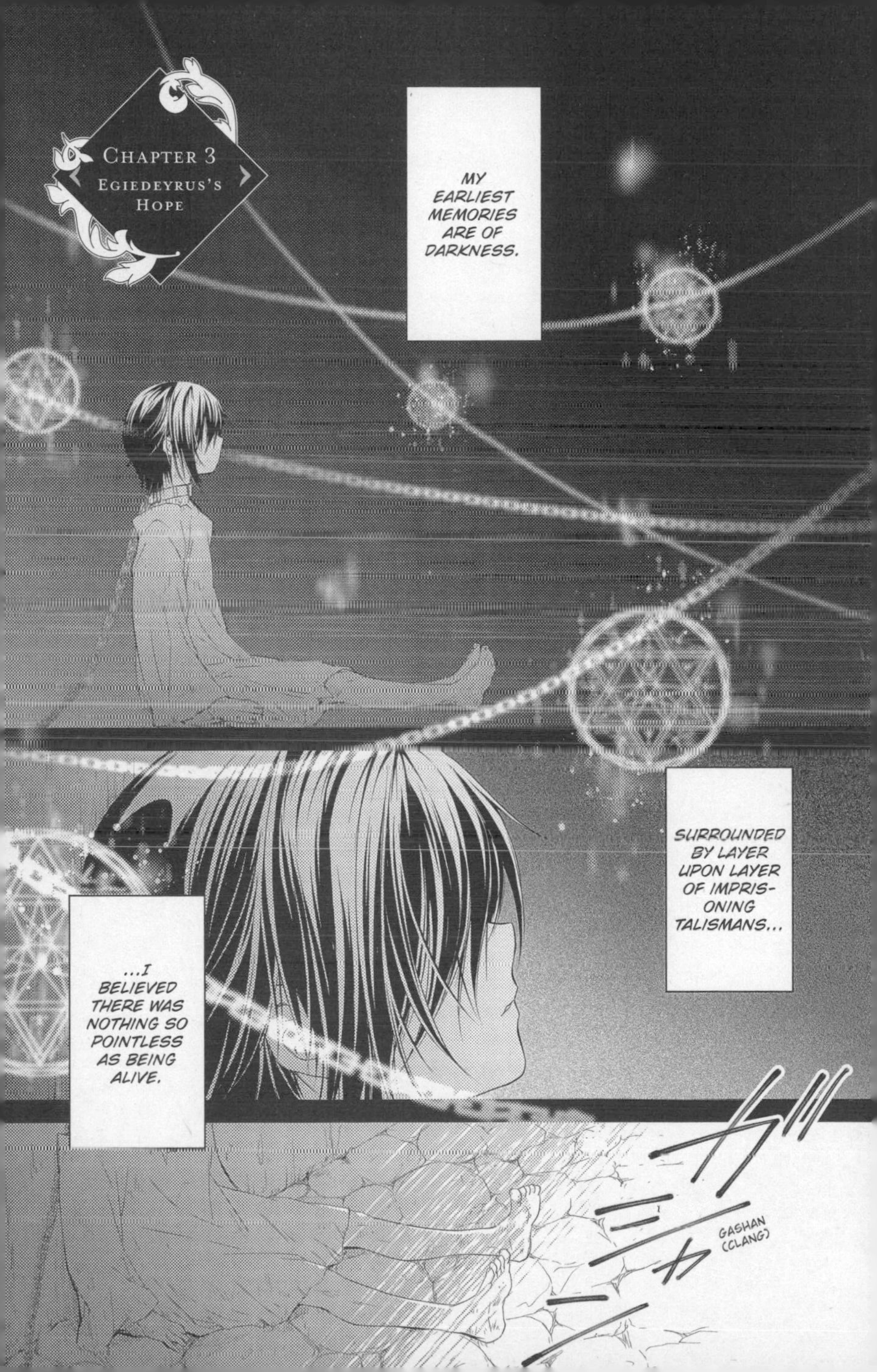

MY EARLIEST MEMORIES ARE OF DARKNESS.
SURROUNDED BY LAYER UPON LAYER OF IMPRIS-ONING TALISMANS...
...I BELIEVED THERE WAS NOTHING SO POINTLESS AS BEING ALIVE.
GASHAN (CLANG)

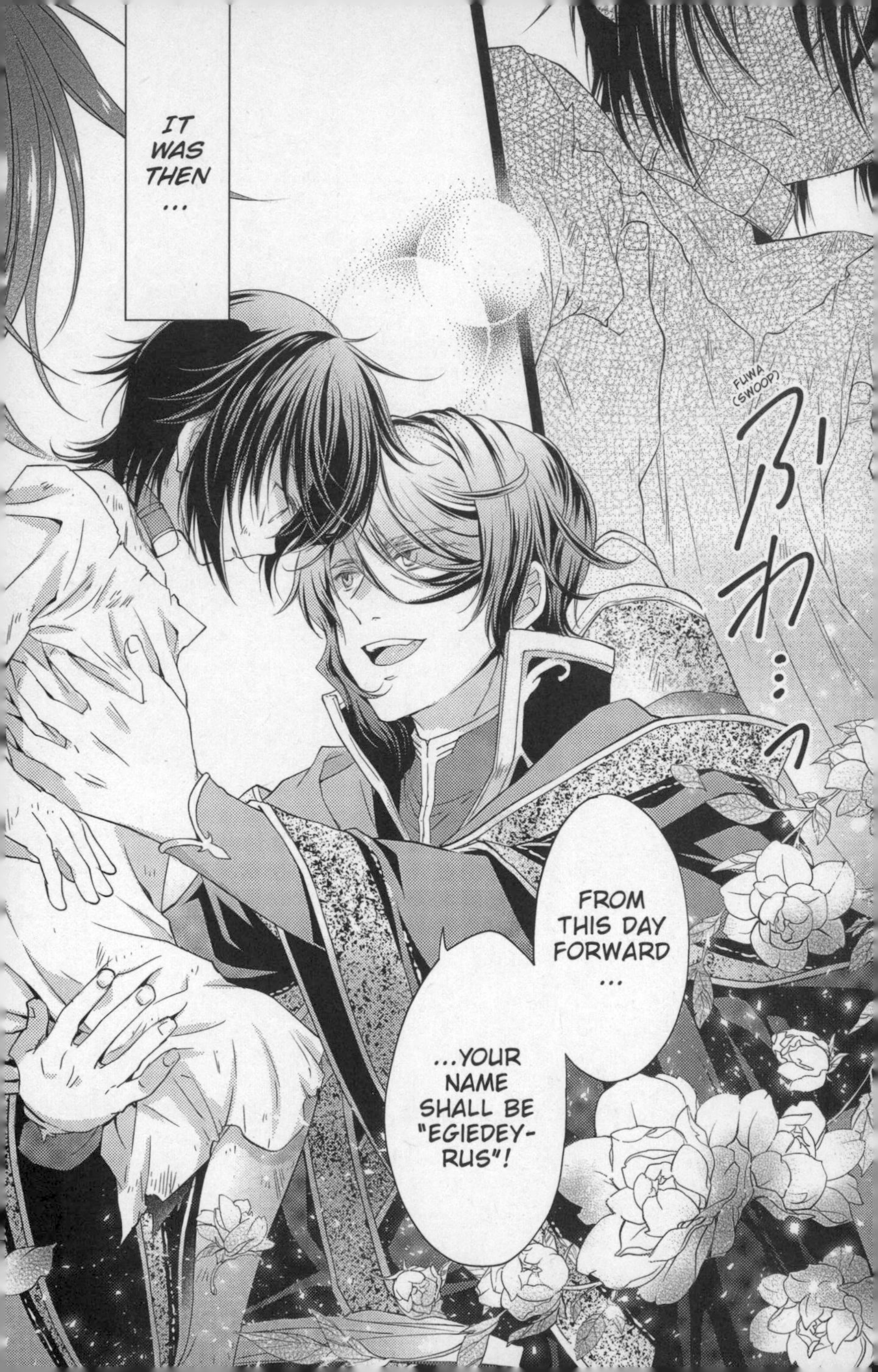
IT WAS THEN ...
FUWA (SWOOP)
ふわ…っ
FROM THIS DAY FORWARD ...
...YOUR NAME SHALL BE "EGIEDEY-RUS"!

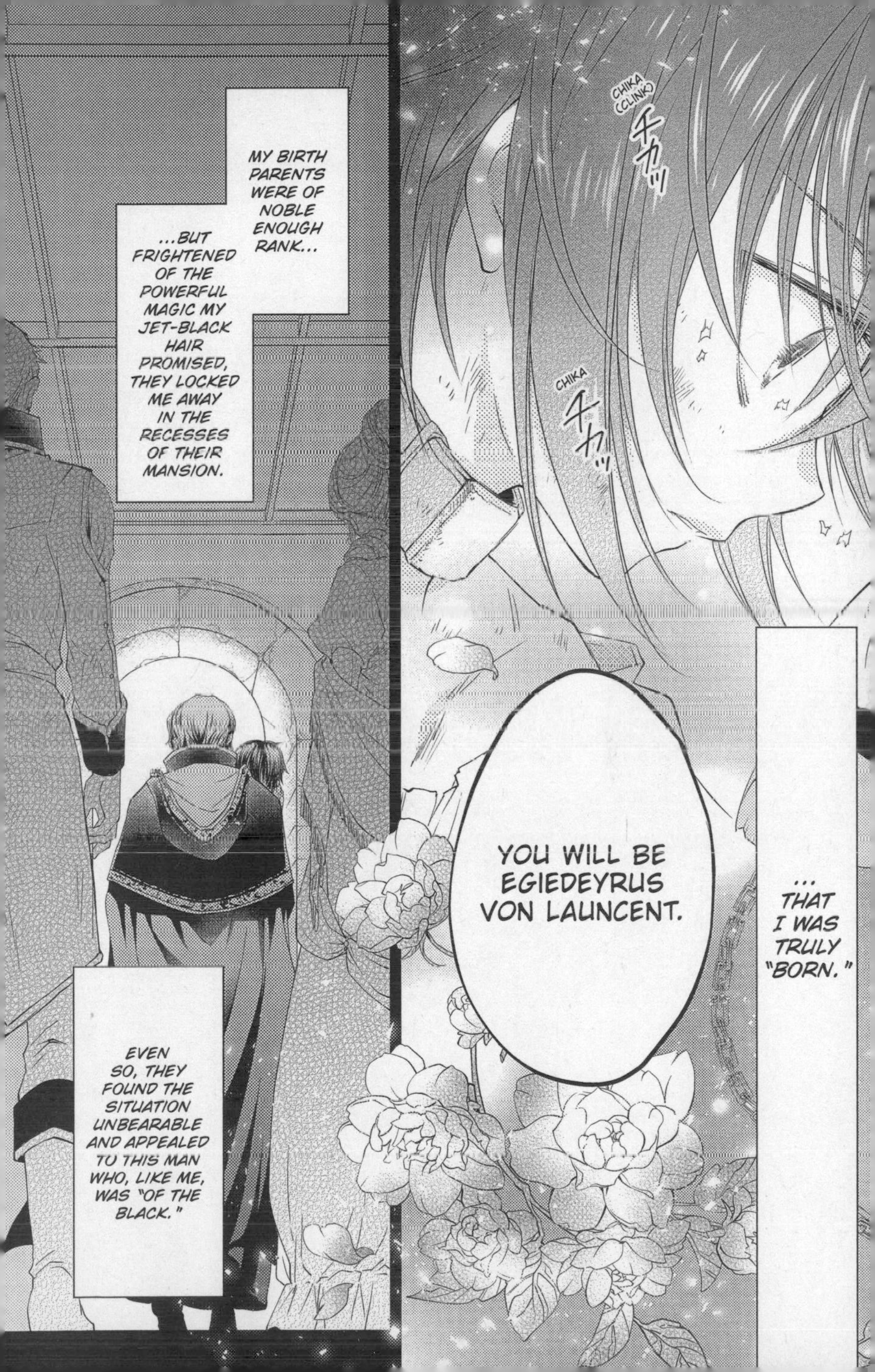
CHIKA (CLINK)
チカッ
CHIKA
チカッ
YOU WILL BE EGIEDEYRUS VON LAUNCENT.
... THAT I WAS TRULY "BORN."
MY BIRTH PARENTS WERE OF NOBLE ENOUGH RANK...
...BUT FRIGHTENED OF THE POWERFUL MAGIC MY JET-BLACK HAIR PROMISED, THEY LOCKED ME AWAY IN THE RECESSES OF THEIR MANSION.
EVEN SO, THEY FOUND THE SITUATION UNBEARABLE AND APPEALED TO THIS MAN WHO, LIKE ME, WAS "OF THE BLACK."

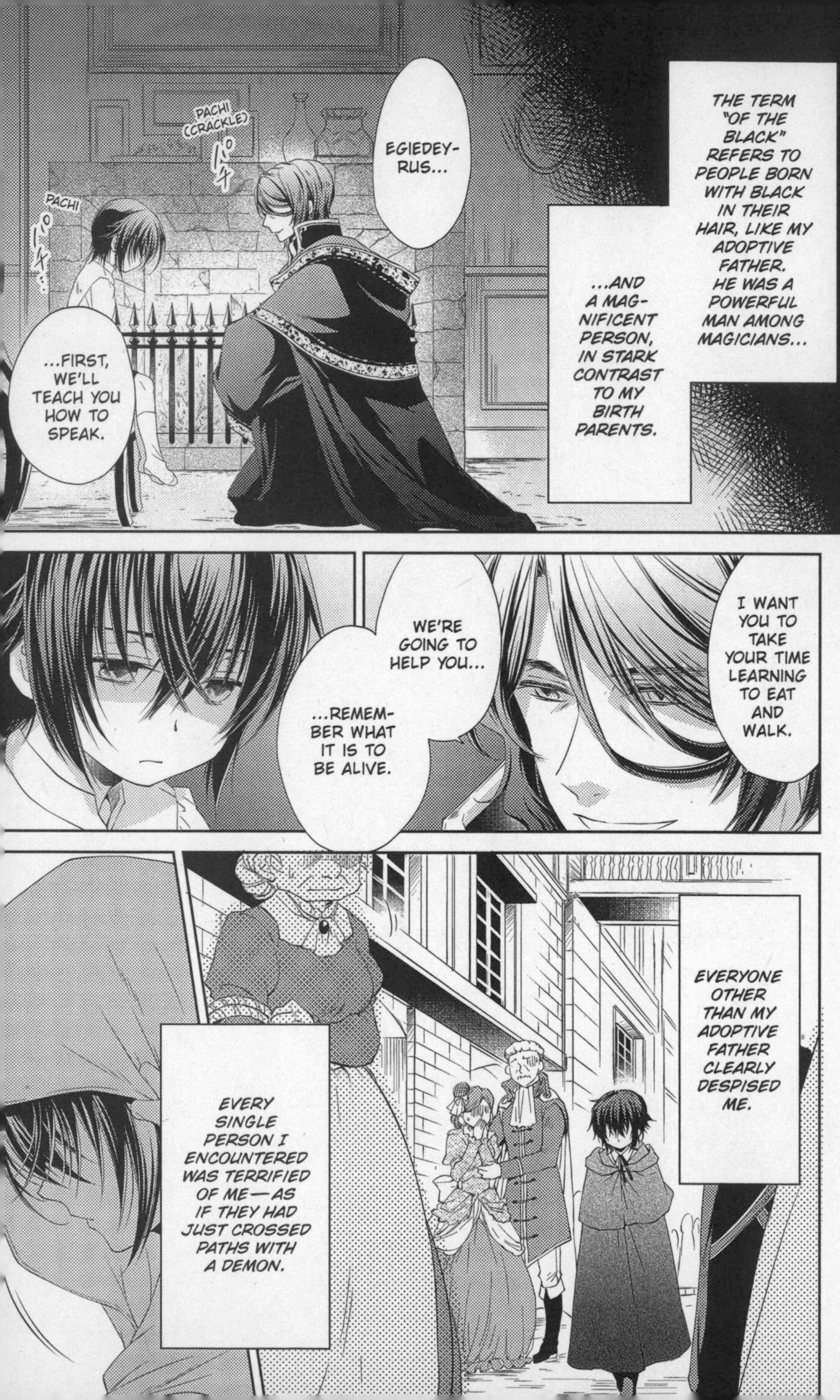
THE TERM "OF THE BLACK" REFERS TO PEOPLE BORN WITH BLACK IN THEIR HAIR, LIKE MY ADOPTIVE FATHER. HE WAS A POWERFUL MAN AMONG MAGICIANS...
...AND A MAGNIFICENT PERSON, IN STARK CONTRAST TO MY BIRTH PARENTS.
EGIEDEYRUS...
PACHI (CRACKLE)
PACHI
...FIRST, WE'LL TEACH YOU HOW TO SPEAK.
I WANT YOU TO TAKE YOUR TIME LEARNING TO EAT AND WALK.
WE'RE GOING TO HELP YOU...
...REMEMBER WHAT IT IS TO BE ALIVE.
EVERYONE OTHER THAN MY ADOPTIVE FATHER CLEARLY DESPISED ME.
EVERY SINGLE PERSON I ENCOUNTERED WAS TERRIFIED OF ME—AS IF THEY HAD JUST CROSSED PATHS WITH A DEMON.

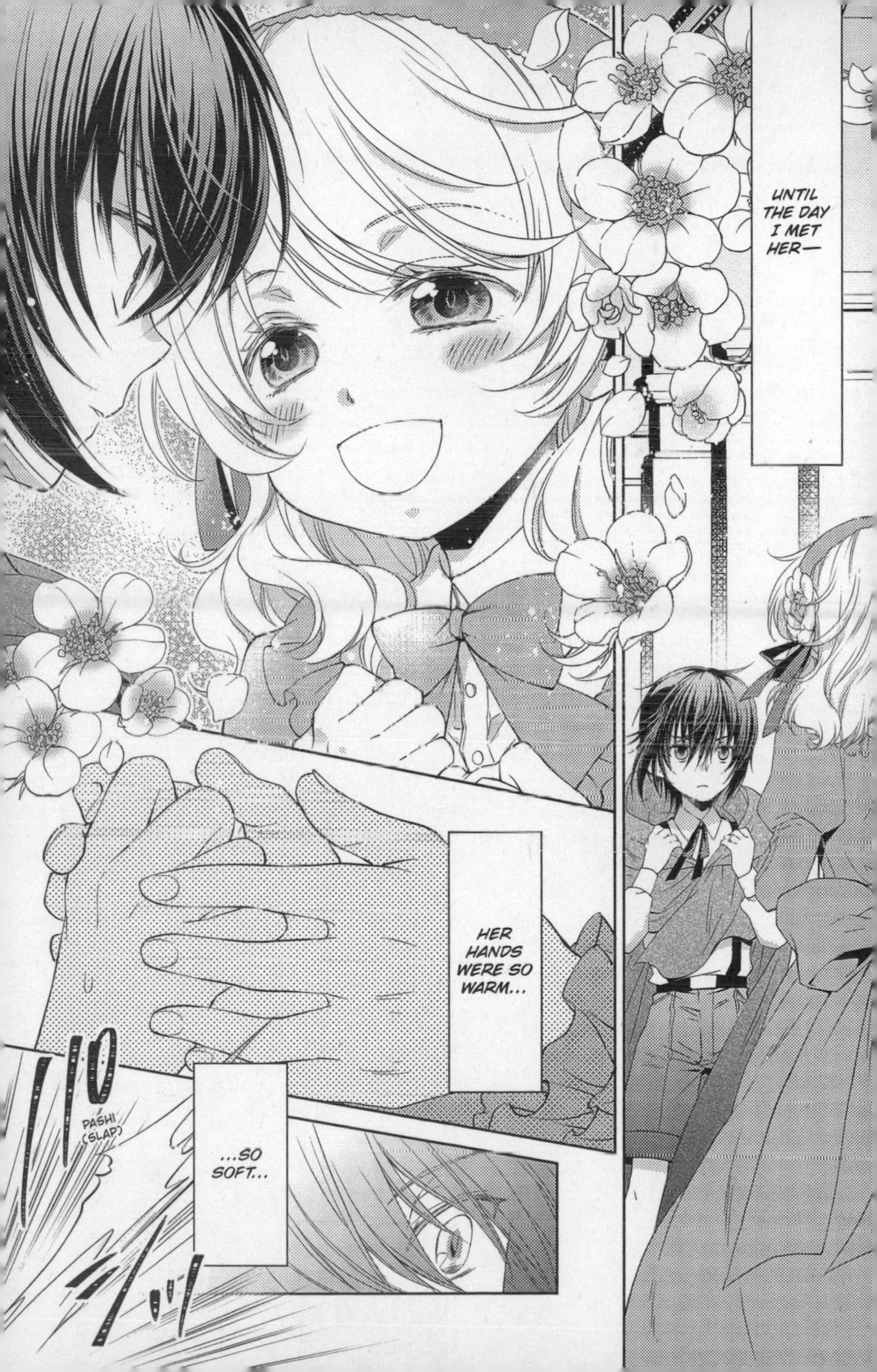
UNTIL THE DAY I MET HER—
HER HANDS WERE SO WARM...
...SO SOFT...
PASHI (SLAP)

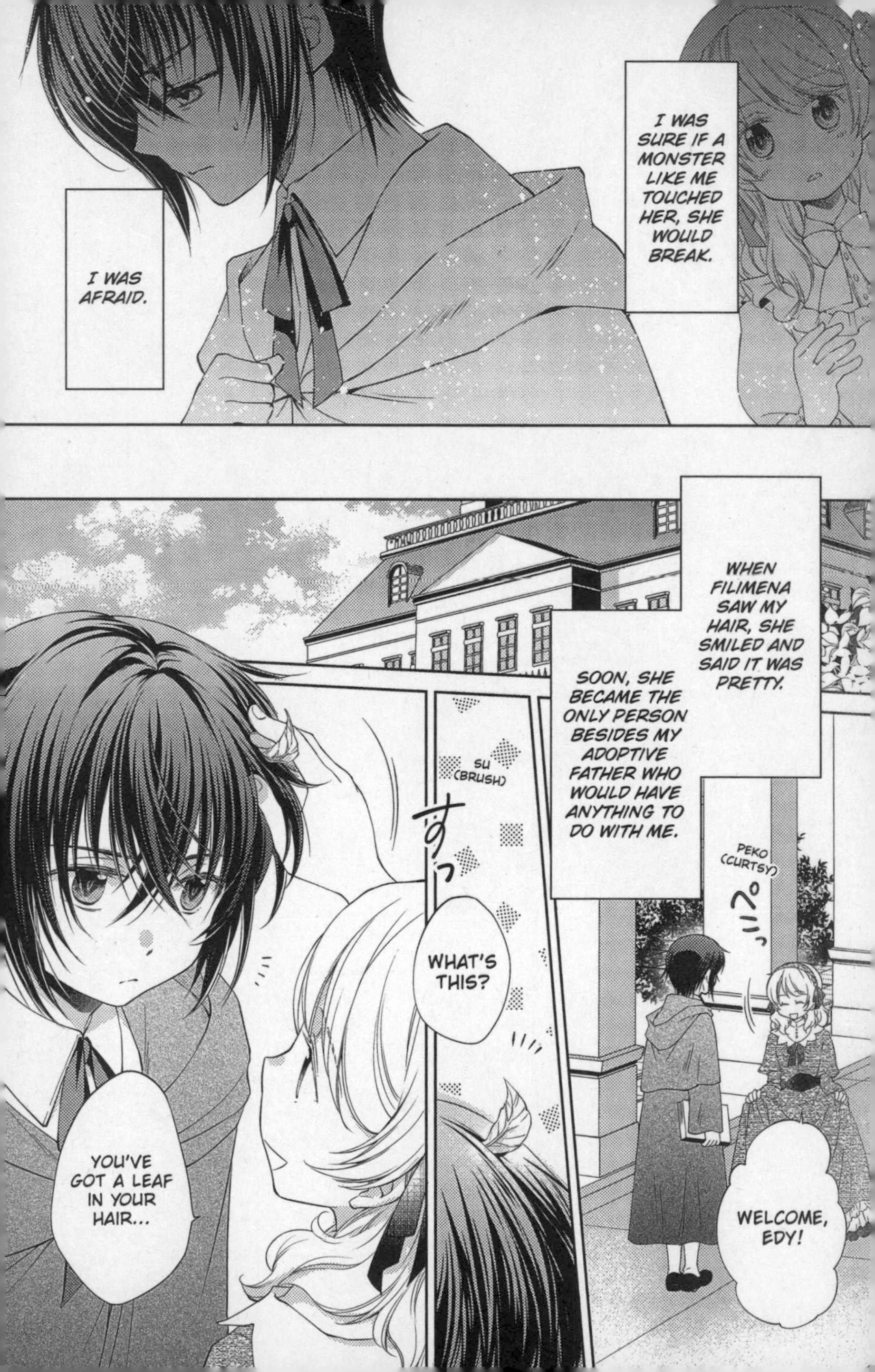
I WAS SURE IF A MONSTER LIKE ME TOUCHED HER, SHE WOULD BREAK.
I WAS AFRAID.
WHEN FILIMENA SAW MY HAIR, SHE SMILED AND SAID IT WAS PRETTY.
SOON, SHE BECAME THE ONLY PERSON BESIDES MY ADOPTIVE FATHER WHO WOULD HAVE ANYTHING TO DO WITH ME.
PEKO (CURTSY)
WELCOME, EDY!
SU (BRUSH)
WHAT'S THIS?
YOU'VE GOT A LEAF IN YOUR HAIR...

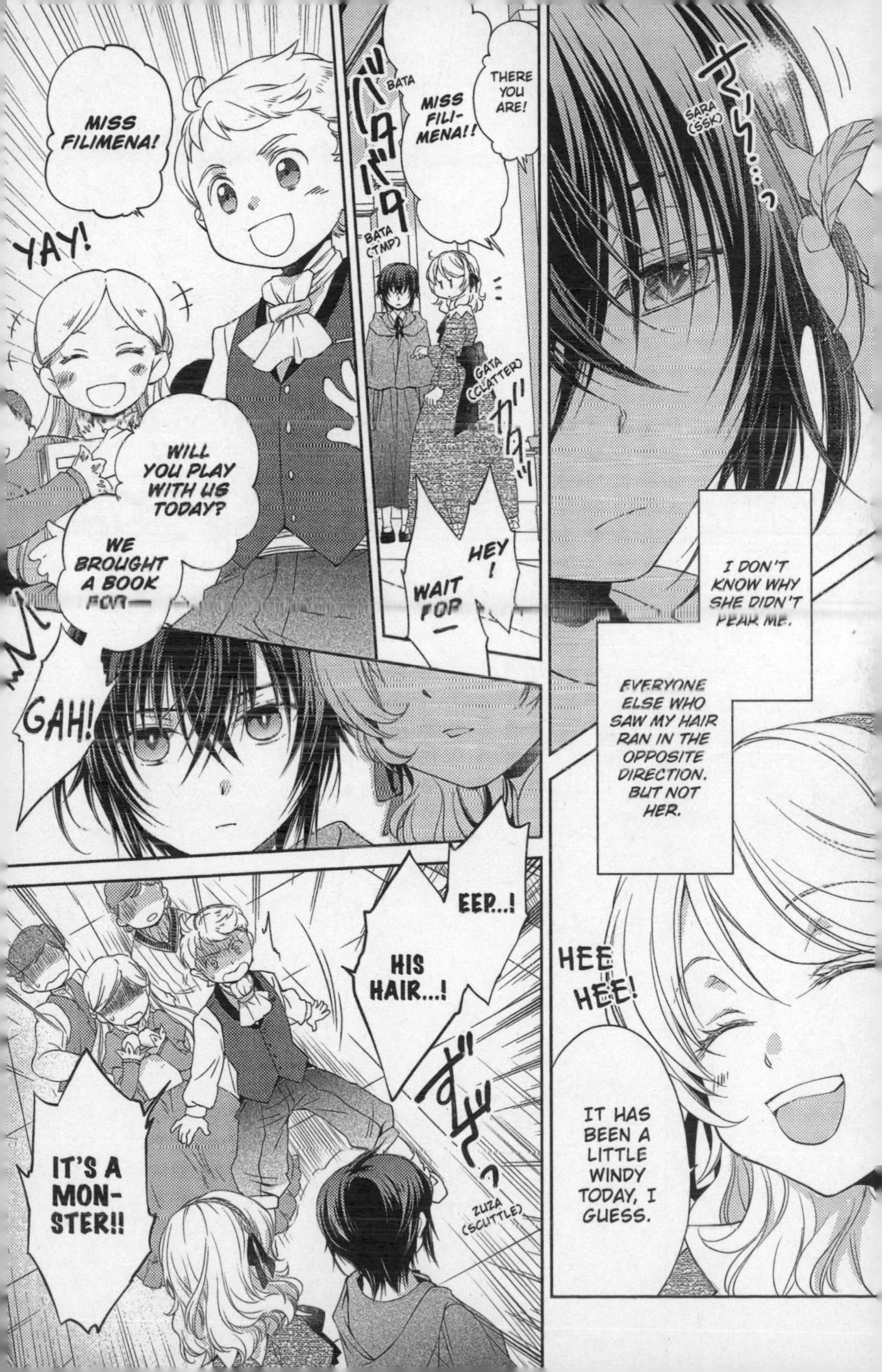
SARA (SSK)
I DON'T KNOW WHY SHE DIDN'T FEAR ME.
EVERYONE ELSE WHO SAW MY HAIR RAN IN THE OPPOSITE DIRECTION. BUT NOT HER.
THERE YOU ARE!
MISS FILI-MENA!!
BATA
BATA (TMP)
GATA (CLATTER)
HEY!
WAIT FOR—
MISS FILIMENA!
YAY!
WILL YOU PLAY WITH US TODAY?
WE BROUGHT A BOOK FOR—
GAH!
HEE HEE!
IT HAS BEEN A LITTLE WINDY TODAY, I GUESS.
EEP...!
HIS HAIR...!
IT'S A MON-STER!!
ZUZA (SCUTTLE)

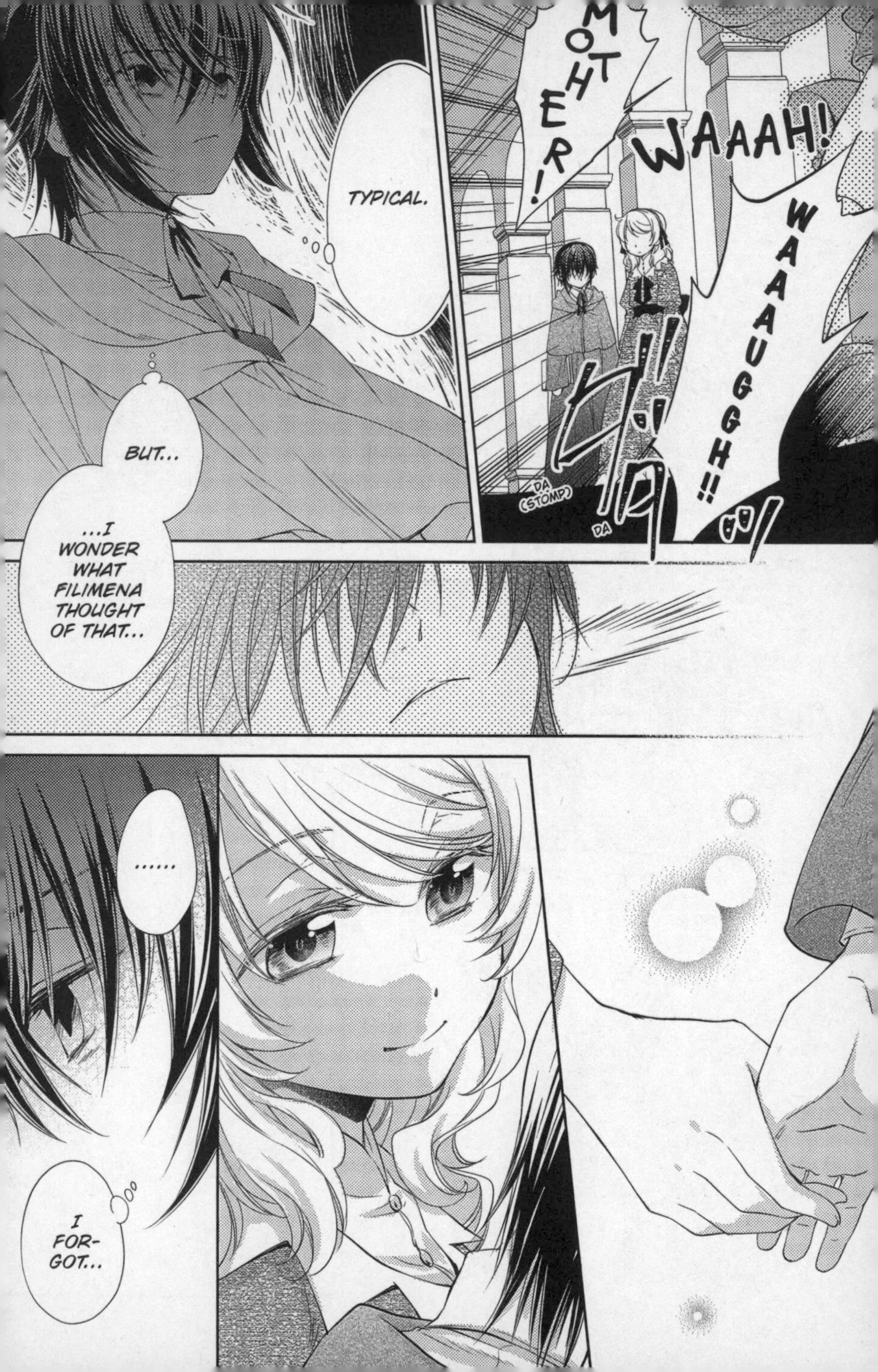
MOTHER!
WAAAH!
WAAAAUGGH!!
DA (STOMP)
DA
TYPICAL.
BUT...
...I WONDER WHAT FILIMENA THOUGHT OF THAT...
......
I FOR-GOT...

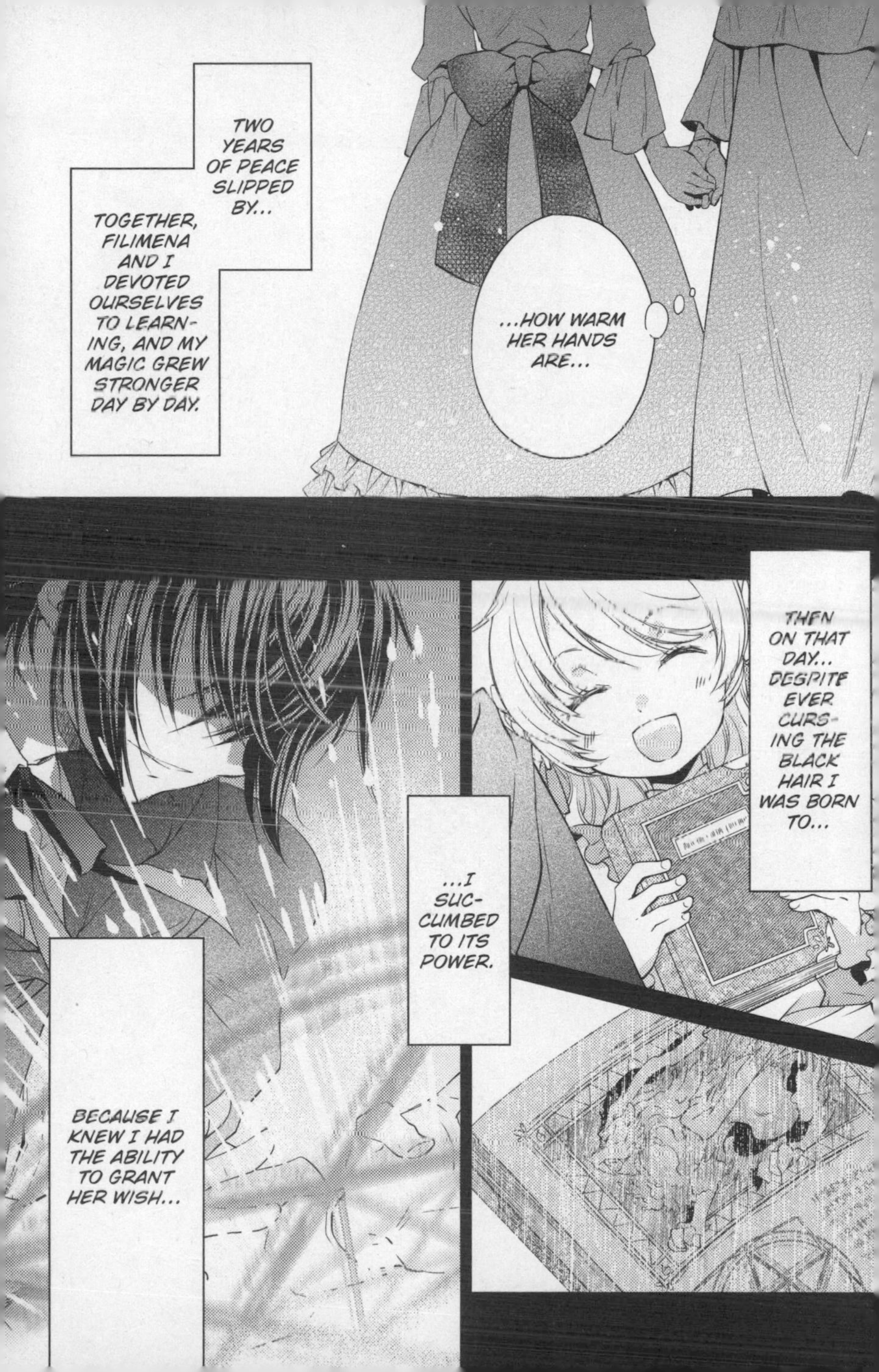
TWO YEARS OF PEACE SLIPPED BY...
TOGETHER, FILIMENA AND I DEVOTED OURSELVES TO LEARNING, AND MY MAGIC GREW STRONGER DAY BY DAY.
...HOW WARM HER HANDS ARE...
THEN ON THAT DAY... DESPITE EVER CURSING THE BLACK HAIR I WAS BORN TO...
...I SUCCUMBED TO ITS POWER.
BECAUSE I KNEW I HAD THE ABILITY TO GRANT HER WISH...

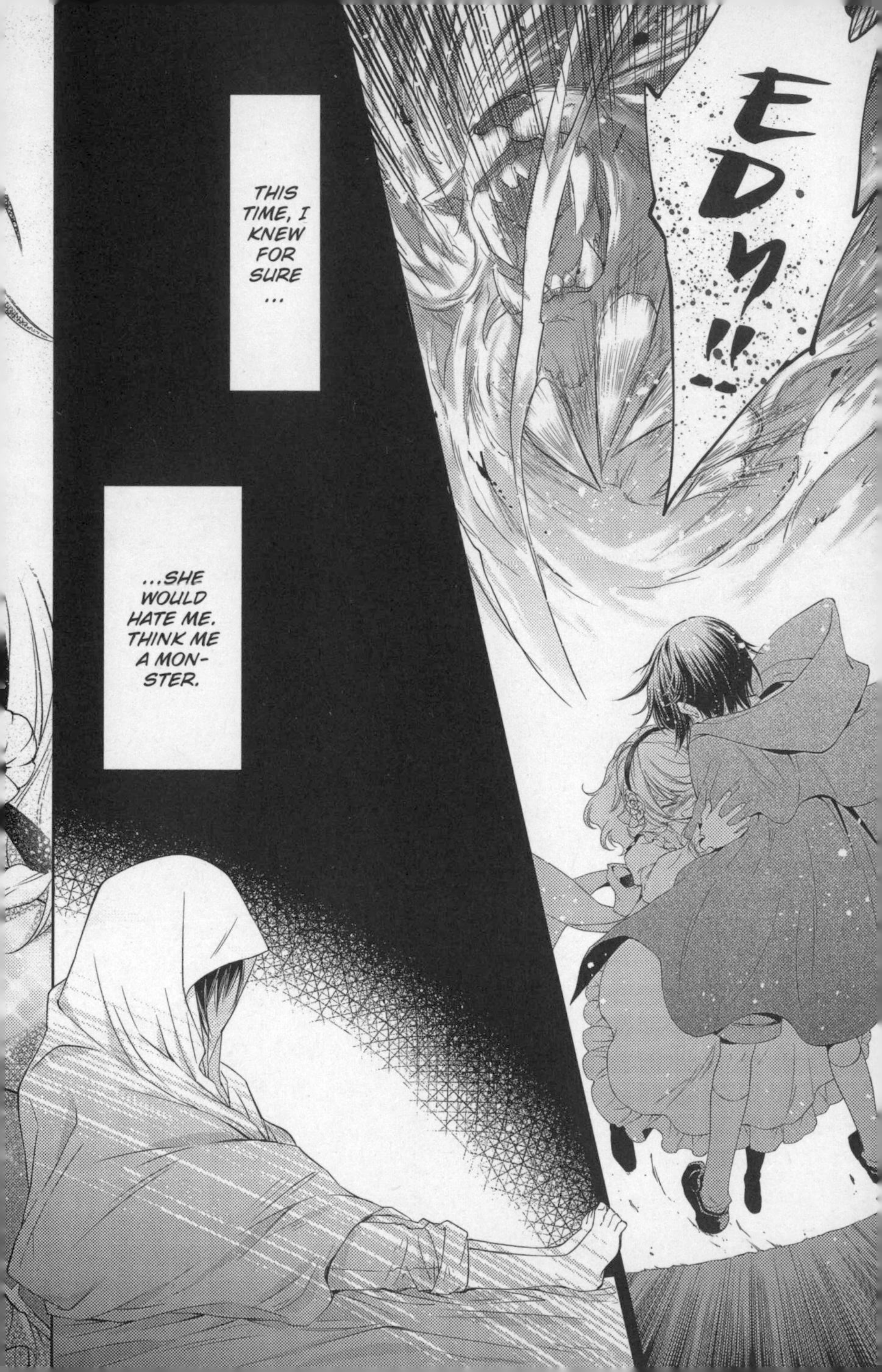
EDY!!
THIS TIME, I KNEW FOR SURE...
...SHE WOULD HATE ME. THINK ME A MONSTER.

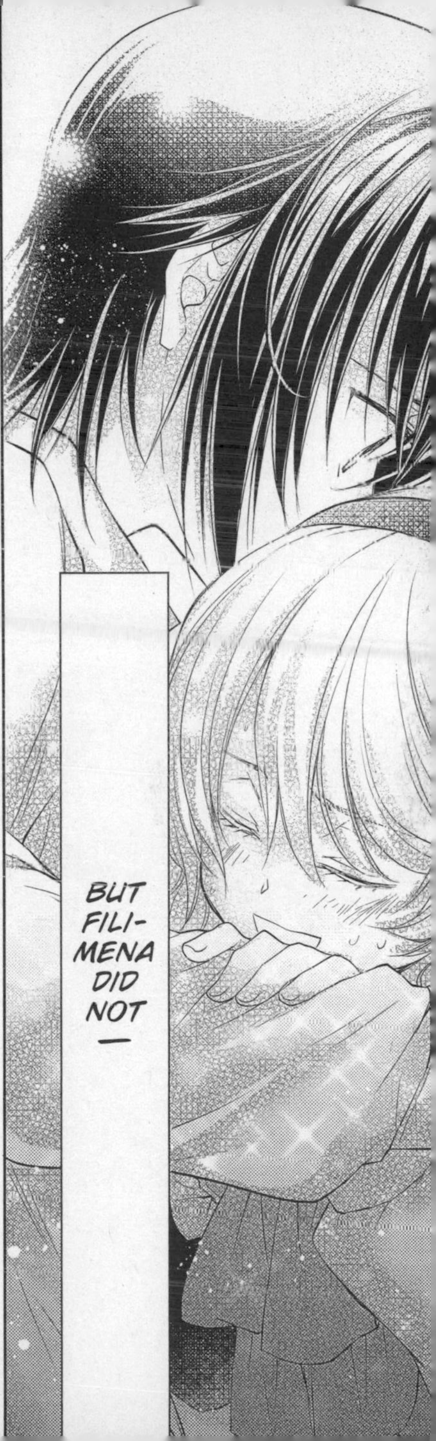
BUT FILI-MENA DID NOT —

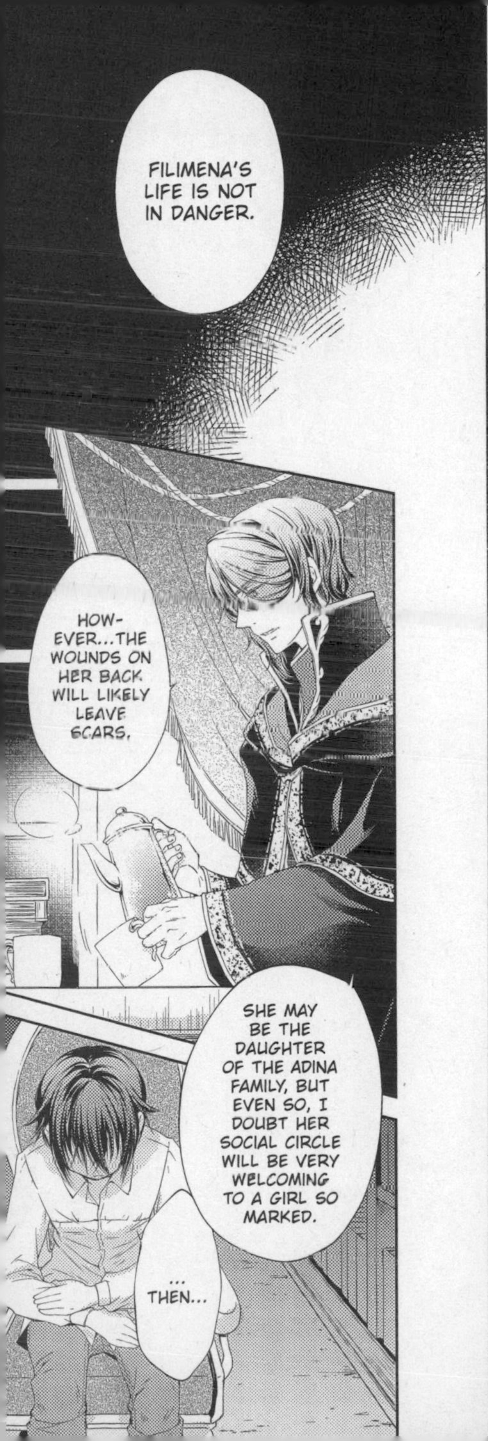
FILIMENA'S LIFE IS NOT IN DANGER.
HOW-EVER...THE WOUNDS ON HER BACK WILL LIKELY LEAVE SCARS.
SHE MAY BE THE DAUGHTER OF THE ADINA FAMILY, BUT EVEN SO, I DOUBT HER SOCIAL CIRCLE WILL BE VERY WELCOMING TO A GIRL SO MARKED.
...THEN...

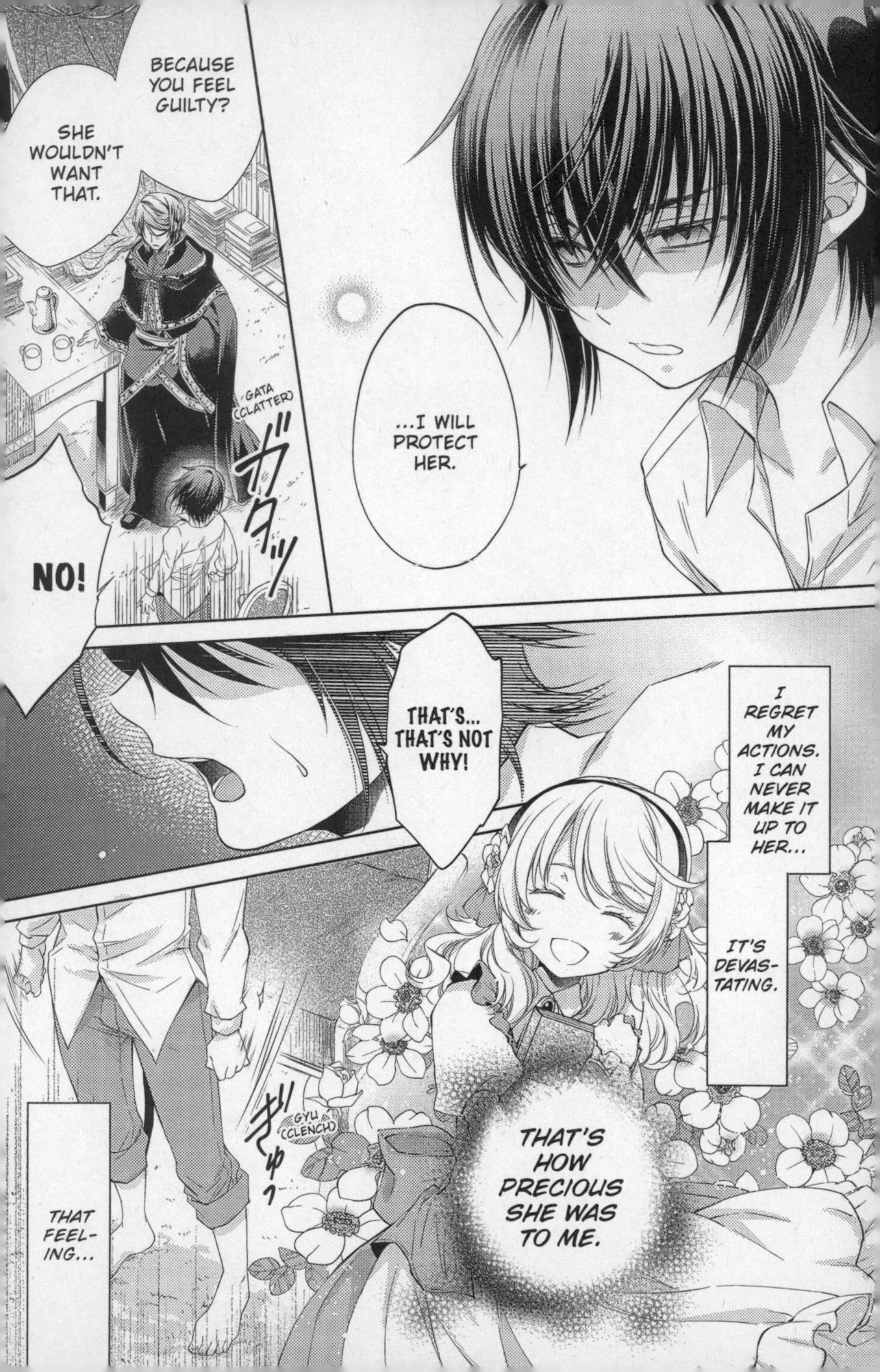
...I WILL PROTECT HER.
BECAUSE YOU FEEL GUILTY?
SHE WOULDN'T WANT THAT.
GATA (CLATTER)
NO!
THAT'S... THAT'S NOT WHY!
I REGRET MY ACTIONS. I CAN NEVER MAKE IT UP TO HER...
IT'S DEVAS-TATING.
THAT'S HOW PRECIOUS SHE WAS TO ME.
GYU (CLENCH)
THAT FEEL-ING...

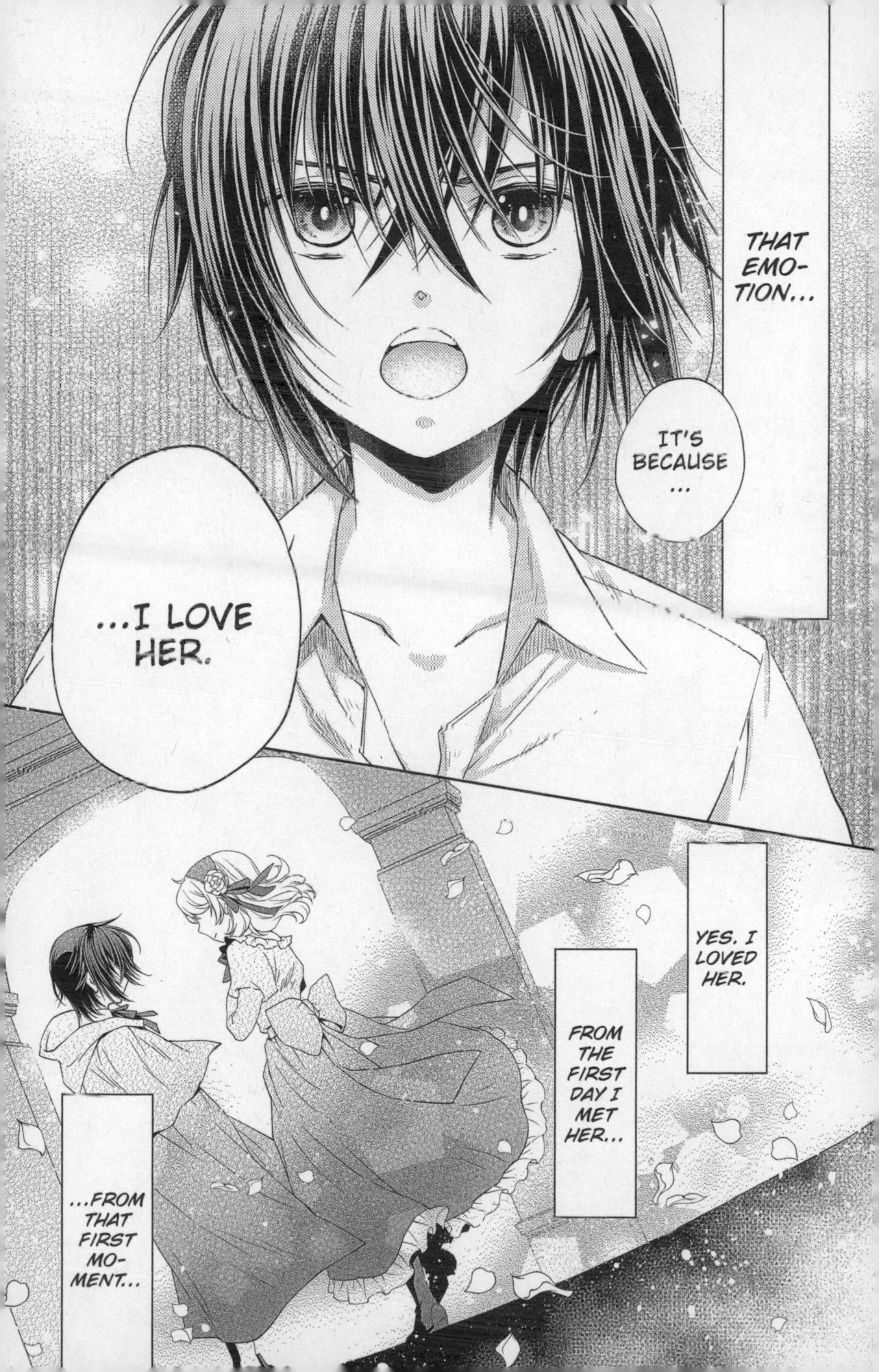
THAT EMOTION...
IT'S BECAUSE ...
...I LOVE HER.
YES. I LOVED HER.
FROM THE FIRST DAY I MET HER...
...FROM THAT FIRST MOMENT...

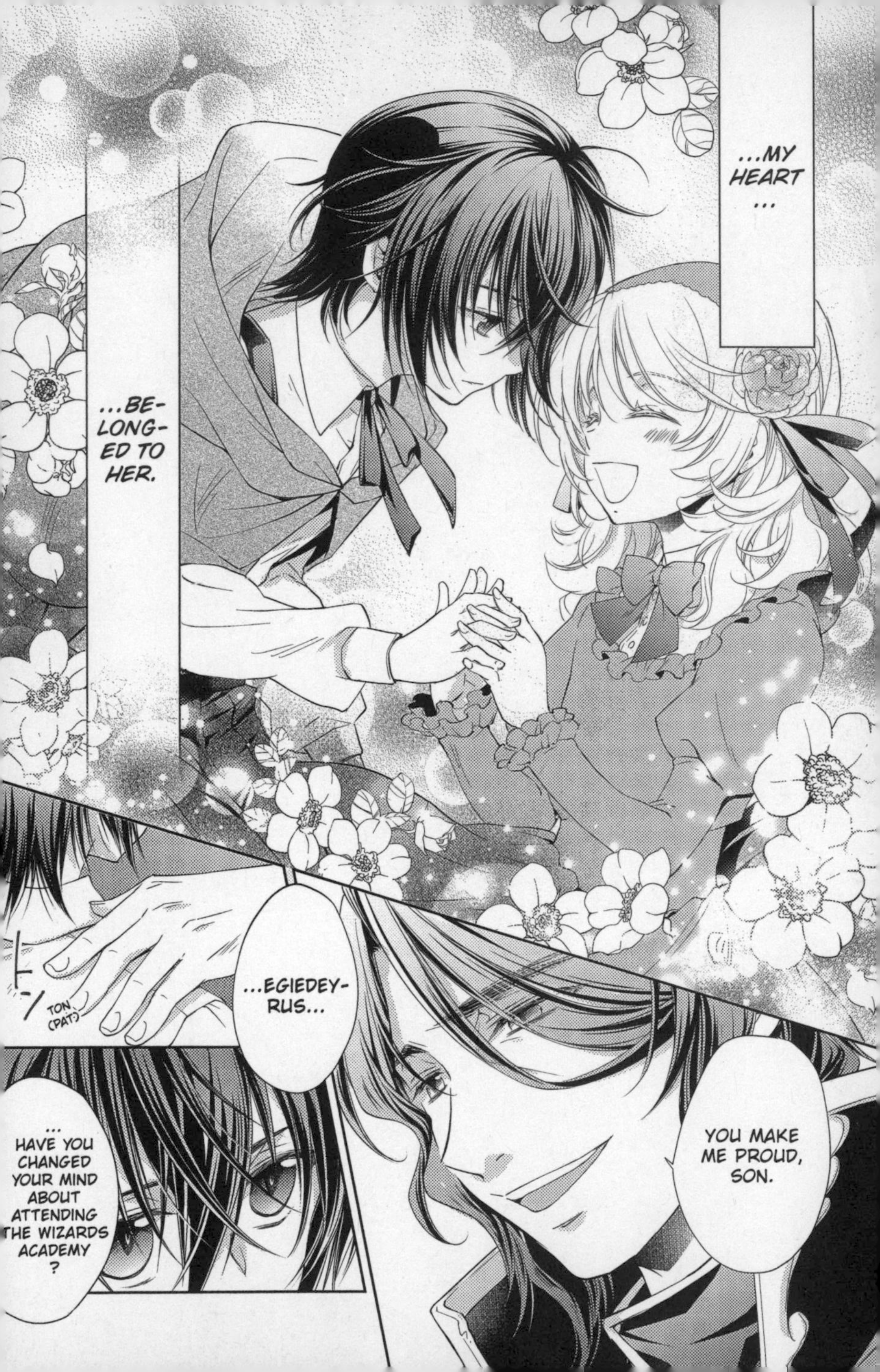
...MY HEART...
...BE-LONGED TO HER.
...EGIEDEY-RUS...
TON (PAT)
YOU MAKE ME PROUD, SON.
...HAVE YOU CHANGED YOUR MIND ABOUT ATTENDING THE WIZARDS ACADEMY?

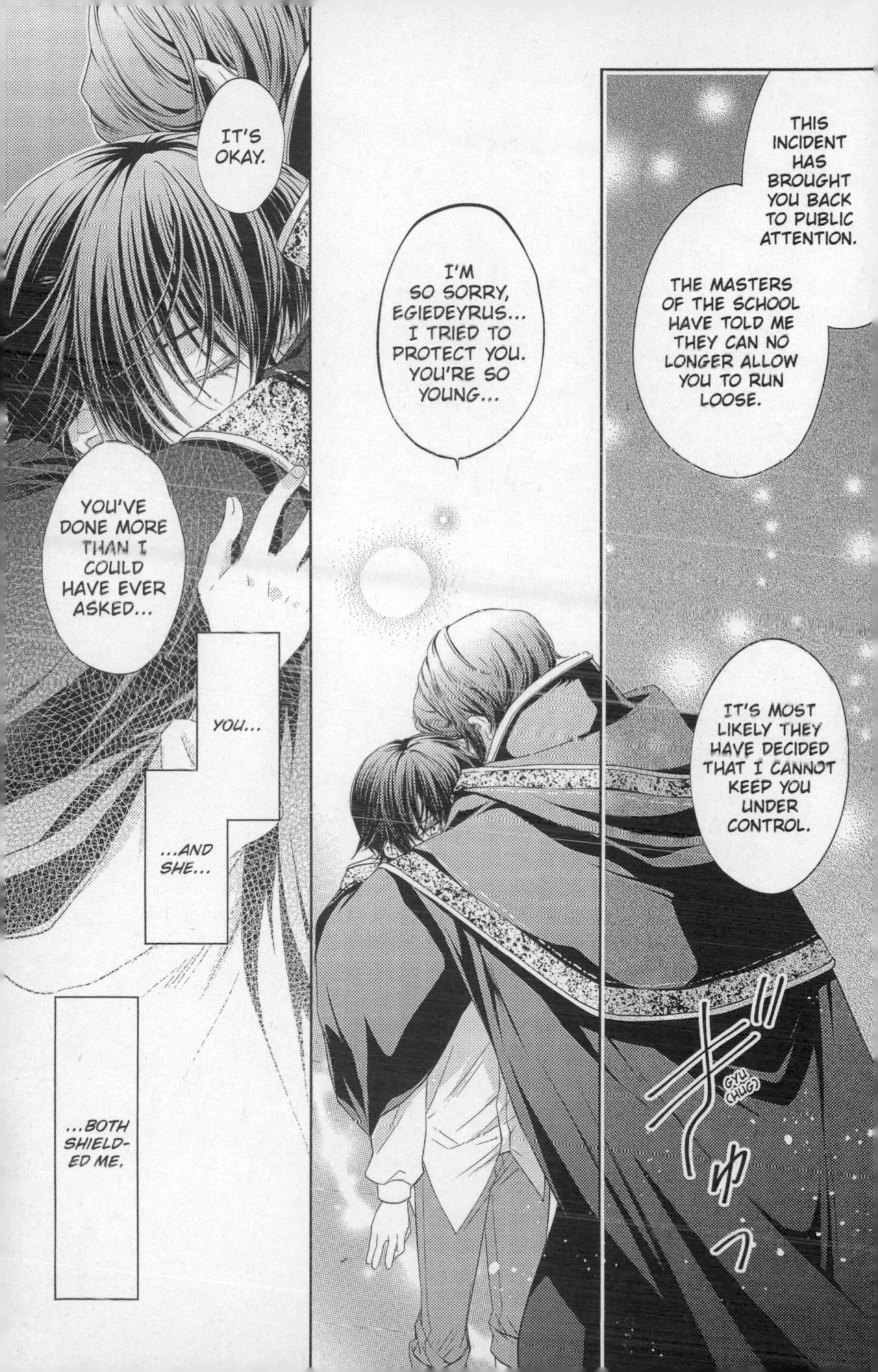
THIS INCIDENT HAS BROUGHT YOU BACK TO PUBLIC ATTENTION.
THE MASTERS OF THE SCHOOL HAVE TOLD ME THEY CAN NO LONGER ALLOW YOU TO RUN LOOSE.
IT'S MOST LIKELY THEY HAVE DECIDED THAT I CANNOT KEEP YOU UNDER CONTROL.
ぎゅっ
GYU (HUG)
I'M SO SORRY, EGIEDEYRUS... I TRIED TO PROTECT YOU. YOU'RE SO YOUNG...
IT'S OKAY.
YOU'VE DONE MORE THAN I COULD HAVE EVER ASKED...
YOU...
...AND SHE...
...BOTH SHIELD-ED ME.

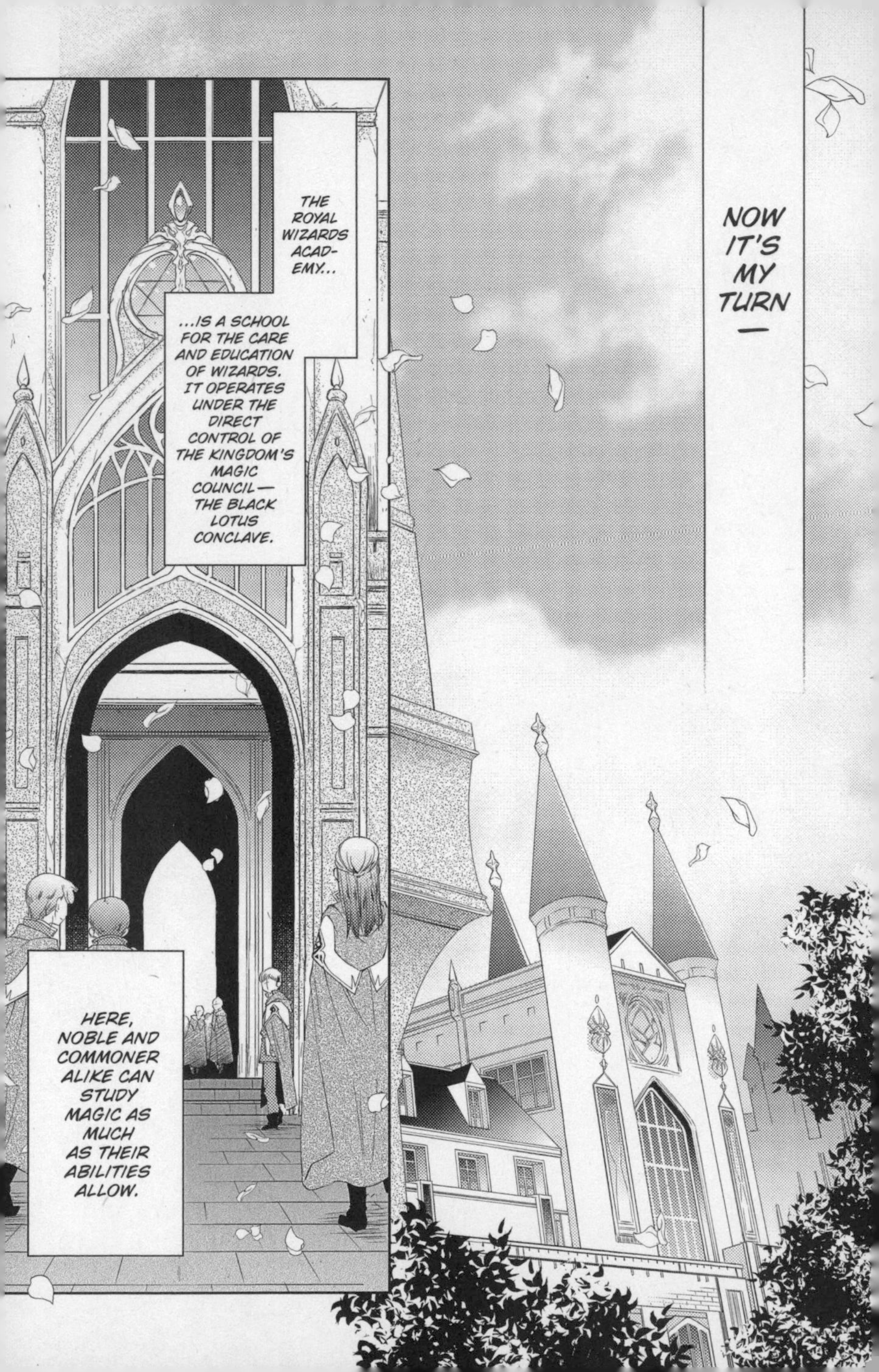
NOW IT'S MY TURN—
THE ROYAL WIZARDS ACADEMY...
...IS A SCHOOL FOR THE CARE AND EDUCATION OF WIZARDS. IT OPERATES UNDER THE DIRECT CONTROL OF THE KINGDOM'S MAGIC COUNCIL—THE BLACK LOTUS CONCLAVE.
HERE, NOBLE AND COMMONER ALIKE CAN STUDY MAGIC AS MUCH AS THEIR ABILITIES ALLOW.

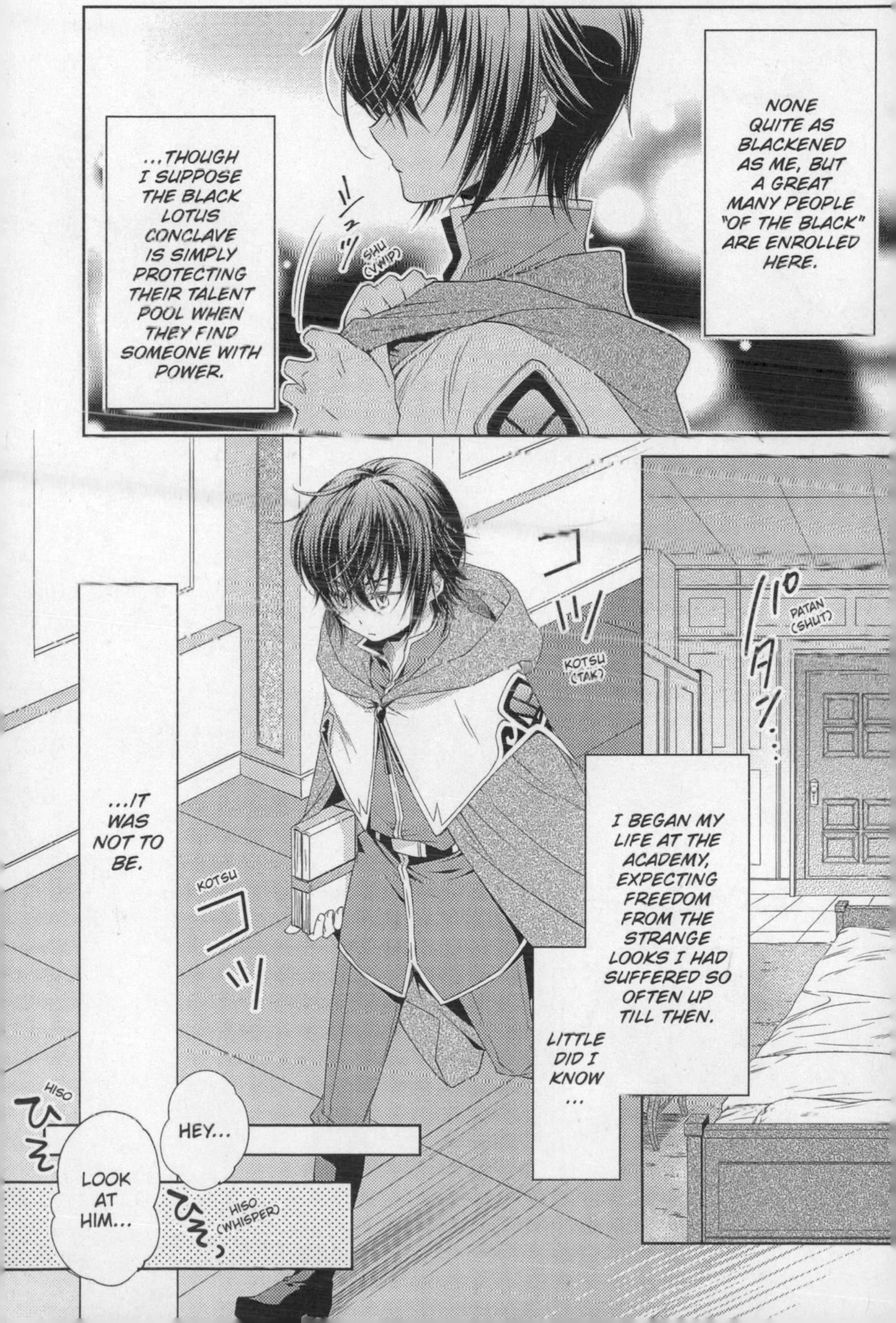
NONE QUITE AS BLACKENED AS ME, BUT A GREAT MANY PEOPLE "OF THE BLACK" ARE ENROLLED HERE.
...THOUGH I SUPPOSE THE BLACK LOTUS CONCLAVE IS SIMPLY PROTECTING THEIR TALENT POOL WHEN THEY FIND SOMEONE WITH POWER.
SHU (VWIP)
PATAN (SHUT)
KOTSU (TAK)
I BEGAN MY LIFE AT THE ACADEMY, EXPECTING FREEDOM FROM THE STRANGE LOOKS I HAD SUFFERED SO OFTEN UP TILL THEN.
LITTLE DID I KNOW ...
...IT WAS NOT TO BE.
KOTSU
HEY...
LOOK AT HIM...
HISO
HISO (WHISPER)

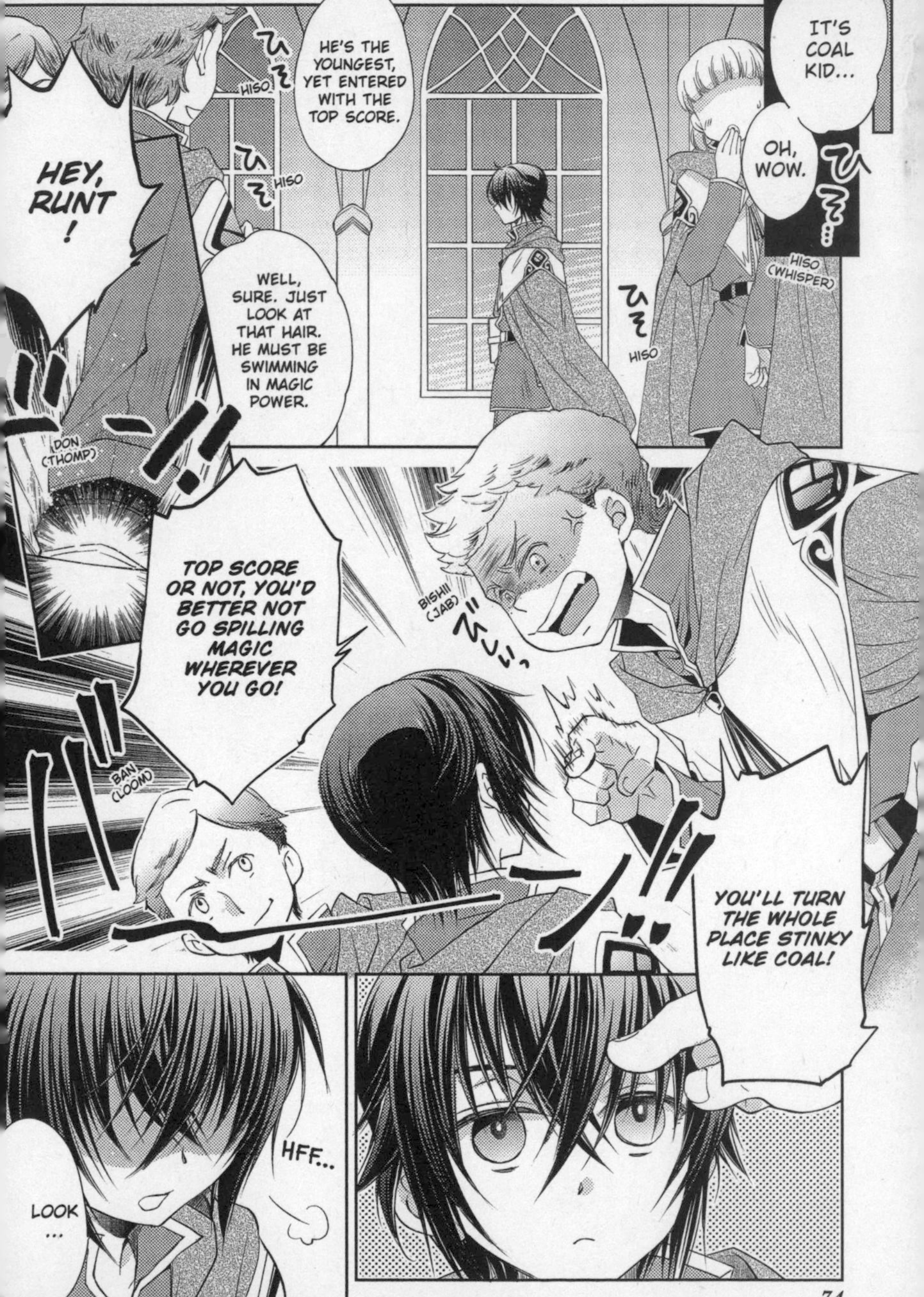
IT'S COAL KID...
OH, WOW.
HISO (WHISPER)
HISO
HE'S THE YOUNGEST, YET ENTERED WITH THE TOP SCORE.
HISO
HISO
WELL, SURE. JUST LOOK AT THAT HAIR. HE MUST BE SWIMMING IN MAGIC POWER.
HEY, RUNT!
BISHI (JAB)
TOP SCORE OR NOT, YOU'D BETTER NOT GO SPILLING MAGIC WHEREVER YOU GO!
YOU'LL TURN THE WHOLE PLACE STINKY LIKE COAL!
DON (THOMP)
BAN (LOOM)
HFF...
LOOK...

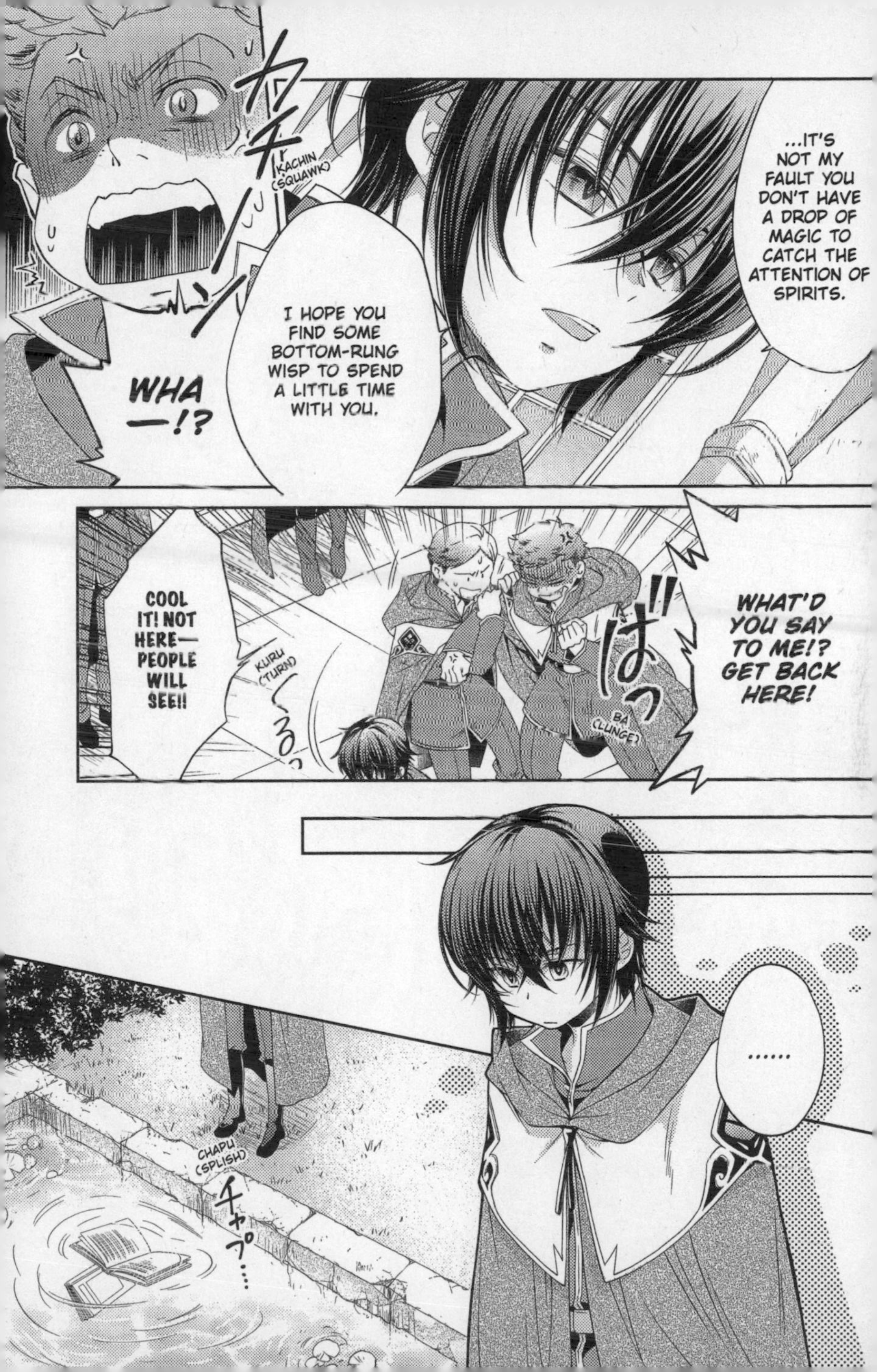
...IT'S NOT MY FAULT YOU DON'T HAVE A DROP OF MAGIC TO CATCH THE ATTENTION OF SPIRITS.
I HOPE YOU FIND SOME BOTTOM-RUNG WISP TO SPEND A LITTLE TIME WITH YOU.
KACHIN (SQUAWK)
WHA—!?
WHAT'D YOU SAY TO ME!? GET BACK HERE!
BA (LUNGE)
KURU (TURN)
COOL IT! NOT HERE— PEOPLE WILL SEE!!
......
CHAPU (SPLISH)

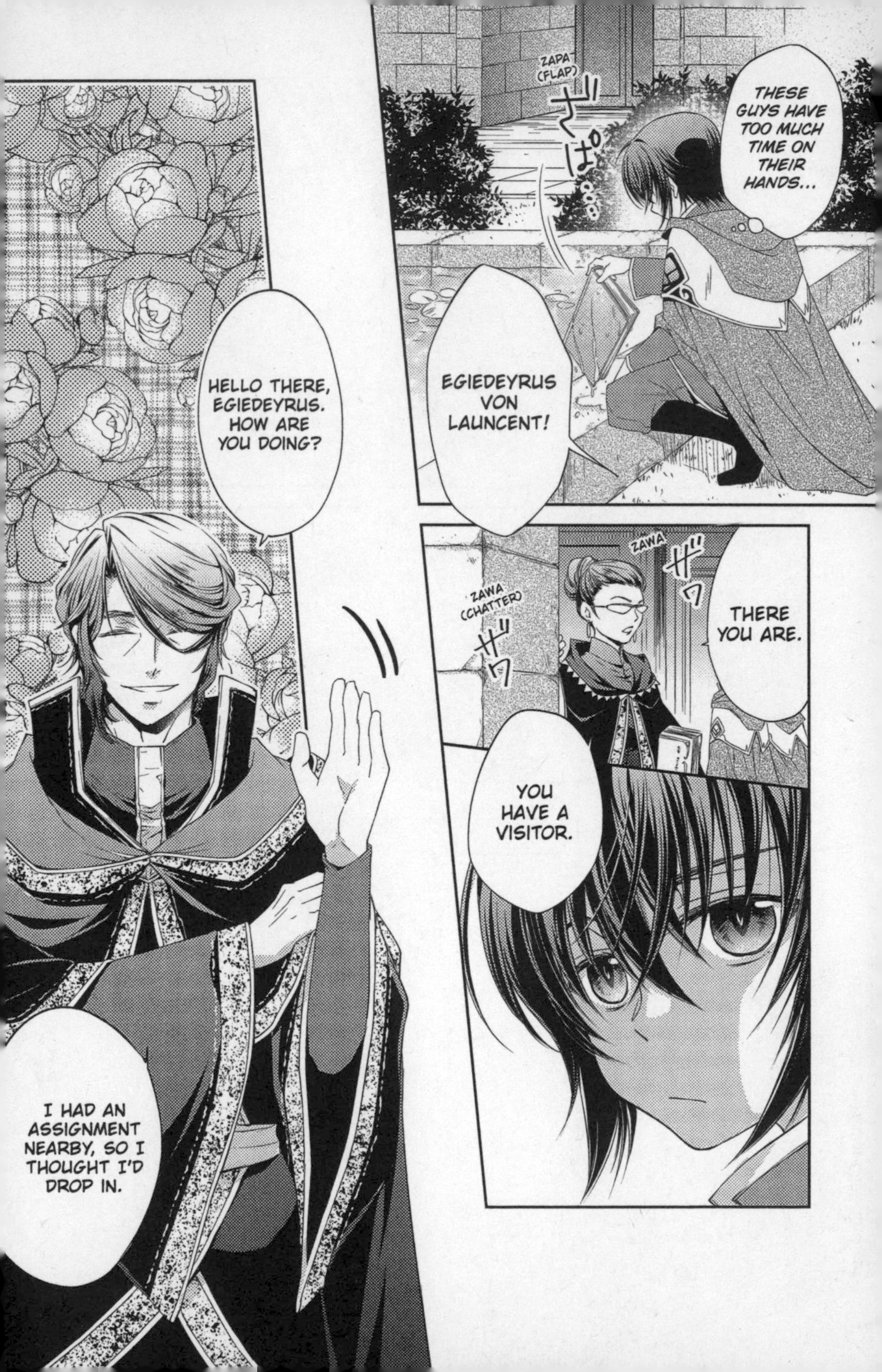
THESE GUYS HAVE TOO MUCH TIME ON THEIR HANDS...
ZAPA (FLAP)
ざぱ
EGIEDEYRUS VON LAUNCENT!
ZAWA
ザワ
ZAWA (CHATTER)
ザワ
THERE YOU ARE.
YOU HAVE A VISITOR.
HELLO THERE, EGIEDEYRUS. HOW ARE YOU DOING?
I HAD AN ASSIGNMENT NEARBY, SO I THOUGHT I'D DROP IN.

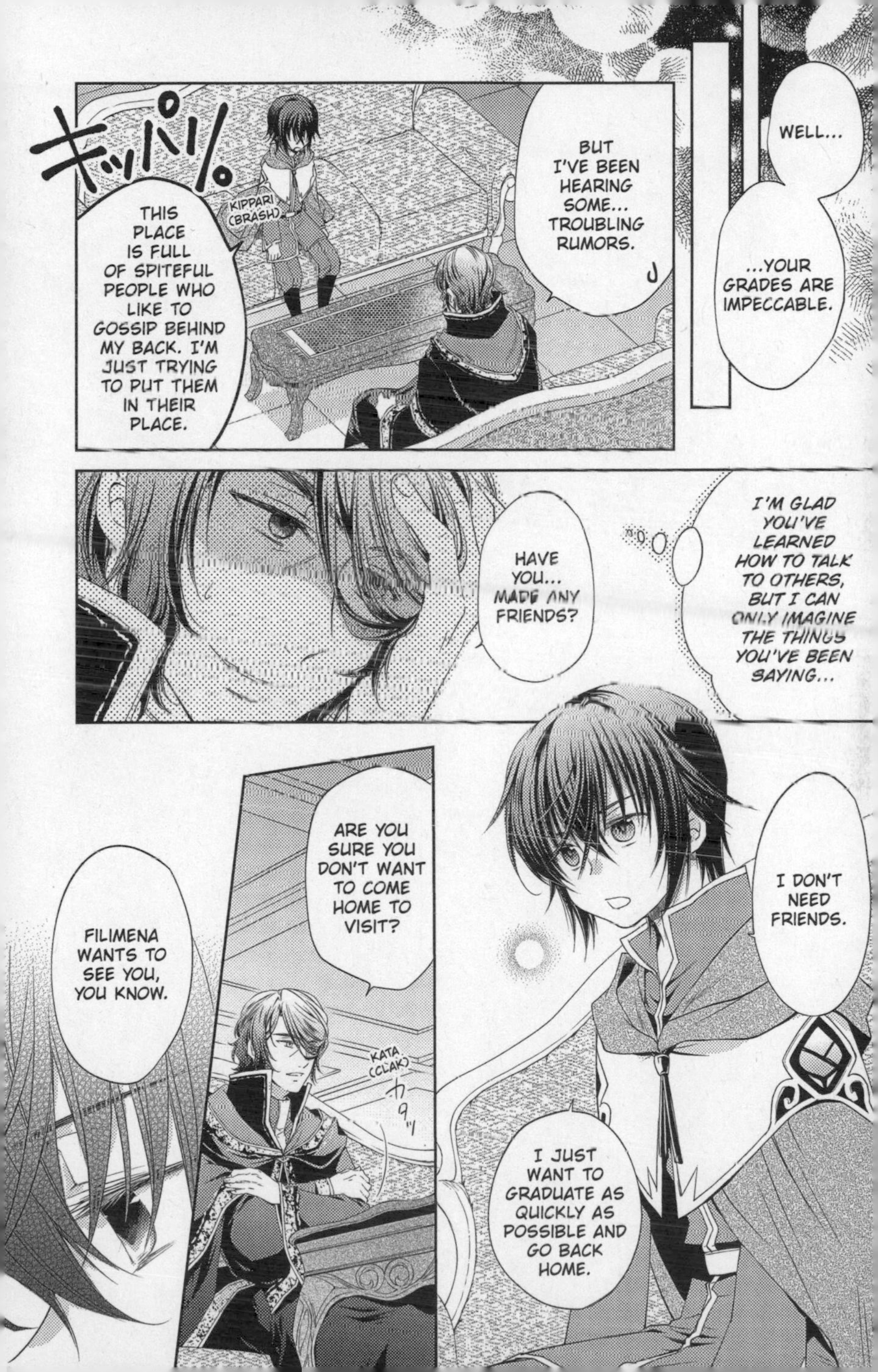
WELL...
...YOUR GRADES ARE IMPECCABLE.
BUT I'VE BEEN HEARING SOME... TROUBLING RUMORS.
キッパリ
KIPPARI (BRASH)
THIS PLACE IS FULL OF SPITEFUL PEOPLE WHO LIKE TO GOSSIP BEHIND MY BACK. I'M JUST TRYING TO PUT THEM IN THEIR PLACE.
I'M GLAD YOU'VE LEARNED HOW TO TALK TO OTHERS, BUT I CAN ONLY IMAGINE THE THINGS YOU'VE BEEN SAYING...
HAVE YOU... MADE ANY FRIENDS?
I DON'T NEED FRIENDS.
I JUST WANT TO GRADUATE AS QUICKLY AS POSSIBLE AND GO BACK HOME.
ARE YOU SURE YOU DON'T WANT TO COME HOME TO VISIT?
KATA (CLAK)
カタッ
FILIMENA WANTS TO SEE YOU, YOU KNOW.

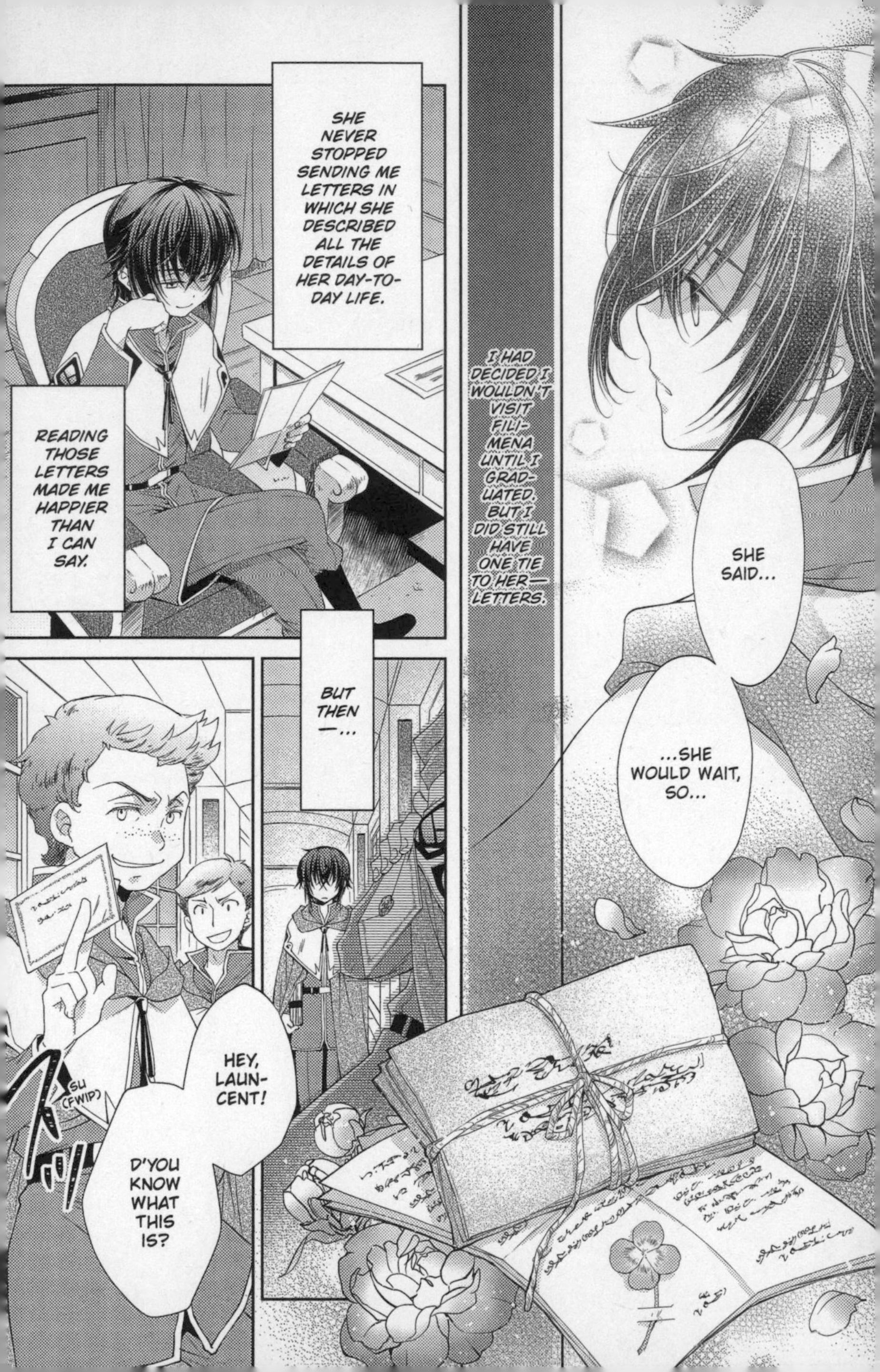
SHE SAID...
...SHE WOULD WAIT, SO...
I HAD DECIDED I WOULDN'T VISIT FILI-MENA UNTIL I GRAD-UATED. BUT I DID STILL HAVE ONE TIE TO HER—LETTERS.
SHE NEVER STOPPED SENDING ME LETTERS IN WHICH SHE DESCRIBED ALL THE DETAILS OF HER DAY-TO-DAY LIFE.
READING THOSE LETTERS MADE ME HAPPIER THAN I CAN SAY.
BUT THEN—...
HEY, LAUN-CENT!
SU (FWIP)
D'YOU KNOW WHAT THIS IS?

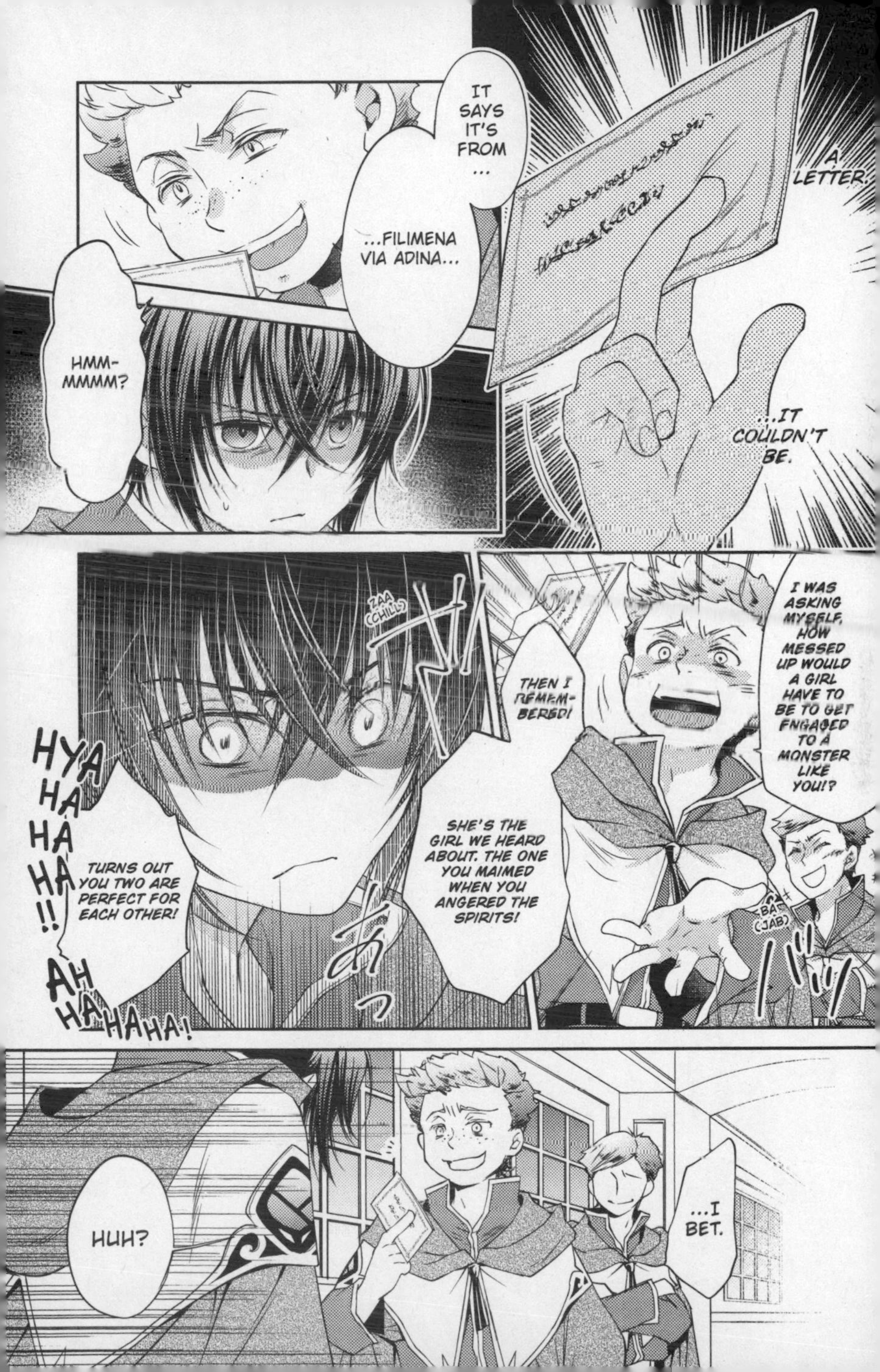
A LETTER.
IT SAYS IT'S FROM ...
...FILIMENA VIA ADINA...
HMM-MMMM?
...IT COULDN'T BE.
I WAS ASKING MYSELF, HOW MESSED UP WOULD A GIRL HAVE TO BE TO GET ENGAGED TO A MONSTER LIKE YOU!?
THEN I REMEMBERED!
BA (JAB)
SHE'S THE GIRL WE HEARD ABOUT. THE ONE YOU MAIMED WHEN YOU ANGERED THE SPIRITS!
ZAA (CHILL)
TURNS OUT YOU TWO ARE PERFECT FOR EACH OTHER!
HYA HA HA HA HA!!
AH HA HA HA HA!
...I BET.
HUH?

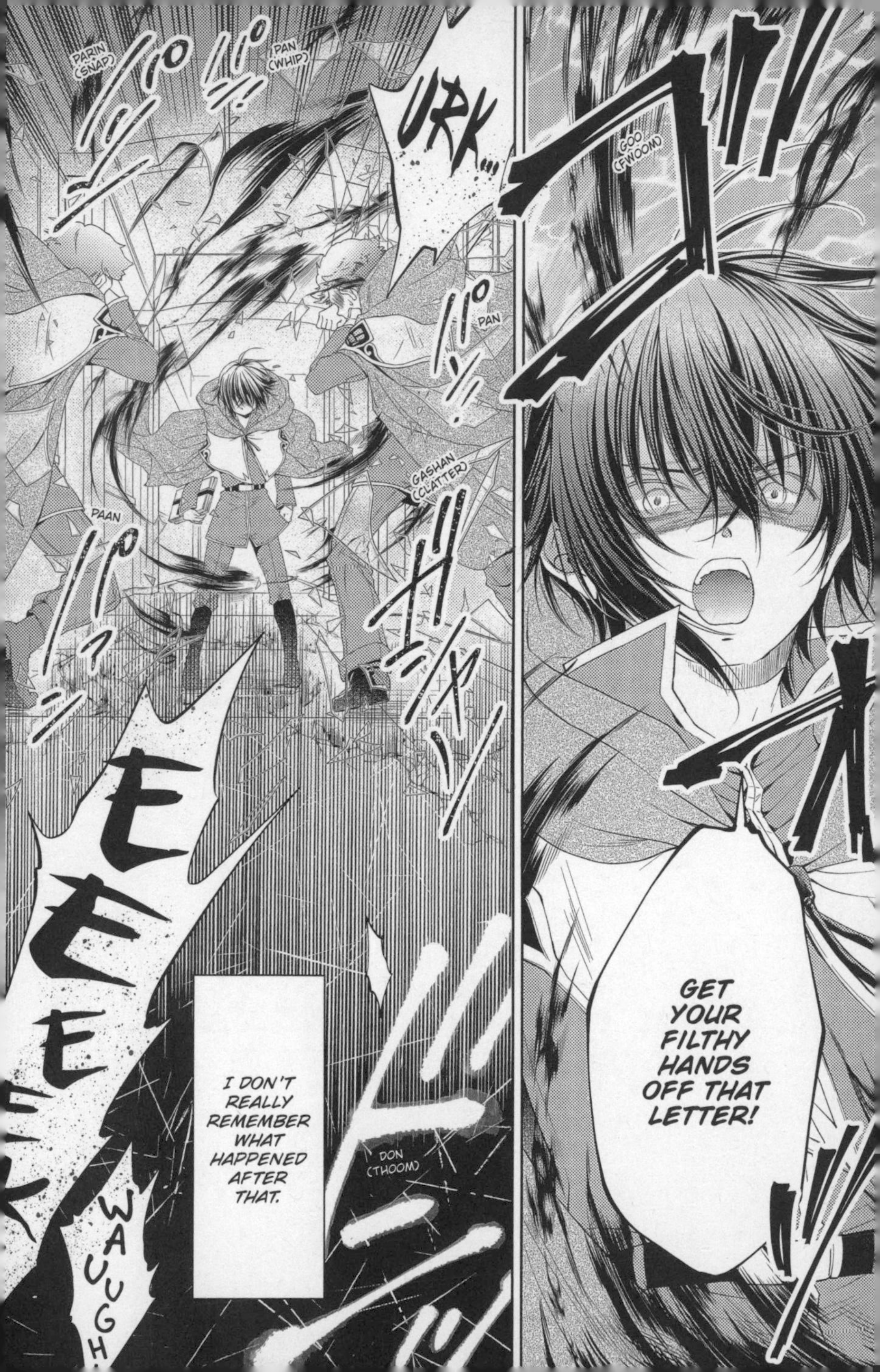
GOO (FWOOM)
GET YOUR FILTHY HANDS OFF THAT LETTER!
URK...
PAN (WHIP)
PARIN (SNAP)
PAN
GASHAN (CLATTER)
PAAN
DON (THOOM)
I DON'T REALLY REMEMBER WHAT HAPPENED AFTER THAT.
WAUUGH.

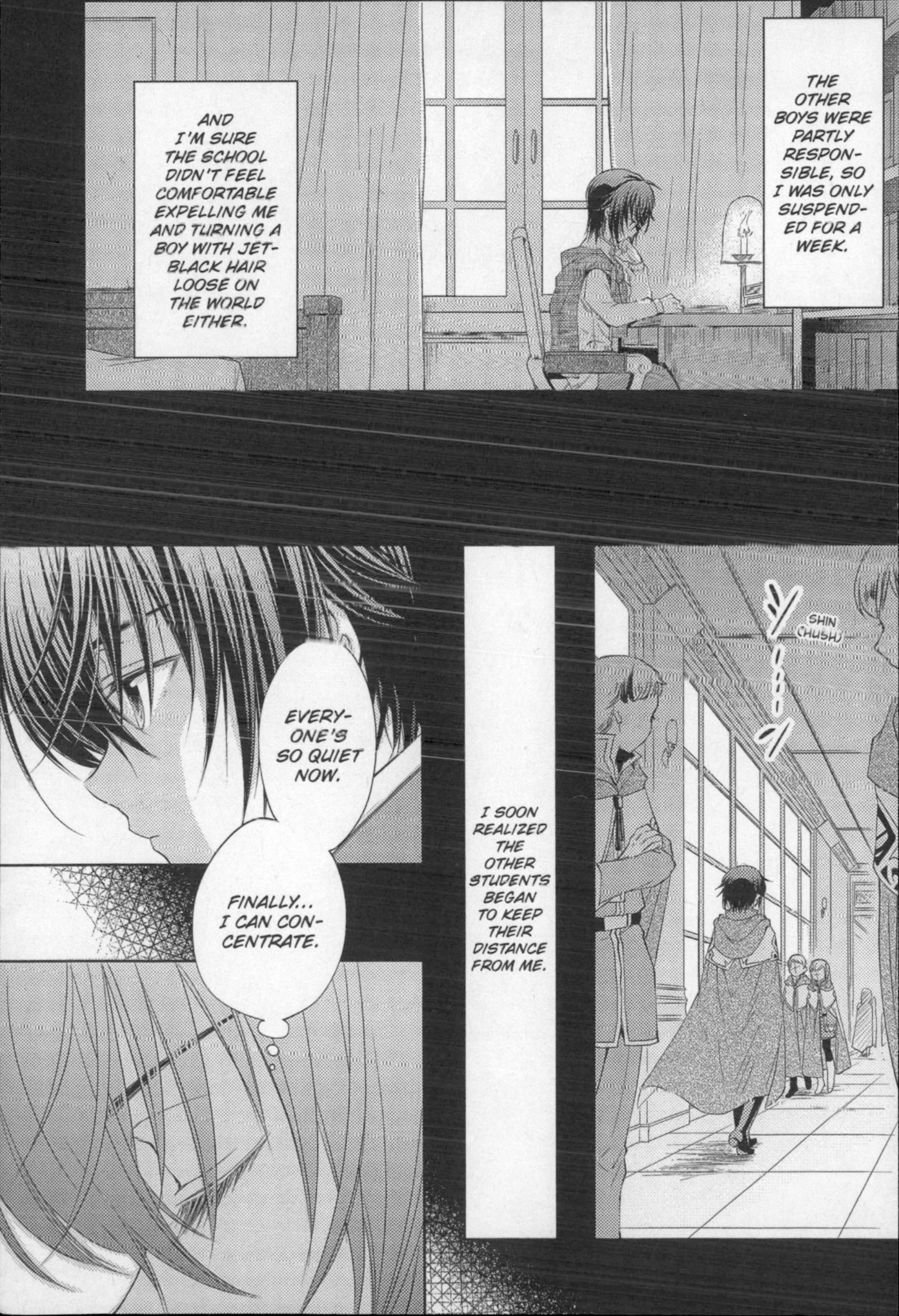
THE OTHER BOYS WERE PARTLY RESPONSIBLE, SO I WAS ONLY SUSPENDED FOR A WEEK.
AND I'M SURE THE SCHOOL DIDN'T FEEL COMFORTABLE EXPELLING ME AND TURNING A BOY WITH JET-BLACK HAIR LOOSE ON THE WORLD EITHER.
SHIN (HUSH)
I SOON REALIZED THE OTHER STUDENTS BEGAN TO KEEP THEIR DISTANCE FROM ME.
EVERYONE'S SO QUIET NOW.
FINALLY... I CAN CONCENTRATE.

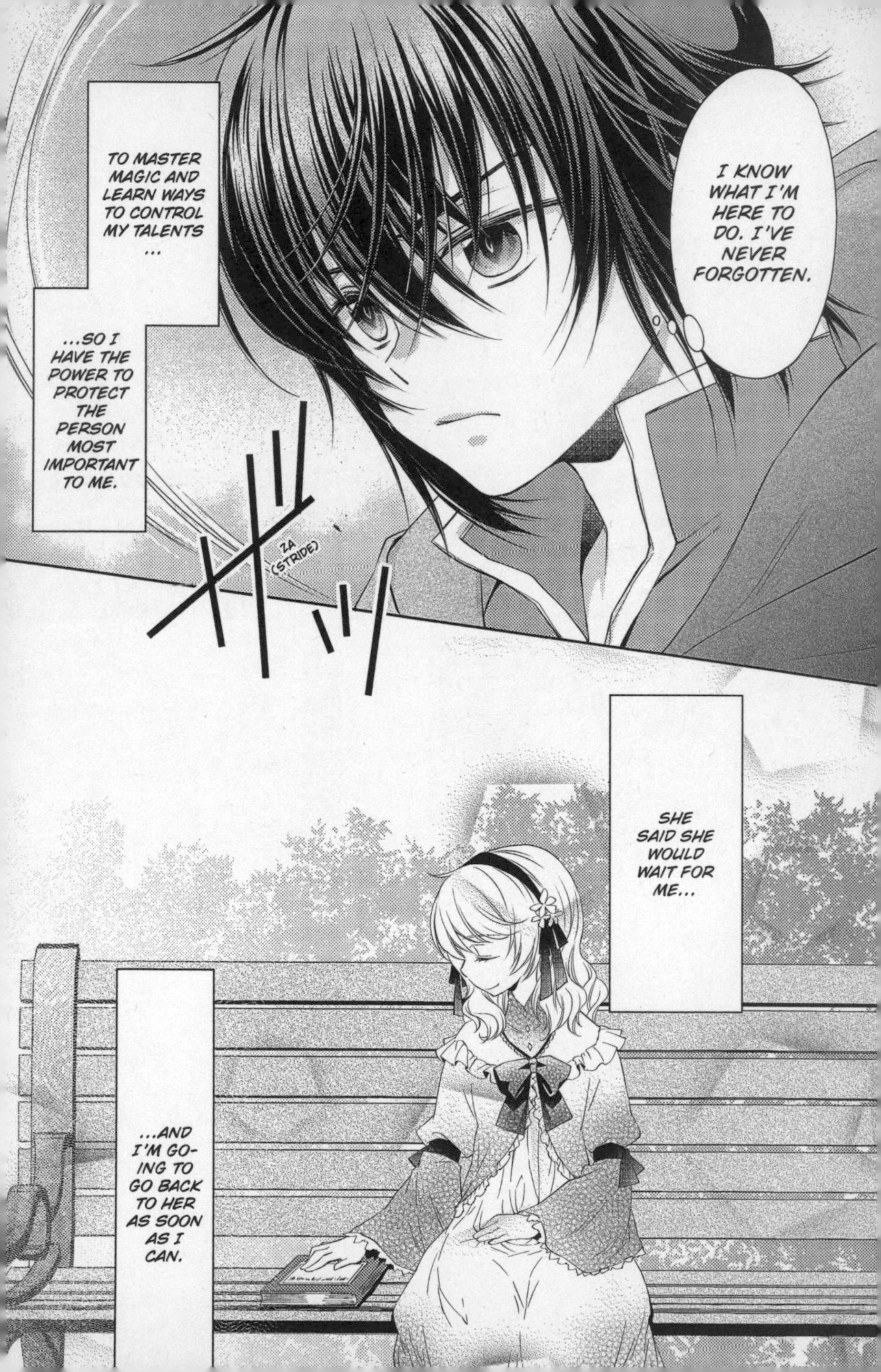
I KNOW WHAT I'M HERE TO DO. I'VE NEVER FORGOTTEN.
TO MASTER MAGIC AND LEARN WAYS TO CONTROL MY TALENTS...
...SO I HAVE THE POWER TO PROTECT THE PERSON MOST IMPORTANT TO ME.
ZA (STRIDE)
SHE SAID SHE WOULD WAIT FOR ME...
...AND I'M GO-ING TO GO BACK TO HER AS SOON AS I CAN.

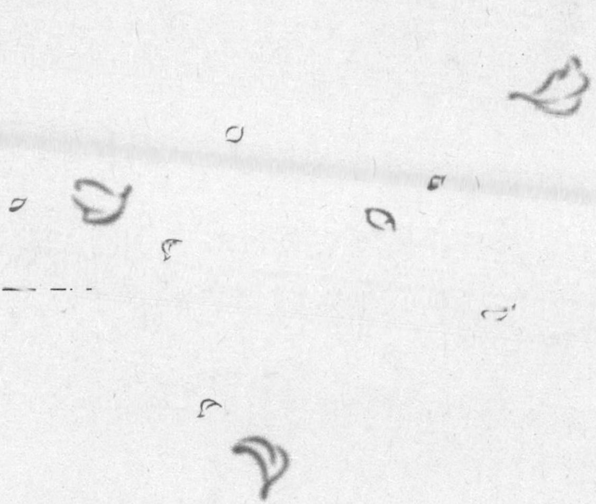

FIANCÉE OF THE WIZARD

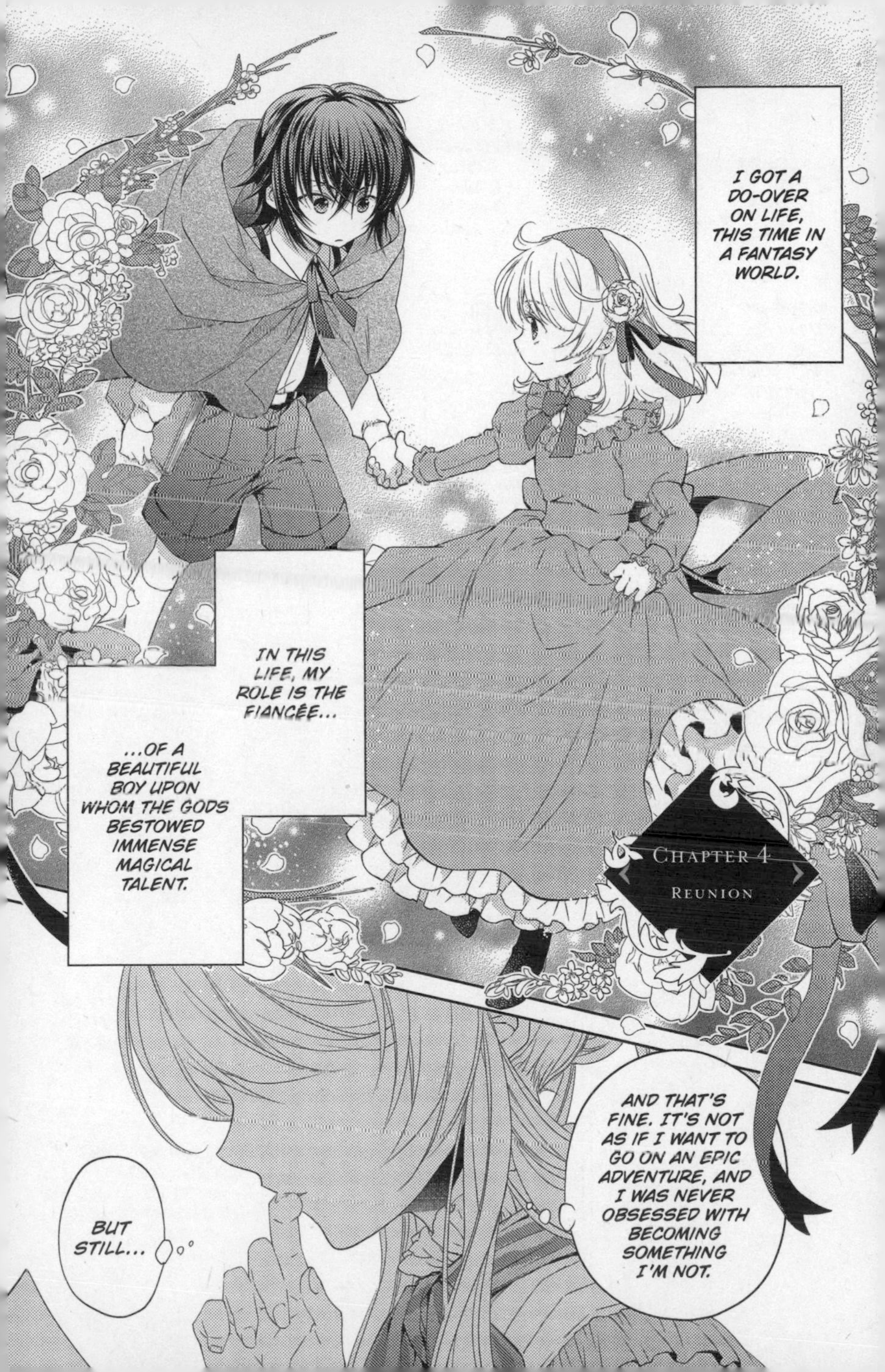
I GOT A DO-OVER ON LIFE, THIS TIME IN A FANTASY WORLD.
IN THIS LIFE, MY ROLE IS THE FIANCÉE...
...OF A BEAUTIFUL BOY UPON WHOM THE GODS BESTOWED IMMENSE MAGICAL TALENT.
CHAPTER 4
REUNION
AND THAT'S FINE. IT'S NOT AS IF I WANT TO GO ON AN EPIC ADVENTURE, AND I WAS NEVER OBSESSED WITH BECOMING SOMETHING I'M NOT.
BUT STILL...

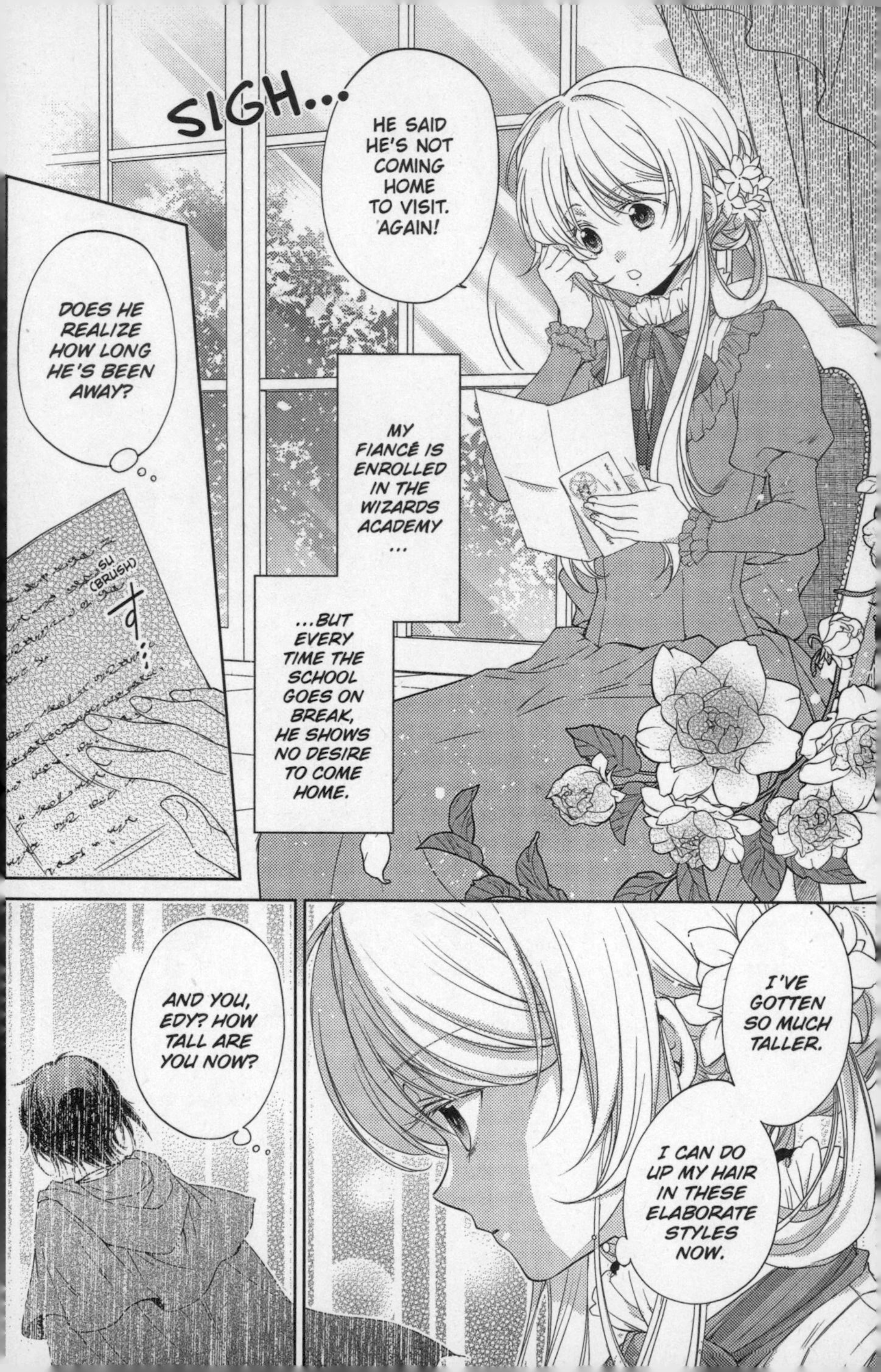
SIGH...
HE SAID HE'S NOT COMING HOME TO VISIT. AGAIN!
MY FIANCÉ IS ENROLLED IN THE WIZARDS ACADEMY ...
...BUT EVERY TIME THE SCHOOL GOES ON BREAK, HE SHOWS NO DESIRE TO COME HOME.
DOES HE REALIZE HOW LONG HE'S BEEN AWAY?
SU (BRUSH)
I'VE GOTTEN SO MUCH TALLER.
I CAN DO UP MY HAIR IN THESE ELABORATE STYLES NOW.
AND YOU, EDY? HOW TALL ARE YOU NOW?

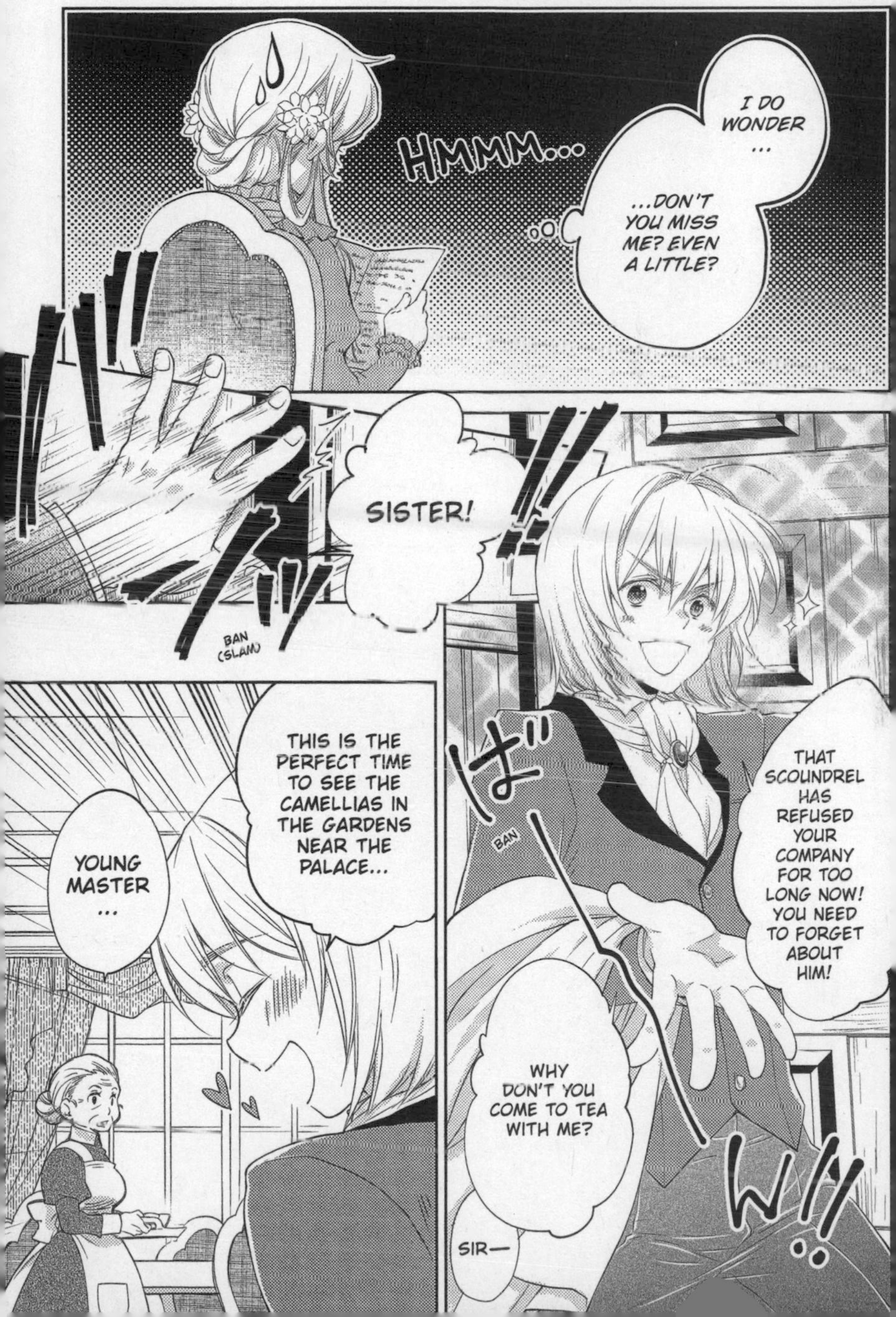
I DO WONDER ...
...DON'T YOU MISS ME? EVEN A LITTLE?
HMMM...
THAT SCOUNDREL HAS REFUSED YOUR COMPANY FOR TOO LONG NOW! YOU NEED TO FORGET ABOUT HIM!
BAN
WHY DON'T YOU COME TO TEA WITH ME?
SIR—
SISTER!
BAN (SLAM)
THIS IS THE PERFECT TIME TO SEE THE CAMELLIAS IN THE GARDENS NEAR THE PALACE...
YOUNG MASTER ...

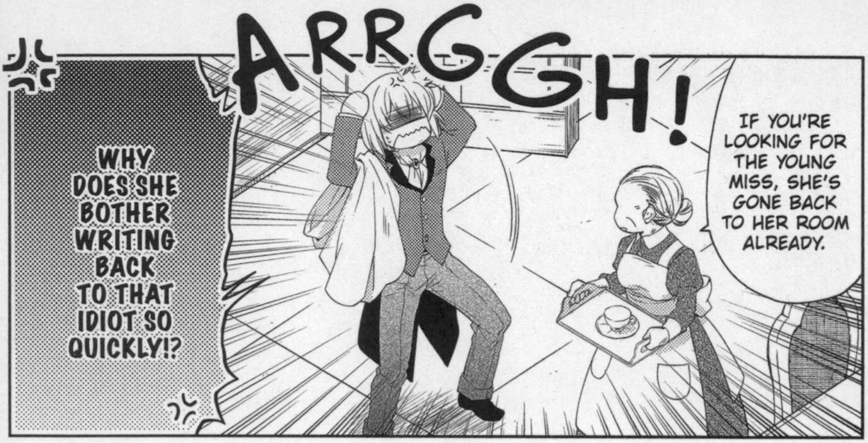
ARRGGH!
IF YOU'RE LOOKING FOR THE YOUNG MISS, SHE'S GONE BACK TO HER ROOM ALREADY.
WHY DOES SHE BOTHER WRITING BACK TO THAT IDIOT SO QUICKLY!?

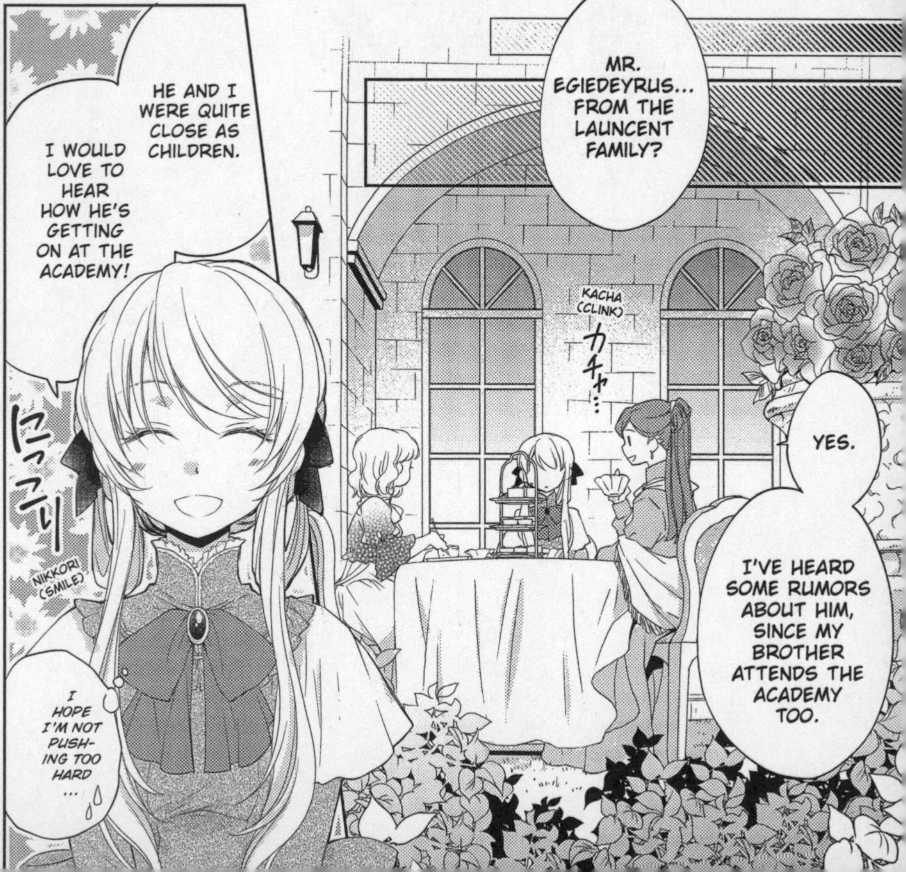
MR. EGIEDEYRUS... FROM THE LAUNCENT FAMILY?
YES.
I'VE HEARD SOME RUMORS ABOUT HIM, SINCE MY BROTHER ATTENDS THE ACADEMY TOO.
KACHA (CLINK)
カチャ…
HE AND I WERE QUITE CLOSE AS CHILDREN.
I WOULD LOVE TO HEAR HOW HE'S GETTING ON AT THE ACADEMY!
にっこり
NIKKORI (SMILE)
I HOPE I'M NOT PUSHING TOO HARD...

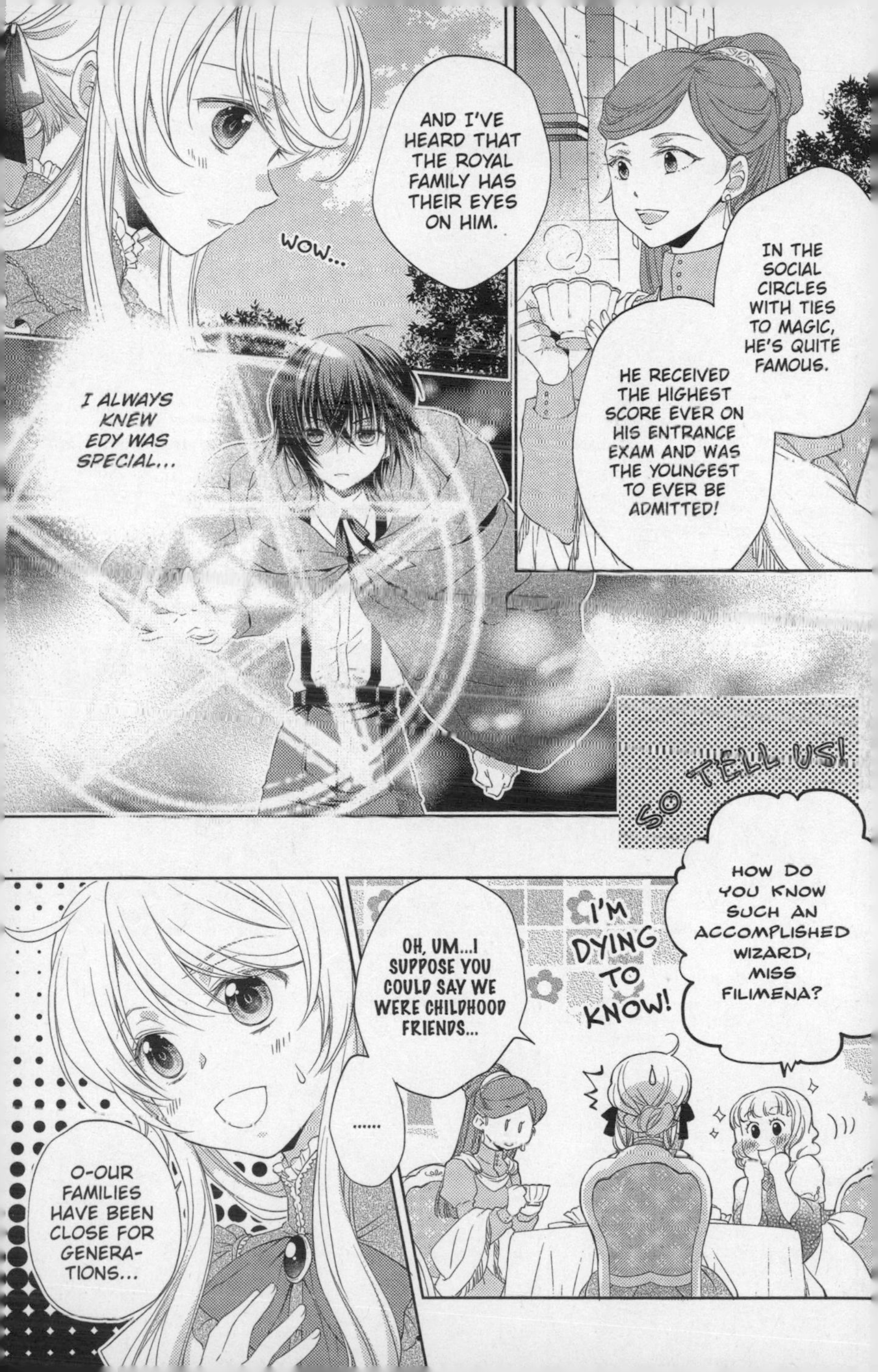
IN THE SOCIAL CIRCLES WITH TIES TO MAGIC, HE'S QUITE FAMOUS.
HE RECEIVED THE HIGHEST SCORE EVER ON HIS ENTRANCE EXAM AND WAS THE YOUNGEST TO EVER BE ADMITTED!
AND I'VE HEARD THAT THE ROYAL FAMILY HAS THEIR EYES ON HIM.
WOW...
I ALWAYS KNEW EDY WAS SPECIAL...
SO TELL US!
HOW DO YOU KNOW SUCH AN ACCOMPLISHED WIZARD, MISS FILIMENA?
I'M DYING TO KNOW!
......
OH, UM...I SUPPOSE YOU COULD SAY WE WERE CHILDHOOD FRIENDS...
O-OUR FAMILIES HAVE BEEN CLOSE FOR GENERA-TIONS...

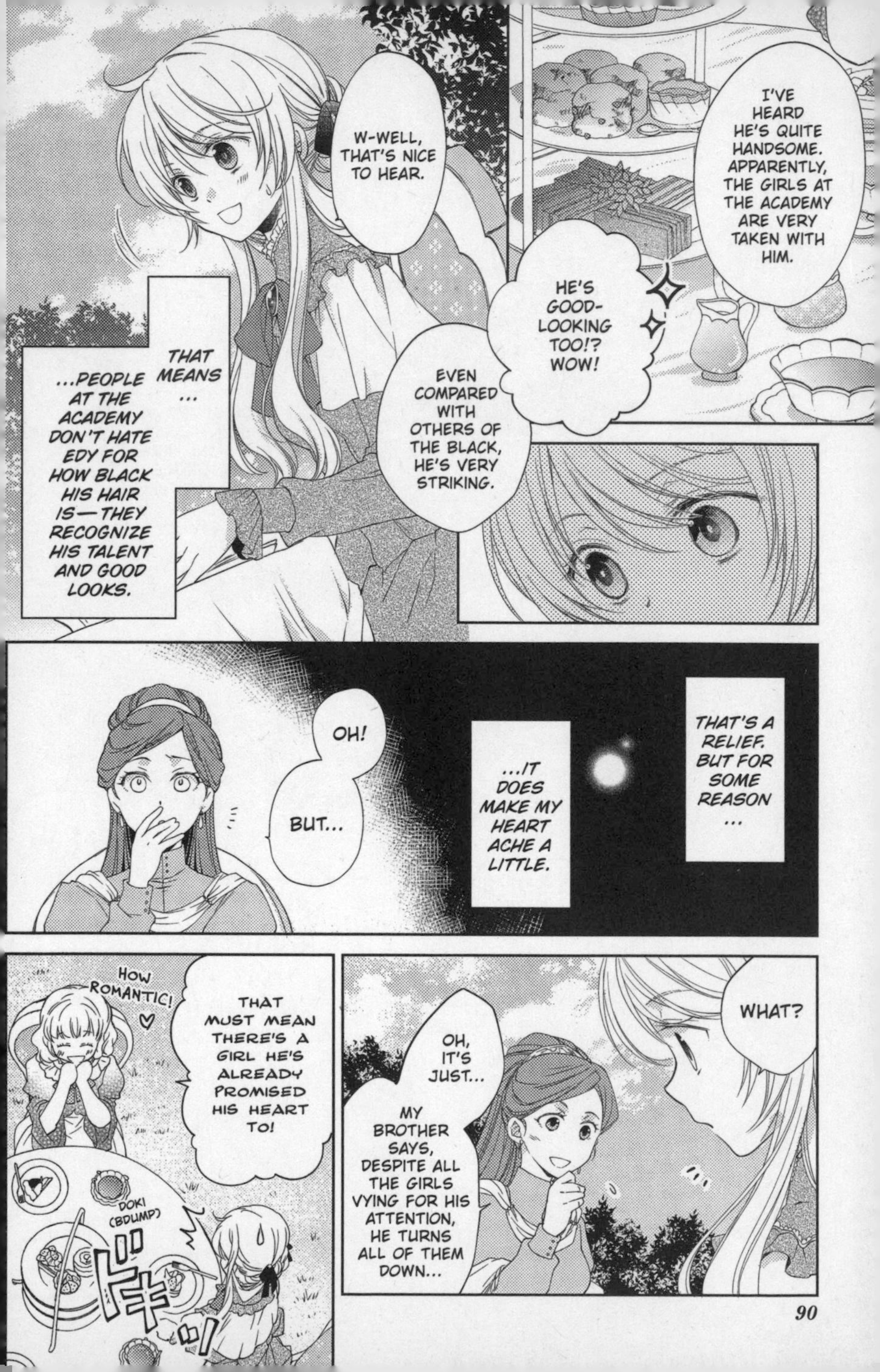
I'VE HEARD HE'S QUITE HANDSOME. APPARENTLY, THE GIRLS AT THE ACADEMY ARE VERY TAKEN WITH HIM.
HE'S GOOD-LOOKING TOO!? WOW!
EVEN COMPARED WITH OTHERS OF THE BLACK, HE'S VERY STRIKING.
W-WELL, THAT'S NICE TO HEAR.
THAT MEANS...
...PEOPLE AT THE ACADEMY DON'T HATE EDY FOR HOW BLACK HIS HAIR IS—THEY RECOGNIZE HIS TALENT AND GOOD LOOKS.
THAT'S A RELIEF. BUT FOR SOME REASON...
...IT DOES MAKE MY HEART ACHE A LITTLE.
OH!
BUT...
WHAT?
OH, IT'S JUST...
MY BROTHER SAYS, DESPITE ALL THE GIRLS VYING FOR HIS ATTENTION, HE TURNS ALL OF THEM DOWN...
THAT MUST MEAN THERE'S A GIRL HE'S ALREADY PROMISED HIS HEART TO!
HOW ROMANTIC! ♥
DOKI (BDUMP)
ドキッ!

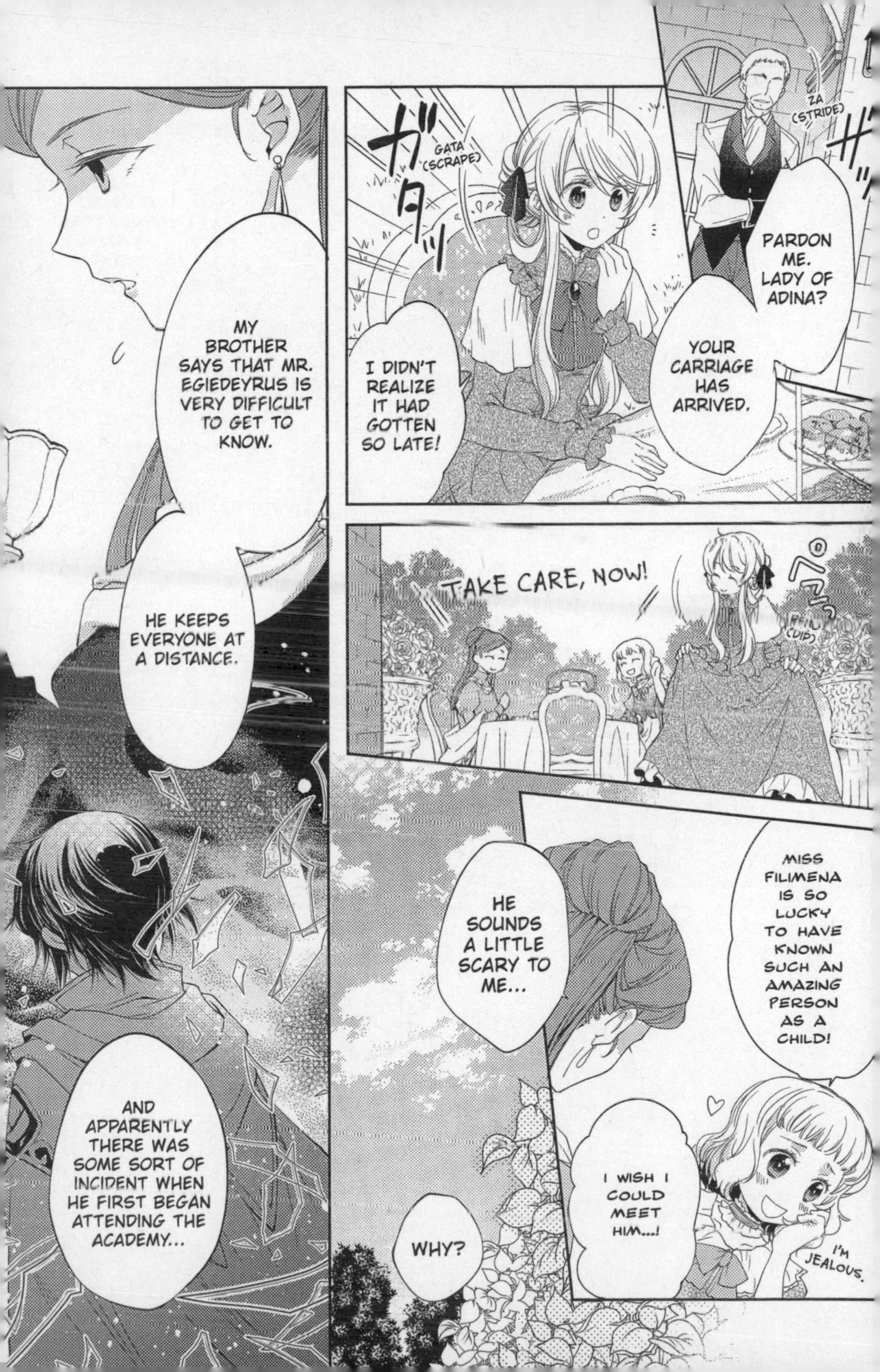
ZA (STRIDE)
PARDON ME. LADY OF ADINA?
YOUR CARRIAGE HAS ARRIVED.
GATA (SCRAPE)
I DIDN'T REALIZE IT HAD GOTTEN SO LATE!
(DIP)
TAKE CARE, NOW!
MISS FILIMENA IS SO LUCKY TO HAVE KNOWN SUCH AN AMAZING PERSON AS A CHILD!
HE SOUNDS A LITTLE SCARY TO ME...
I'M JEALOUS.
I WISH I COULD MEET HIM...!
WHY?
MY BROTHER SAYS THAT MR. EGIEDEYRUS IS VERY DIFFICULT TO GET TO KNOW.
HE KEEPS EVERYONE AT A DISTANCE.
AND APPARENTLY THERE WAS SOME SORT OF INCIDENT WHEN HE FIRST BEGAN ATTENDING THE ACADEMY...

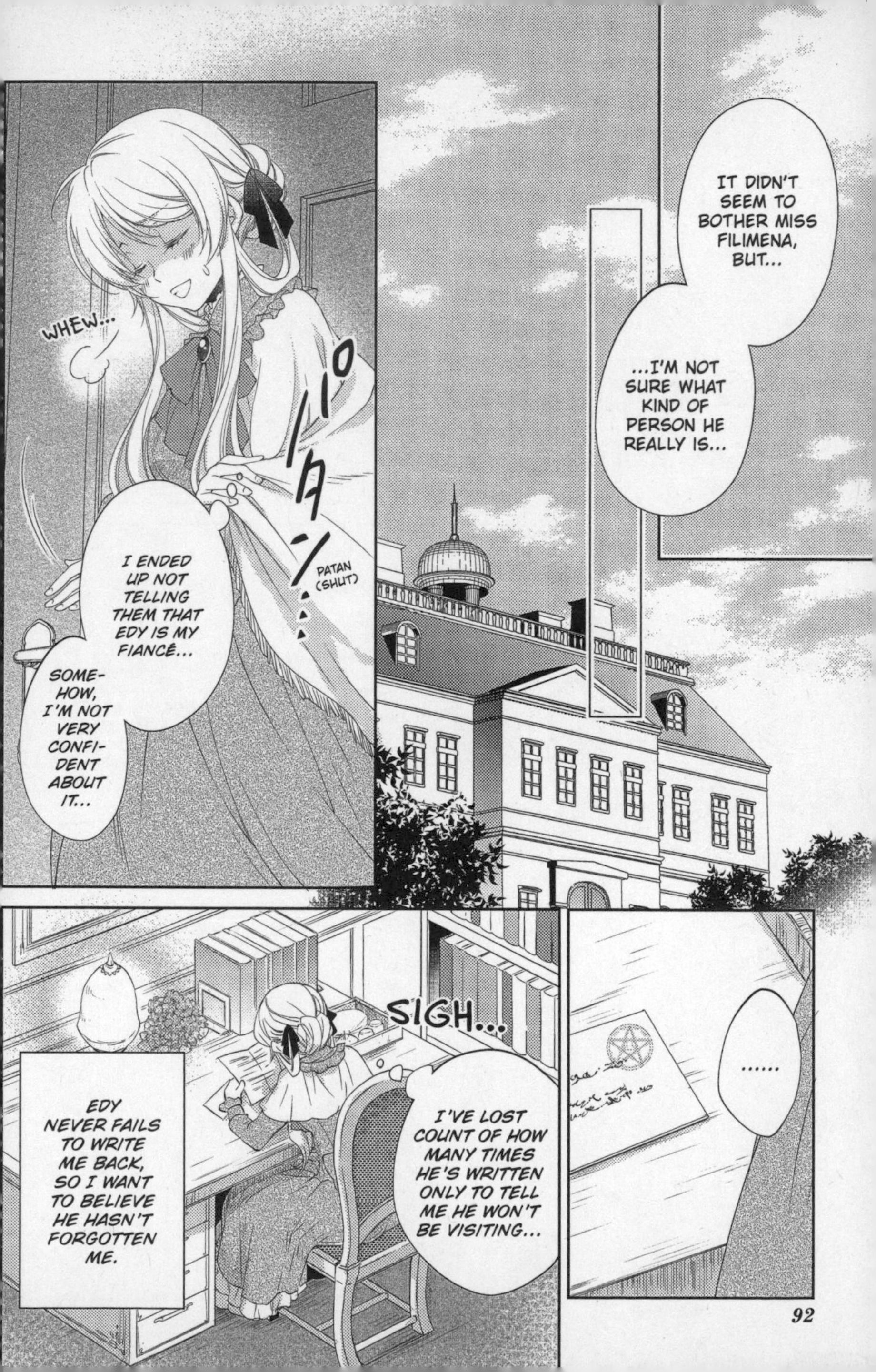
IT DIDN'T SEEM TO BOTHER MISS FILIMENA, BUT...
...I'M NOT SURE WHAT KIND OF PERSON HE REALLY IS...
WHEW...
パタン
PATAN (SHUT)
I ENDED UP NOT TELLING THEM THAT EDY IS MY FIANCÉ...
SOME-HOW, I'M NOT VERY CONFI-DENT ABOUT IT...
......
SIGH...
I'VE LOST COUNT OF HOW MANY TIMES HE'S WRITTEN ONLY TO TELL ME HE WON'T BE VISITING...
EDY NEVER FAILS TO WRITE ME BACK, SO I WANT TO BELIEVE HE HASN'T FORGOTTEN ME.

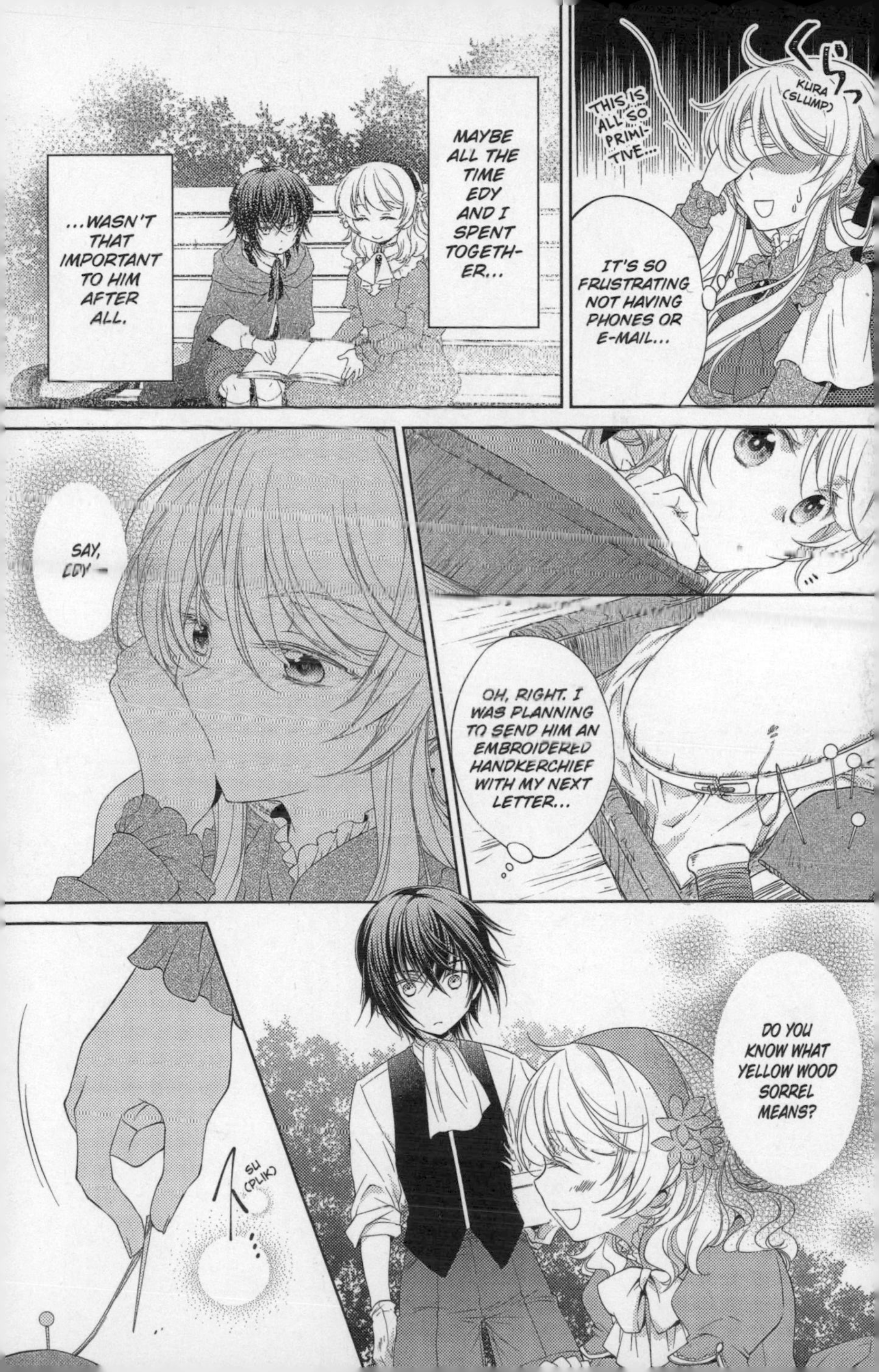
KURA (SLUMP)
THIS IS ALL SO PRIMI-TIVE...
IT'S SO FRUSTRATING NOT HAVING PHONES OR E-MAIL...
MAYBE ALL THE TIME EDY AND I SPENT TOGETH-ER...
...WASN'T THAT IMPORTANT TO HIM AFTER ALL.
OH, RIGHT. I WAS PLANNING TO SEND HIM AN EMBROIDERED HANDKERCHIEF WITH MY NEXT LETTER...
SAY, EDY—
DO YOU KNOW WHAT YELLOW WOOD SORREL MEANS?
SU (PLIK)
...

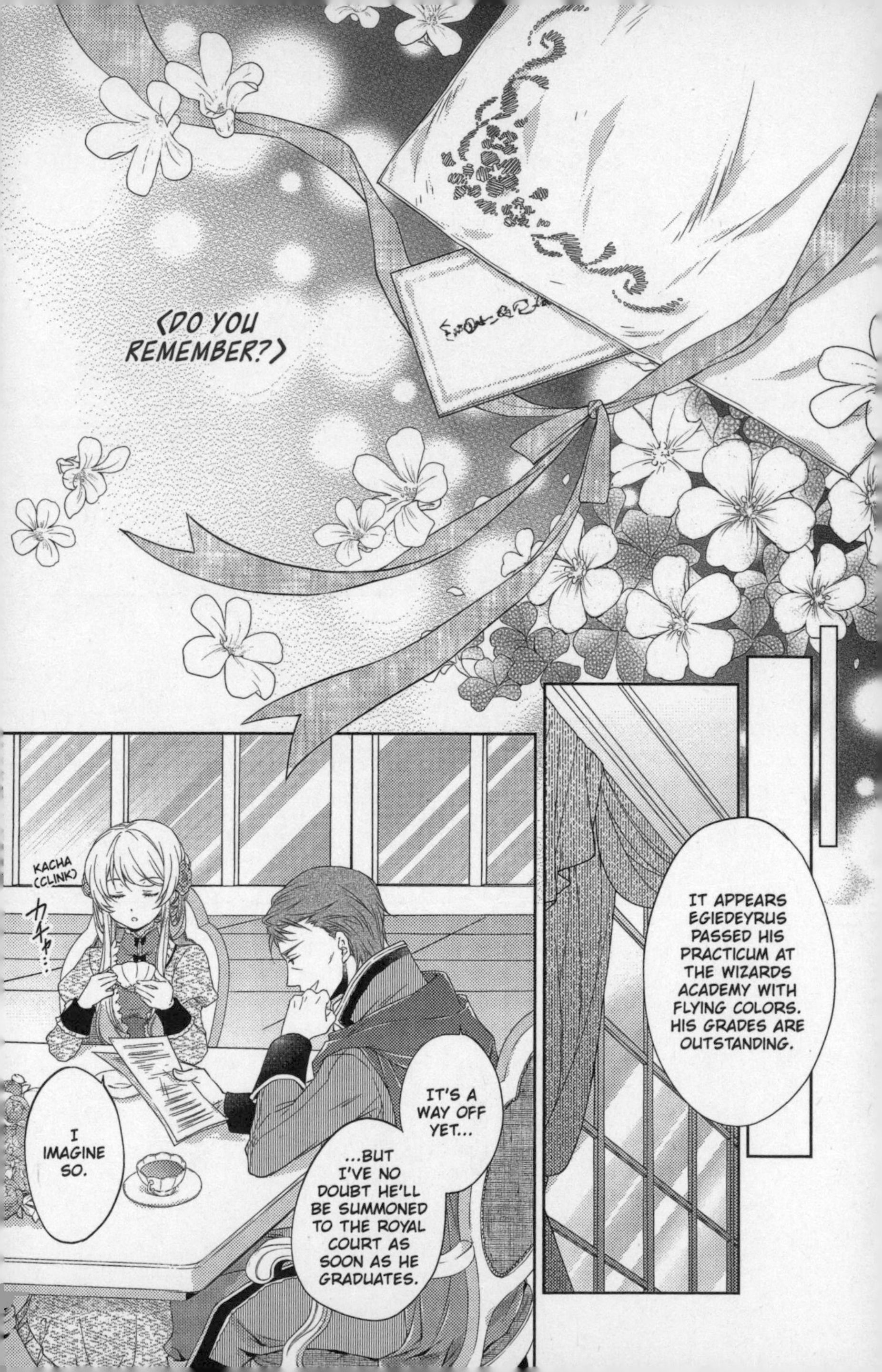

<DO YOU REMEMBER?>
IT APPEARS EGIEDEYRUS PASSED HIS PRACTICUM AT THE WIZARDS ACADEMY WITH FLYING COLORS. HIS GRADES ARE OUTSTANDING.
IT'S A WAY OFF YET...
...BUT I'VE NO DOUBT HE'LL BE SUMMONED TO THE ROYAL COURT AS SOON AS HE GRADUATES.
KACHA (CLINK)
カチャ…
I IMAGINE SO.

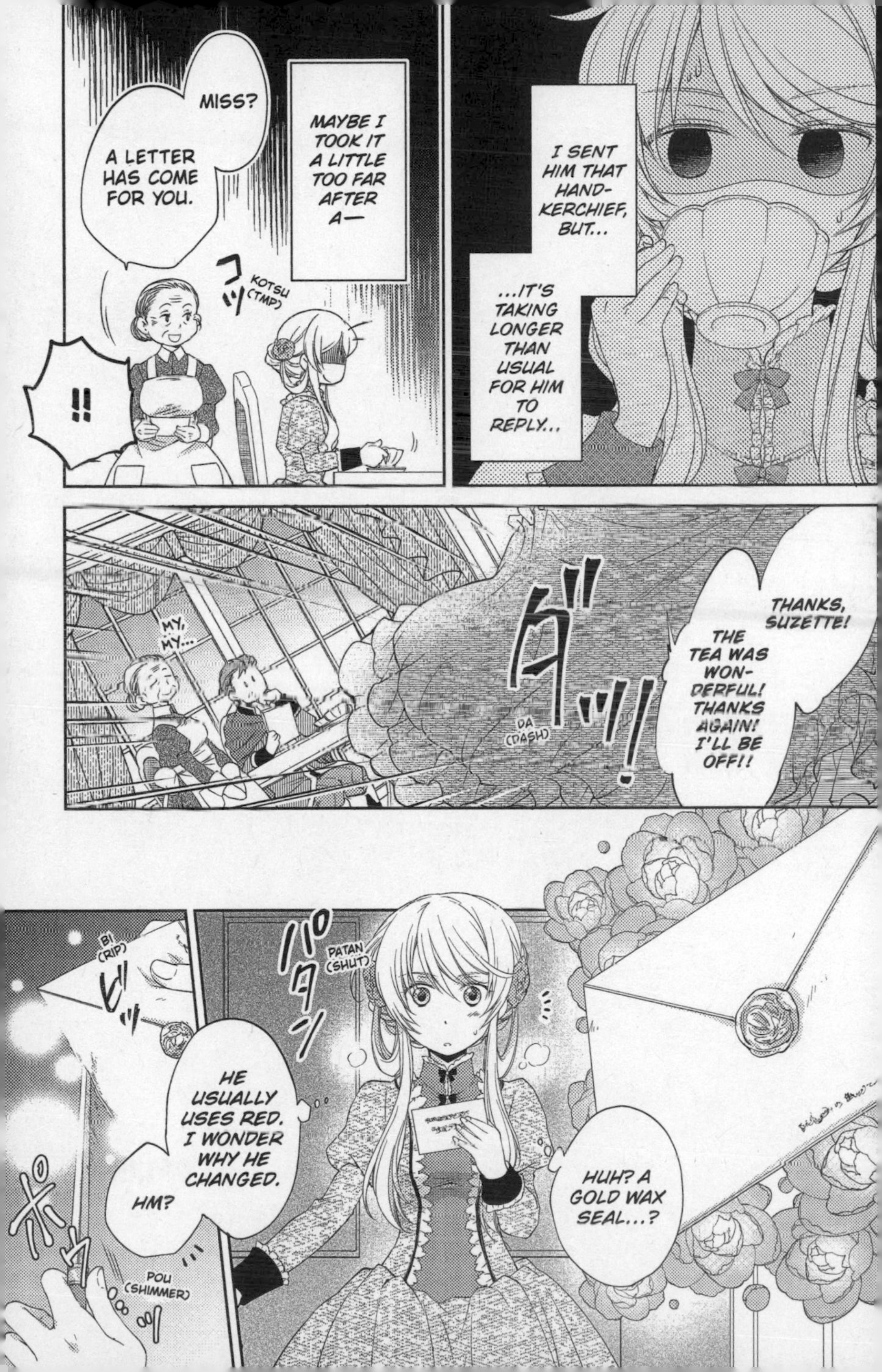
I SENT HIM THAT HAND-KERCHIEF, BUT...
...IT'S TAKING LONGER THAN USUAL FOR HIM TO REPLY...
MAYBE I TOOK IT A LITTLE TOO FAR AFTER A—
KOTSU (TMP)
MISS?
A LETTER HAS COME FOR YOU.
!!
THANKS, SUZETTE!
THE TEA WAS WON-DERFUL! THANKS AGAIN! I'LL BE OFF!!
DA (DASH)
MY, MY...
HUH? A GOLD WAX SEAL...?
PATAN (SHUT)
HE USUALLY USES RED. I WONDER WHY HE CHANGED.
HM?
BI (RIP)
POU (SHIMMER)

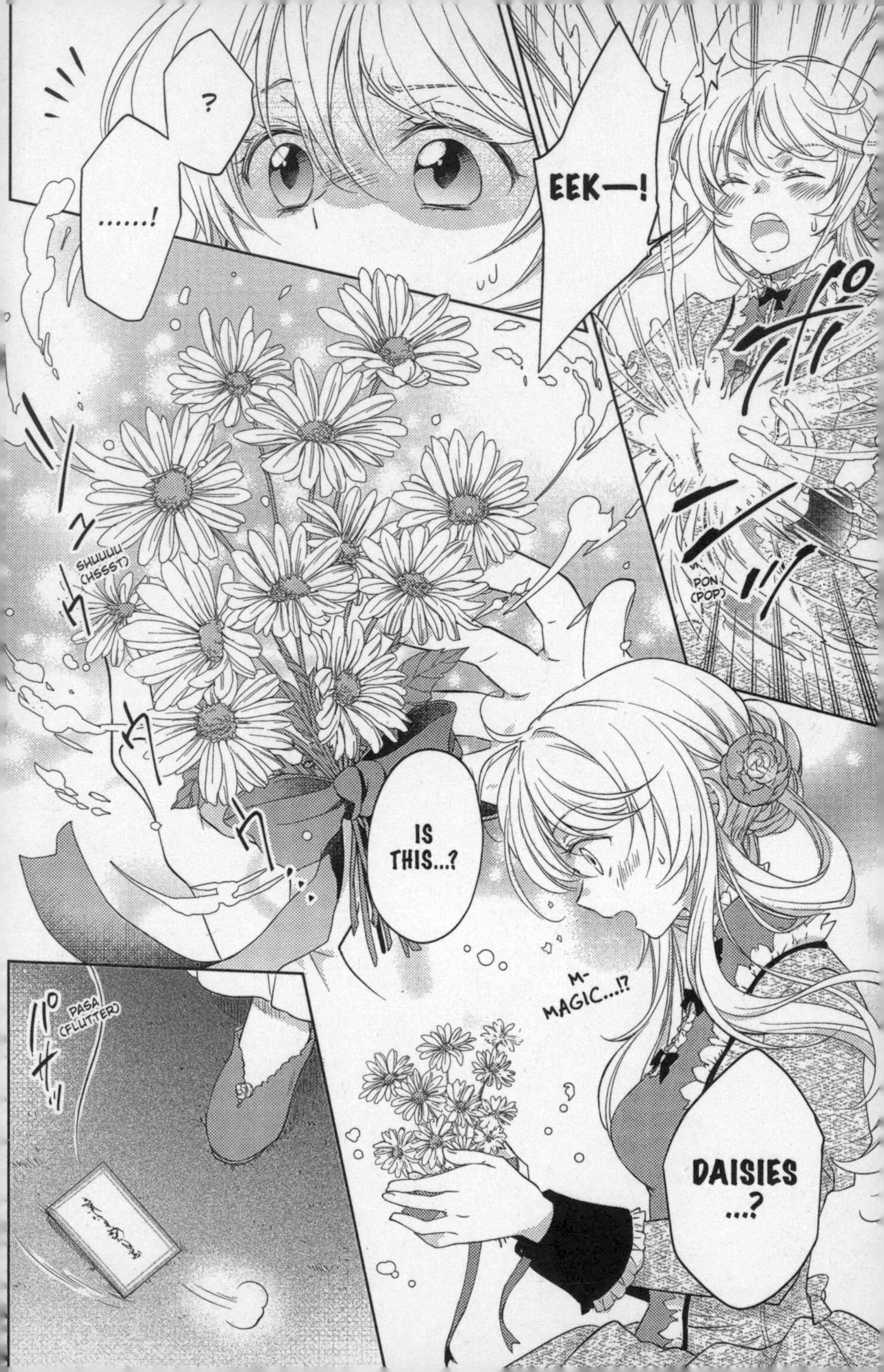
EEK—!
PON (POP)
?
......!
SHUUUU (HSSST)
IS THIS...?
M-MAGIC...!?
DAISIES ...?
PASA (FLUTTER)

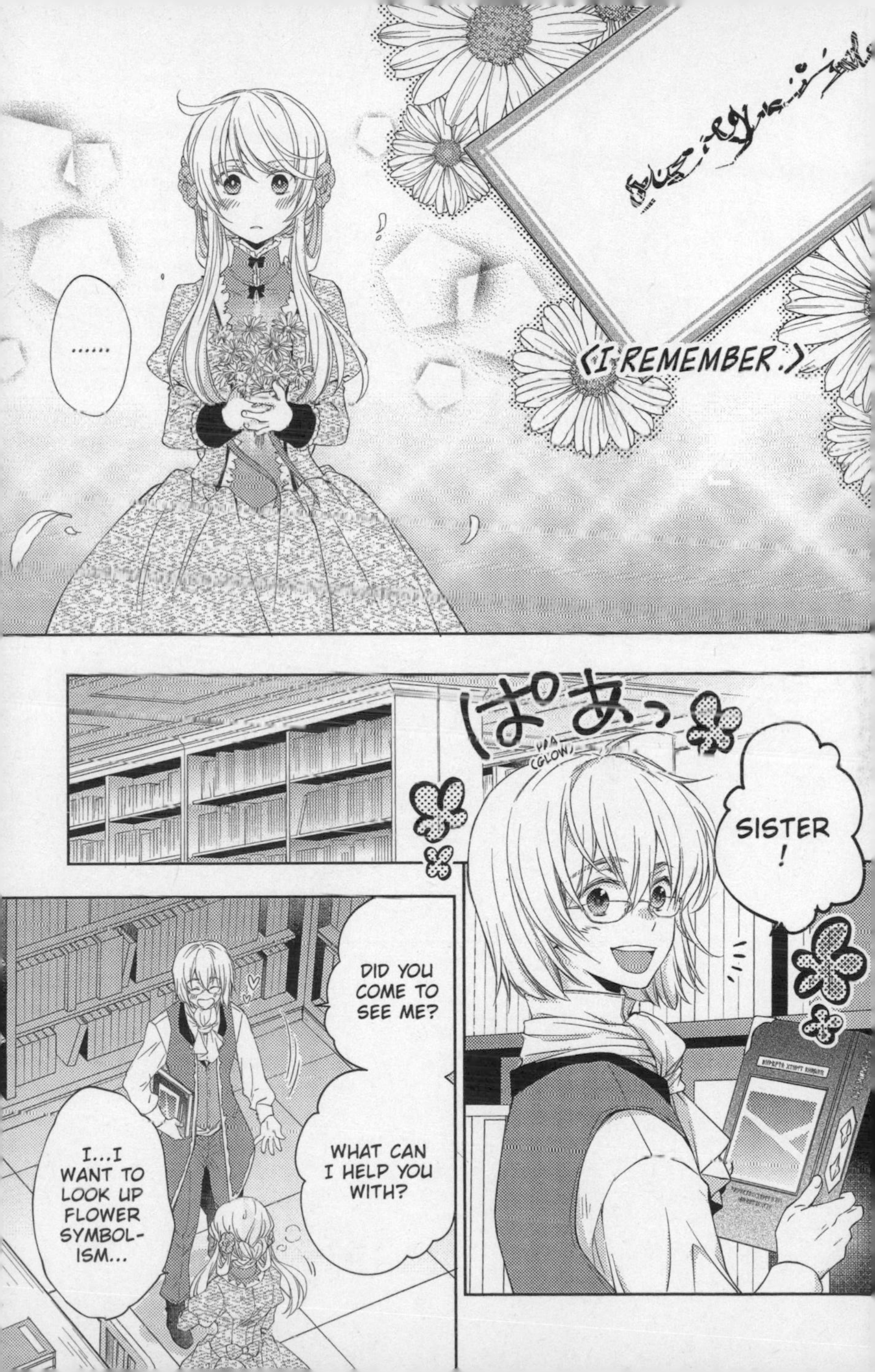
〈I REMEMBER.〉
......
ぱあっ
PA (GLOW)
SISTER!
DID YOU COME TO SEE ME?
WHAT CAN I HELP YOU WITH?
I...I WANT TO LOOK UP FLOWER SYMBOLISM...

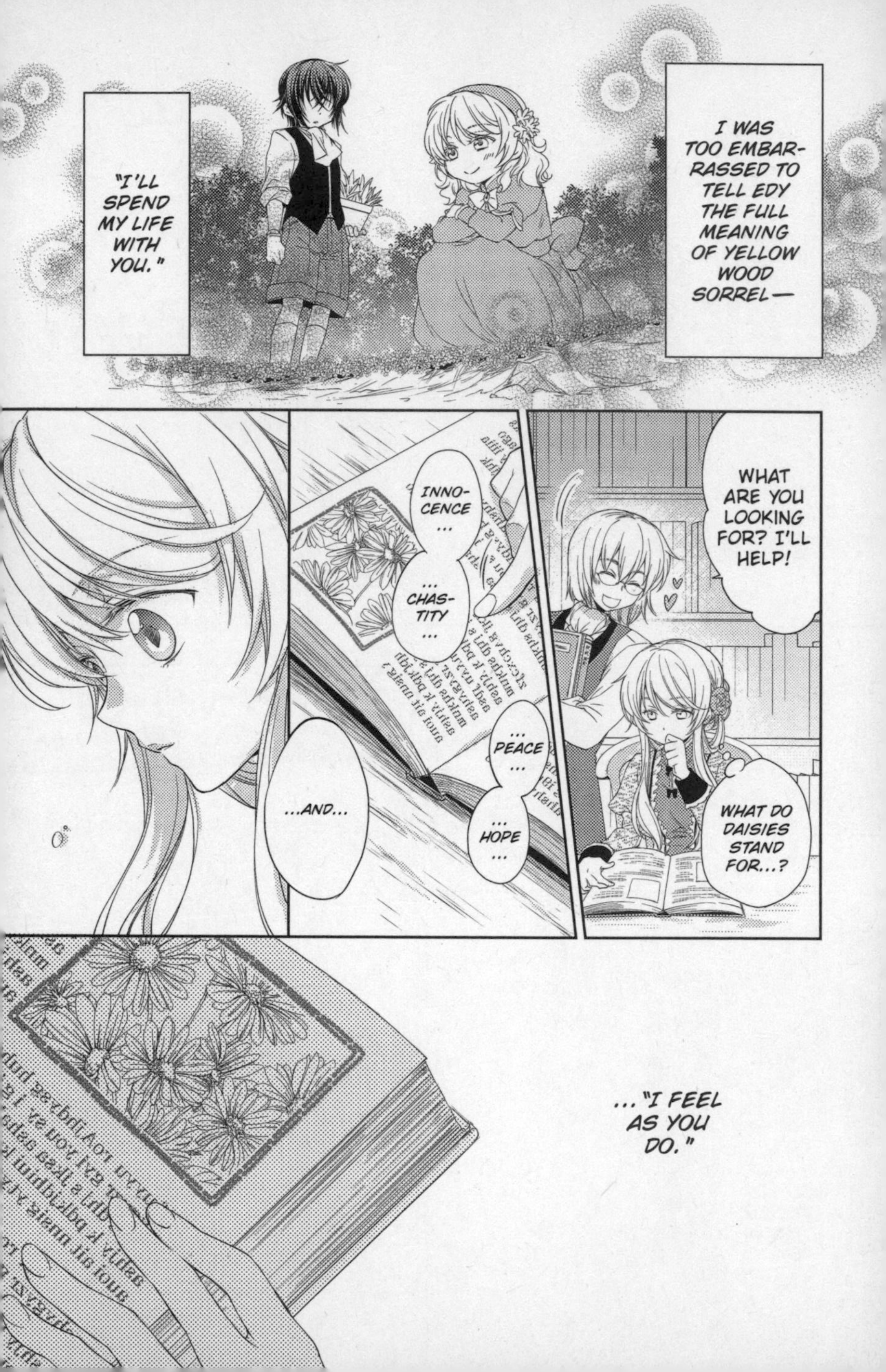
I WAS TOO EMBARRASSED TO TELL EDY THE FULL MEANING OF YELLOW WOOD SORREL—
"I'LL SPEND MY LIFE WITH YOU."
WHAT ARE YOU LOOKING FOR? I'LL HELP!
WHAT DO DAISIES STAND FOR...?
INNOCENCE...
...CHASTITY...
...PEACE...
...HOPE...
...AND...
..."I FEEL AS YOU DO."

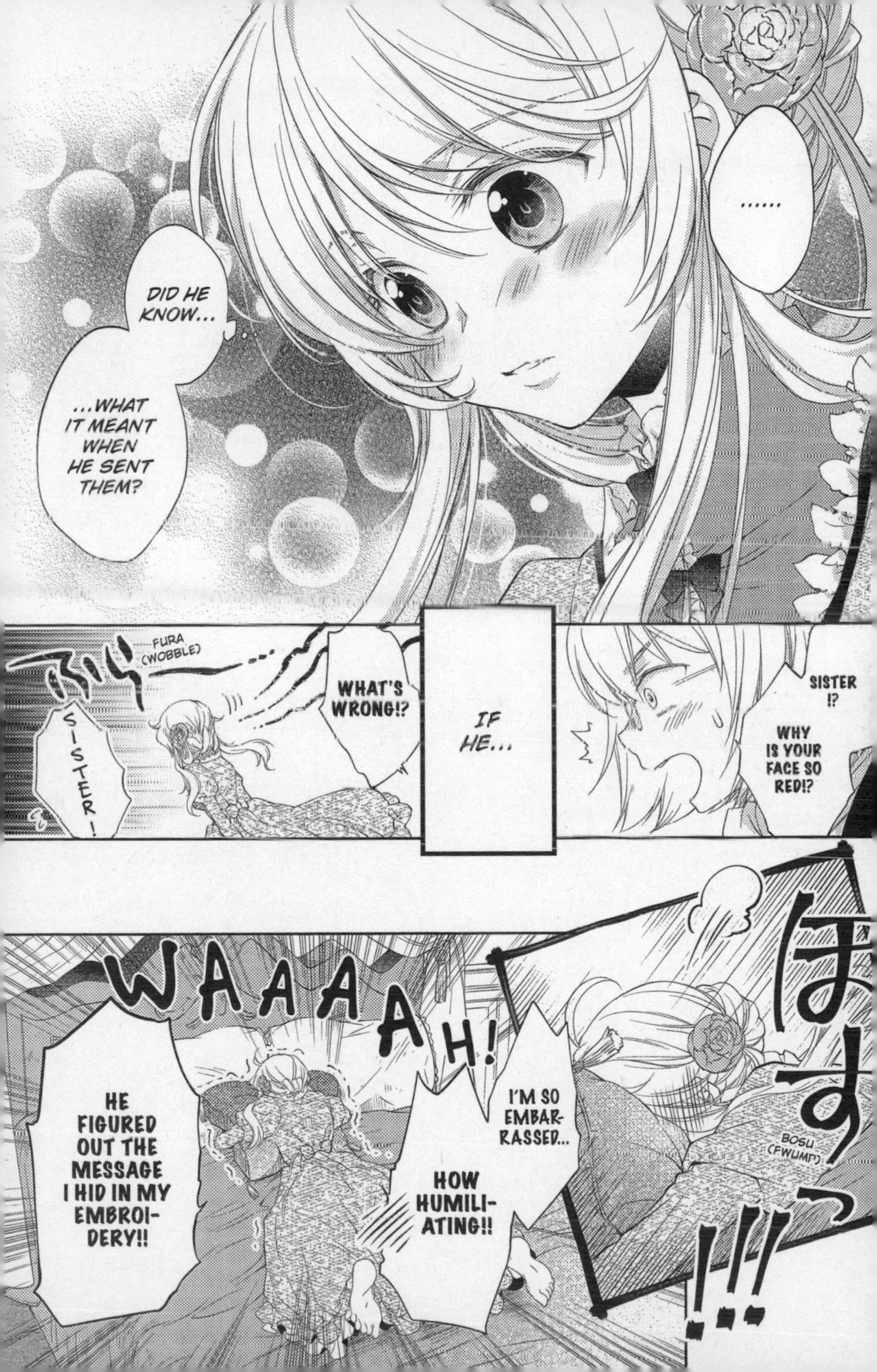
......
DID HE KNOW...
...WHAT IT MEANT WHEN HE SENT THEM?
SISTER!?
WHY IS YOUR FACE SO RED!?
IF HE...
WHAT'S WRONG!?
FURA (WOBBLE)
SISTER!
BOSU (FWUMP)
I'M SO EMBARRASSED...
HOW HUMILIATING!!
WAAAAAH!
HE FIGURED OUT THE MESSAGE I HID IN MY EMBROIDERY!!

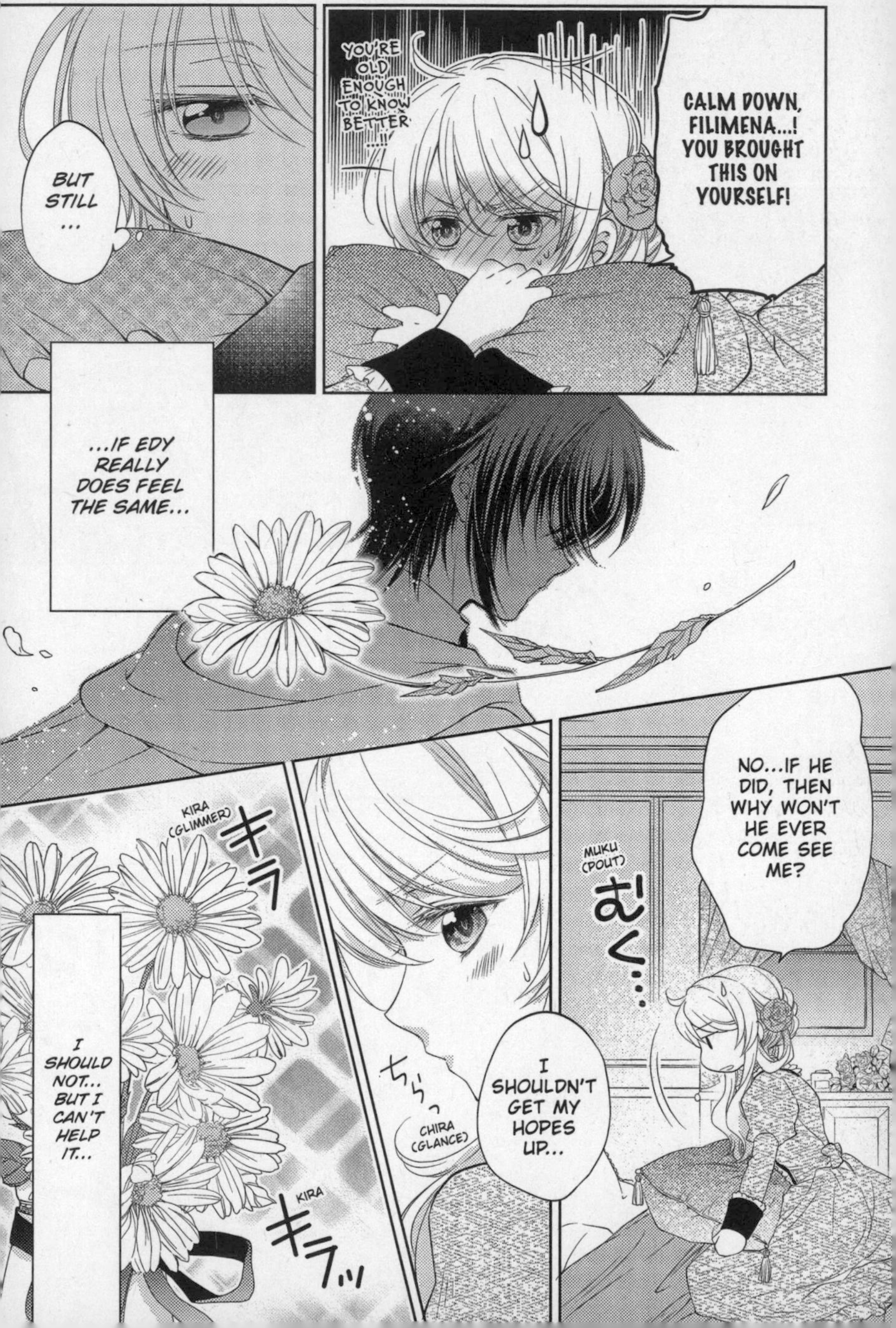
CALM DOWN, FILIMENA...! YOU BROUGHT THIS ON YOURSELF!
YOU'RE OLD ENOUGH TO KNOW BETTER...!!
BUT STILL...
...IF EDY REALLY DOES FEEL THE SAME...
NO...IF HE DID, THEN WHY WON'T HE EVER COME SEE ME?
MUKU (POUT)
むく…
I SHOULDN'T GET MY HOPES UP...
ちらっ
CHIRA (GLANCE)
KIRA (GLIMMER)
キラ
I SHOULD NOT... BUT I CAN'T HELP IT...
KIRA
キラッ

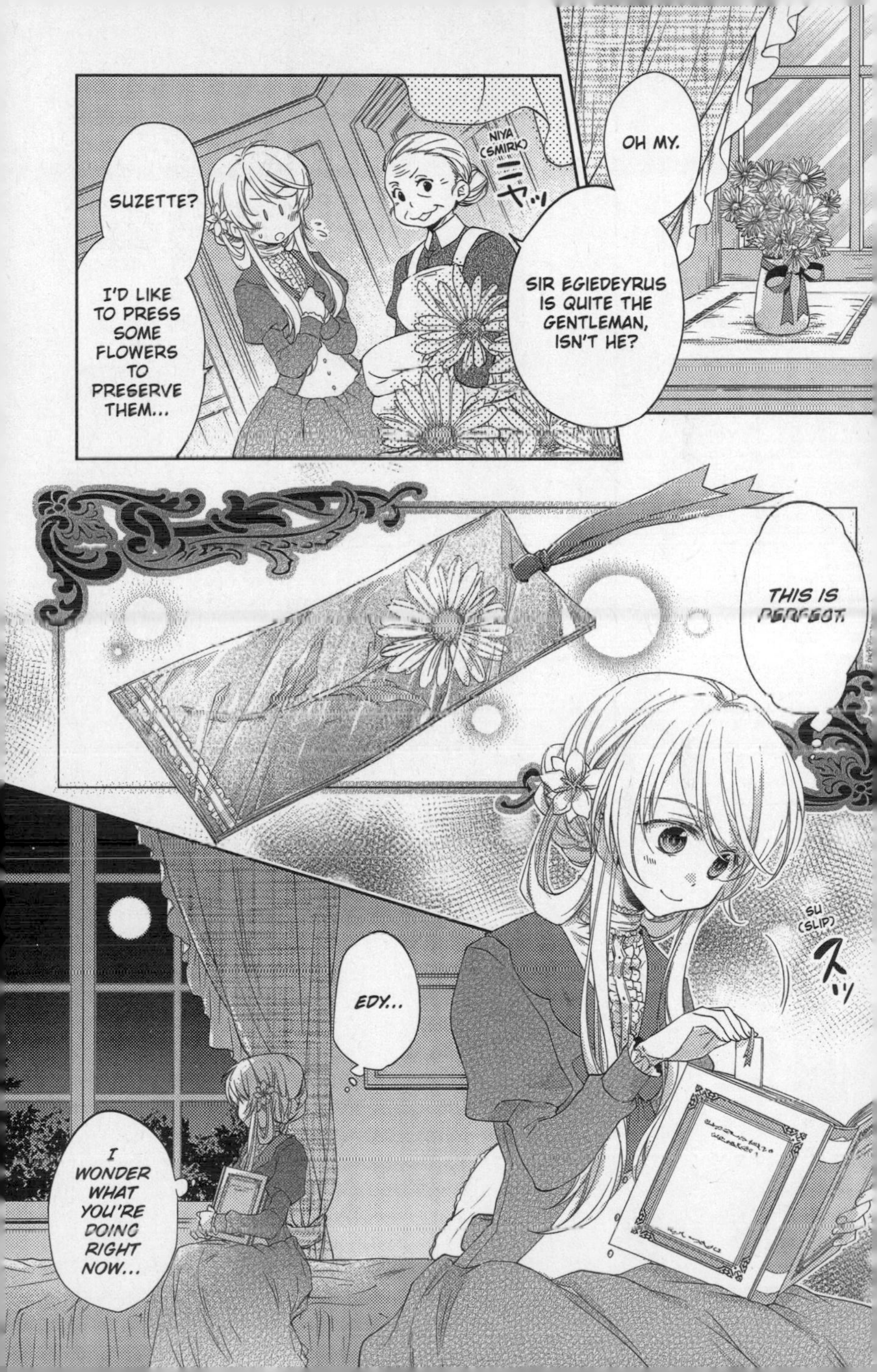
SUZETTE?
I'D LIKE TO PRESS SOME FLOWERS TO PRESERVE THEM...
NIYA (SMIRK)
ニヤッ
OH MY.
SIR EGIEDEYRUS IS QUITE THE GENTLEMAN, ISN'T HE?
THIS IS PERFECT.
SU (SLIP)
スッ
EDY...
I WONDER WHAT YOU'RE DOING RIGHT NOW...

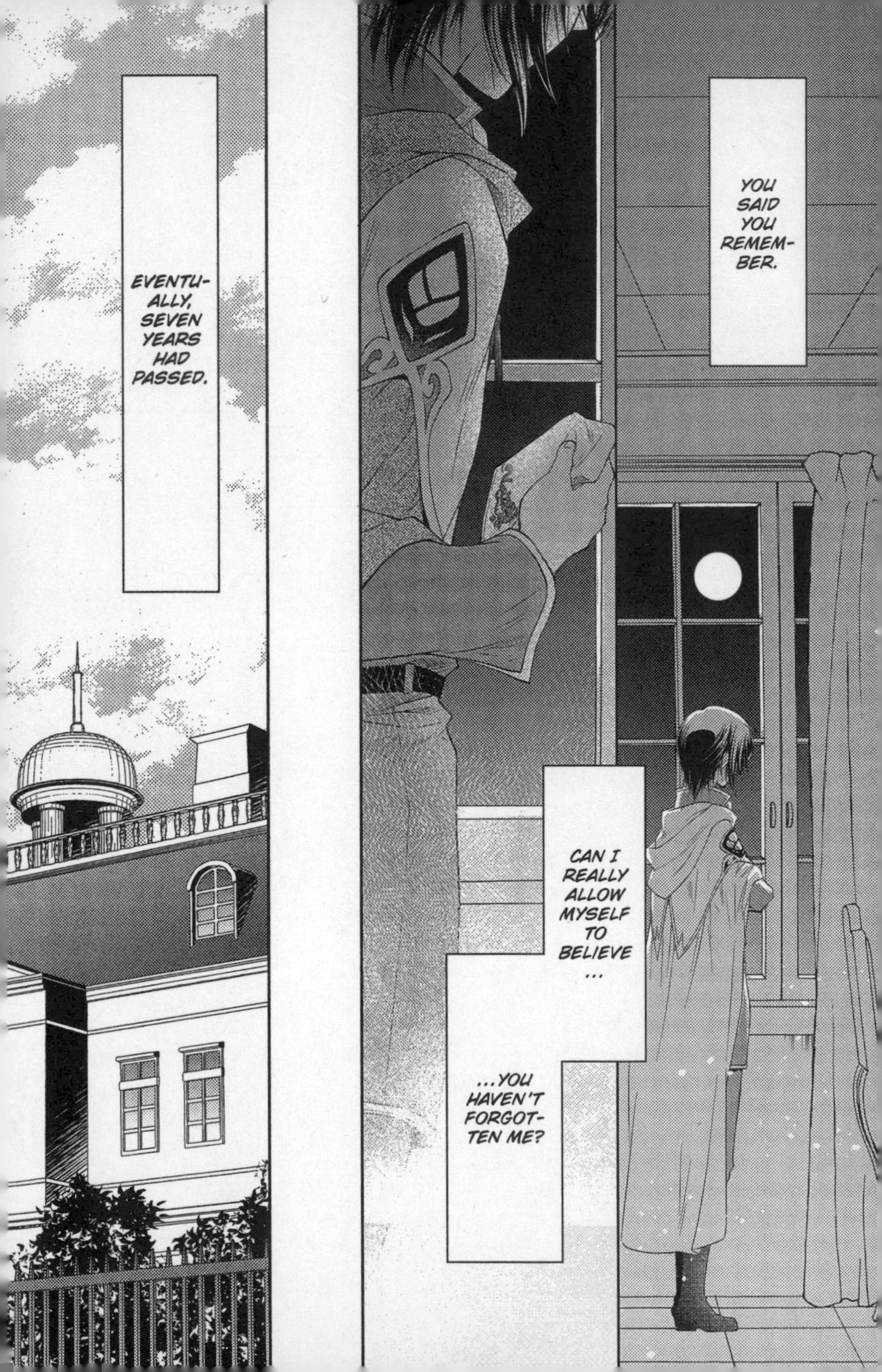
YOU SAID YOU REMEMBER.
CAN I REALLY ALLOW MYSELF TO BELIEVE...
...YOU HAVEN'T FORGOTTEN ME?
EVENTUALLY, SEVEN YEARS HAD PASSED.

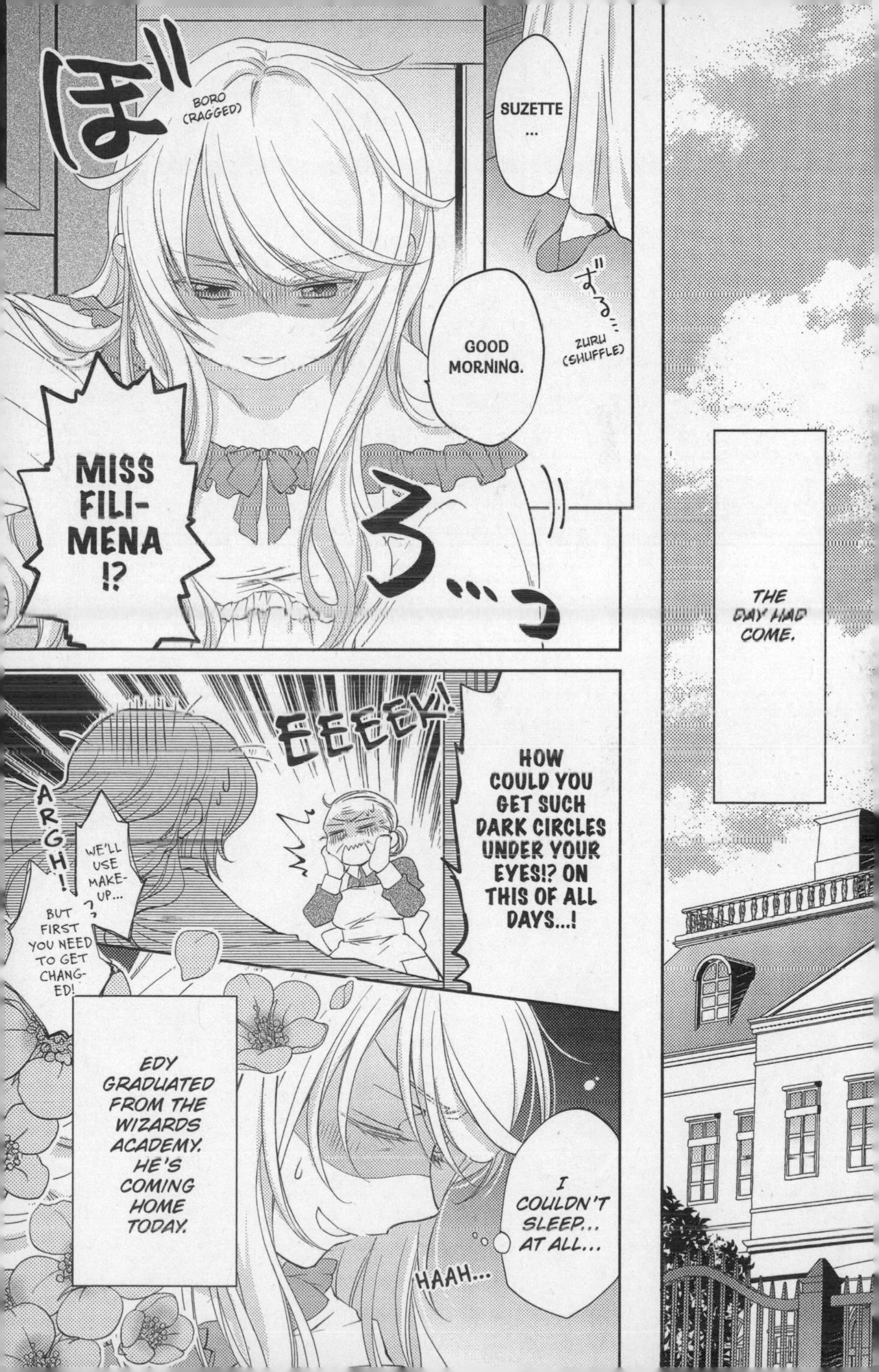
THE DAY HAD COME.
SUZETTE ...
GOOD MORNING.
ずる…
ZURU (SHUFFLE)
ぼ
BORO (RAGGED)
ろ…っ
MISS FILI-MENA !?
EEEEEK!
HOW COULD YOU GET SUCH DARK CIRCLES UNDER YOUR EYES!? ON THIS OF ALL DAYS...!
ARGH!
WE'LL USE MAKE-UP...
BUT FIRST YOU NEED TO GET CHANG-ED!
I COULDN'T SLEEP... AT ALL...
HAAH...
EDY GRADUATED FROM THE WIZARDS ACADEMY. HE'S COMING HOME TODAY.

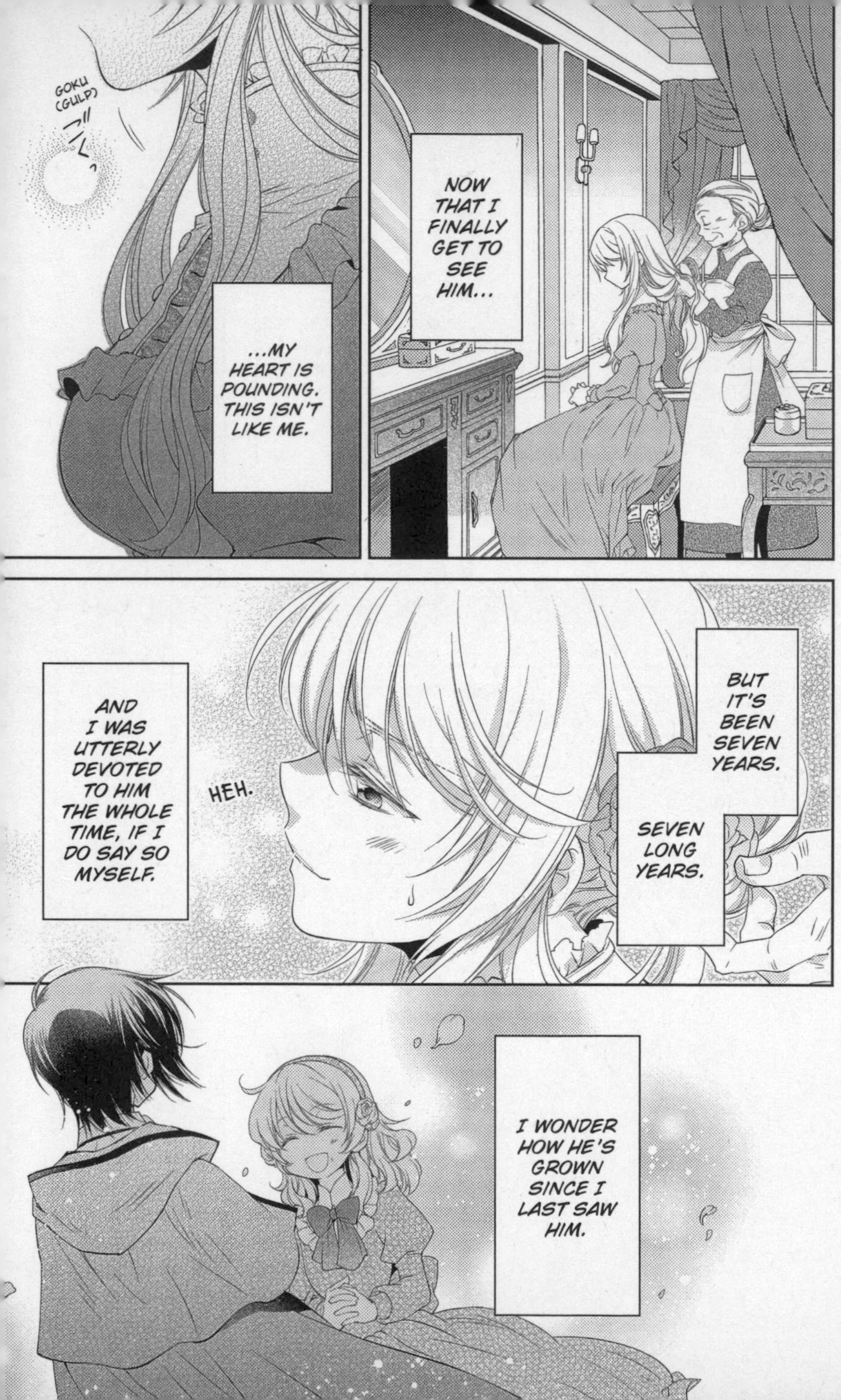
NOW THAT I FINALLY GET TO SEE HIM...
...MY HEART IS POUNDING. THIS ISN'T LIKE ME.
GOKU (GULP)
BUT IT'S BEEN SEVEN YEARS.
SEVEN LONG YEARS.
HEH.
AND I WAS UTTERLY DEVOTED TO HIM THE WHOLE TIME, IF I DO SAY SO MYSELF.
I WONDER HOW HE'S GROWN SINCE I LAST SAW HIM.

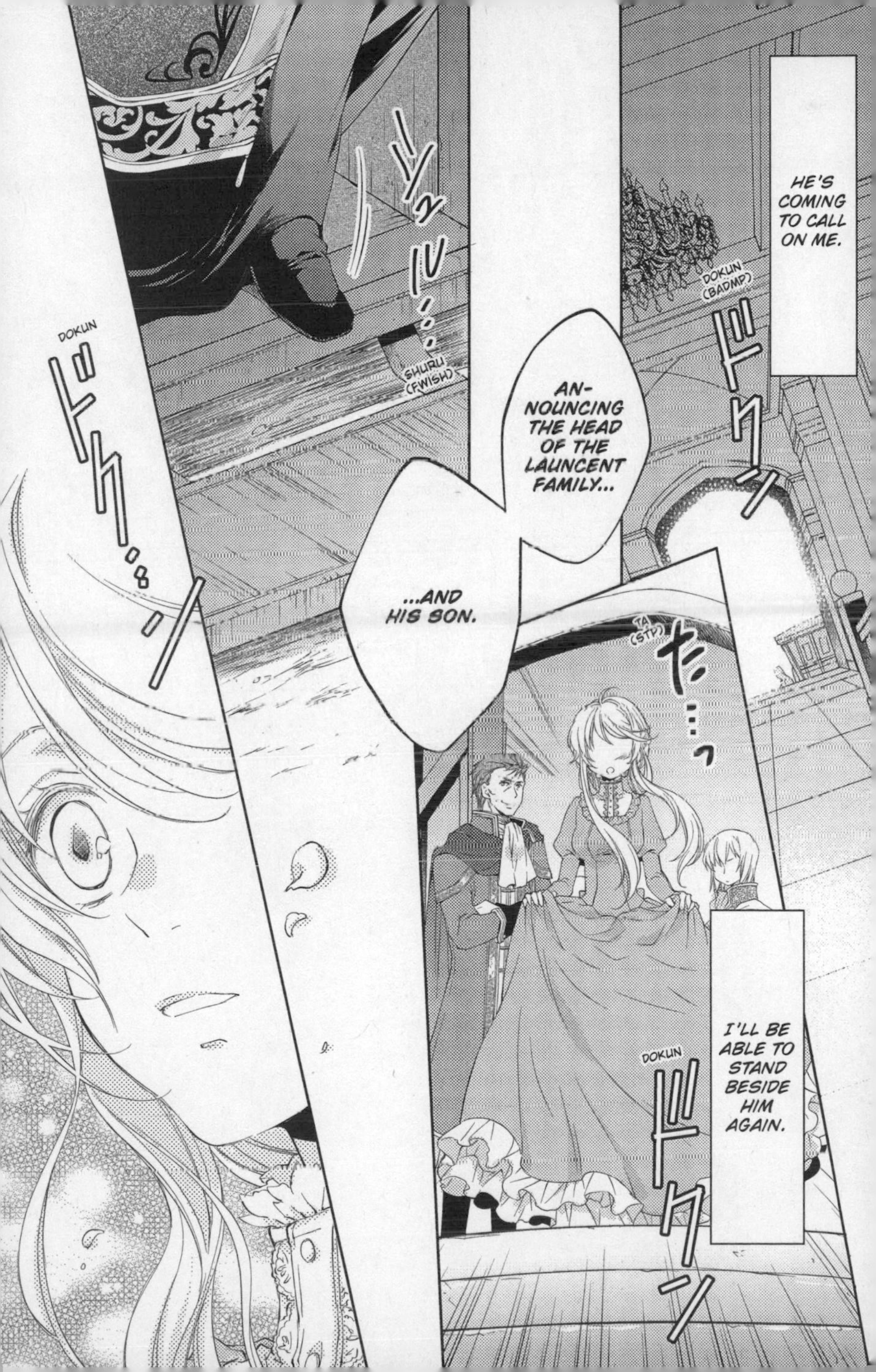
HE'S COMING TO CALL ON ME.
DOKUN (BADMP)
SHURU (FWISH)
AN-NOUNCING THE HEAD OF THE LAUNCENT FAMILY...
...AND HIS SON.
TA (STP)
I'LL BE ABLE TO STAND BESIDE HIM AGAIN.
DOKUN
DOKUN

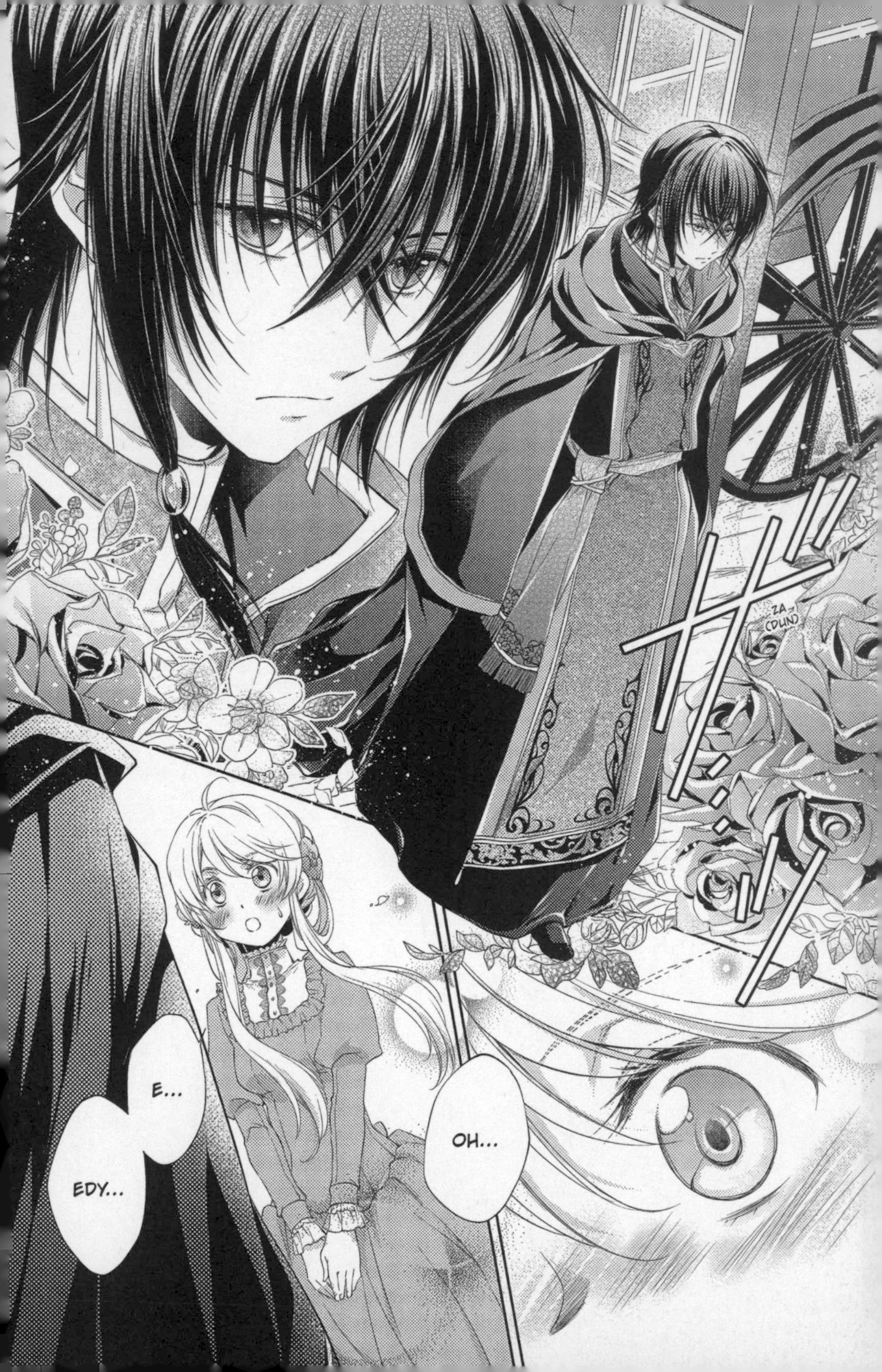
ZA (DUN)
OH...
E...
EDY...

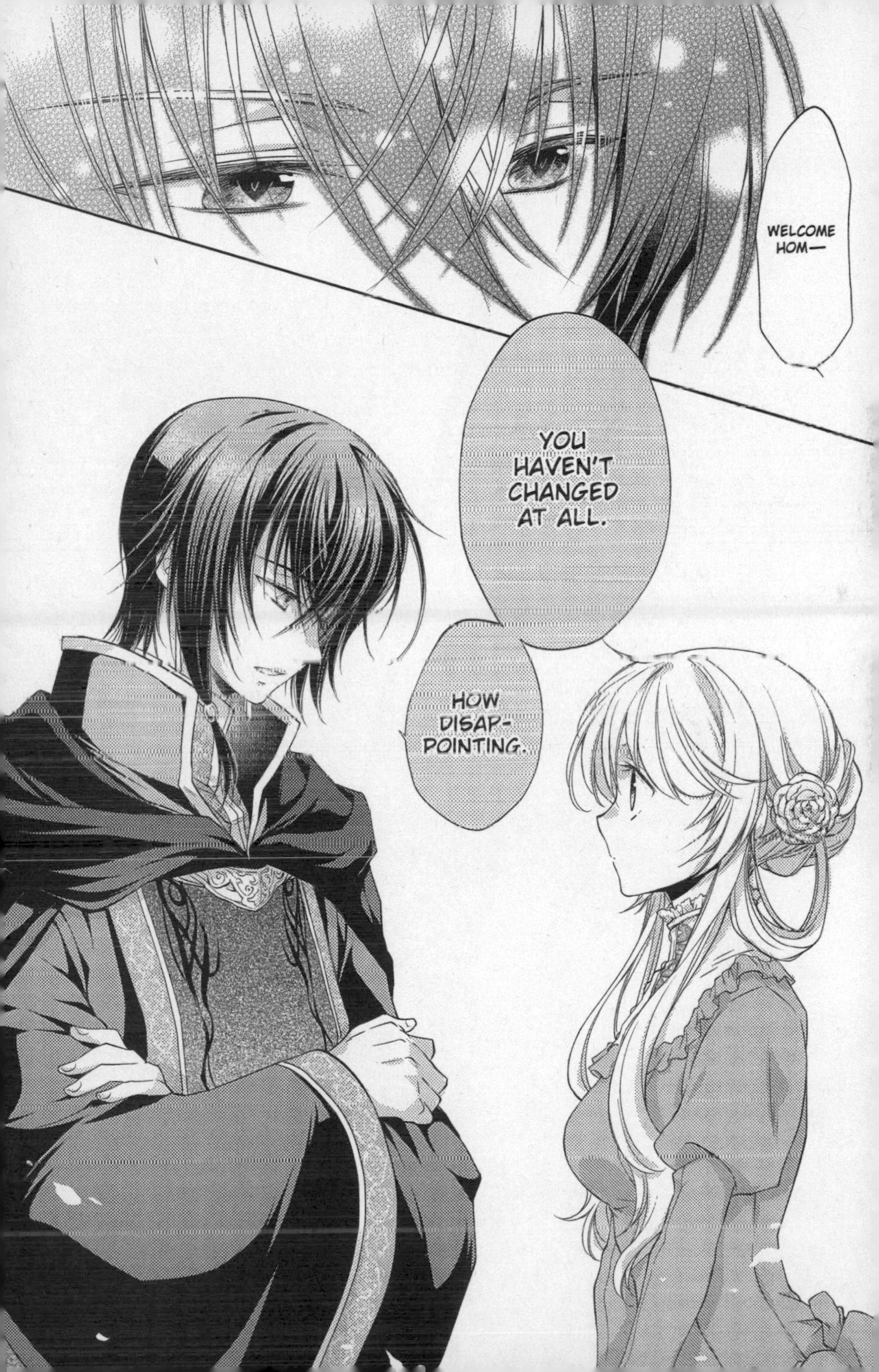
WELCOME HOM—
YOU HAVEN'T CHANGED AT ALL.
HOW DISAP-POINTING.

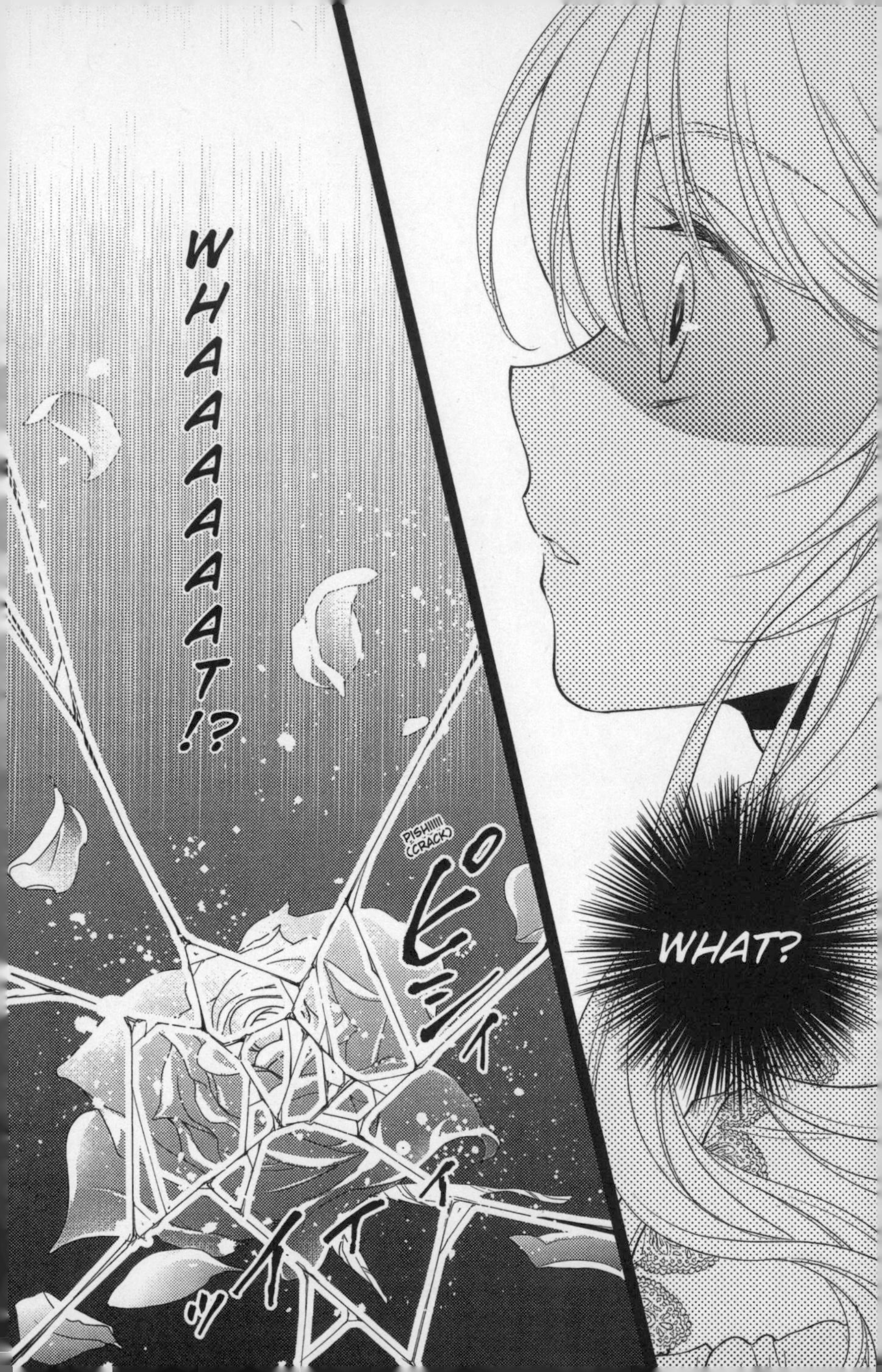
WHAT?
WHAAAAAAAT!?
PISHIIIIII (CRACK)

FIANCÉE OF THE WIZARD

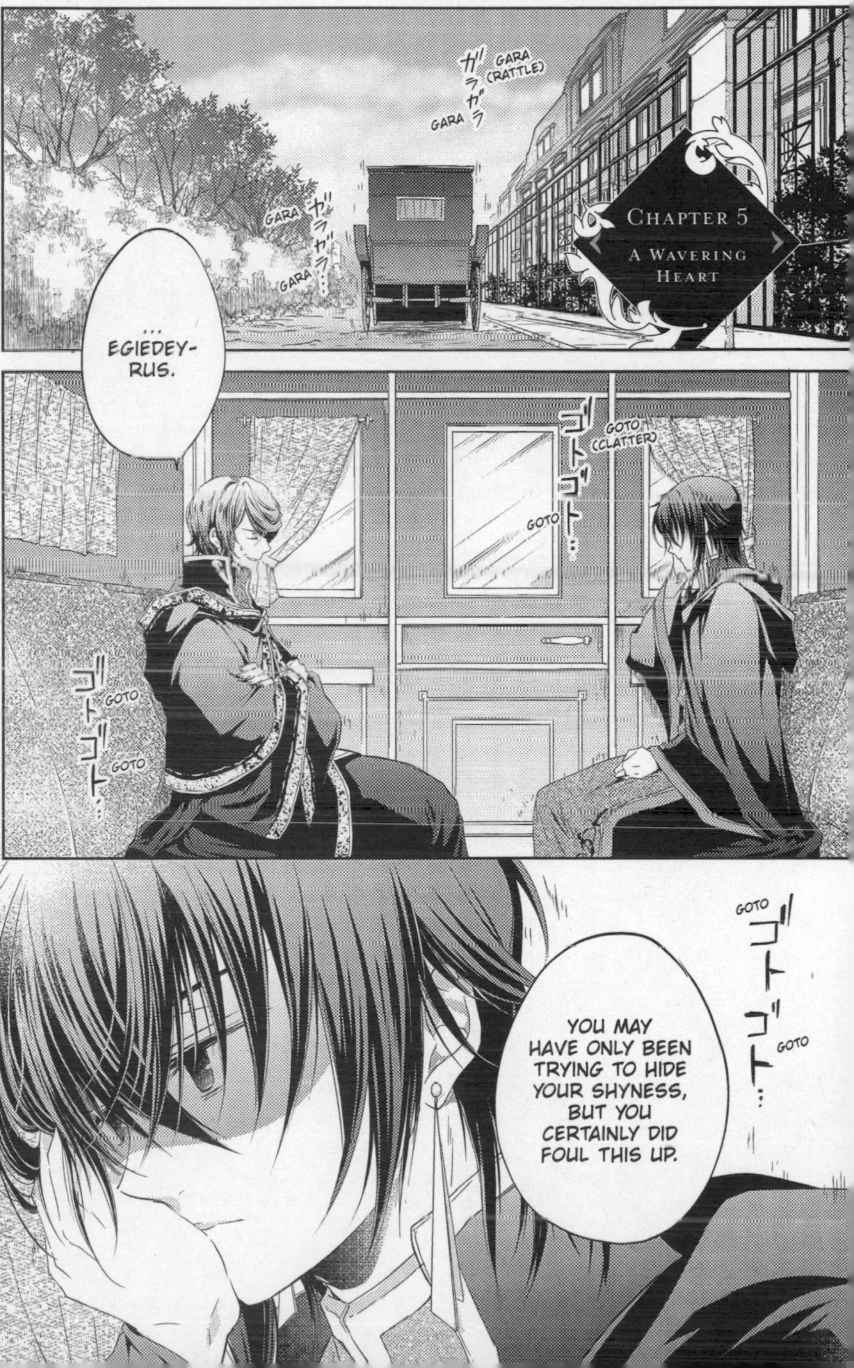
Chapter 5
A Wavering Heart
ガラガラ GARA (RATTLE) GARA
ガラガラ… GARA GARA
…EGIEDEY-RUS.
ゴトゴト… GOTO (CLATTER) GOTO
ゴトゴト… GOTO GOTO
ゴトゴト… GOTO GOTO
YOU MAY HAVE ONLY BEEN TRYING TO HIDE YOUR SHYNESS, BUT YOU CERTAINLY DID FOUL THIS UP.

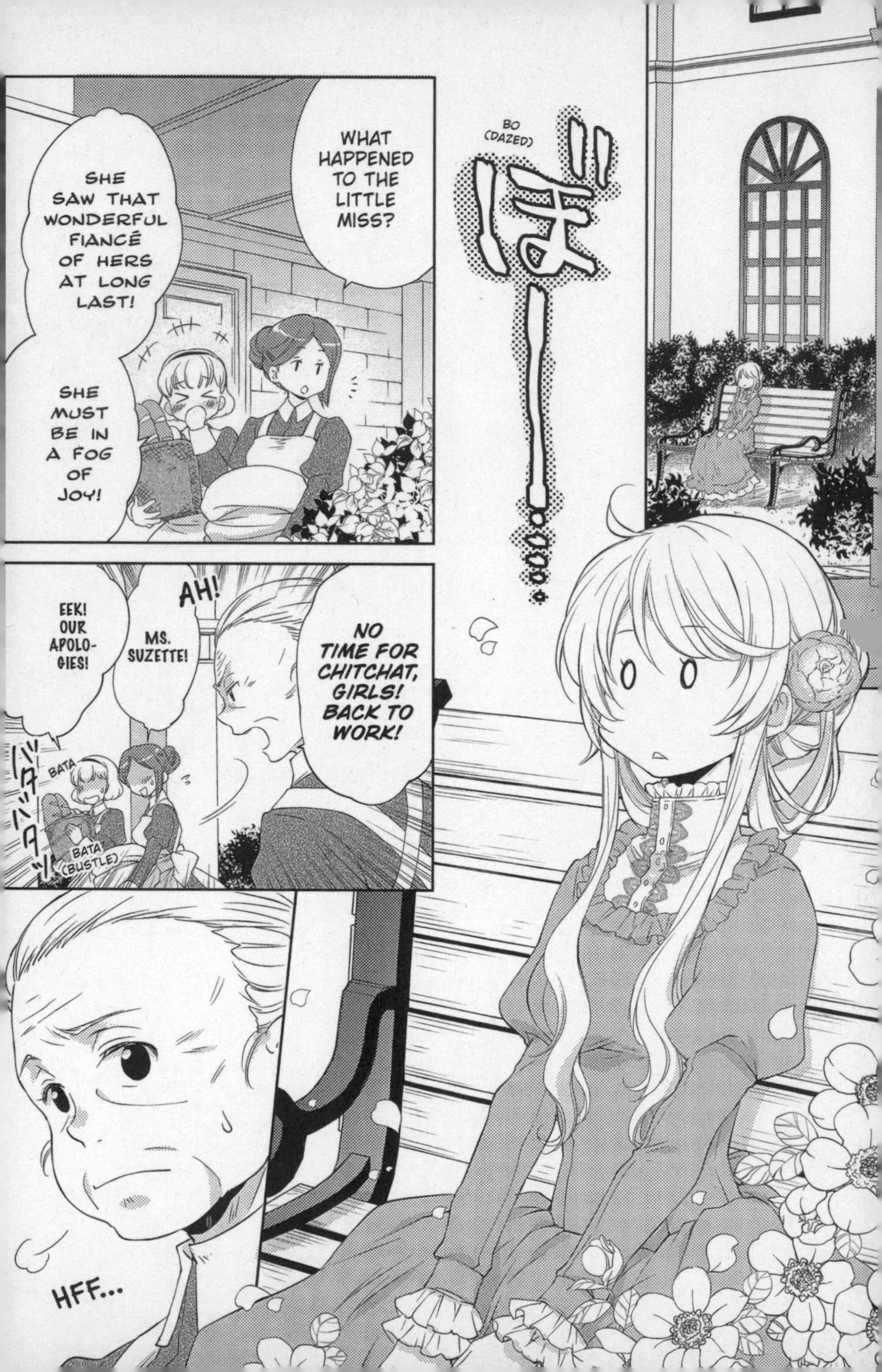
BO (DAZED)
WHAT HAPPENED TO THE LITTLE MISS?
SHE SAW THAT WONDERFUL FIANCÉ OF HERS AT LONG LAST!
SHE MUST BE IN A FOG OF JOY!
NO TIME FOR CHITCHAT, GIRLS! BACK TO WORK!
AH!
MS. SUZETTE!
EEK! OUR APOLOGIES!
BATA BATA (BUSTLE)
HFF...

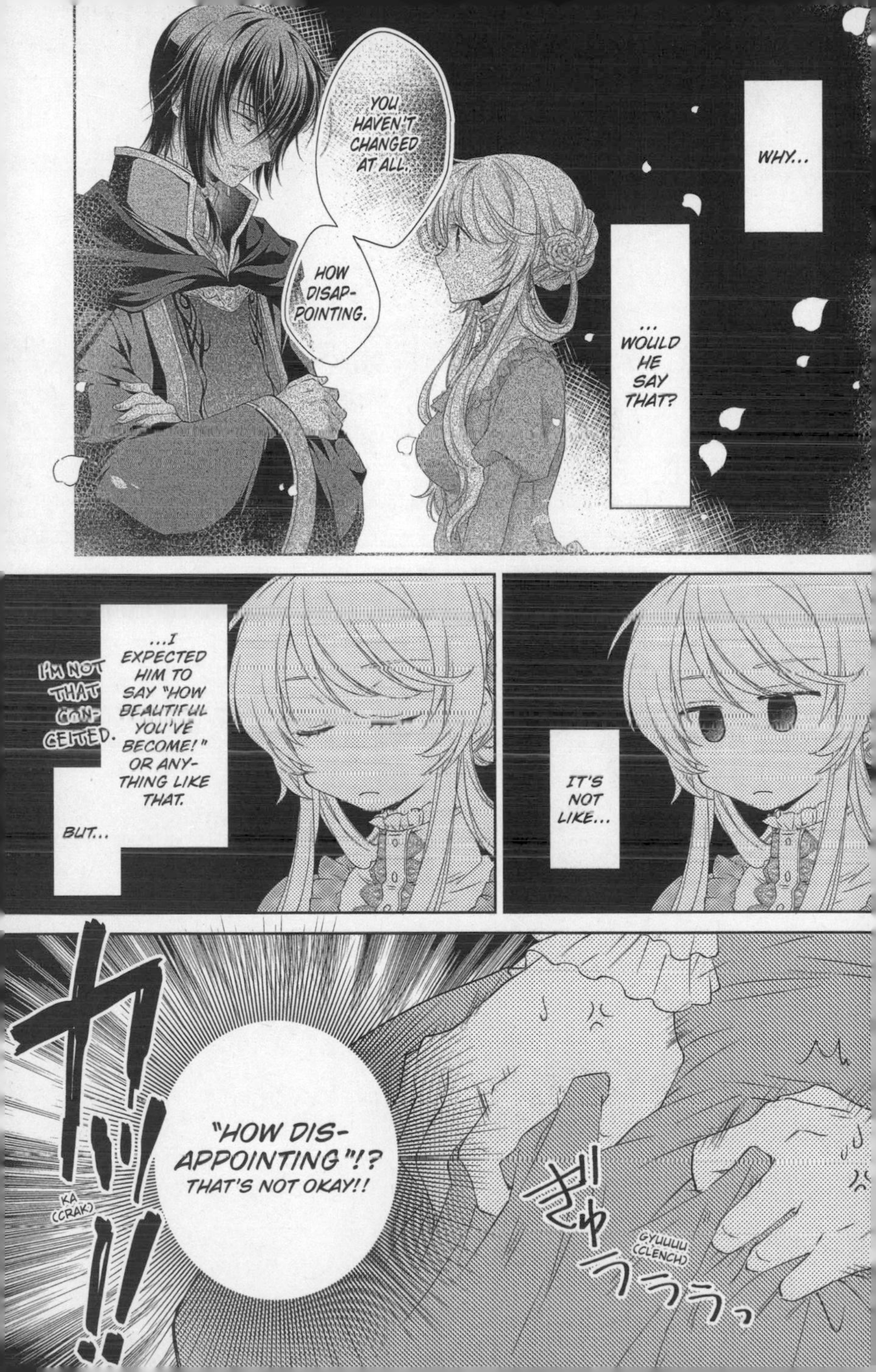
YOU HAVEN'T CHANGED AT ALL.
HOW DISAP-POINTING.
WHY...
...WOULD HE SAY THAT?
IT'S NOT LIKE...
...I EXPECTED HIM TO SAY "HOW BEAUTIFUL YOU'VE BECOME!" OR ANY-THING LIKE THAT.
I'M NOT THAT CON-CEITED.
BUT...
GYUUUU (CLENCH)
"HOW DIS-APPOINTING"!? THAT'S NOT OKAY!!
KA (CRAK)

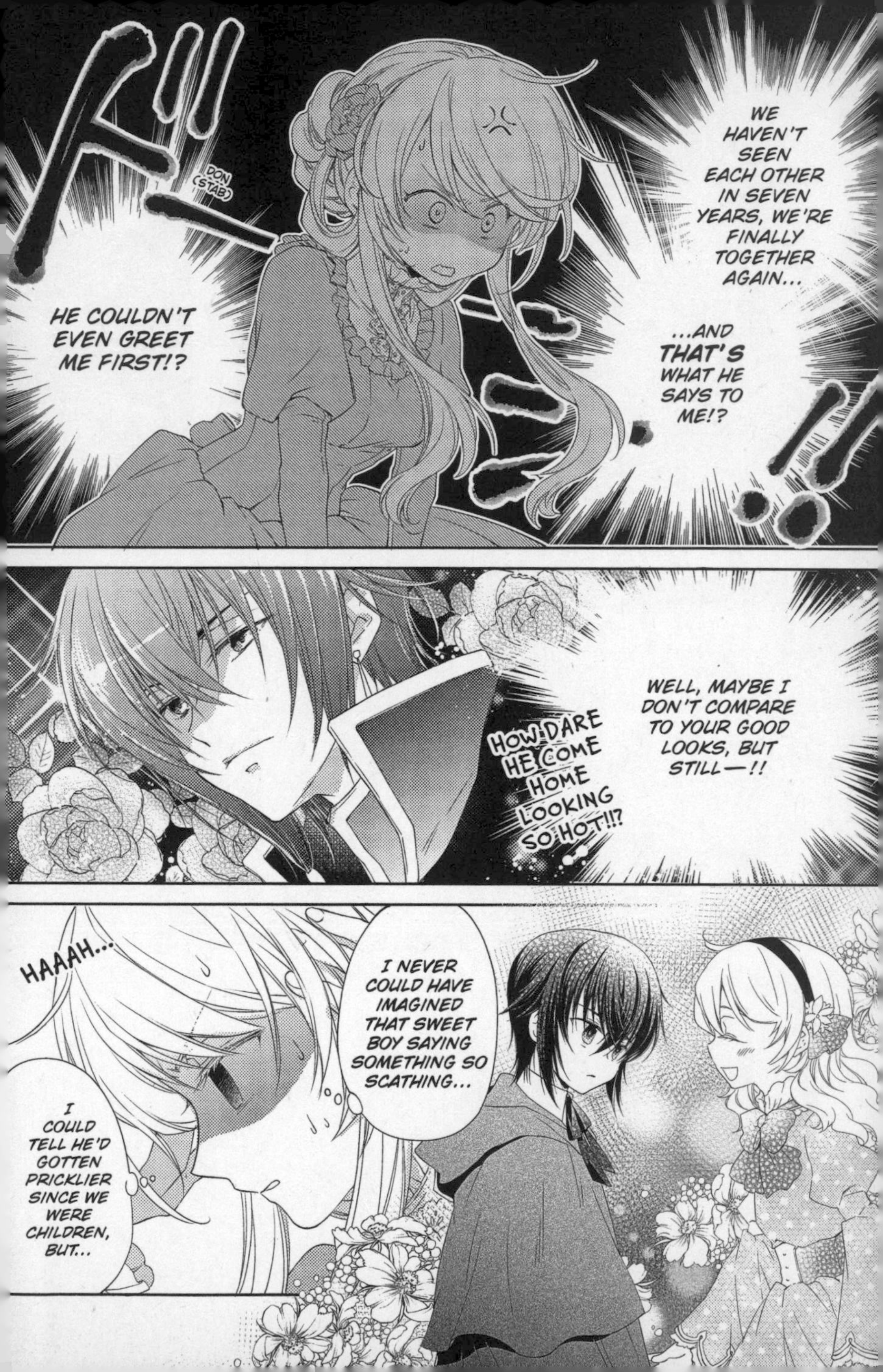

WE HAVEN'T SEEN EACH OTHER IN SEVEN YEARS, WE'RE FINALLY TOGETHER AGAIN...
...AND THAT'S WHAT HE SAYS TO ME!?
DON (STAB)
HE COULDN'T EVEN GREET ME FIRST!?
WELL, MAYBE I DON'T COMPARE TO YOUR GOOD LOOKS, BUT STILL—!!
HOW DARE HE COME HOME LOOKING SO HOT!!?
I NEVER COULD HAVE IMAGINED THAT SWEET BOY SAYING SOMETHING SO SCATHING...
HAAAH...
I COULD TELL HE'D GOTTEN PRICKLIER SINCE WE WERE CHILDREN, BUT...

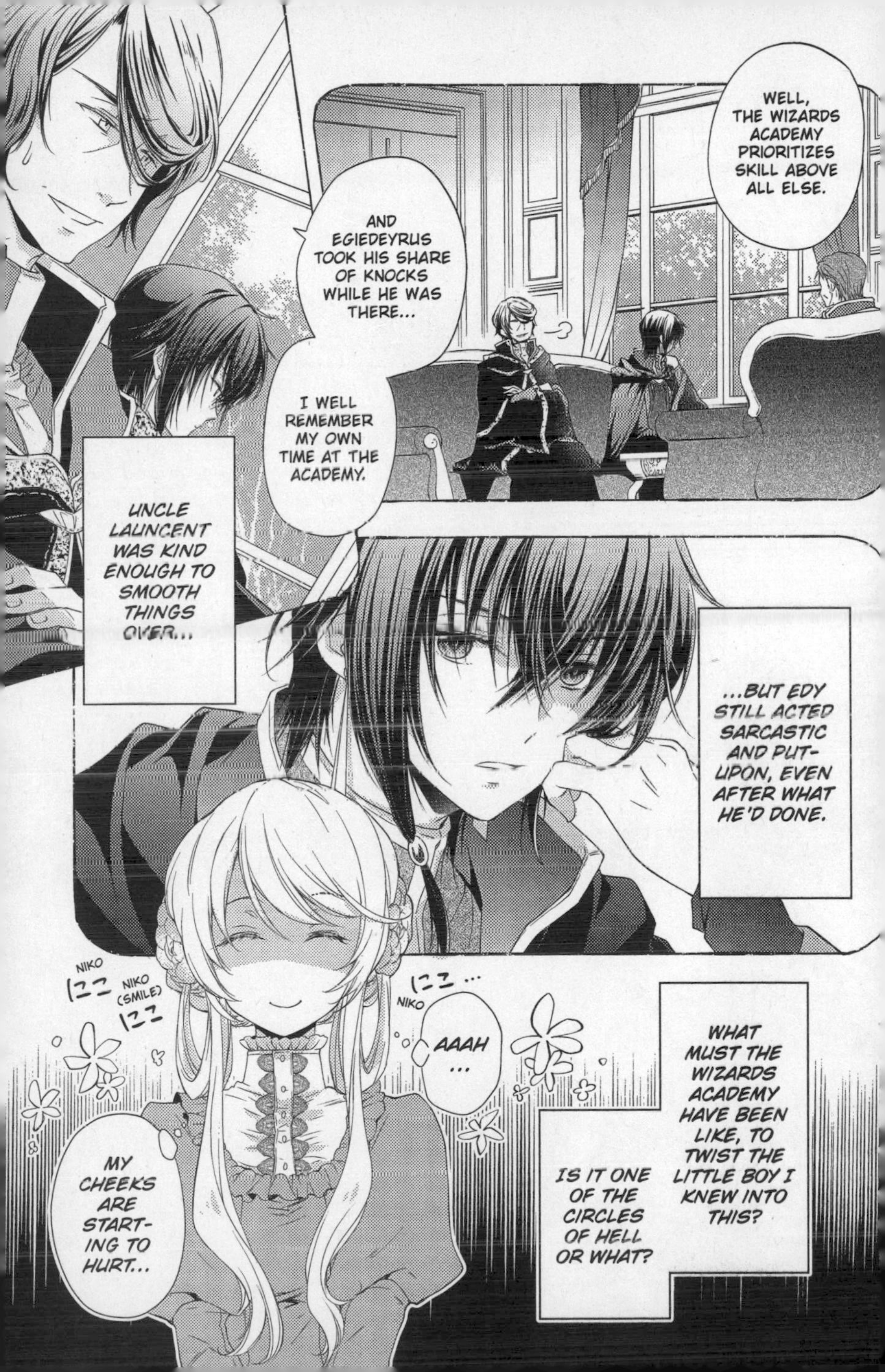
WELL, THE WIZARDS ACADEMY PRIORITIZES SKILL ABOVE ALL ELSE.
AND EGIEDEYRUS TOOK HIS SHARE OF KNOCKS WHILE HE WAS THERE...
I WELL REMEMBER MY OWN TIME AT THE ACADEMY.
UNCLE LAUNCENT WAS KIND ENOUGH TO SMOOTH THINGS OVER...
...BUT EDY STILL ACTED SARCASTIC AND PUT-UPON, EVEN AFTER WHAT HE'D DONE.
WHAT MUST THE WIZARDS ACADEMY HAVE BEEN LIKE, TO TWIST THE LITTLE BOY I KNEW INTO THIS?
IS IT ONE OF THE CIRCLES OF HELL OR WHAT?
にこ… NIKO
AAAH …
にこ NIKO
にこ NIKO (SMILE)
MY CHEEKS ARE STARTING TO HURT...

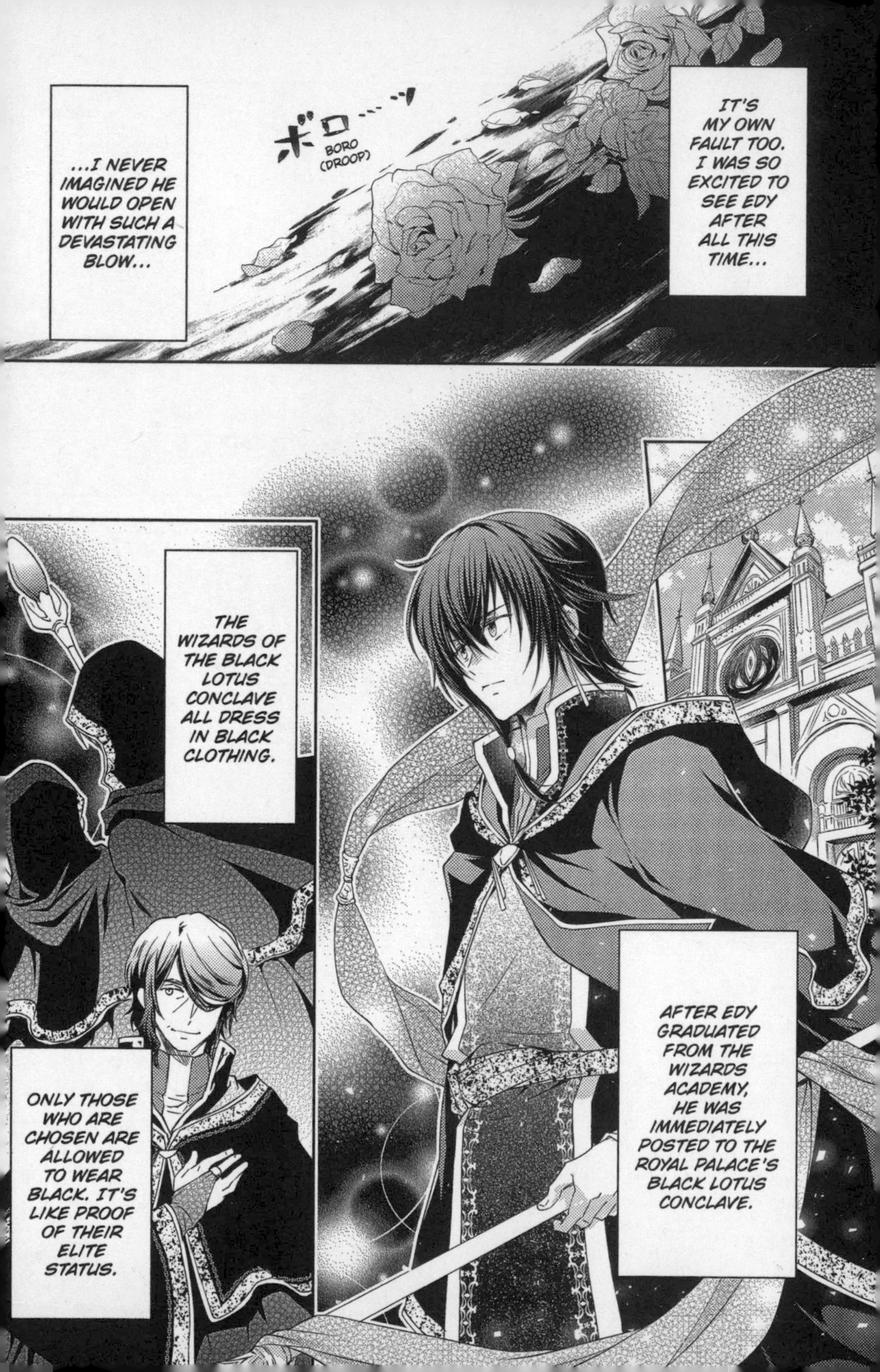
IT'S MY OWN FAULT TOO. I WAS SO EXCITED TO SEE EDY AFTER ALL THIS TIME...
ボロ…ッ
BORO (DROOP)
...I NEVER IMAGINED HE WOULD OPEN WITH SUCH A DEVASTATING BLOW...
AFTER EDY GRADUATED FROM THE WIZARDS ACADEMY, HE WAS IMMEDIATELY POSTED TO THE ROYAL PALACE'S BLACK LOTUS CONCLAVE.
THE WIZARDS OF THE BLACK LOTUS CONCLAVE ALL DRESS IN BLACK CLOTHING.
ONLY THOSE WHO ARE CHOSEN ARE ALLOWED TO WEAR BLACK. IT'S LIKE PROOF OF THEIR ELITE STATUS.

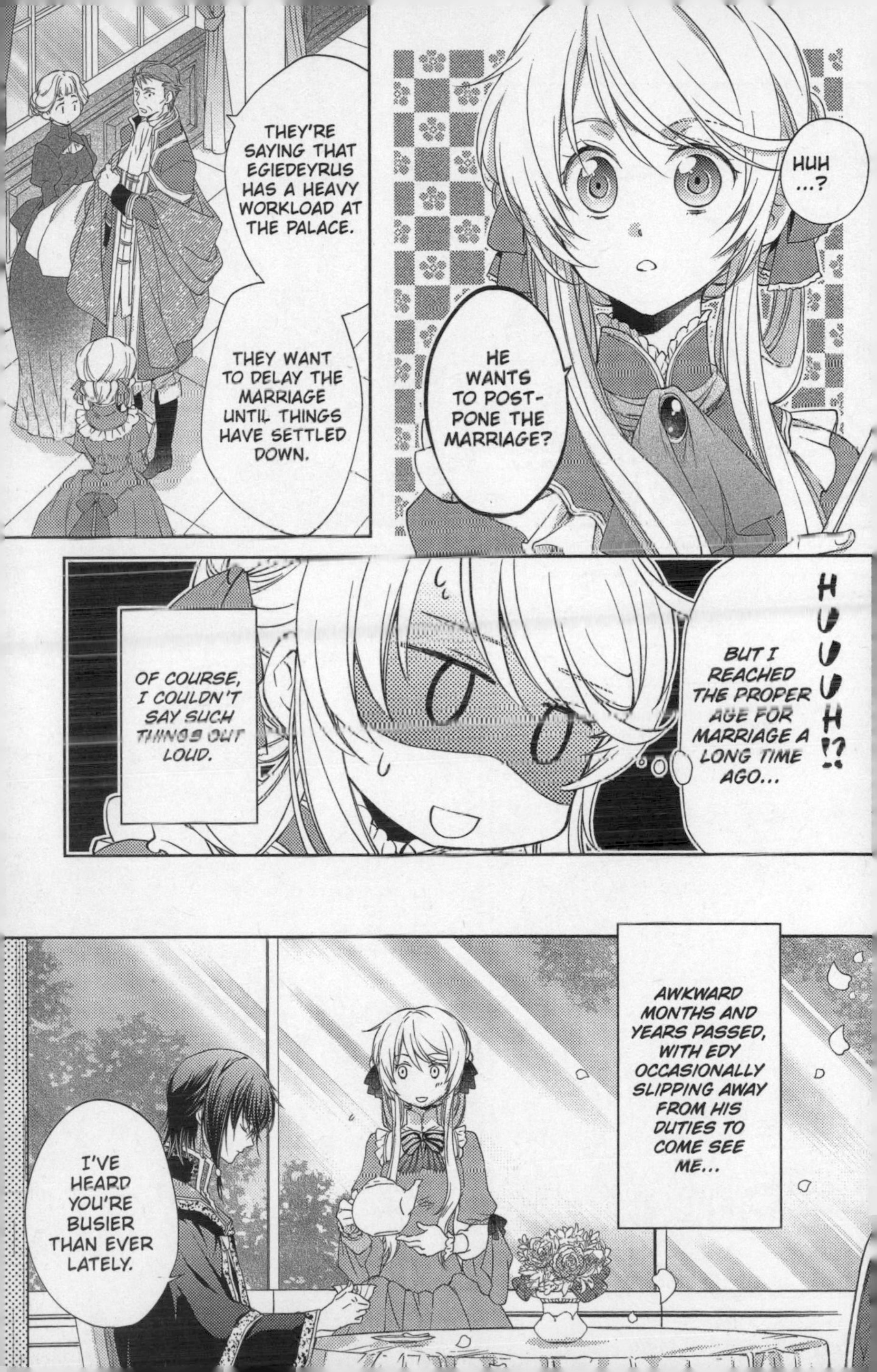
HUH ...?
HE WANTS TO POST-PONE THE MARRIAGE?
THEY'RE SAYING THAT EGIEDEYRUS HAS A HEAVY WORKLOAD AT THE PALACE.
THEY WANT TO DELAY THE MARRIAGE UNTIL THINGS HAVE SETTLED DOWN.
HUUUH!?
BUT I REACHED THE PROPER AGE FOR MARRIAGE A LONG TIME AGO...
OF COURSE, I COULDN'T SAY SUCH THINGS OUT LOUD.
AWKWARD MONTHS AND YEARS PASSED, WITH EDY OCCASIONALLY SLIPPING AWAY FROM HIS DUTIES TO COME SEE ME...
I'VE HEARD YOU'RE BUSIER THAN EVER LATELY.

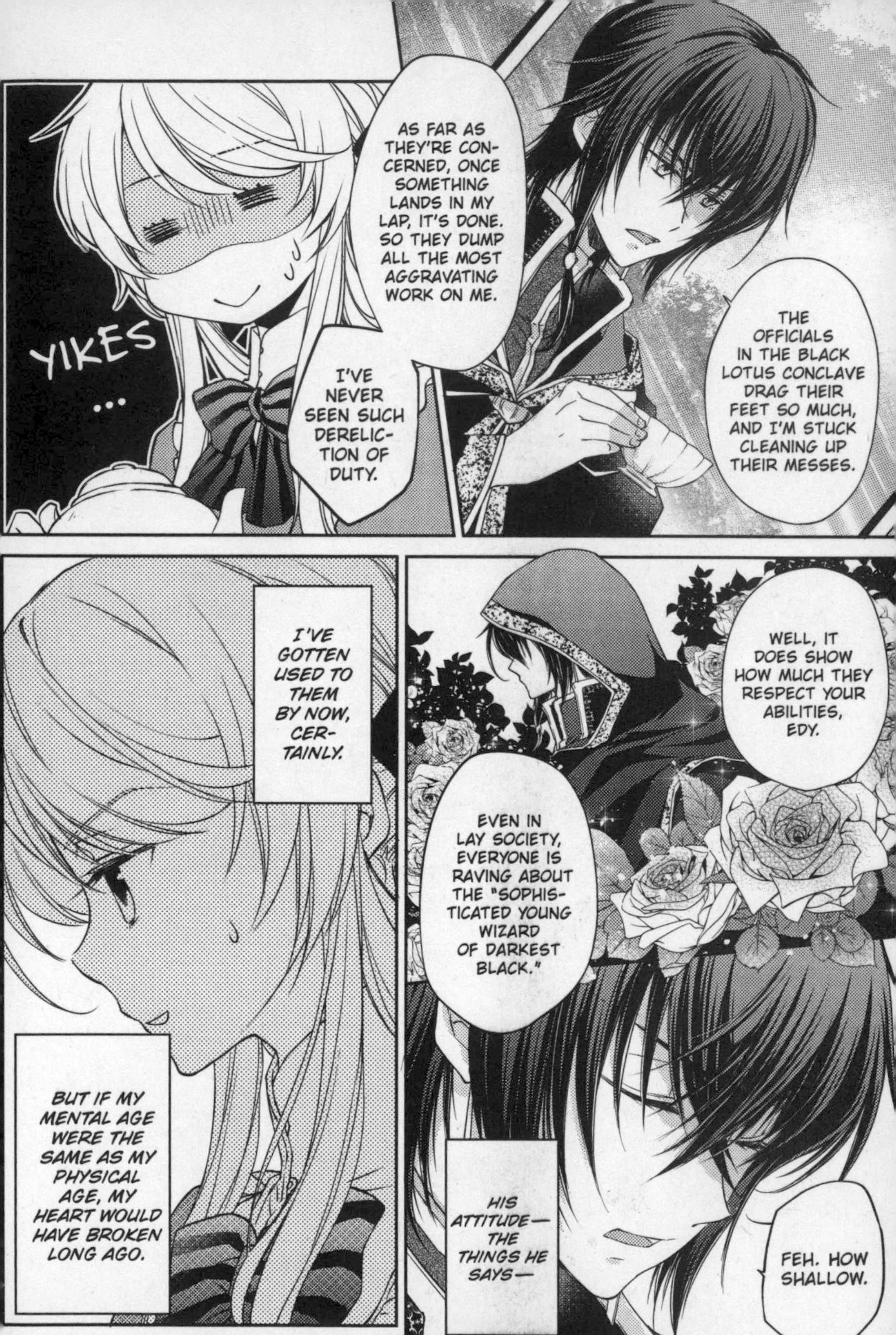
THE OFFICIALS IN THE BLACK LOTUS CONCLAVE DRAG THEIR FEET SO MUCH, AND I'M STUCK CLEANING UP THEIR MESSES.
AS FAR AS THEY'RE CONCERNED, ONCE SOMETHING LANDS IN MY LAP, IT'S DONE. SO THEY DUMP ALL THE MOST AGGRAVATING WORK ON ME.
I'VE NEVER SEEN SUCH DERELICTION OF DUTY.
YIKES...
WELL, IT DOES SHOW HOW MUCH THEY RESPECT YOUR ABILITIES, EDY.
EVEN IN LAY SOCIETY, EVERYONE IS RAVING ABOUT THE "SOPHISTICATED YOUNG WIZARD OF DARKEST BLACK."
FEH. HOW SHALLOW.
HIS ATTITUDE—THE THINGS HE SAYS—
I'VE GOTTEN USED TO THEM BY NOW, CERTAINLY.
BUT IF MY MENTAL AGE WERE THE SAME AS MY PHYSICAL AGE, MY HEART WOULD HAVE BROKEN LONG AGO.

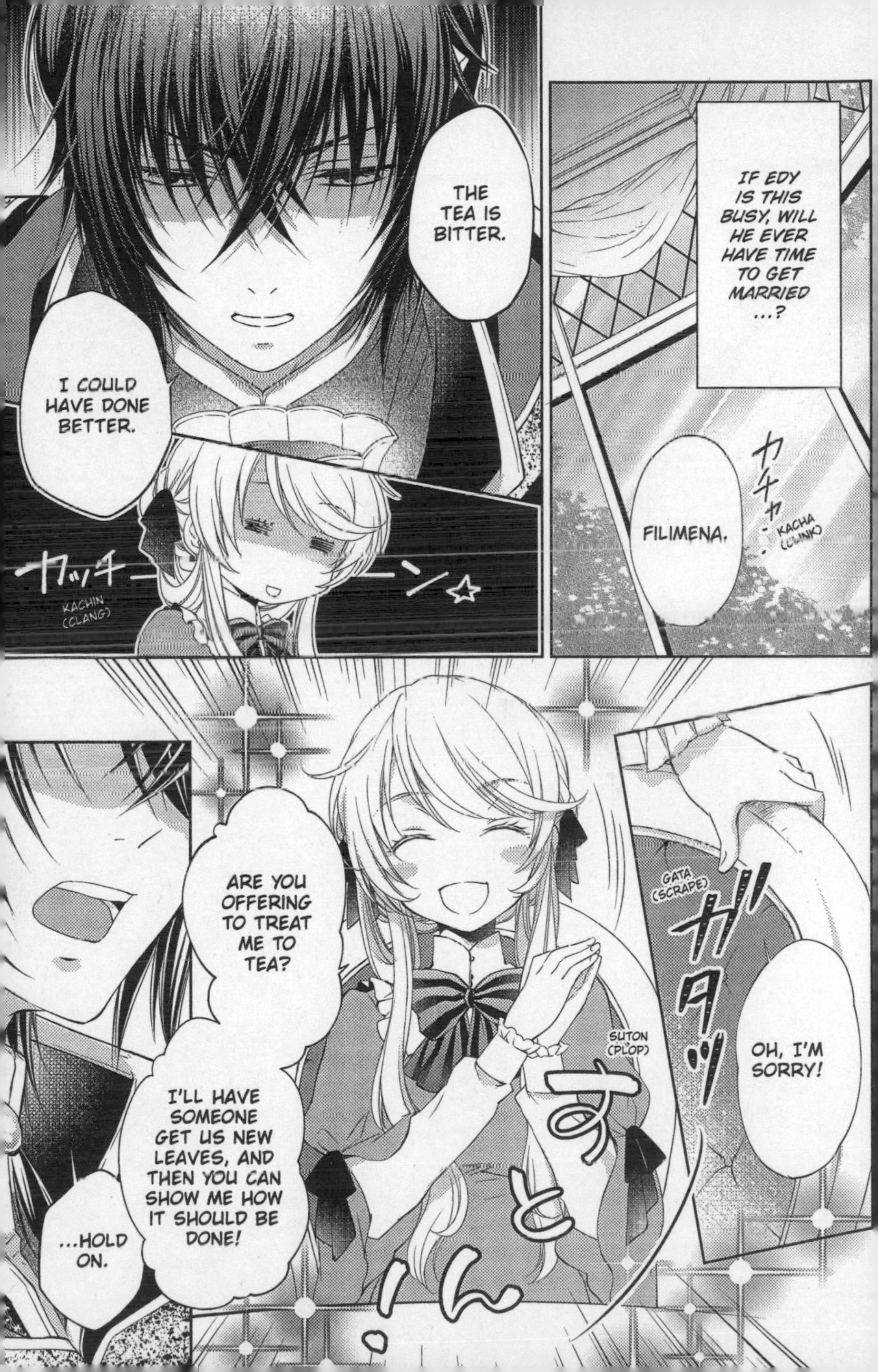
IF EDY IS THIS BUSY, WILL HE EVER HAVE TIME TO GET MARRIED ...?
KACHA (CLINK)
FILIMENA.
THE TEA IS BITTER.
I COULD HAVE DONE BETTER.
KACHIN (CLANG)
GATA (SCRAPE)
OH, I'M SORRY!
SUTON (PLOP)
ARE YOU OFFERING TO TREAT ME TO TEA?
I'LL HAVE SOMEONE GET US NEW LEAVES, AND THEN YOU CAN SHOW ME HOW IT SHOULD BE DONE!
...HOLD ON.

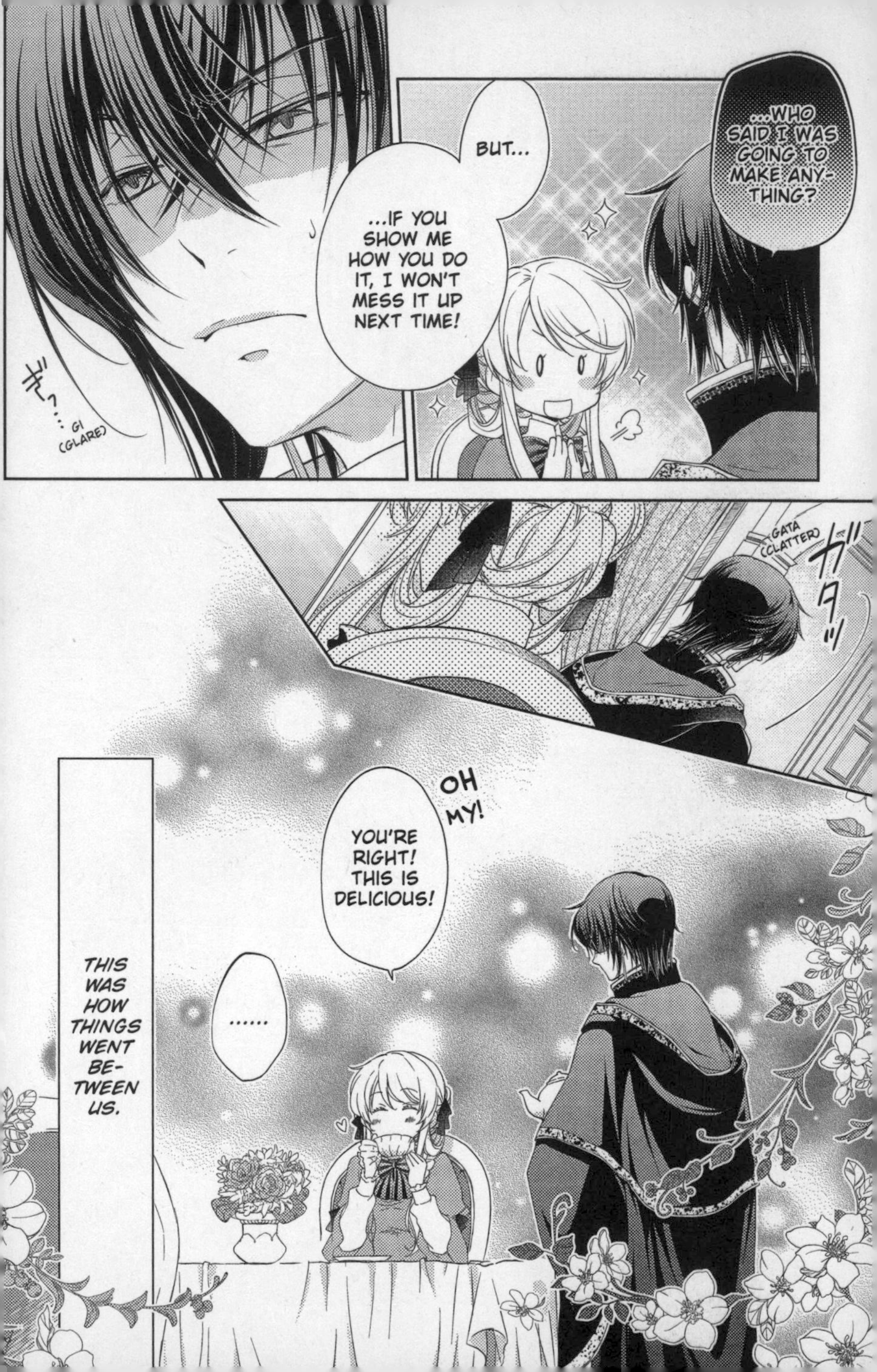
...WHO SAID I WAS GOING TO MAKE ANYTHING?
BUT...
...IF YOU SHOW ME HOW YOU DO IT, I WON'T MESS IT UP NEXT TIME!
ぎっ…
GI (GLARE)
GATA (CLATTER)
ガタッ
OH MY!
YOU'RE RIGHT! THIS IS DELICIOUS!
......
THIS WAS HOW THINGS WENT BE-TWEEN US.

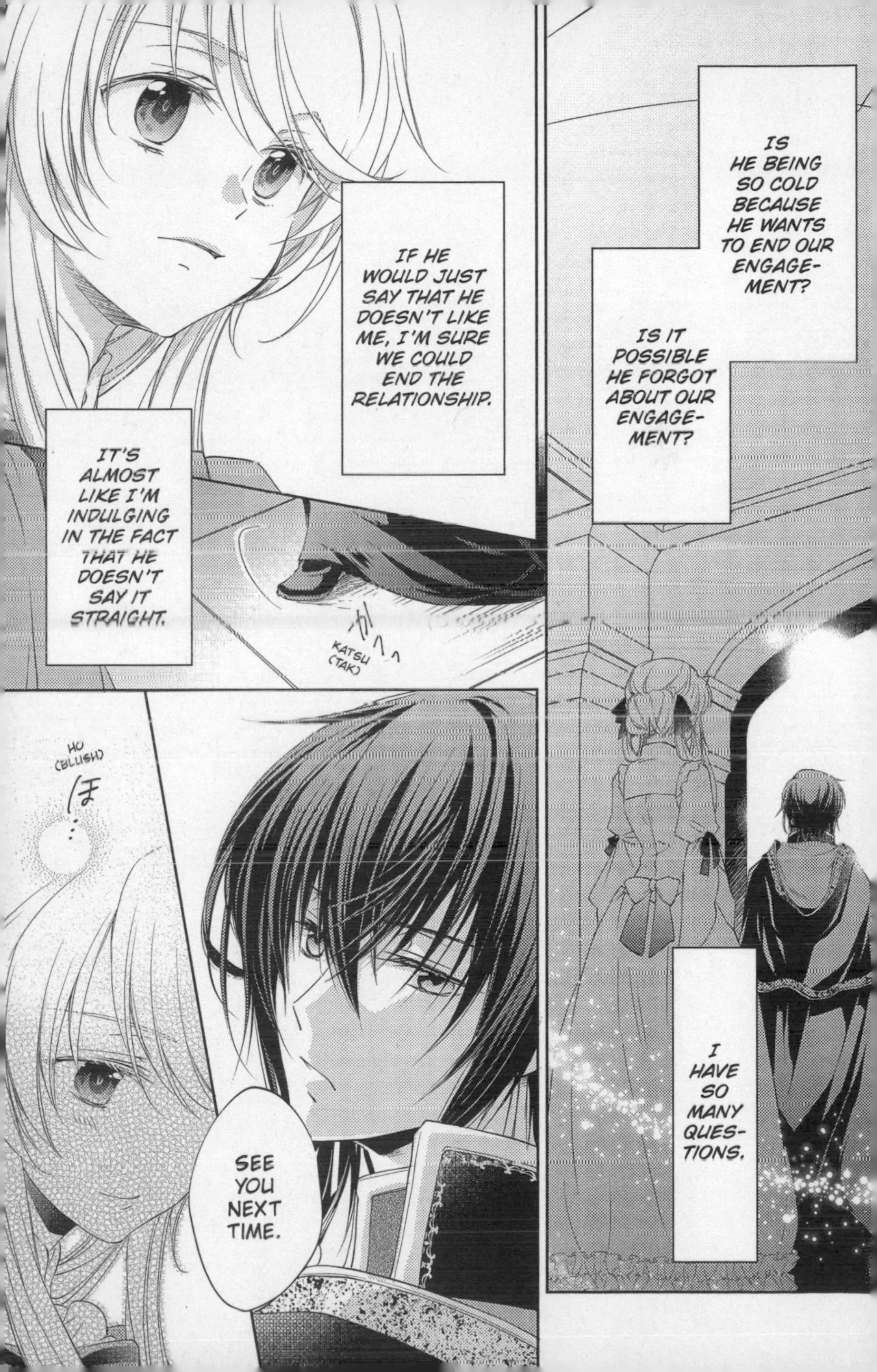
IS HE BEING SO COLD BECAUSE HE WANTS TO END OUR ENGAGE-MENT?
IS IT POSSIBLE HE FORGOT ABOUT OUR ENGAGE-MENT?
I HAVE SO MANY QUES-TIONS.
IF HE WOULD JUST SAY THAT HE DOESN'T LIKE ME, I'M SURE WE COULD END THE RELATIONSHIP.
IT'S ALMOST LIKE I'M INDULGING IN THE FACT THAT HE DOESN'T SAY IT STRAIGHT.
KATSU (TAK)
SEE YOU NEXT TIME.
HO (BLUSH)

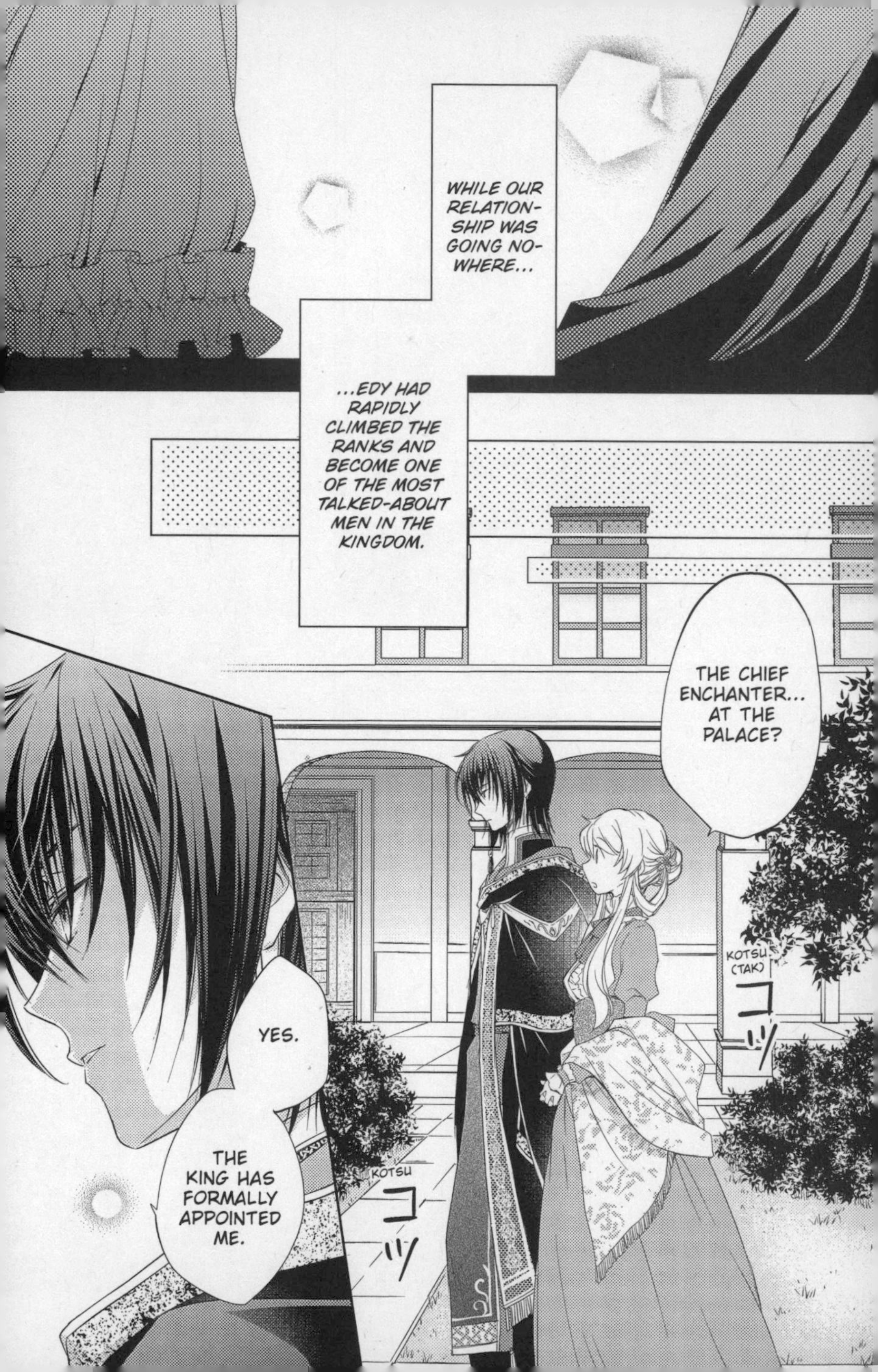
WHILE OUR RELATION-SHIP WAS GOING NO-WHERE...
...EDY HAD RAPIDLY CLIMBED THE RANKS AND BECOME ONE OF THE MOST TALKED-ABOUT MEN IN THE KINGDOM.
THE CHIEF ENCHANTER... AT THE PALACE?
KOTSU (TAK)
コツ
YES.
THE KING HAS FORMALLY APPOINTED ME.
KOTSU
コツ

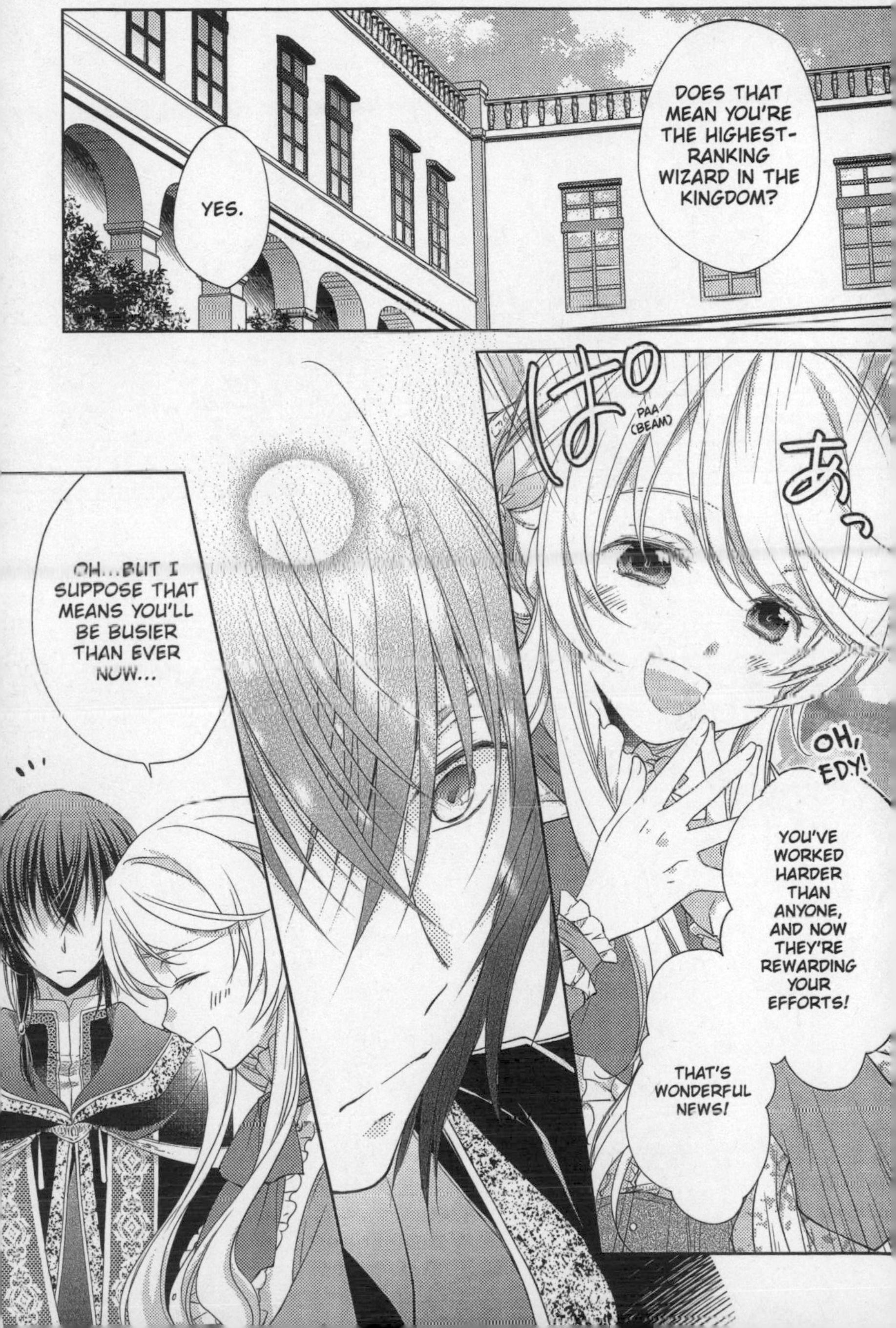
DOES THAT MEAN YOU'RE THE HIGHEST-RANKING WIZARD IN THE KINGDOM?
YES.
ぱあっ
PAA (BEAM)
OH, EDY!
YOU'VE WORKED HARDER THAN ANYONE, AND NOW THEY'RE REWARDING YOUR EFFORTS!
THAT'S WONDERFUL NEWS!
OH...BUT I SUPPOSE THAT MEANS YOU'LL BE BUSIER THAN EVER NOW...
...

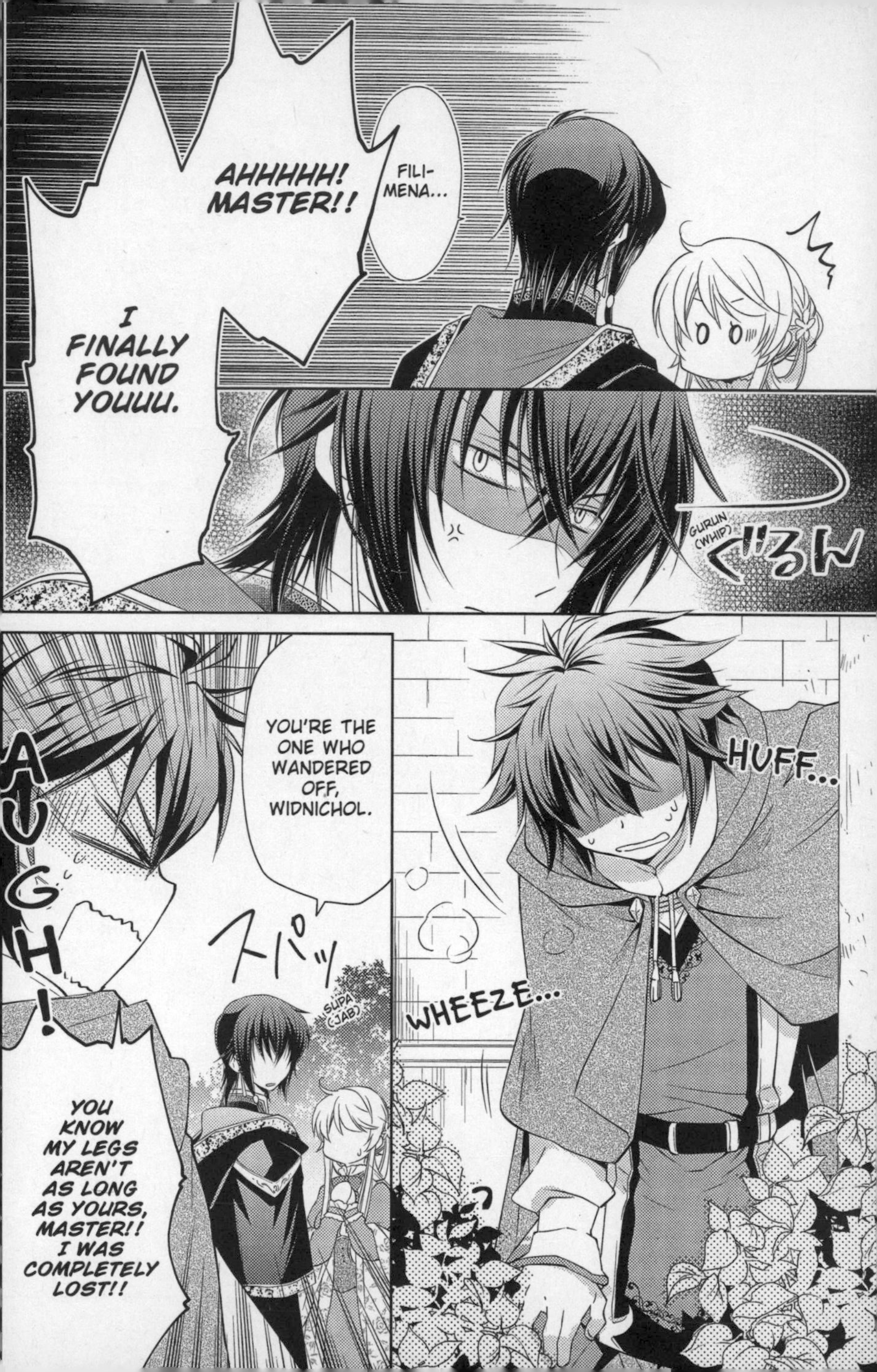
FILI-
MENA...
AHHHHH! MASTER!!
I FINALLY FOUND YOUUU.
GURUN (WHIP)
ぐるん
HUFF...
WHEEZE...
YOU'RE THE ONE WHO WANDERED OFF, WIDNICHOL.
スパッ
SUPA (JAB)
AUGH!
YOU KNOW MY LEGS AREN'T AS LONG AS YOURS, MASTER!! I WAS COMPLETELY LOST!!

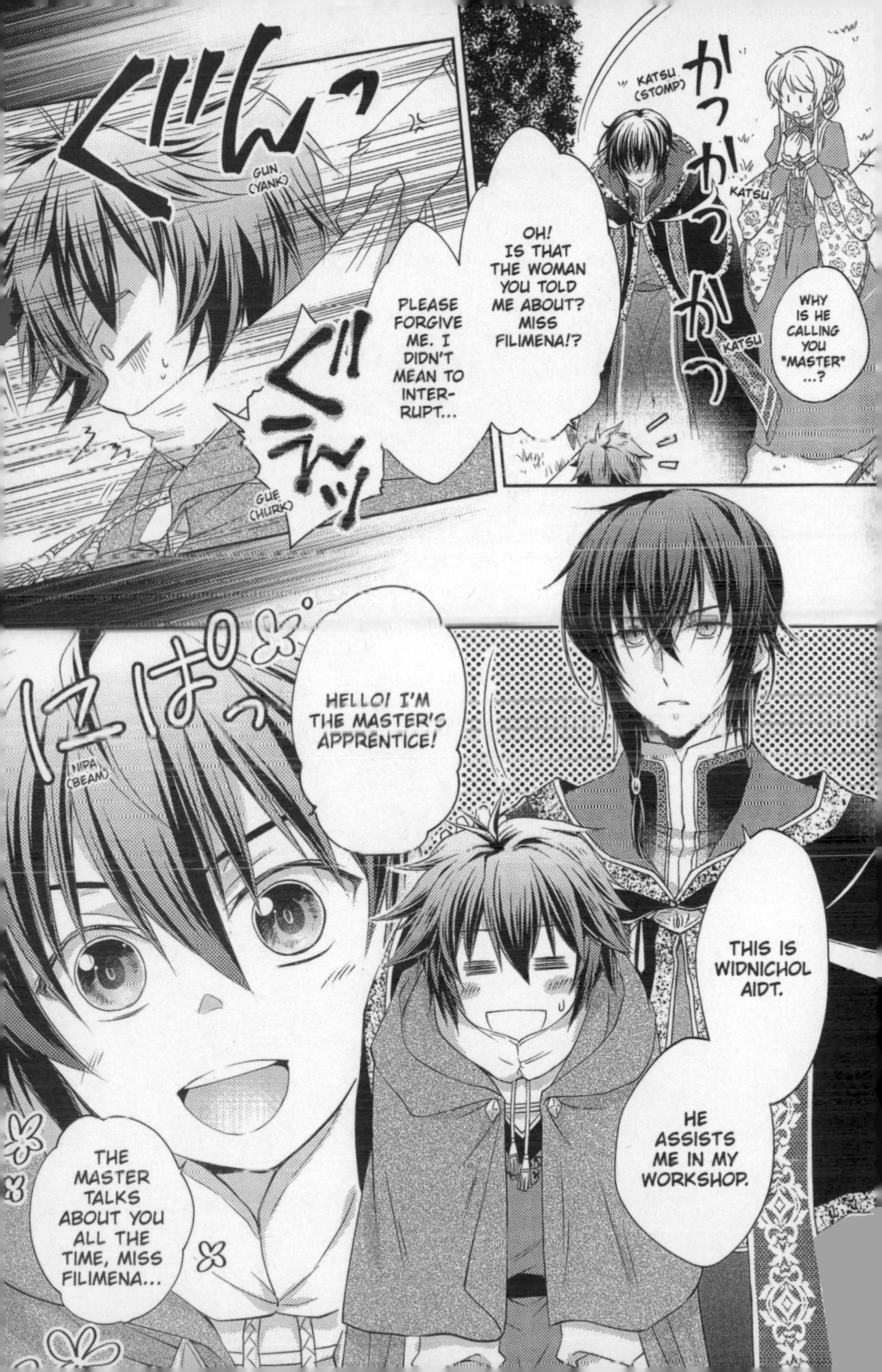
KATSU (STOMP)
KATSU
WHY IS HE CALLING YOU "MASTER" ...?
OH! IS THAT THE WOMAN YOU TOLD ME ABOUT? MISS FILIMENA!?
KATSU
GUN (YANK)
PLEASE FORGIVE ME. I DIDN'T MEAN TO INTER-RUPT...
GUE (HURK)
HELLO! I'M THE MASTER'S APPRENTICE!
NIPA (BEAM)
THIS IS WIDNICHOL AIDT.
HE ASSISTS ME IN MY WORKSHOP.
THE MASTER TALKS ABOUT YOU ALL THE TIME, MISS FILIMENA...

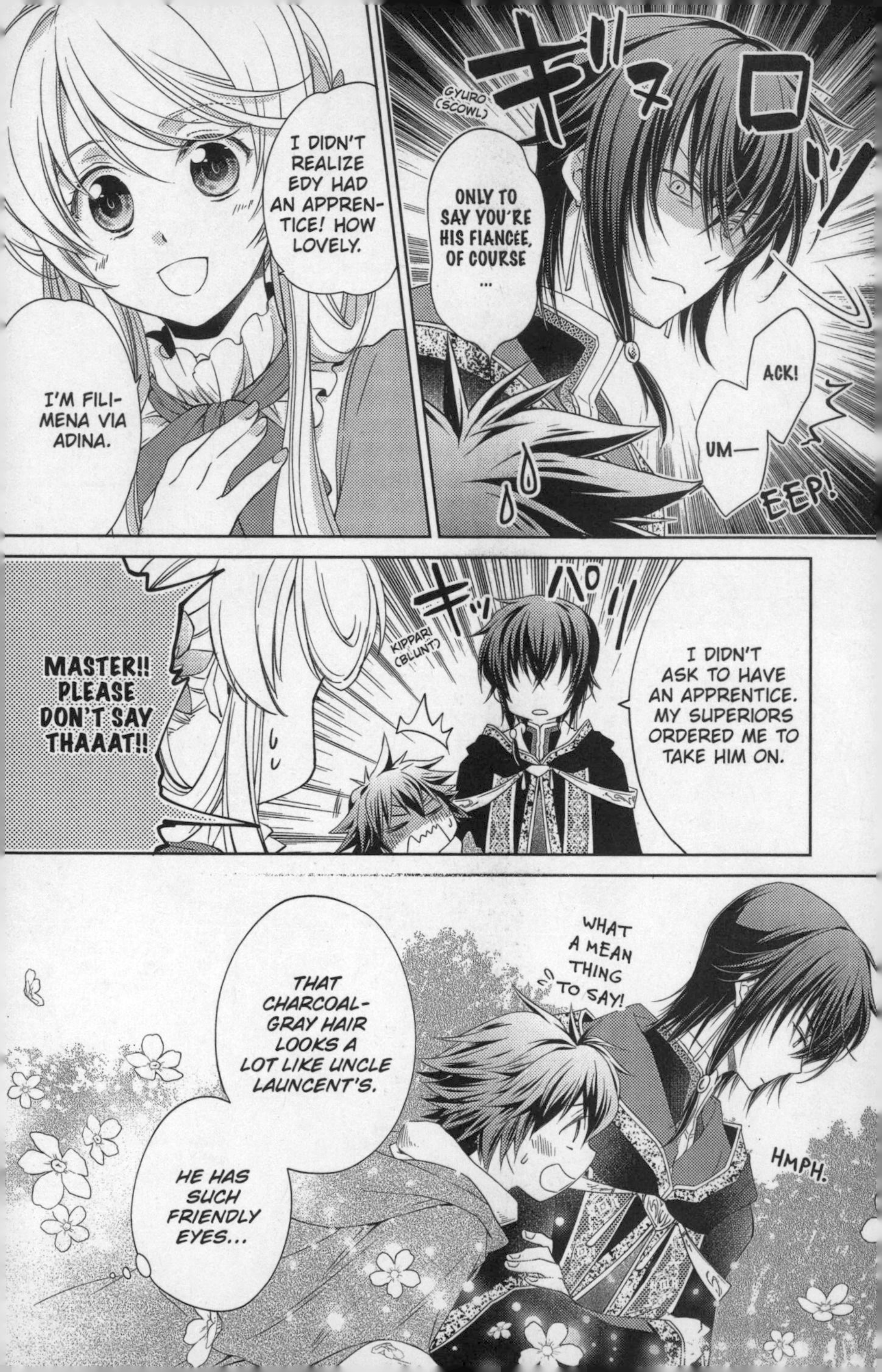
GYURO (SCOWL)
ONLY TO SAY YOU'RE HIS FIANCÉE, OF COURSE ...
ACK!
UM—
EEP!
I DIDN'T REALIZE EDY HAD AN APPREN-TICE! HOW LOVELY.
I'M FILI-MENA VIA ADINA.
I DIDN'T ASK TO HAVE AN APPRENTICE. MY SUPERIORS ORDERED ME TO TAKE HIM ON.
KIPPARI (BLUNT)
MASTER!! PLEASE DON'T SAY THAAAT!!
WHAT A MEAN THING TO SAY!
HMPH.
THAT CHARCOAL-GRAY HAIR LOOKS A LOT LIKE UNCLE LAUNCENT'S.
HE HAS SUCH FRIENDLY EYES...

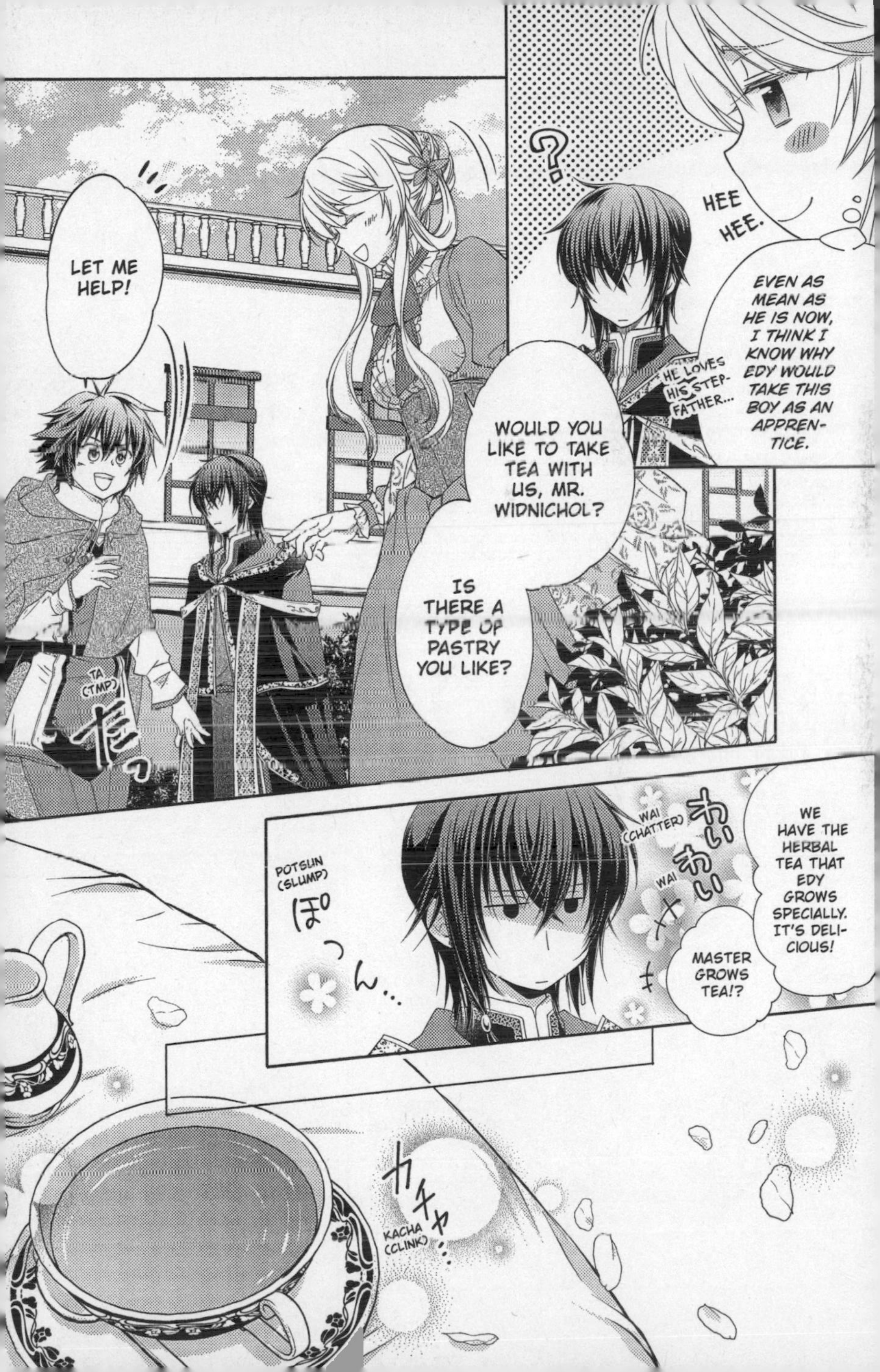

?
HEE HEE.
EVEN AS MEAN AS HE IS NOW, I THINK I KNOW WHY EDY WOULD TAKE THIS BOY AS AN APPRENTICE.
HE LOVES HIS STEP-FATHER...
WOULD YOU LIKE TO TAKE TEA WITH US, MR. WIDNICHOL?
IS THERE A TYPE OF PASTRY YOU LIKE?
LET ME HELP!
TA (TMP)
WE HAVE THE HERBAL TEA THAT EDY GROWS SPECIALLY. IT'S DELICIOUS!
MASTER GROWS TEA!?
WAI (CHATTER)
WAI
POTSUN (SLUMP)
KACHA (CLINK)

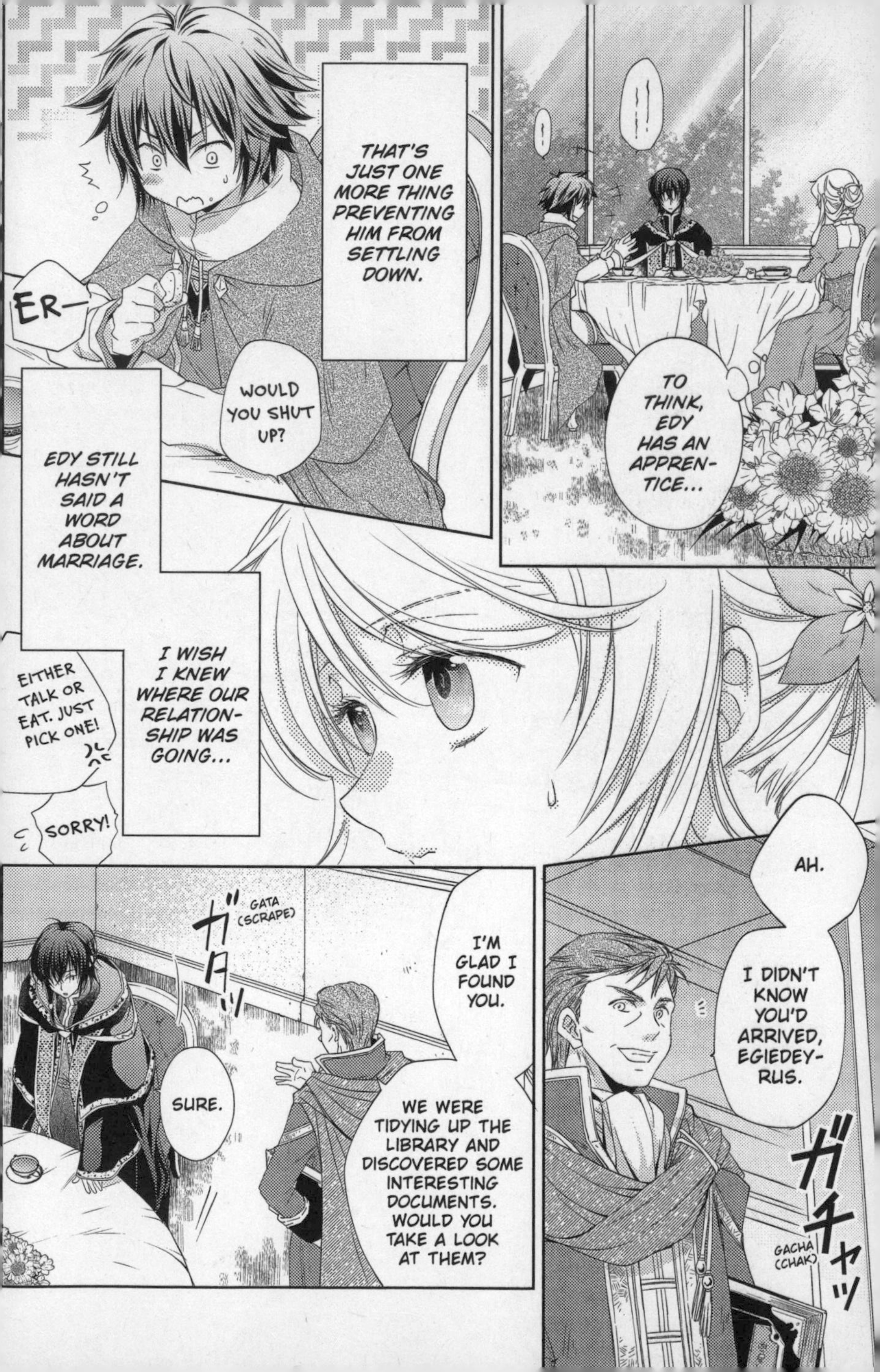
TO THINK, EDY HAS AN APPRENTICE...
THAT'S JUST ONE MORE THING PREVENTING HIM FROM SETTLING DOWN.
ER—
WOULD YOU SHUT UP?
EDY STILL HASN'T SAID A WORD ABOUT MARRIAGE.
I WISH I KNEW WHERE OUR RELATIONSHIP WAS GOING...
EITHER TALK OR EAT. JUST PICK ONE!
SORRY!
AH.
I DIDN'T KNOW YOU'D ARRIVED, EGIEDEYRUS.
GACHA (CHAK)
I'M GLAD I FOUND YOU.
GATA (SCRAPE)
WE WERE TIDYING UP THE LIBRARY AND DISCOVERED SOME INTERESTING DOCUMENTS. WOULD YOU TAKE A LOOK AT THEM?
SURE.

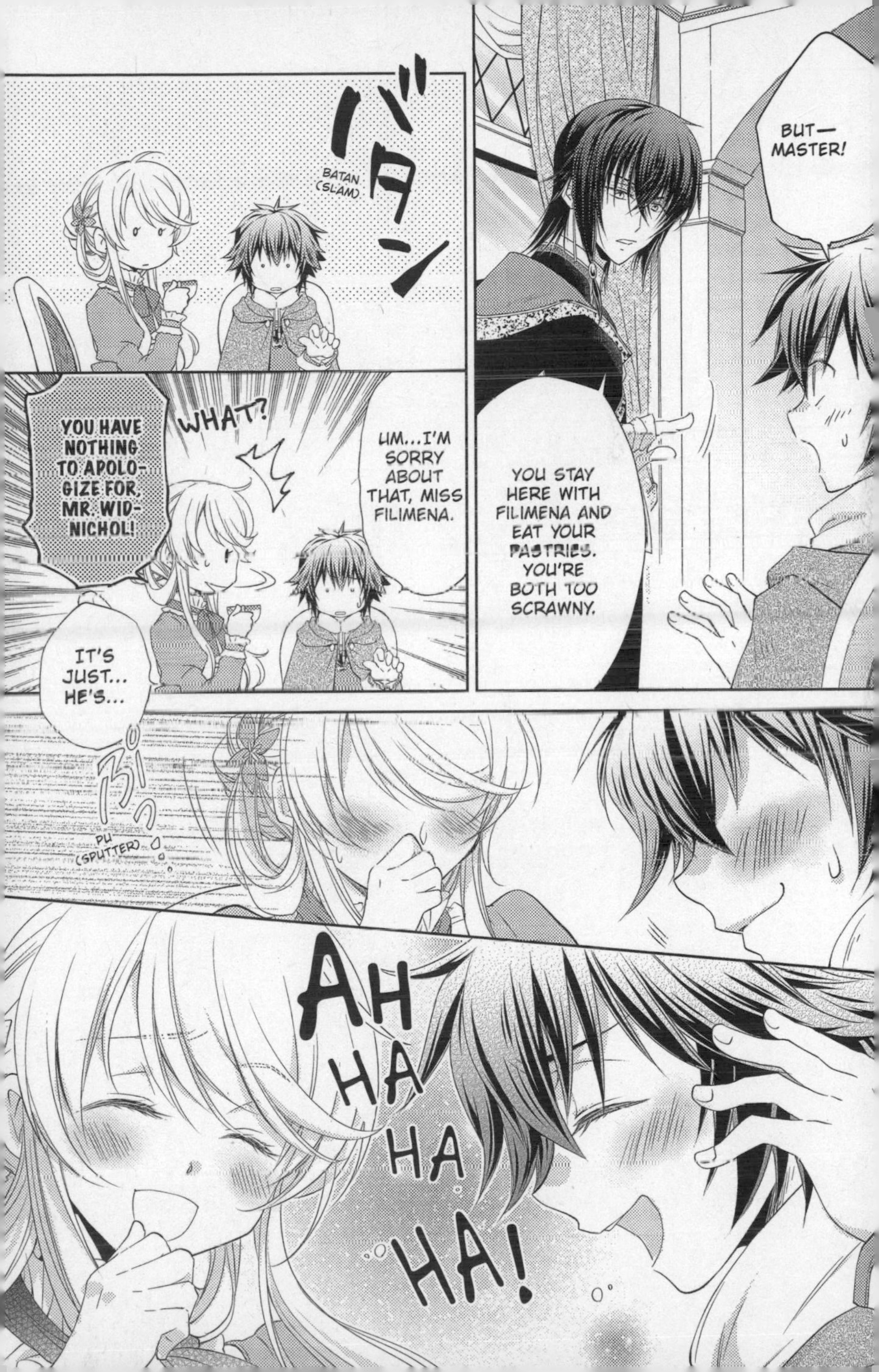

BUT— MASTER!
YOU STAY HERE WITH FILIMENA AND EAT YOUR PASTRIES. YOU'RE BOTH TOO SCRAWNY.
BATAN (SLAM)
UM...I'M SORRY ABOUT THAT, MISS FILIMENA.
WHAT?!
YOU HAVE NOTHING TO APOLO-GIZE FOR, MR. WID-NICHOL!
IT'S JUST... HE'S...
PU (SPUTTER)
AH HA HA HA!

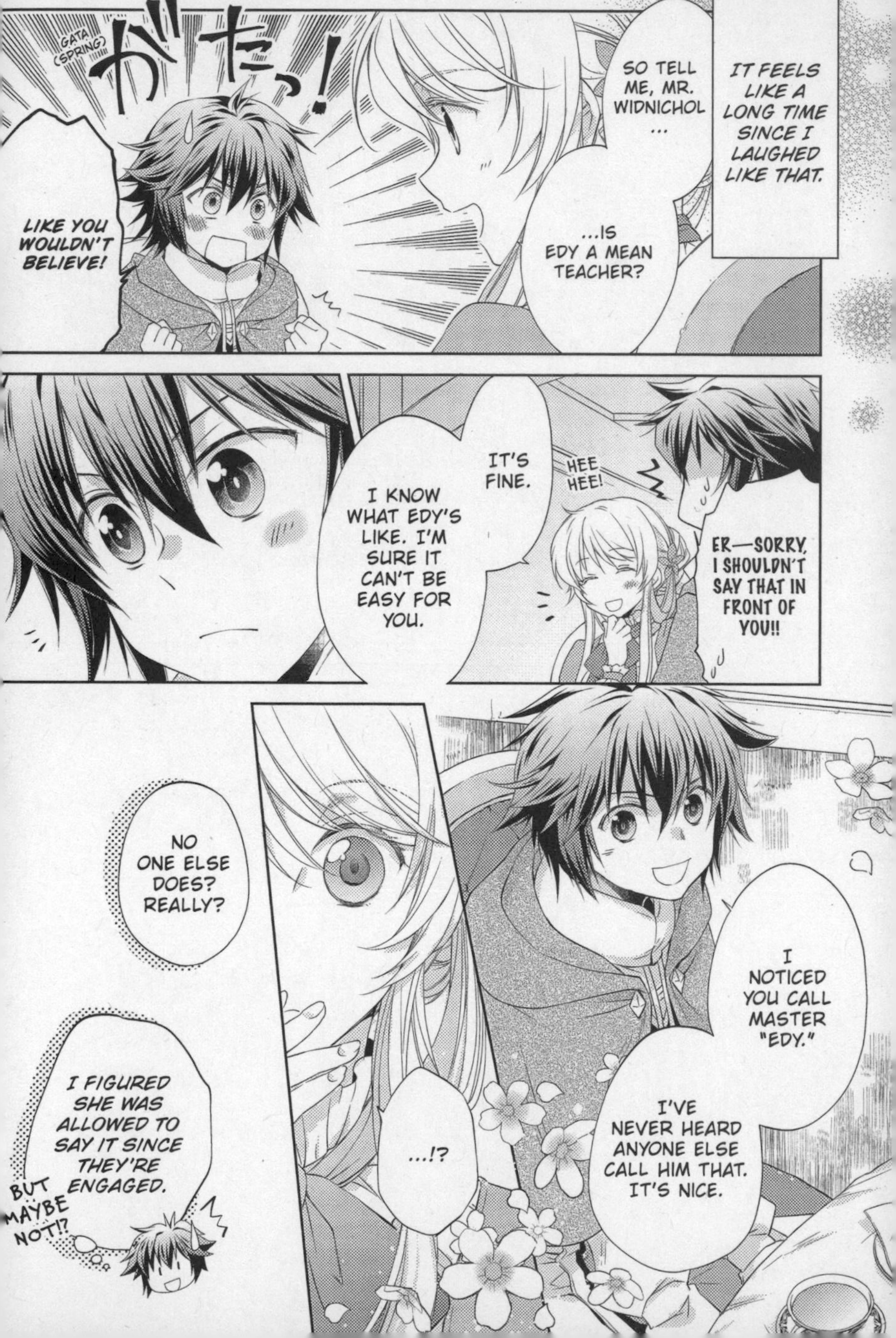
IT FEELS LIKE A LONG TIME SINCE I LAUGHED LIKE THAT.
SO TELL ME, MR. WIDNICHOL ...
...IS EDY A MEAN TEACHER?
GATA (SPRING)
LIKE YOU WOULDN'T BELIEVE!
ER—SORRY, I SHOULDN'T SAY THAT IN FRONT OF YOU!!
HEE HEE!
IT'S FINE.
I KNOW WHAT EDY'S LIKE. I'M SURE IT CAN'T BE EASY FOR YOU.
I NOTICED YOU CALL MASTER "EDY."
I'VE NEVER HEARD ANYONE ELSE CALL HIM THAT. IT'S NICE.
...!?
NO ONE ELSE DOES? REALLY?
I FIGURED SHE WAS ALLOWED TO SAY IT SINCE THEY'RE ENGAGED.
BUT MAYBE NOT!?

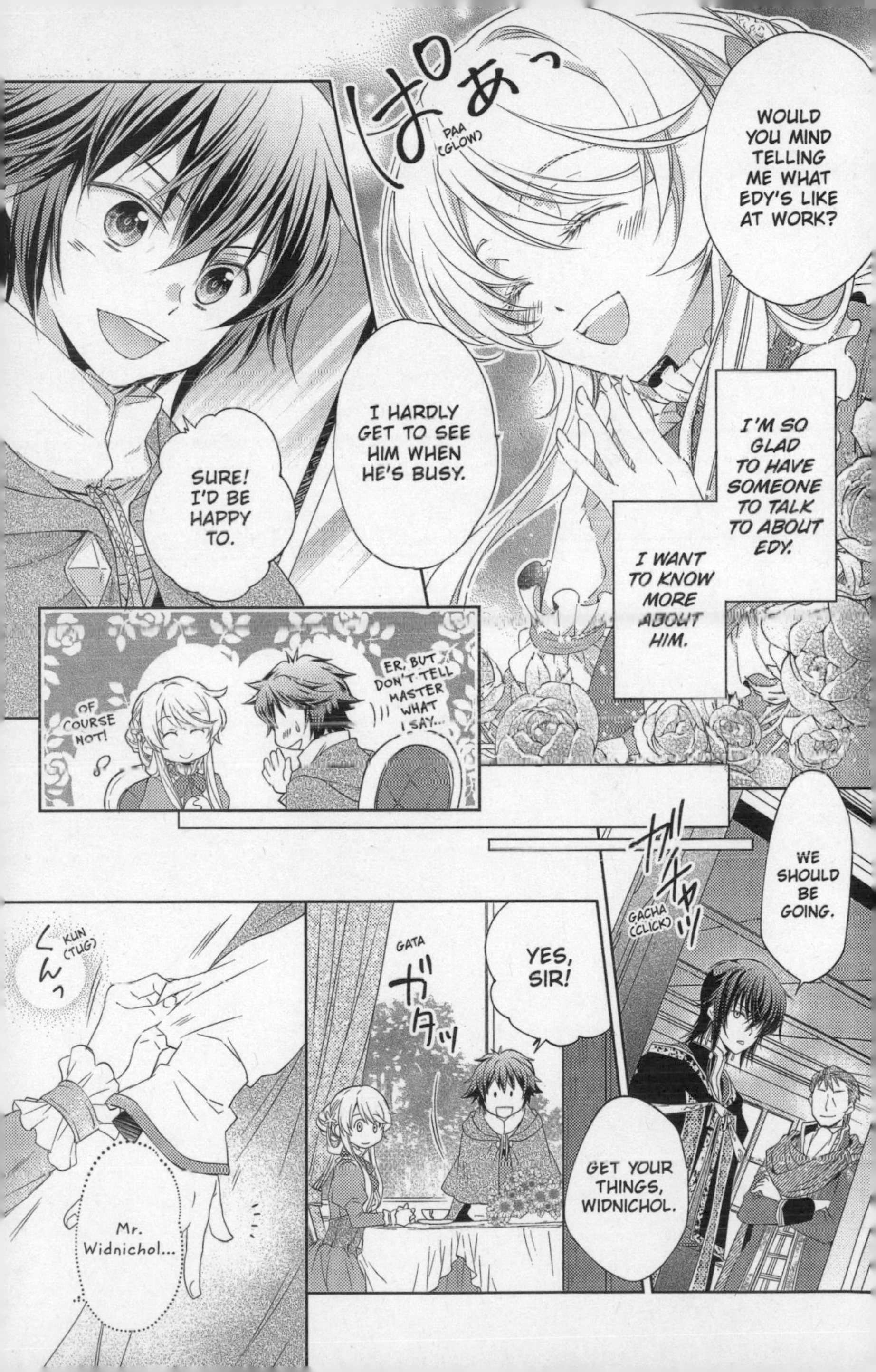
WOULD YOU MIND TELLING ME WHAT EDY'S LIKE AT WORK?
PAA (GLOW)
I HARDLY GET TO SEE HIM WHEN HE'S BUSY.
I'M SO GLAD TO HAVE SOMEONE TO TALK TO ABOUT EDY.
I WANT TO KNOW MORE ABOUT HIM.
SURE! I'D BE HAPPY TO.
ER, BUT DON'T TELL MASTER WHAT I SAY...
OF COURSE NOT!
GACHA (CLICK)
WE SHOULD BE GOING.
GET YOUR THINGS, WIDNICHOL.
YES, SIR!
GATA
KUN (TUG)
Mr. Widnichol...

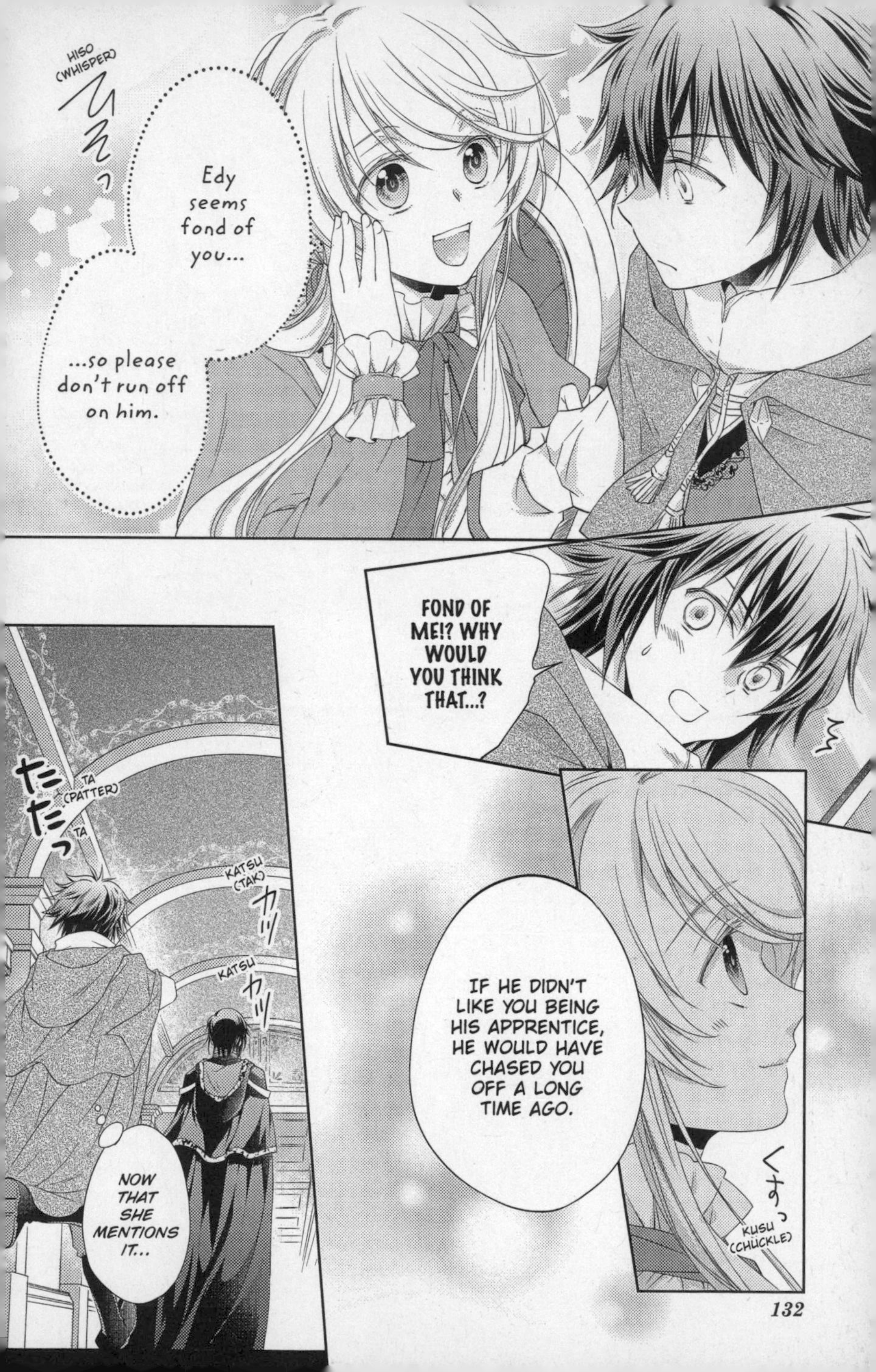
Edy seems fond of you...
HISO (WHISPER)
...so please don't run off on him.
FOND OF ME!? WHY WOULD YOU THINK THAT...?
IF HE DIDN'T LIKE YOU BEING HIS APPRENTICE, HE WOULD HAVE CHASED YOU OFF A LONG TIME AGO.
KUSU (CHUCKLE)
TA TA (PATTER)
KATSU (TAK)
KATSU
NOW THAT SHE MENTIONS IT...

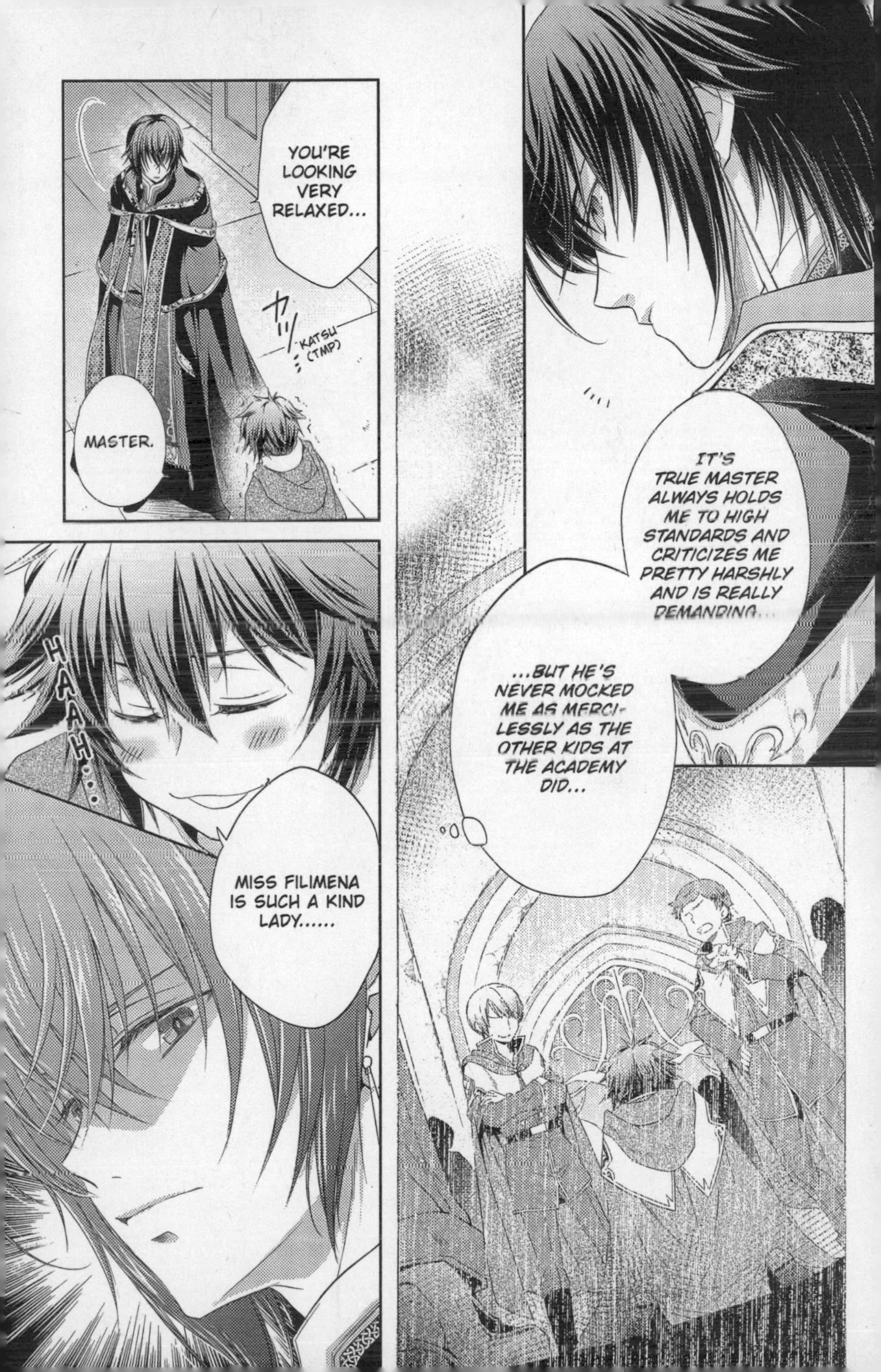
...
YOU'RE LOOKING VERY RELAXED...
KATSU (TMP)
MASTER.
HAAAH...
MISS FILIMENA IS SUCH A KIND LADY......
IT'S TRUE MASTER ALWAYS HOLDS ME TO HIGH STANDARDS AND CRITICIZES ME PRETTY HARSHLY AND IS REALLY DEMANDING...
...BUT HE'S NEVER MOCKED ME AS MERCILESSLY AS THE OTHER KIDS AT THE ACADEMY DID...

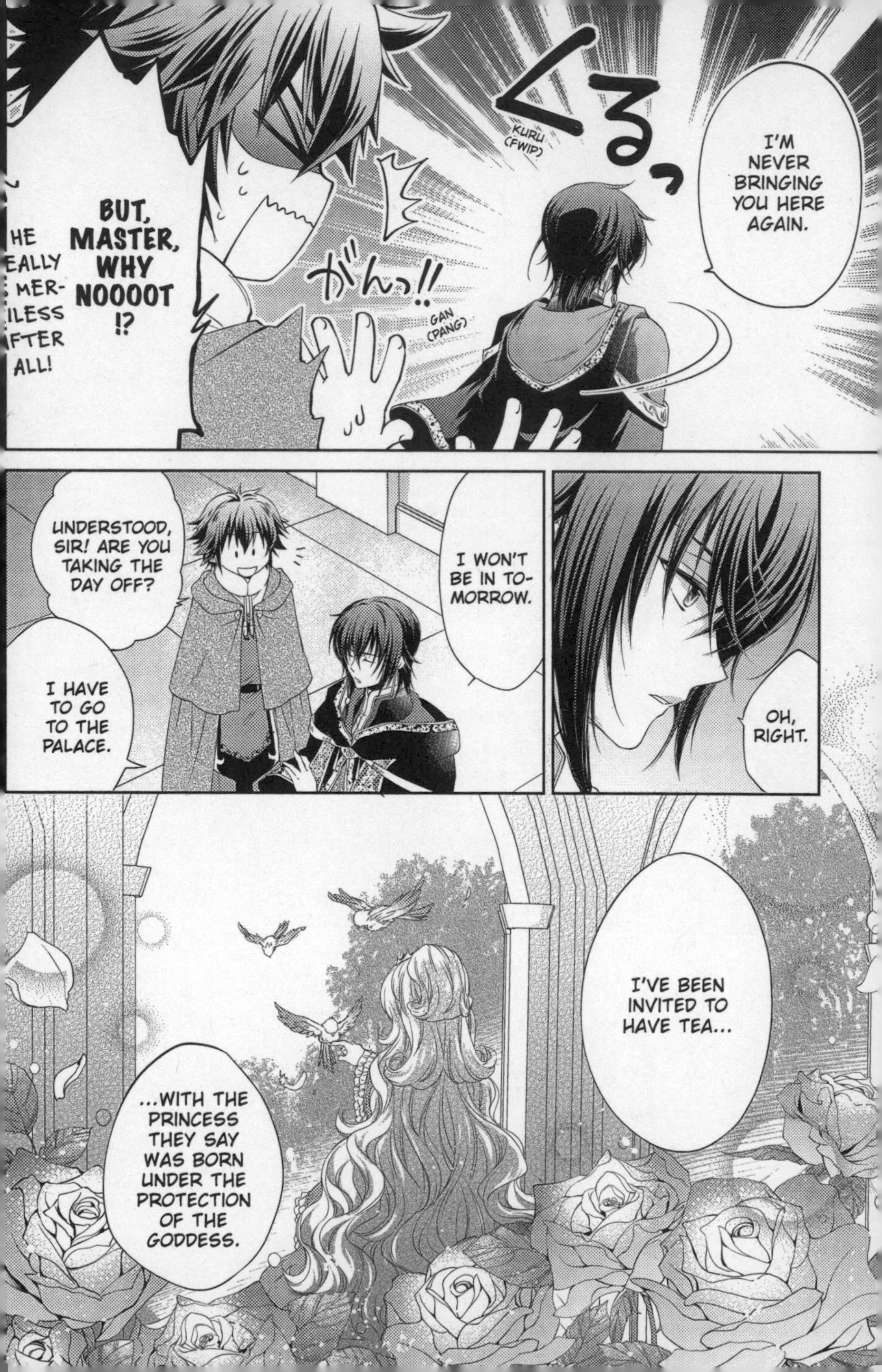

I'M NEVER BRINGING YOU HERE AGAIN.
くるっ
KURU (FWIP)
がんっ!!
GAN (PANG)
BUT, MASTER, WHY NOOOOT !?
HE EALLY MER- ILESS FTER ALL!
OH, RIGHT.
I WON'T BE IN TO-MORROW.
UNDERSTOOD, SIR! ARE YOU TAKING THE DAY OFF?
I HAVE TO GO TO THE PALACE.
I'VE BEEN INVITED TO HAVE TEA...
...WITH THE PRINCESS THEY SAY WAS BORN UNDER THE PROTECTION OF THE GODDESS.

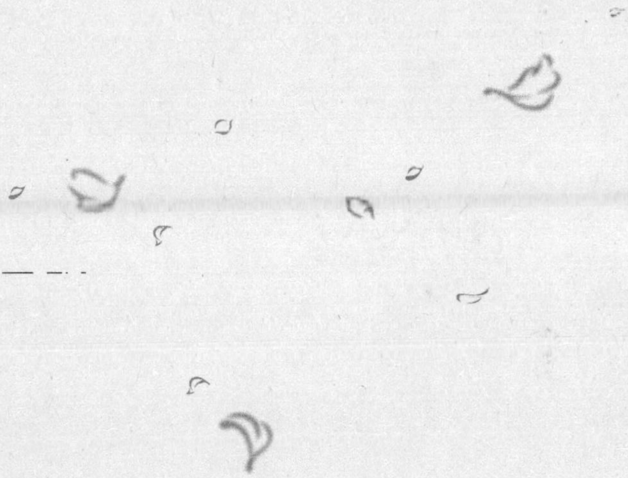

FIANCÉE OF THE WIZARD

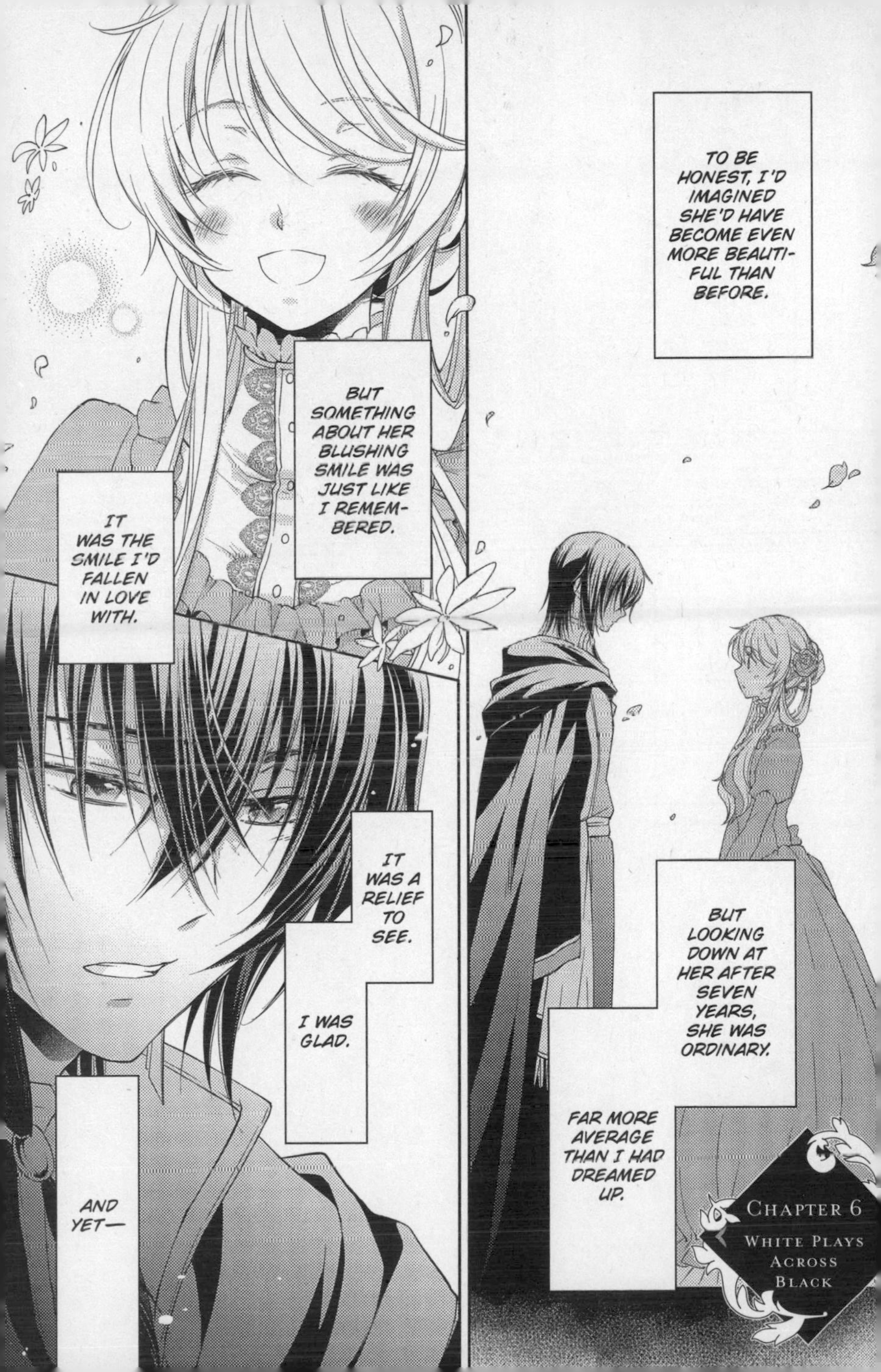
TO BE HONEST, I'D IMAGINED SHE'D HAVE BECOME EVEN MORE BEAUTIFUL THAN BEFORE.
BUT LOOKING DOWN AT HER AFTER SEVEN YEARS, SHE WAS ORDINARY.
FAR MORE AVERAGE THAN I HAD DREAMED UP.
CHAPTER 6
WHITE PLAYS ACROSS BLACK
BUT SOMETHING ABOUT HER BLUSHING SMILE WAS JUST LIKE I REMEMBERED.
IT WAS THE SMILE I'D FALLEN IN LOVE WITH.
IT WAS A RELIEF TO SEE.
I WAS GLAD.
AND YET—

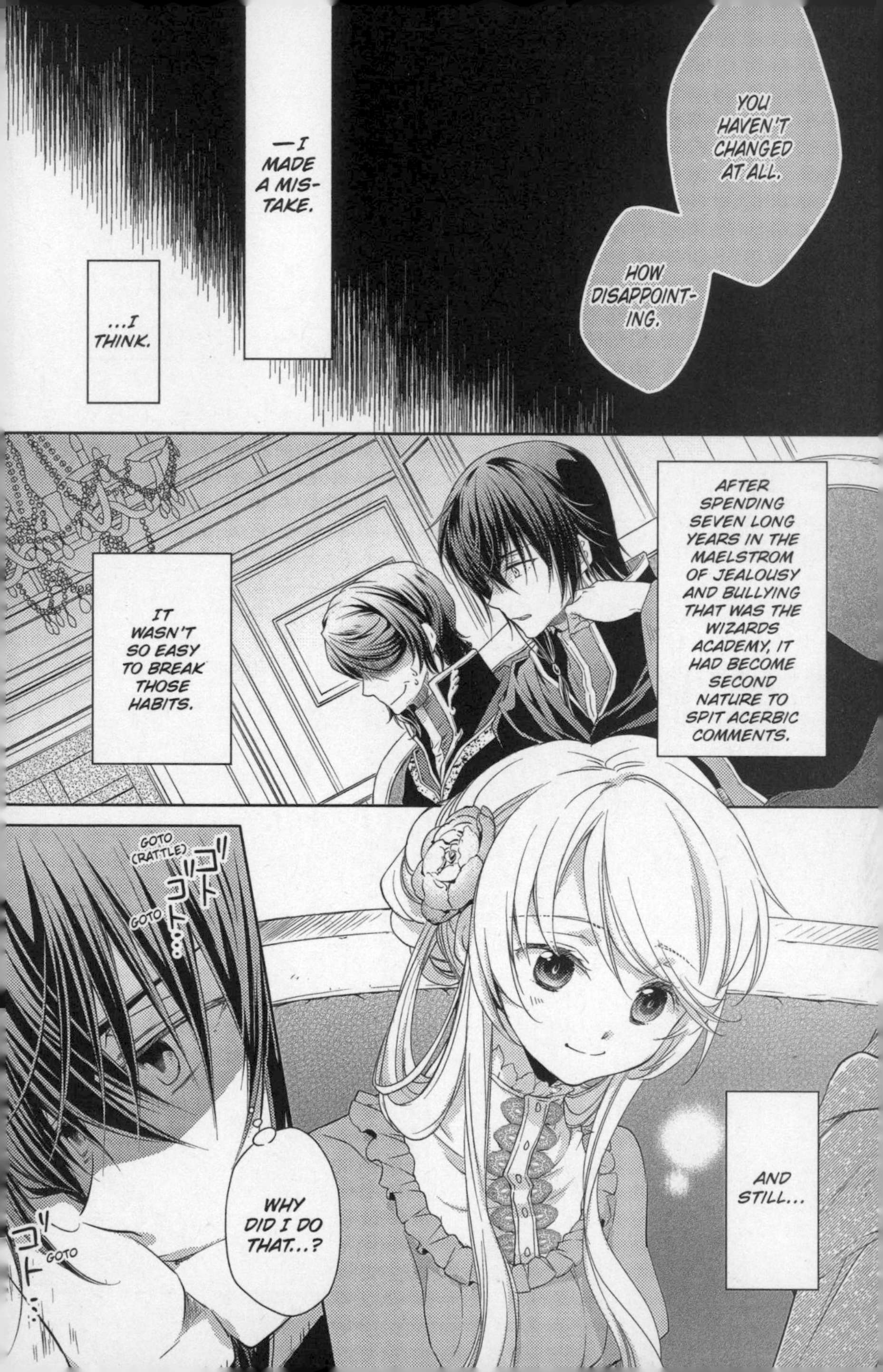

YOU HAVEN'T CHANGED AT ALL.
HOW DISAPPOINTING.
—I MADE A MISTAKE.
...I THINK.
AFTER SPENDING SEVEN LONG YEARS IN THE MAELSTROM OF JEALOUSY AND BULLYING THAT WAS THE WIZARDS ACADEMY, IT HAD BECOME SECOND NATURE TO SPIT ACERBIC COMMENTS.
IT WASN'T SO EASY TO BREAK THOSE HABITS.
AND STILL...
GOTO (RATTLE)
GOTO
WHY DID I DO THAT...?
GOTO

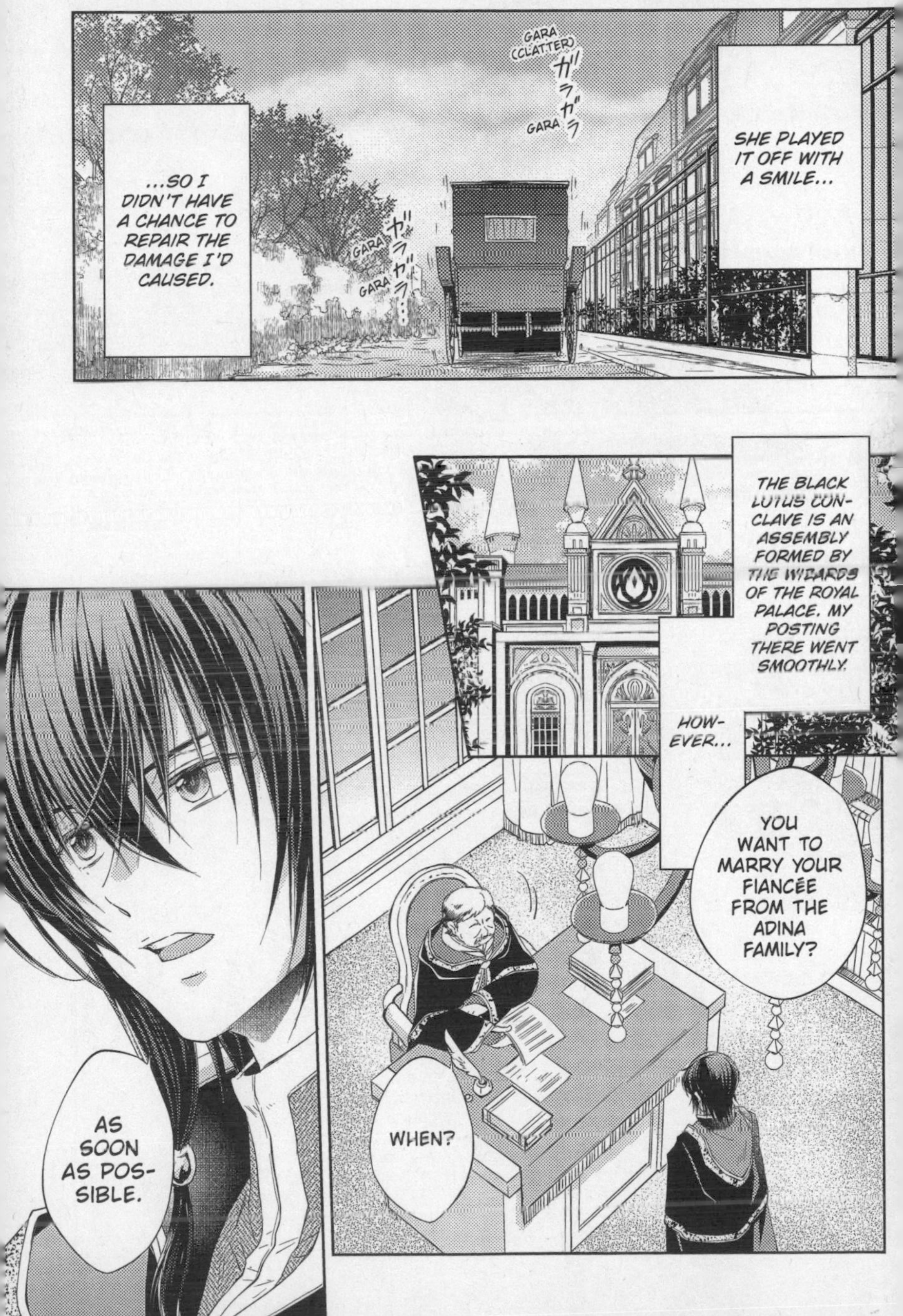
SHE PLAYED IT OFF WITH A SMILE...
GARA (CLATTER) ガラガラ GARA
GARA ガラガラ... GARA
...SO I DIDN'T HAVE A CHANCE TO REPAIR THE DAMAGE I'D CAUSED.
THE BLACK LOTUS CONCLAVE IS AN ASSEMBLY FORMED BY THE WIZARDS OF THE ROYAL PALACE. MY POSTING THERE WENT SMOOTHLY.
HOWEVER...
YOU WANT TO MARRY YOUR FIANCÉE FROM THE ADINA FAMILY?
WHEN?
AS SOON AS POSSIBLE.

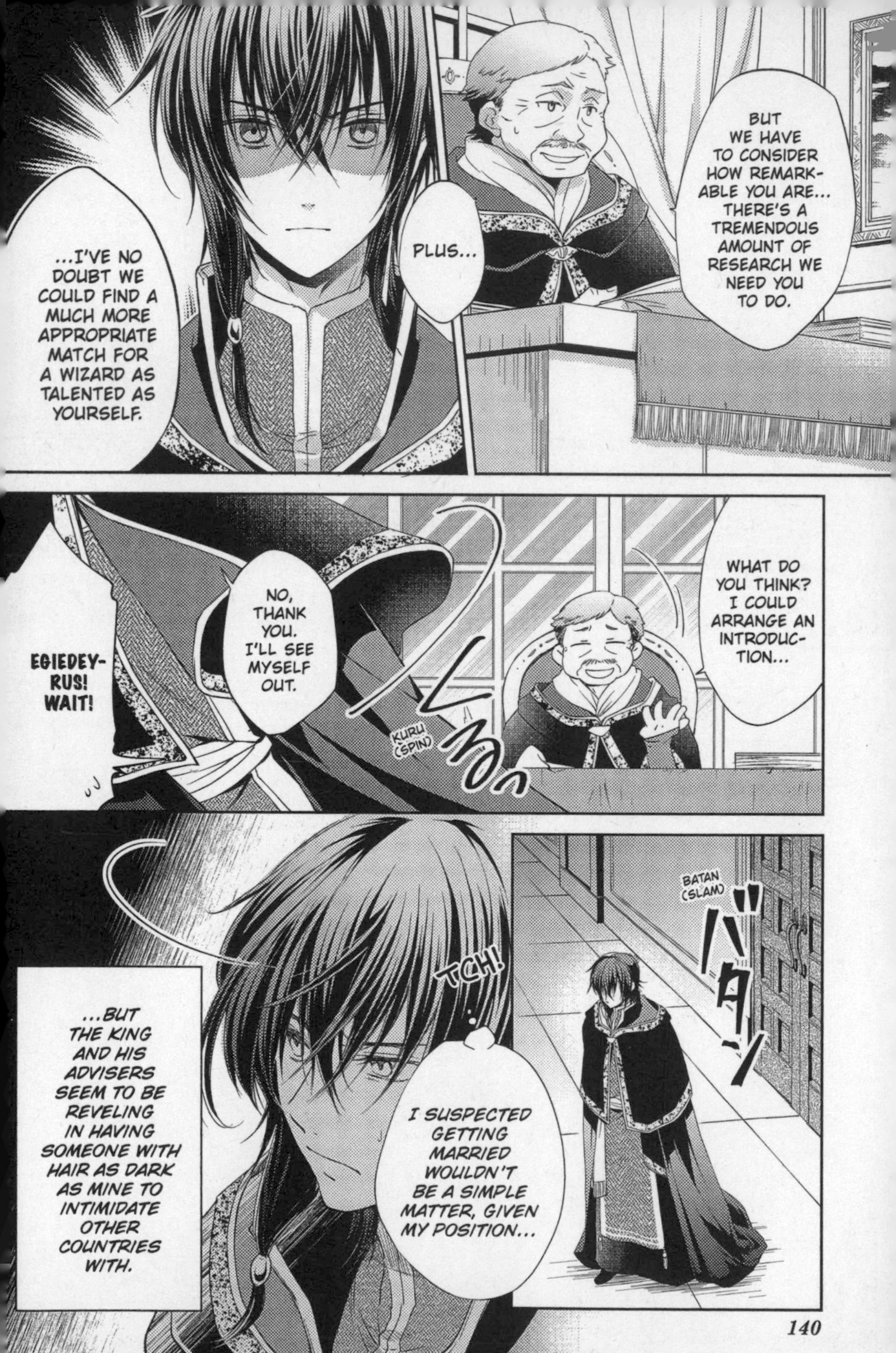
BUT WE HAVE TO CONSIDER HOW REMARKABLE YOU ARE... THERE'S A TREMENDOUS AMOUNT OF RESEARCH WE NEED YOU TO DO.
PLUS...
...I'VE NO DOUBT WE COULD FIND A MUCH MORE APPROPRIATE MATCH FOR A WIZARD AS TALENTED AS YOURSELF.
WHAT DO YOU THINK? I COULD ARRANGE AN INTRODUCTION...
KURU (SPIN)
NO, THANK YOU. I'LL SEE MYSELF OUT.
EGIEDEY-RUS! WAIT!
BATAN (SLAM)
TCH!
I SUSPECTED GETTING MARRIED WOULDN'T BE A SIMPLE MATTER, GIVEN MY POSITION...
...BUT THE KING AND HIS ADVISERS SEEM TO BE REVELING IN HAVING SOMEONE WITH HAIR AS DARK AS MINE TO INTIMIDATE OTHER COUNTRIES WITH.

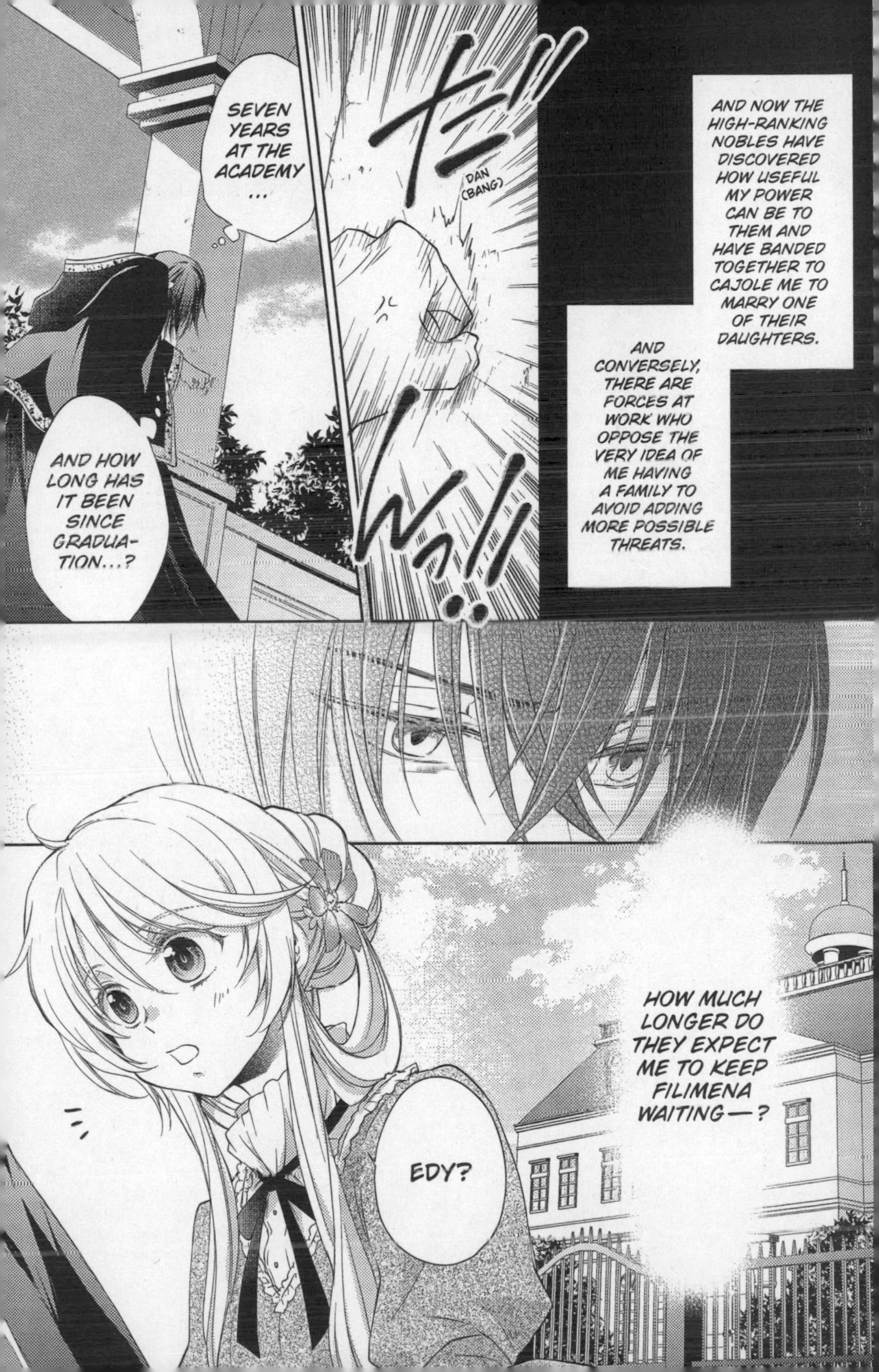
AND NOW THE HIGH-RANKING NOBLES HAVE DISCOVERED HOW USEFUL MY POWER CAN BE TO THEM AND HAVE BANDED TOGETHER TO CAJOLE ME TO MARRY ONE OF THEIR DAUGHTERS.
AND CONVERSELY, THERE ARE FORCES AT WORK WHO OPPOSE THE VERY IDEA OF ME HAVING A FAMILY TO AVOID ADDING MORE POSSIBLE THREATS.
DAN (BANG)
SEVEN YEARS AT THE ACADEMY ...
AND HOW LONG HAS IT BEEN SINCE GRADUATION...?
HOW MUCH LONGER DO THEY EXPECT ME TO KEEP FILIMENA WAITING—?
EDY?

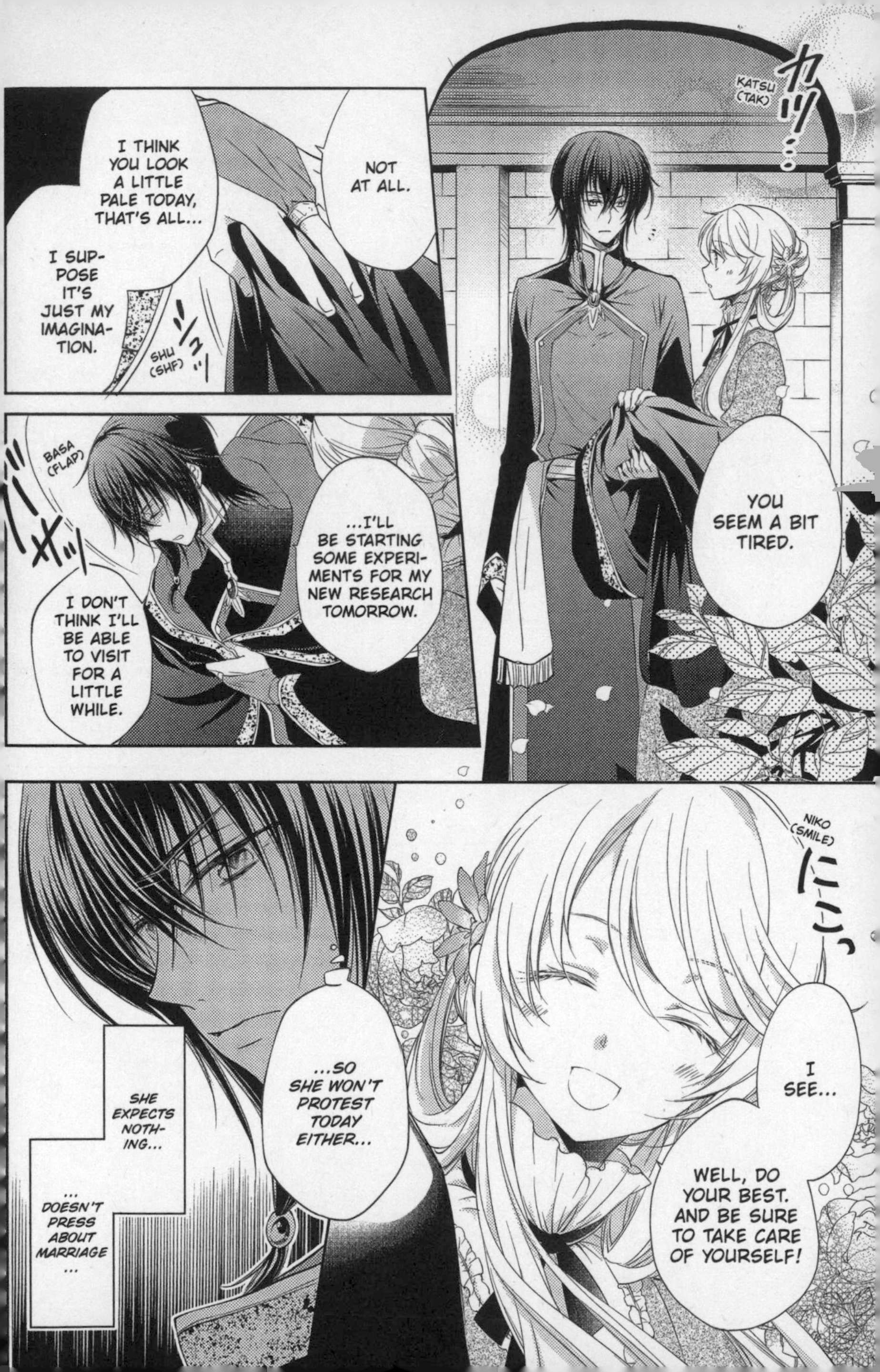
KATSU (TAK)
YOU SEEM A BIT TIRED.
NOT AT ALL.
I THINK YOU LOOK A LITTLE PALE TODAY, THAT'S ALL...
I SUPPOSE IT'S JUST MY IMAGINATION.
SHU (SHF)
...I'LL BE STARTING SOME EXPERIMENTS FOR MY NEW RESEARCH TOMORROW.
BASA (FLAP)
I DON'T THINK I'LL BE ABLE TO VISIT FOR A LITTLE WHILE.
NIKO (SMILE)
I SEE...
WELL, DO YOUR BEST. AND BE SURE TO TAKE CARE OF YOURSELF!
...SO SHE WON'T PROTEST TODAY EITHER...
SHE EXPECTS NOTHING...
...DOESN'T PRESS ABOUT MARRIAGE...

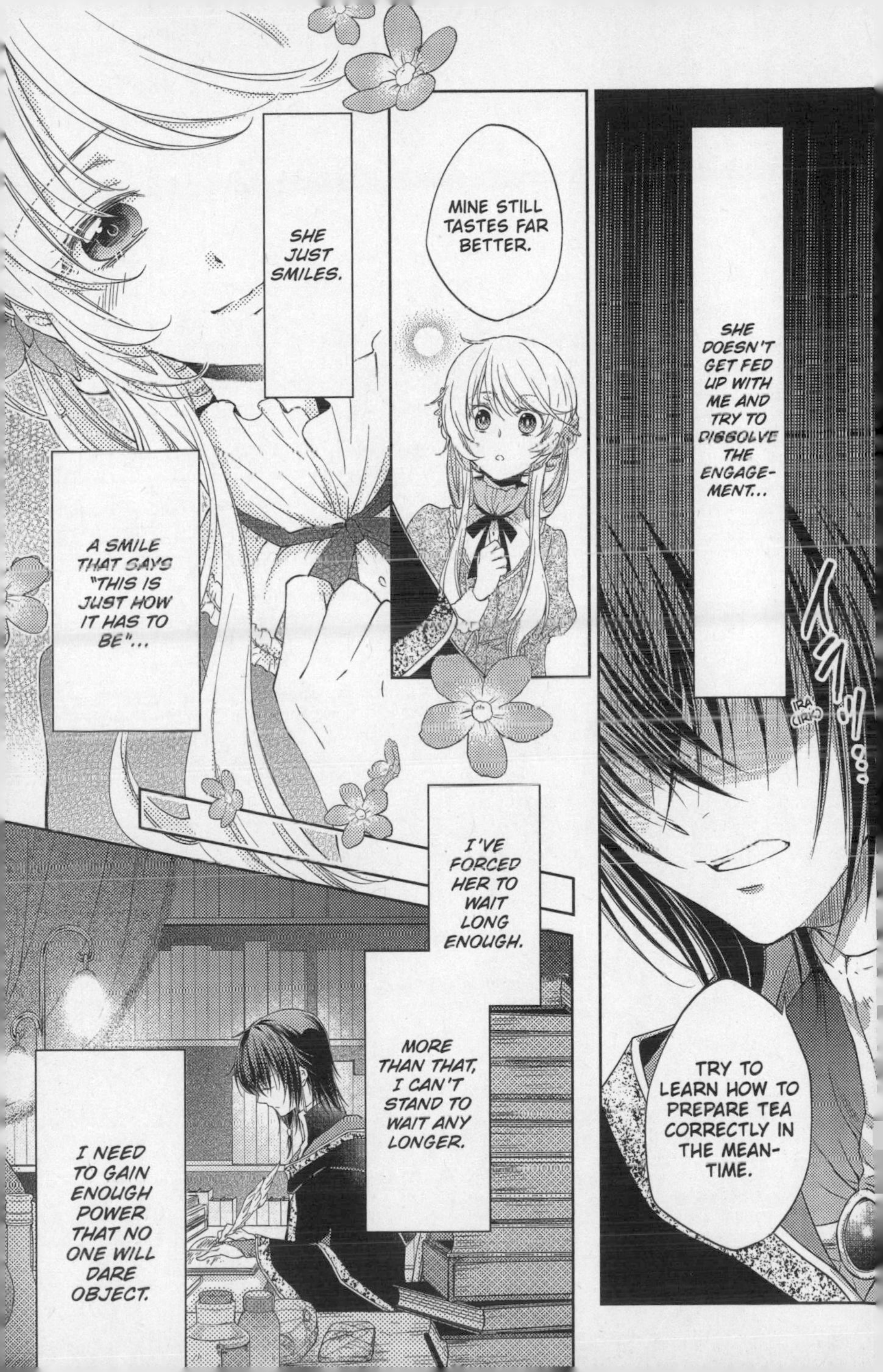
SHE DOESN'T GET FED UP WITH ME AND TRY TO DISSOLVE THE ENGAGEMENT...
IRA IRA
TRY TO LEARN HOW TO PREPARE TEA CORRECTLY IN THE MEAN-TIME.
MINE STILL TASTES FAR BETTER.
SHE JUST SMILES.
A SMILE THAT SAYS "THIS IS JUST HOW IT HAS TO BE"...
I'VE FORCED HER TO WAIT LONG ENOUGH.
MORE THAN THAT, I CAN'T STAND TO WAIT ANY LONGER.
I NEED TO GAIN ENOUGH POWER THAT NO ONE WILL DARE OBJECT.

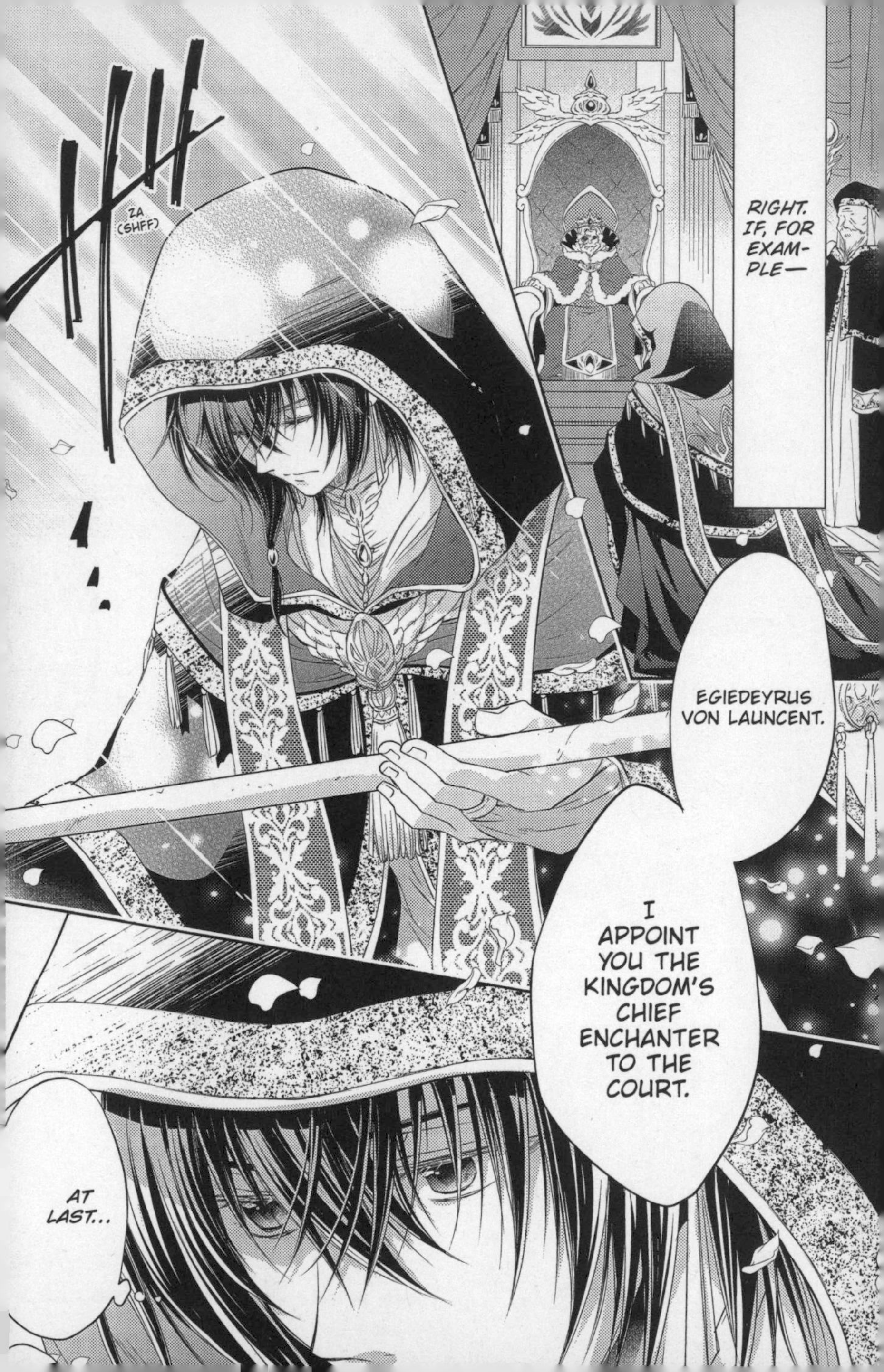
RIGHT. IF, FOR EXAMPLE—
ZA (SHFF)
EGIEDEYRUS VON LAUNCENT.
I APPOINT YOU THE KINGDOM'S CHIEF ENCHANTER TO THE COURT.
AT LAST...

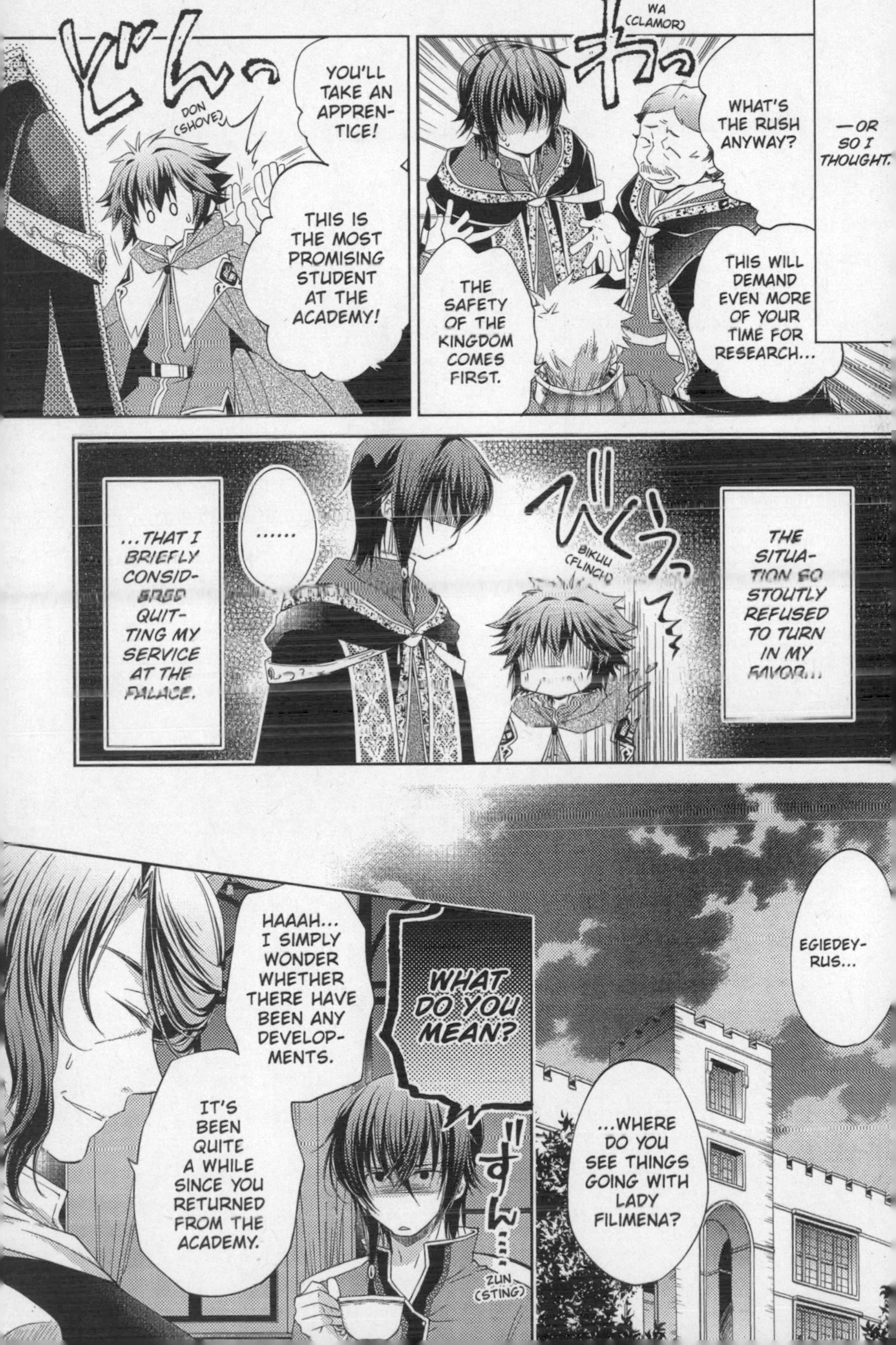
—OR SO I THOUGHT.
WA (CLAMOR)
WHAT'S THE RUSH ANYWAY?
THIS WILL DEMAND EVEN MORE OF YOUR TIME FOR RESEARCH...
THE SAFETY OF THE KINGDOM COMES FIRST.
DON (SHOVE)
YOU'LL TAKE AN APPRENTICE!
THIS IS THE MOST PROMISING STUDENT AT THE ACADEMY!
THE SITUATION SO STOUTLY REFUSED TO TURN IN MY FAVOR...
BIKUU (FLINCH)
......
...THAT I BRIEFLY CONSIDERED QUITTING MY SERVICE AT THE PALACE.
EGIEDEYRUS...
...WHERE DO YOU SEE THINGS GOING WITH LADY FILIMENA?
WHAT DO YOU MEAN?
ZUN (STING)
HAAAH... I SIMPLY WONDER WHETHER THERE HAVE BEEN ANY DEVELOPMENTS.
IT'S BEEN QUITE A WHILE SINCE YOU RETURNED FROM THE ACADEMY.

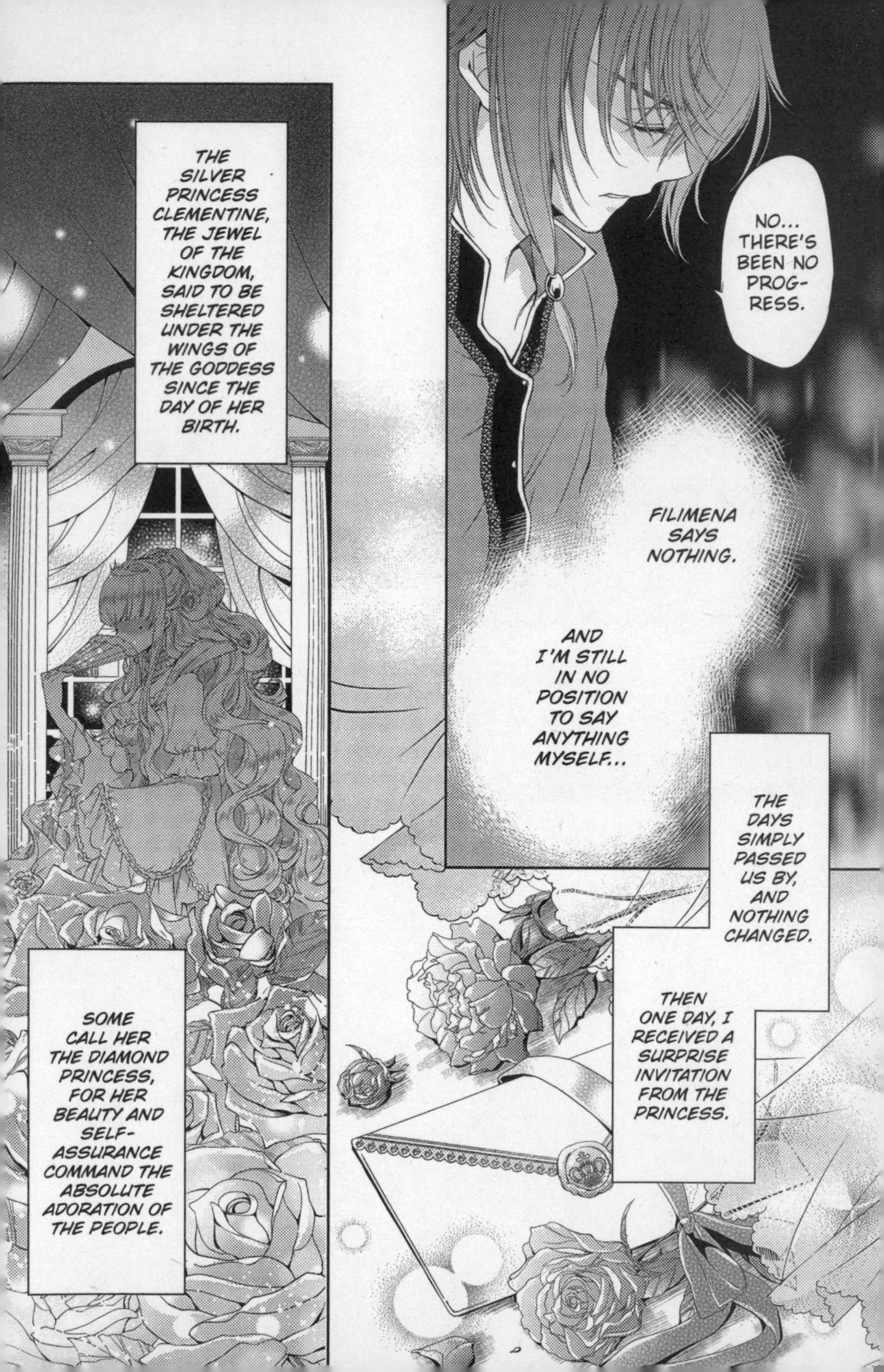
NO... THERE'S BEEN NO PROG-RESS.
FILIMENA SAYS NOTHING.
AND I'M STILL IN NO POSITION TO SAY ANYTHING MYSELF...
THE DAYS SIMPLY PASSED US BY, AND NOTHING CHANGED.
THEN ONE DAY, I RECEIVED A SURPRISE INVITATION FROM THE PRINCESS.
THE SILVER PRINCESS CLEMENTINE, THE JEWEL OF THE KINGDOM, SAID TO BE SHELTERED UNDER THE WINGS OF THE GODDESS SINCE THE DAY OF HER BIRTH.
SOME CALL HER THE DIAMOND PRINCESS, FOR HER BEAUTY AND SELF-ASSURANCE COMMAND THE ABSOLUTE ADORATION OF THE PEOPLE.

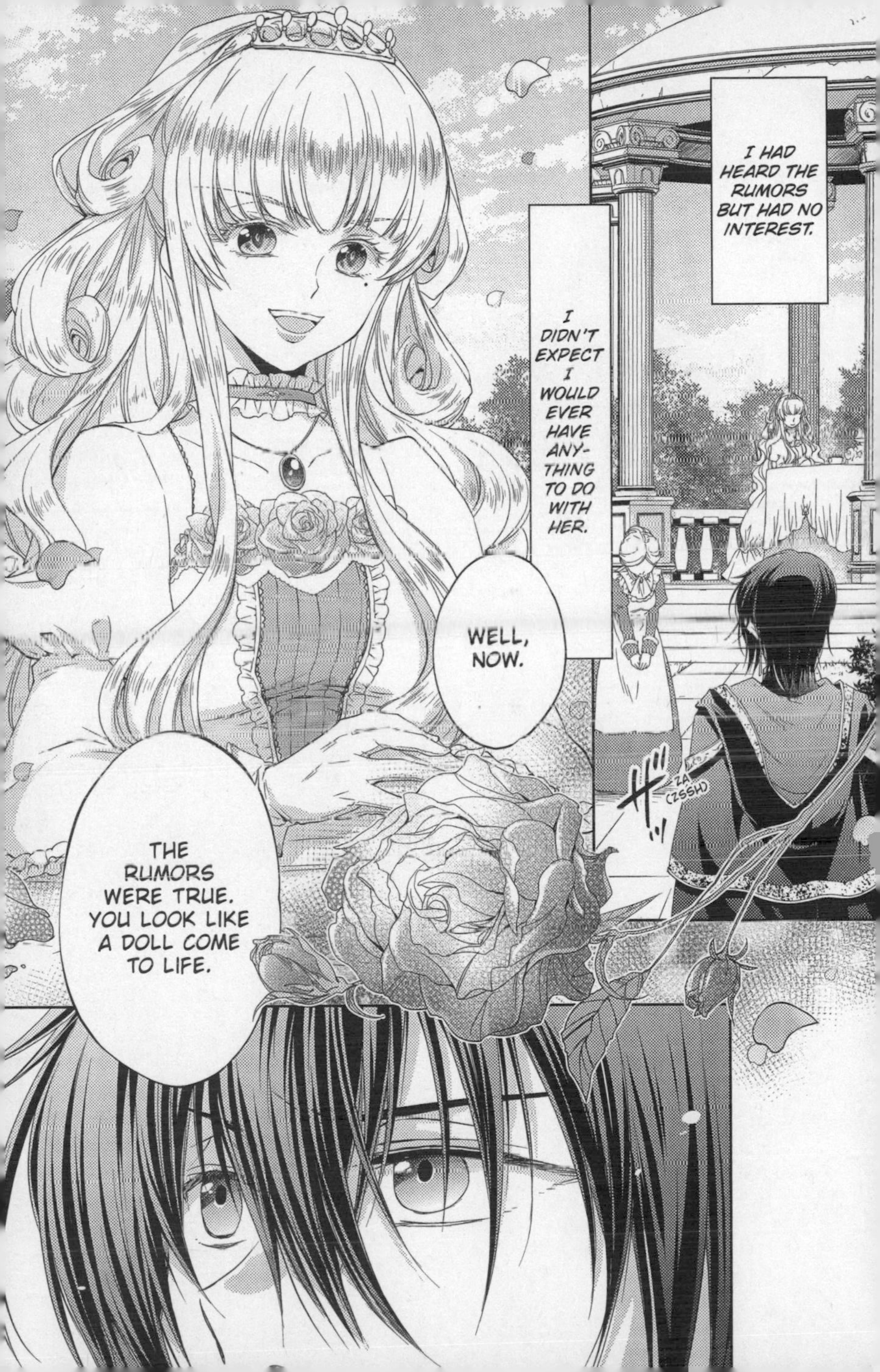
I HAD HEARD THE RUMORS BUT HAD NO INTEREST.
I DIDN'T EXPECT I WOULD EVER HAVE ANYTHING TO DO WITH HER.
ZA (ZSSH)
WELL, NOW.
THE RUMORS WERE TRUE. YOU LOOK LIKE A DOLL COME TO LIFE.

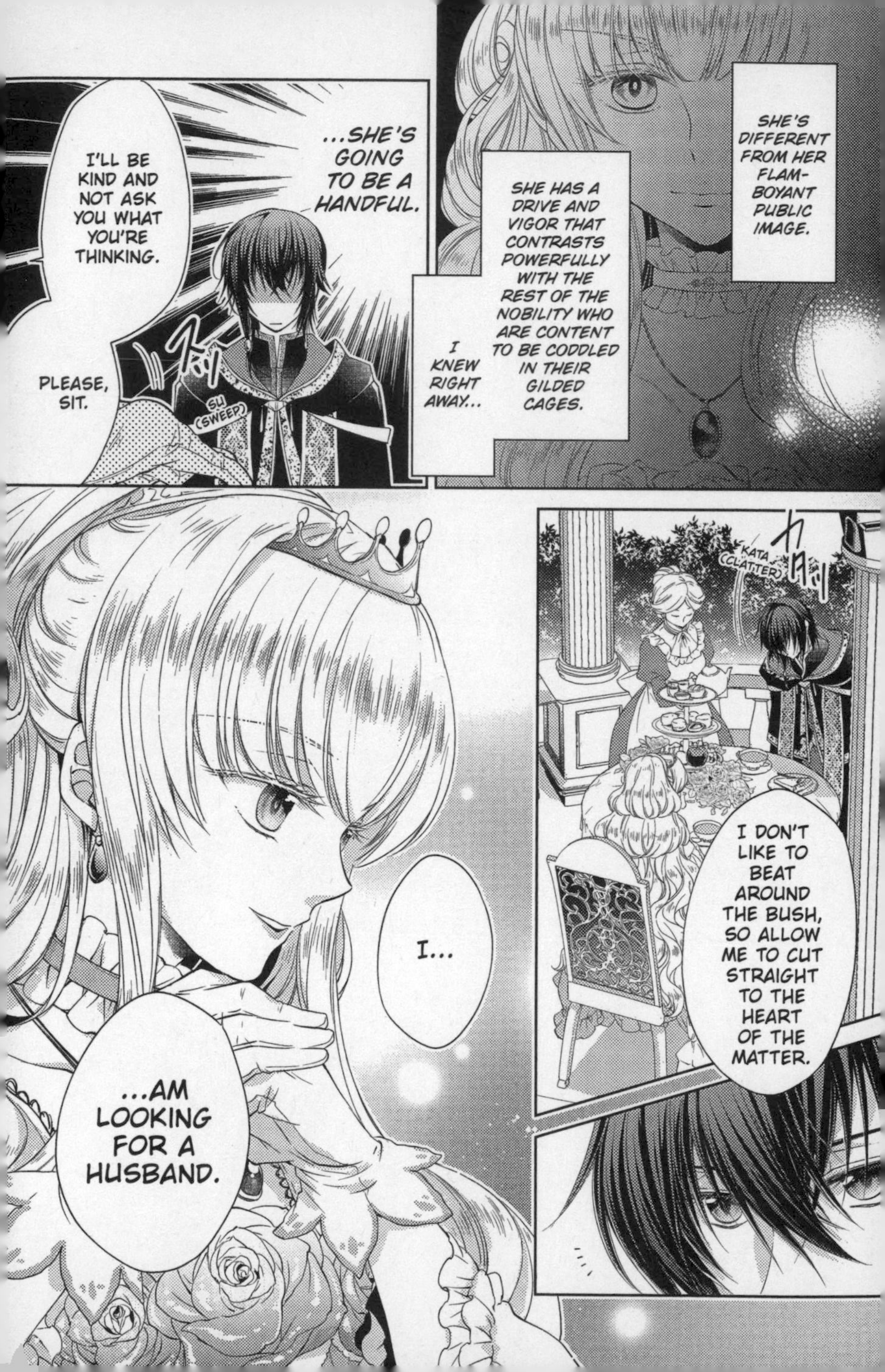
SHE'S DIFFERENT FROM HER FLAM-BOYANT PUBLIC IMAGE.
SHE HAS A DRIVE AND VIGOR THAT CONTRASTS POWERFULLY WITH THE REST OF THE NOBILITY WHO ARE CONTENT TO BE CODDLED IN THEIR GILDED CAGES.
I KNEW RIGHT AWAY...
...SHE'S GOING TO BE A HANDFUL.
I'LL BE KIND AND NOT ASK YOU WHAT YOU'RE THINKING.
SU (SWEEP)
PLEASE, SIT.
KATA (CLATTER)
I DON'T LIKE TO BEAT AROUND THE BUSH, SO ALLOW ME TO CUT STRAIGHT TO THE HEART OF THE MATTER.
...
I...
...AM LOOKING FOR A HUSBAND.

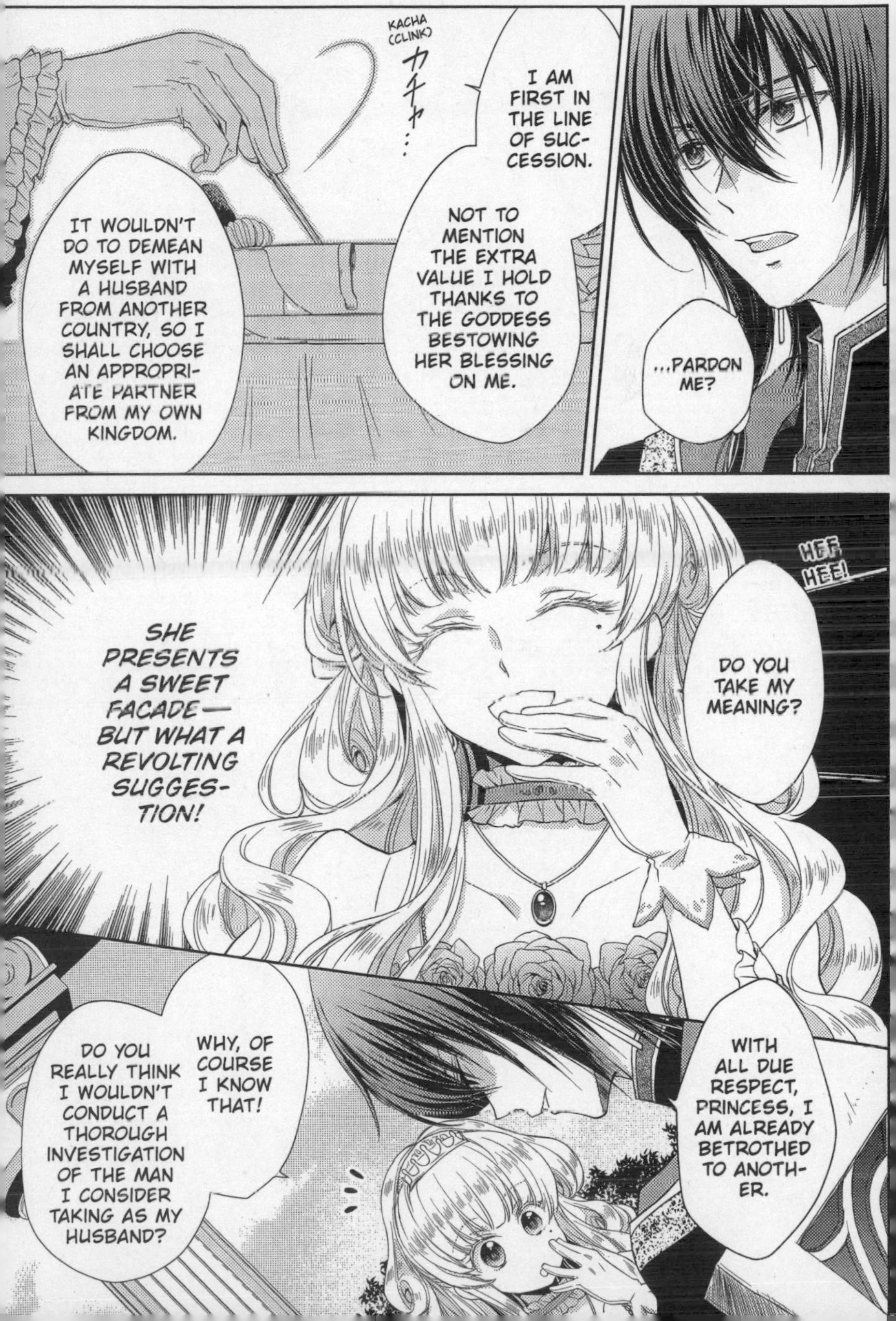
...PARDON ME?
KACHA (CLINK)
カチャ…
I AM FIRST IN THE LINE OF SUC-CESSION.
NOT TO MENTION THE EXTRA VALUE I HOLD THANKS TO THE GODDESS BESTOWING HER BLESSING ON ME.
IT WOULDN'T DO TO DEMEAN MYSELF WITH A HUSBAND FROM ANOTHER COUNTRY, SO I SHALL CHOOSE AN APPROPRI-ATE PARTNER FROM MY OWN KINGDOM.
HEE HEE!
DO YOU TAKE MY MEANING?
SHE PRESENTS A SWEET FACADE— BUT WHAT A REVOLTING SUGGES-TION!
WITH ALL DUE RESPECT, PRINCESS, I AM ALREADY BETROTHED TO ANOTH-ER.
WHY, OF COURSE I KNOW THAT!
DO YOU REALLY THINK I WOULDN'T CONDUCT A THOROUGH INVESTIGATION OF THE MAN I CONSIDER TAKING AS MY HUSBAND?

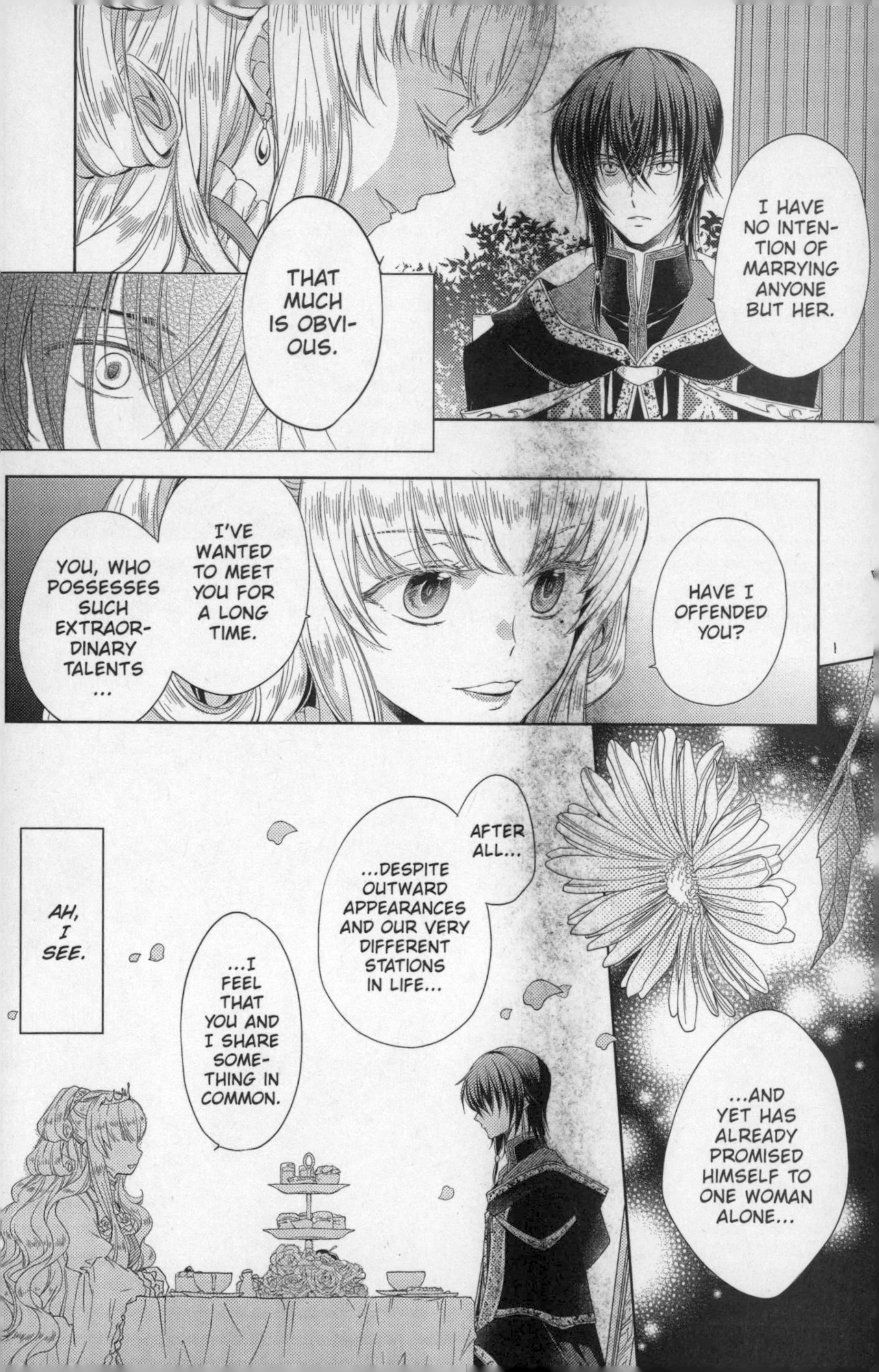
I HAVE NO INTEN-TION OF MARRYING ANYONE BUT HER.
THAT MUCH IS OBVI-OUS.
HAVE I OFFENDED YOU?
I'VE WANTED TO MEET YOU FOR A LONG TIME.
YOU, WHO POSSESSES SUCH EXTRAOR-DINARY TALENTS...
...AND YET HAS ALREADY PROMISED HIMSELF TO ONE WOMAN ALONE...
AFTER ALL...
...DESPITE OUTWARD APPEARANCES AND OUR VERY DIFFERENT STATIONS IN LIFE...
...I FEEL THAT YOU AND I SHARE SOME-THING IN COMMON.
AH, I SEE.

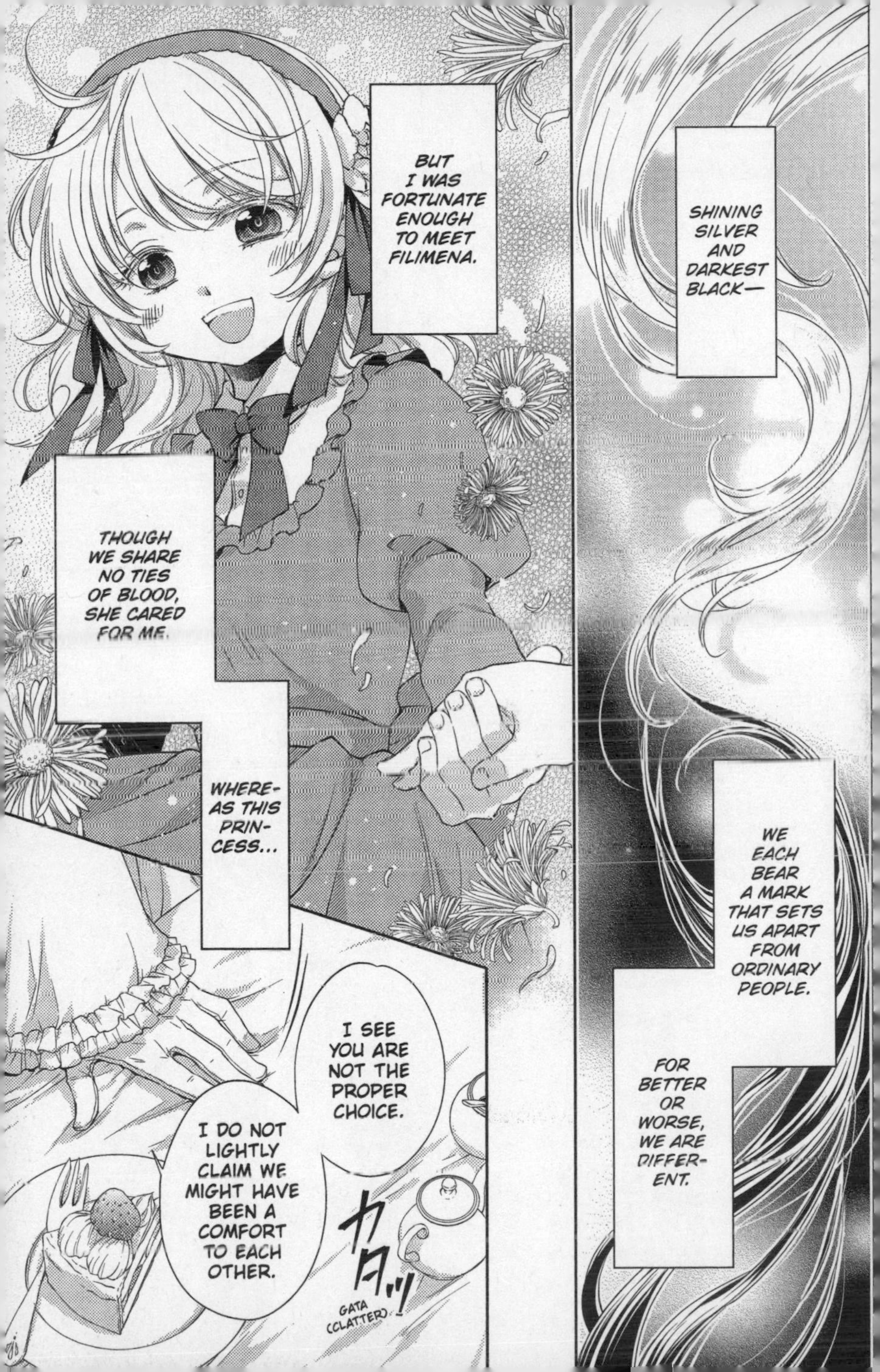
SHINING SILVER AND DARKEST BLACK—
WE EACH BEAR A MARK THAT SETS US APART FROM ORDINARY PEOPLE.
FOR BETTER OR WORSE, WE ARE DIFFER-ENT.
BUT I WAS FORTUNATE ENOUGH TO MEET FILIMENA.
THOUGH WE SHARE NO TIES OF BLOOD, SHE CARED FOR ME.
WHERE-AS THIS PRIN-CESS...
I SEE YOU ARE NOT THE PROPER CHOICE.
I DO NOT LIGHTLY CLAIM WE MIGHT HAVE BEEN A COMFORT TO EACH OTHER.
カタッ!
GATA (CLATTER)

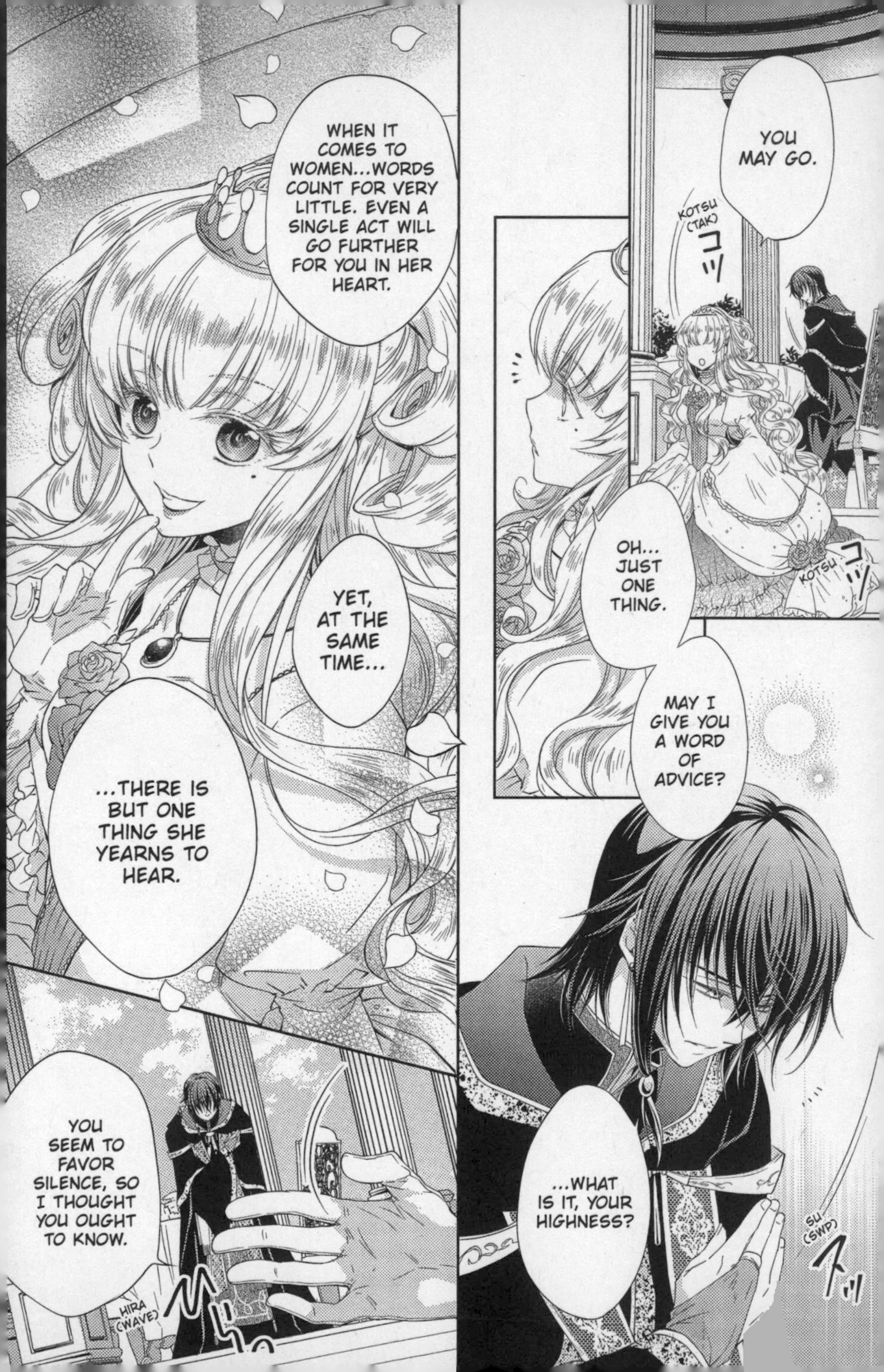
YOU MAY GO.
KOTSU (TAK) コツ
KOTSU コツ
OH... JUST ONE THING.
MAY I GIVE YOU A WORD OF ADVICE?
...WHAT IS IT, YOUR HIGHNESS?
SU (SWP) スッ
WHEN IT COMES TO WOMEN...WORDS COUNT FOR VERY LITTLE. EVEN A SINGLE ACT WILL GO FURTHER FOR YOU IN HER HEART.
YET, AT THE SAME TIME...
...THERE IS BUT ONE THING SHE YEARNS TO HEAR.
YOU SEEM TO FAVOR SILENCE, SO I THOUGHT YOU OUGHT TO KNOW.
HIRA (WAVE)

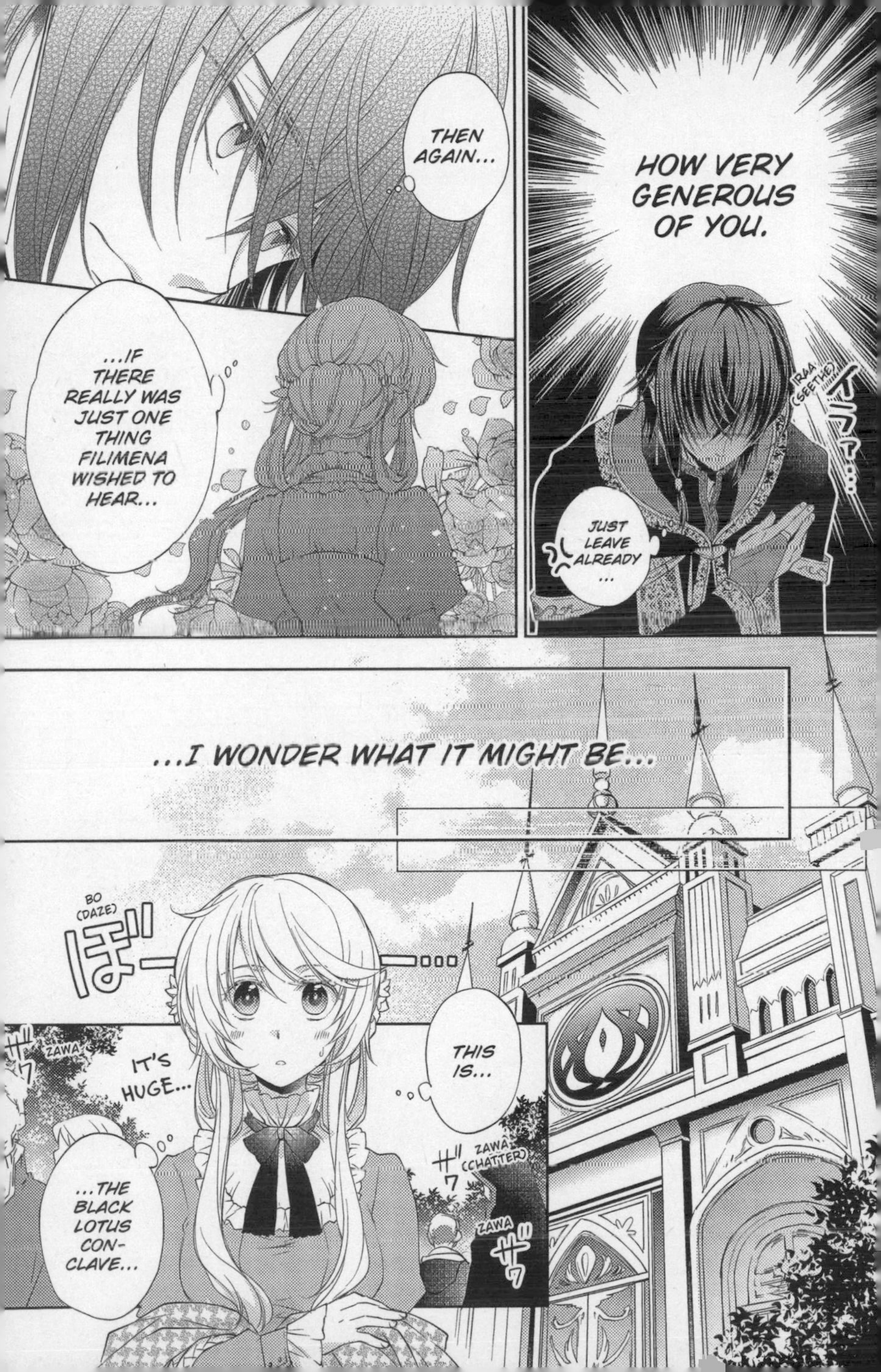
HOW VERY GENEROUS OF YOU.
IRAA (SEETHE)
JUST LEAVE ALREADY...
THEN AGAIN...
...IF THERE REALLY WAS JUST ONE THING FILIMENA WISHED TO HEAR...
...I WONDER WHAT IT MIGHT BE...
BO (DAZE)
THIS IS...
ZAWA (CHATTER)
ZAWA
IT'S HUGE...
ZAWA
...THE BLACK LOTUS CONCLAVE...

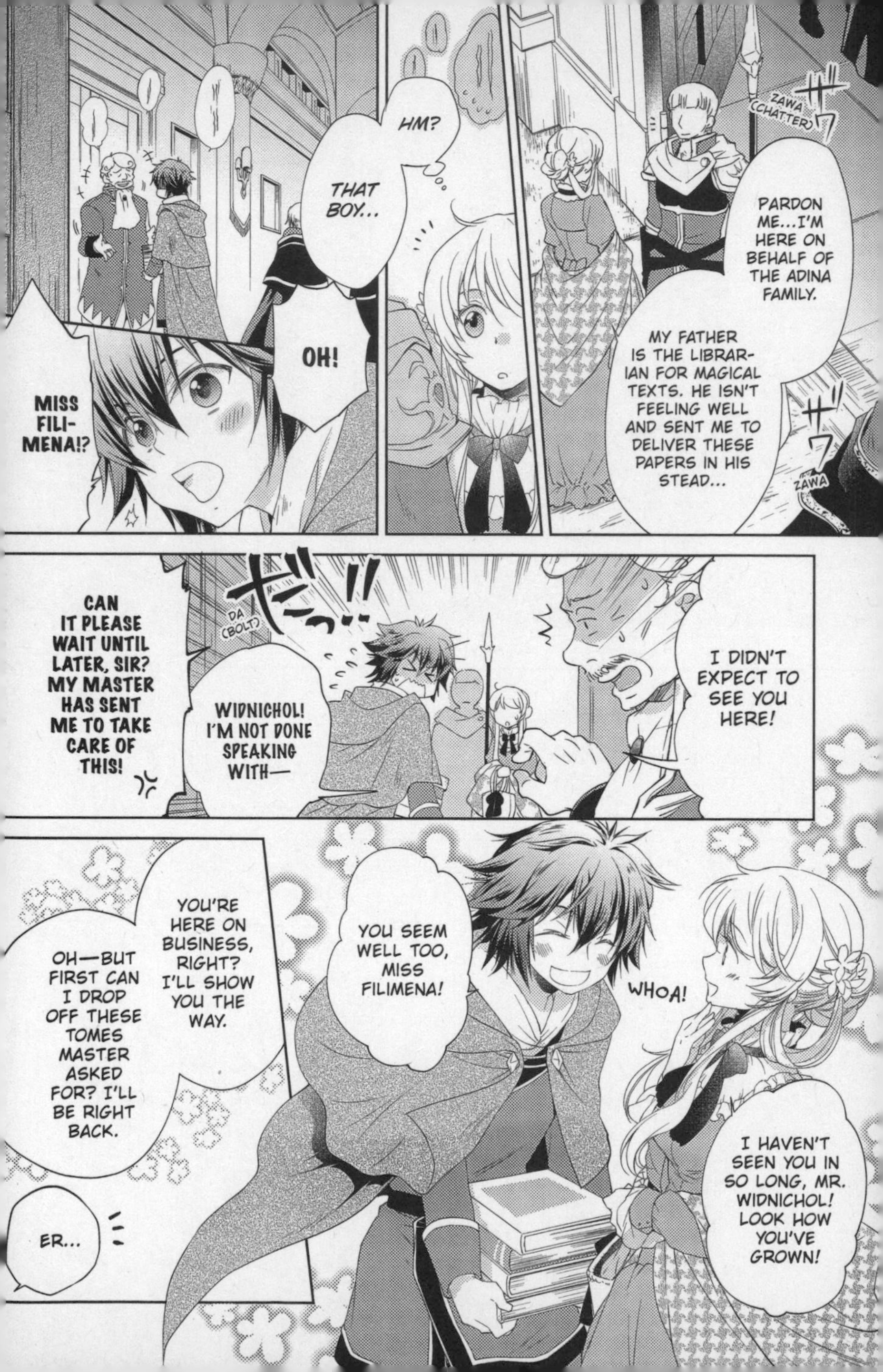
ZAWA (CHATTER)
PARDON ME...I'M HERE ON BEHALF OF THE ADINA FAMILY.
MY FATHER IS THE LIBRARIAN FOR MAGICAL TEXTS. HE ISN'T FEELING WELL AND SENT ME TO DELIVER THESE PAPERS IN HIS STEAD...
ZAWA
HM?
THAT BOY...
OH!
MISS FILIMENA!?
I DIDN'T EXPECT TO SEE YOU HERE!
DA (BOLT)
WIDNICHOL! I'M NOT DONE SPEAKING WITH—
CAN IT PLEASE WAIT UNTIL LATER, SIR? MY MASTER HAS SENT ME TO TAKE CARE OF THIS!
WHOA!
I HAVEN'T SEEN YOU IN SO LONG, MR. WIDNICHOL! LOOK HOW YOU'VE GROWN!
YOU SEEM WELL TOO, MISS FILIMENA!
YOU'RE HERE ON BUSINESS, RIGHT? I'LL SHOW YOU THE WAY.
OH—BUT FIRST CAN I DROP OFF THESE TOMES MASTER ASKED FOR? I'LL BE RIGHT BACK.
ER...

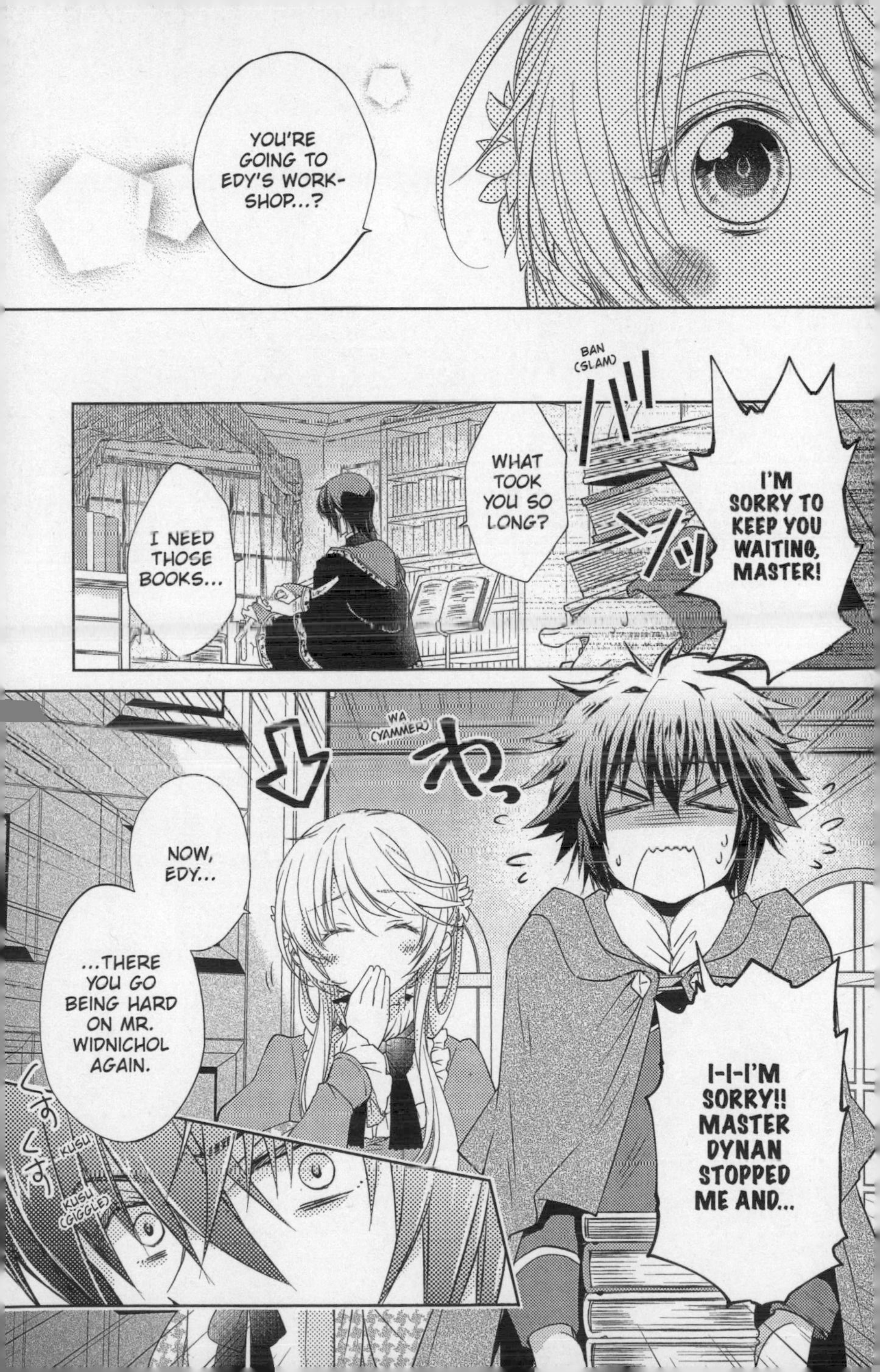
YOU'RE GOING TO EDY'S WORK-SHOP...?
BAN (SLAM)
バッ
I'M SORRY TO KEEP YOU WAITING, MASTER!
WHAT TOOK YOU SO LONG?
I NEED THOSE BOOKS...
WA (YAMMER)
わっ
I-I-I'M SORRY!! MASTER DYNAN STOPPED ME AND...
NOW, EDY...
...THERE YOU GO BEING HARD ON MR. WIDNICHOL AGAIN.
くすくす
KUSU KUSU (GIGGLE)

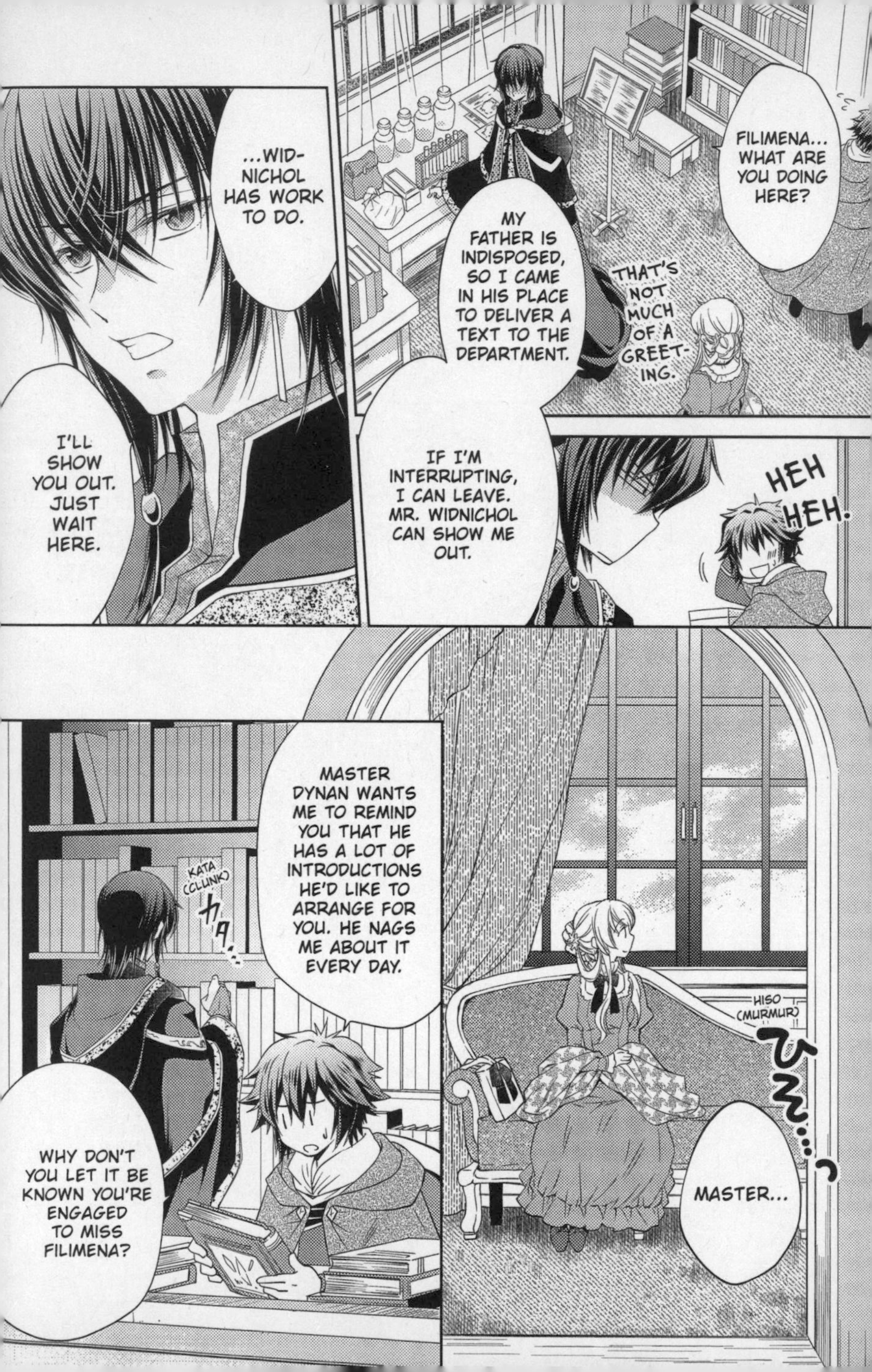
FILIMENA... WHAT ARE YOU DOING HERE?
THAT'S NOT MUCH OF A GREETING.
MY FATHER IS INDISPOSED, SO I CAME IN HIS PLACE TO DELIVER A TEXT TO THE DEPARTMENT.
HEH HEH.
IF I'M INTERRUPTING, I CAN LEAVE. MR. WIDNICHOL CAN SHOW ME OUT.
...WID-NICHOL HAS WORK TO DO.
I'LL SHOW YOU OUT. JUST WAIT HERE.
HISO (MURMUR)
ひそ…
MASTER...
MASTER DYNAN WANTS ME TO REMIND YOU THAT HE HAS A LOT OF INTRODUCTIONS HE'D LIKE TO ARRANGE FOR YOU. HE NAGS ME ABOUT IT EVERY DAY.
KATA (CLUNK)
カタ…
WHY DON'T YOU LET IT BE KNOWN YOU'RE ENGAGED TO MISS FILIMENA?

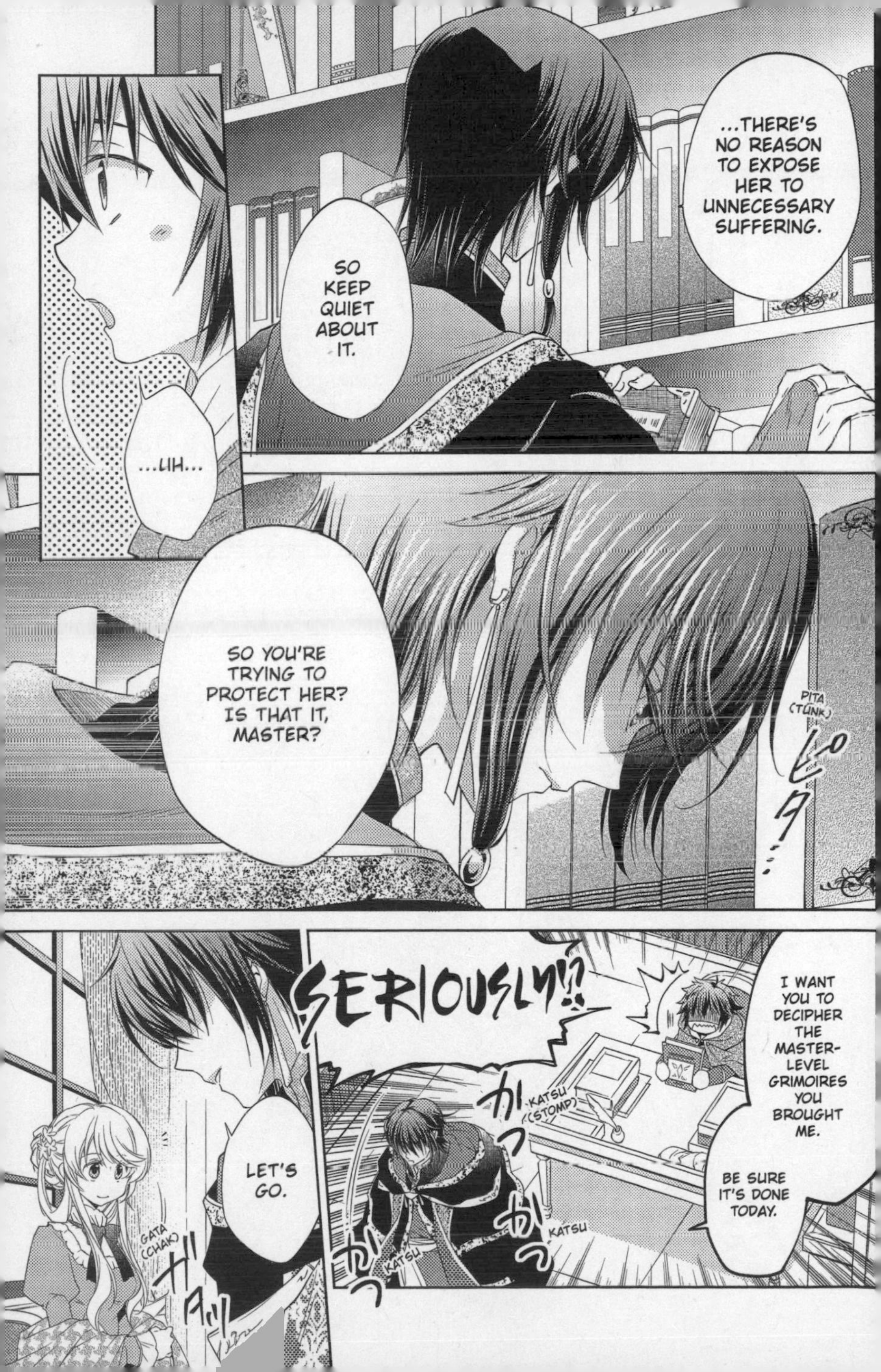
...THERE'S NO REASON TO EXPOSE HER TO UNNECESSARY SUFFERING.
SO KEEP QUIET ABOUT IT.
...UH...
PITA (TUNK)
SO YOU'RE TRYING TO PROTECT HER? IS THAT IT, MASTER?
I WANT YOU TO DECIPHER THE MASTER-LEVEL GRIMOIRES YOU BROUGHT ME.
BE SURE IT'S DONE TODAY.
SERIOUSLY!?
KATSU (STOMP)
KATSU
KATSU
LET'S GO.
GATA (CHAK)

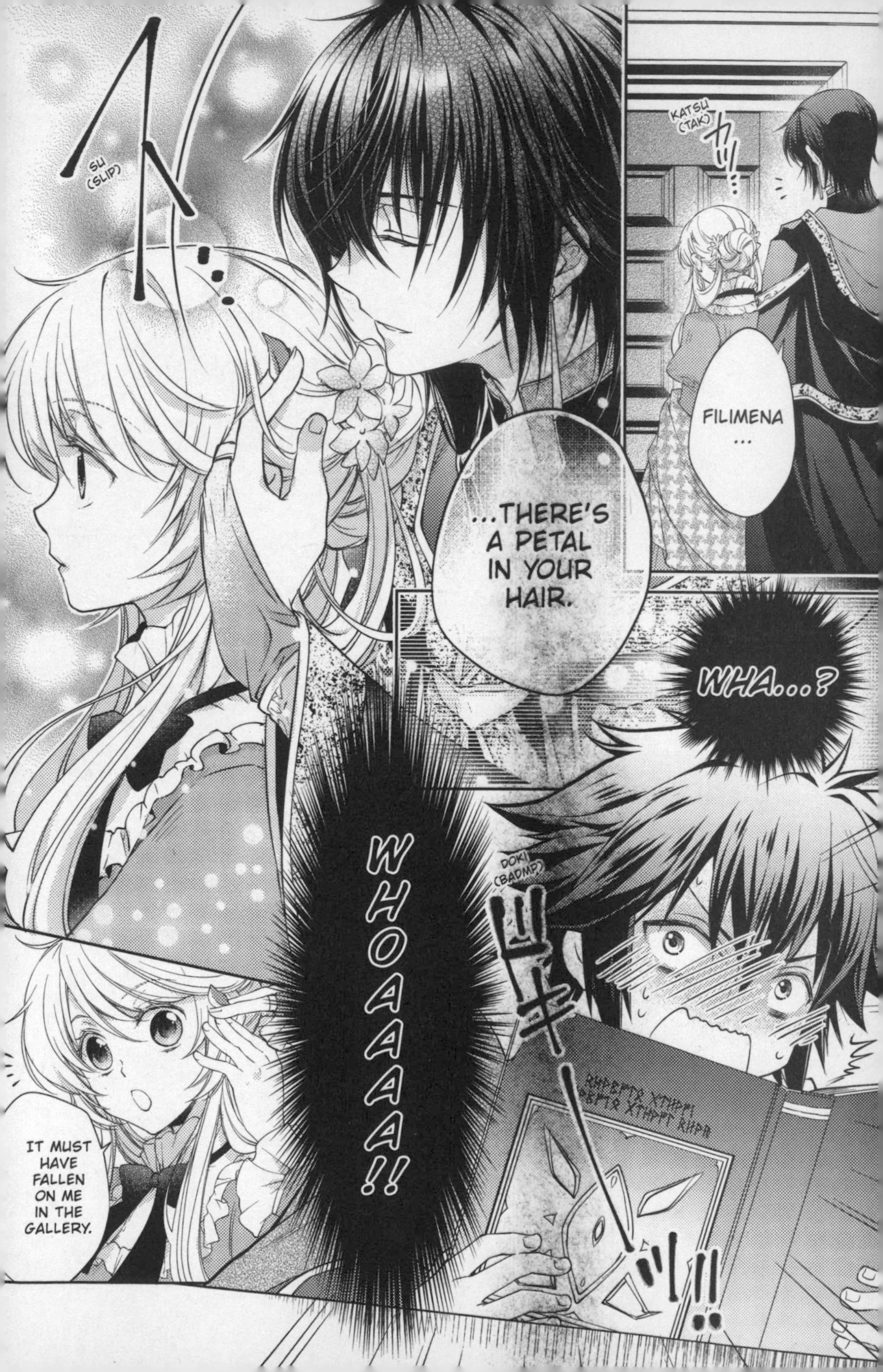
KATSU (TAK)
FILIMENA ...
SU (SLIP)
...THERE'S A PETAL IN YOUR HAIR.
WHA...?
DOKI (BADMP)
WHOAAAAA!!
IT MUST HAVE FALLEN ON ME IN THE GALLERY.

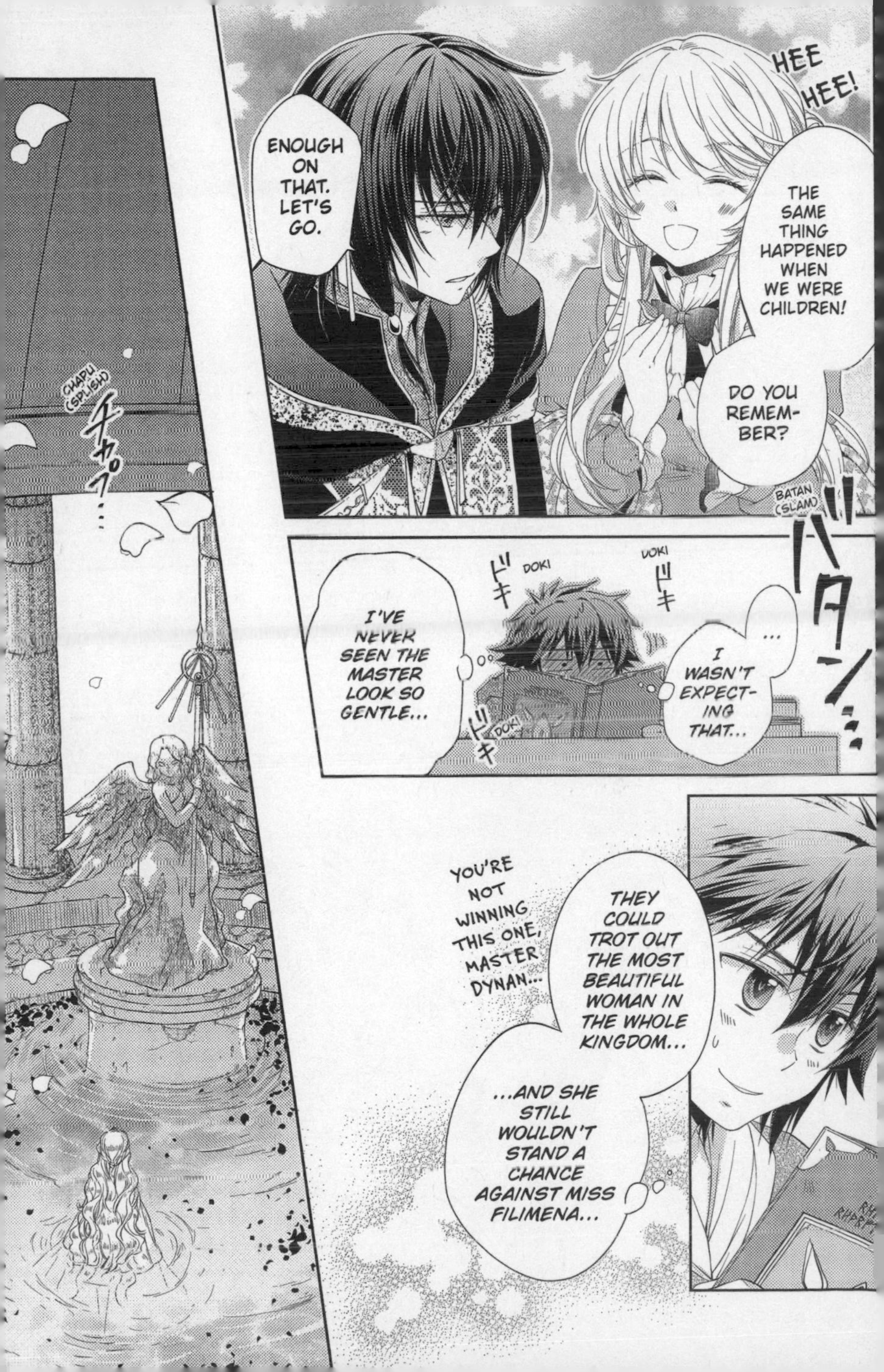
HEE HEE!
THE SAME THING HAPPENED WHEN WE WERE CHILDREN!
DO YOU REMEM-BER?
ENOUGH ON THAT. LET'S GO.
BATAN (SLAM)
... I WASN'T EXPECT-ING THAT...
DOKI
DOKI
I'VE NEVER SEEN THE MASTER LOOK SO GENTLE...
DOKI
THEY COULD TROT OUT THE MOST BEAUTIFUL WOMAN IN THE WHOLE KINGDOM...
...AND SHE STILL WOULDN'T STAND A CHANCE AGAINST MISS FILIMENA...
YOU'RE NOT WINNING THIS ONE, MASTER DYNAN...
CHAPU (SPLISH)

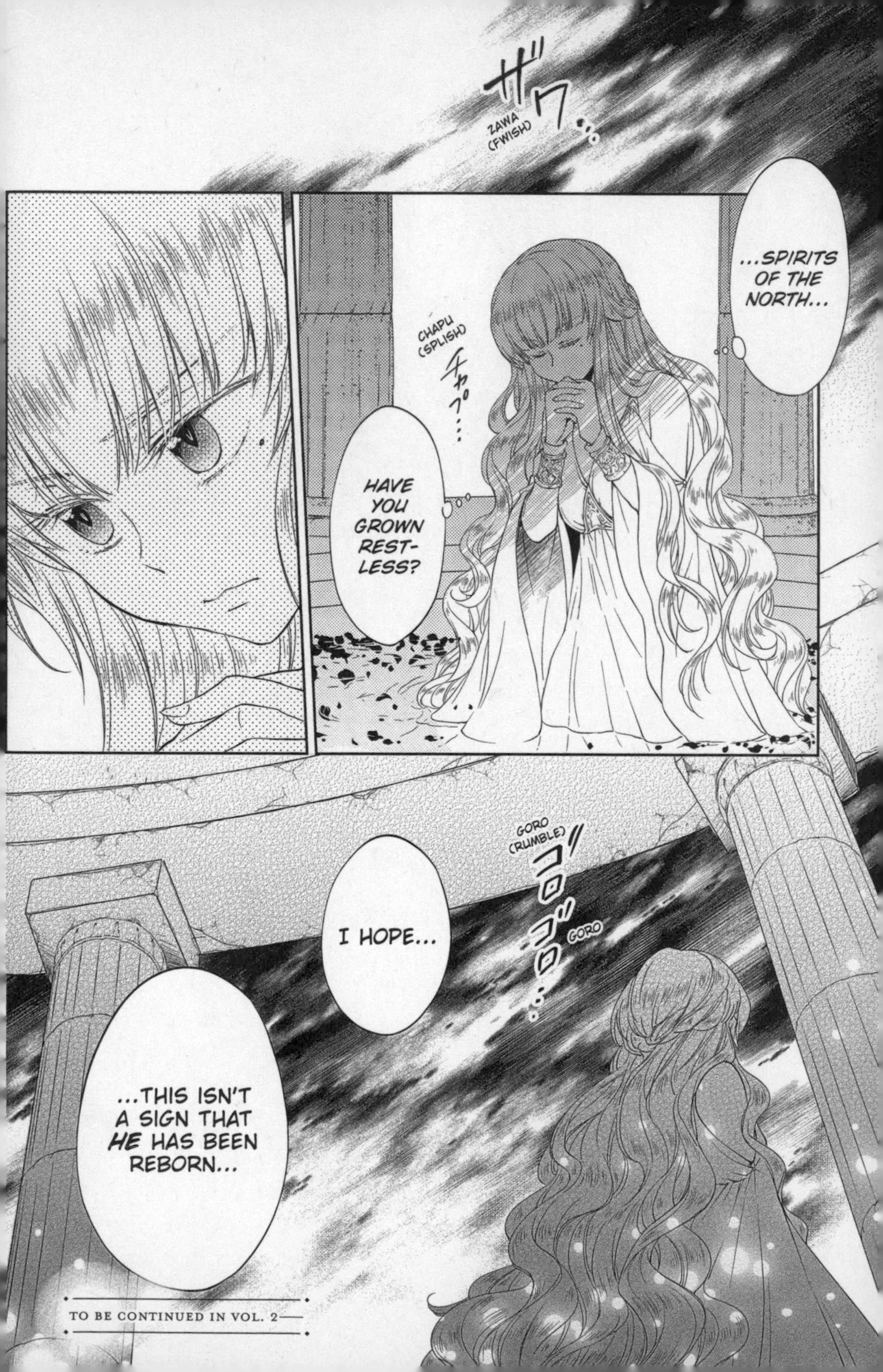
ザワ…
ZAWA (FWISH)
…SPIRITS OF THE NORTH…
CHAPU (SPLISH)
チャプ…
HAVE YOU GROWN RESTLESS?
GORO (RUMBLE)
ゴロゴロ…
GORO
I HOPE…
…THIS ISN'T A SIGN THAT ***HE*** HAS BEEN REBORN…

TO BE CONTINUED IN VOL. 2—

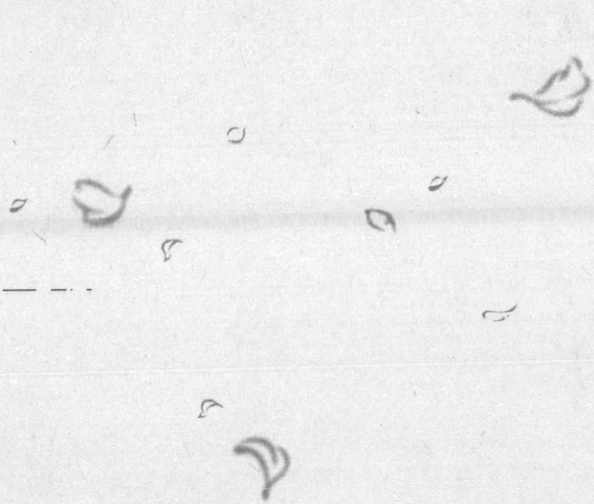

FIANCÉE OF THE WIZARD

ORIGINAL AUTHOR'S AFTERWORD

Volume 1 is now on sale—congratulations!
As both the author of the original novel and as a reader, this fills me with happiness. I can't begin to express my gratitude to Kazuka-sensei, who wove the story together so beautifully, and to you, the readers, who have picked up this book. It's got a little bit of a different flavor from the novel, so I hope you will enjoy this world of *Fiancée of the Wizard* too.

Syuri Nakamura

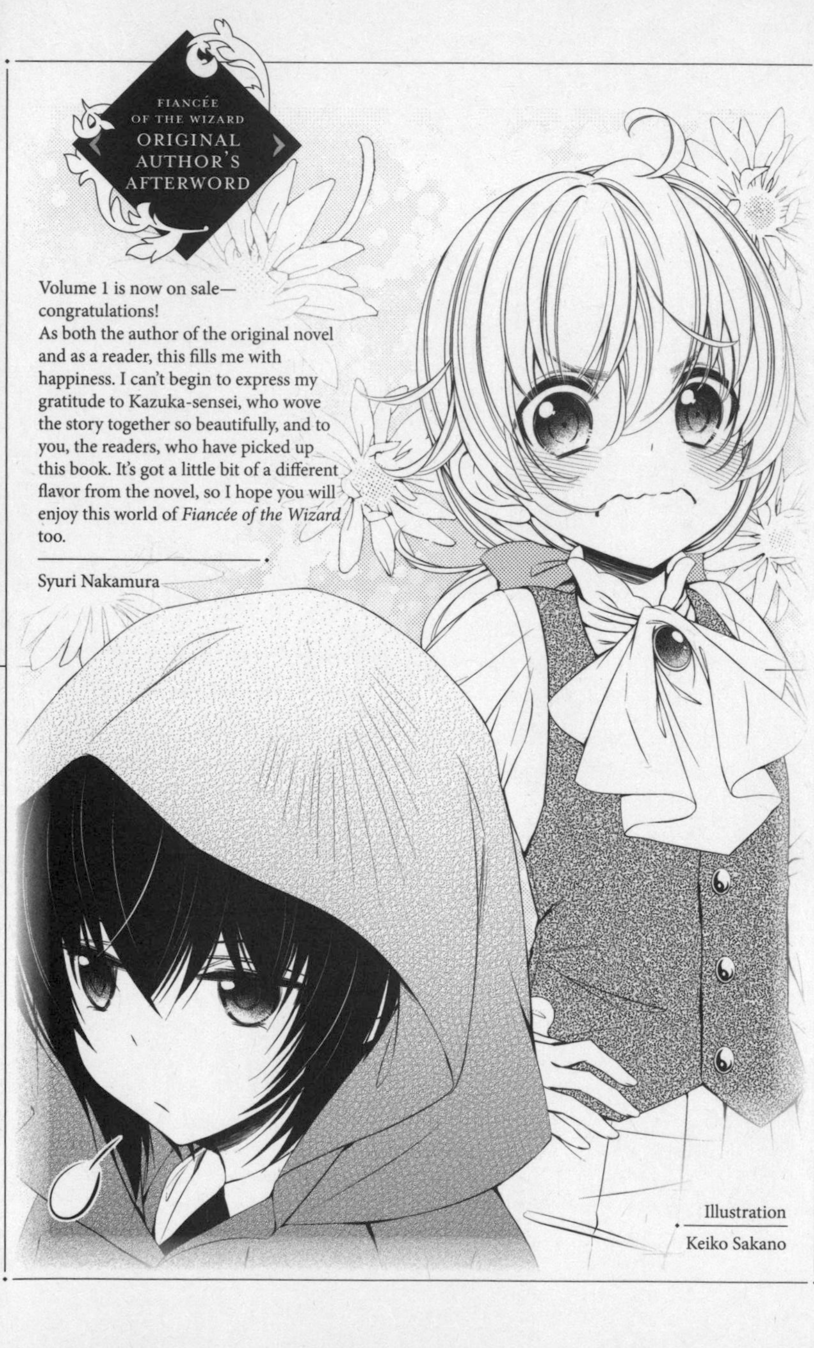

Illustration

Keiko Sakano

FIANCÉE OF THE WIZARD

ARTIST'S AFTERWORD

Thank you for reading Volume 1 of *Fiancée of the Wizard.*

As I was laying out the pages, I tried my best to convey the essence of Nakamura-sensei's delightful characters and jewellike vignettes from her novel in comics form. I would love for people who have read the novel to have a little fun recognizing "Oh! This is that part of the story!" I hope you'll stick with us to watch Filimena and Edy's relationship weather the events of their world, maddeningly unable to tell each other how they truly feel.

Masaki Kazuka

Production Help

Tana-sama
Tomomi Mizuna-sama
Yuno Aoi-sama
Cherry-sama

Editors

K-sama, N-sama

Thank you so much!

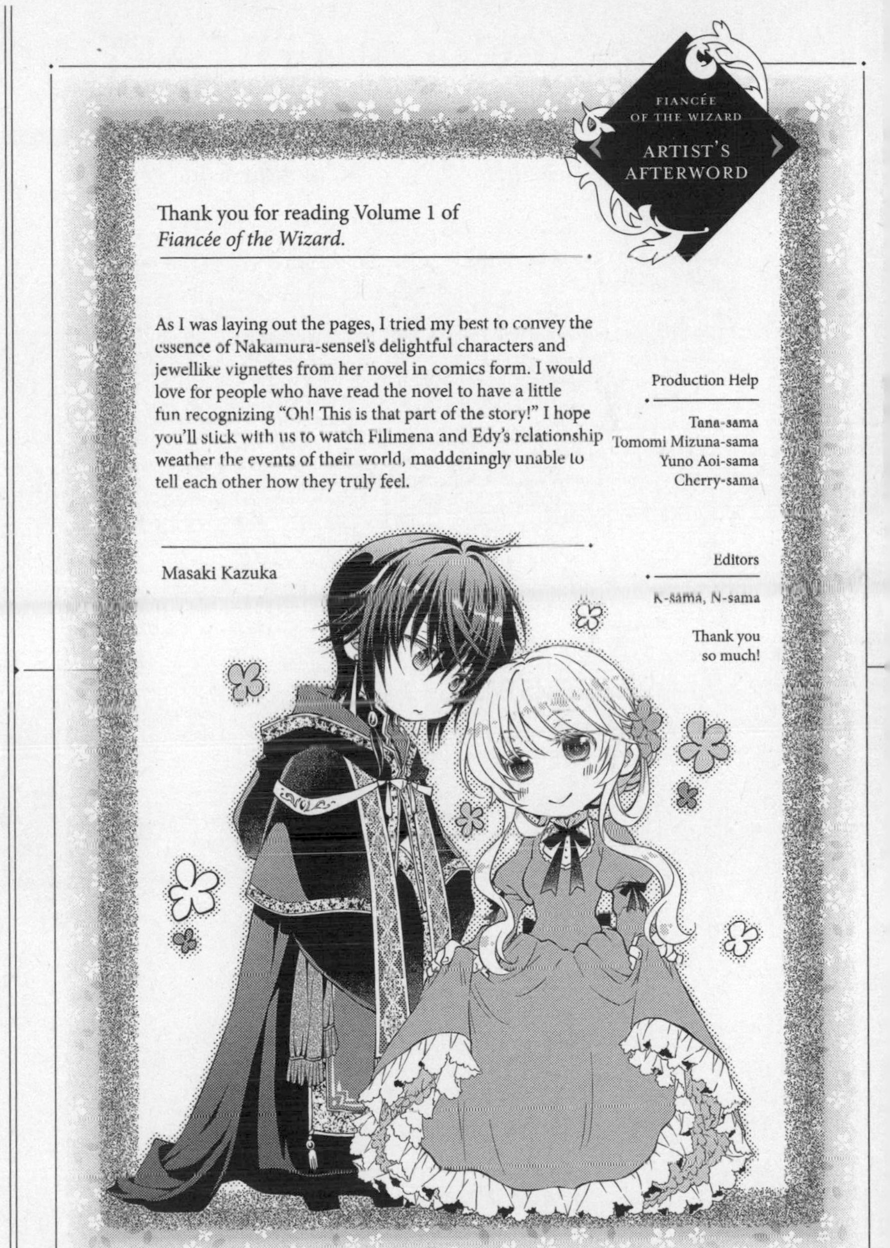

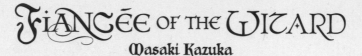

FIANCÉE OF THE WIZARD

Masaki Kazuka

ORIGINAL STORY
Syuri Nakamura ◇ I ◇ CHARACTER DESIGN
Keiko Sakano

Translation: Karen McGillicuddy ❧ Lettering: Elizabeth Kolkman

MAHOTSUKAI NO KONYAKUSHA vol. 1
© Masaki Kazuka 2018
© Syuri Nakamura, Keiko Sakano 2018
First published in Japan in 2018 by KADOKAWA CORPORATION, Tokyo.
English translation rights arranged with KADOKAWA CORPORATION, Tokyo
and Yen Press, LLC through Tuttle-Mori Agency, Inc.

English translation © 2020 by Yen Press, LLC

Yen Press
150 West 30th Street, 19th Floor
New York, NY 10001

Visit us at yenpress.com ❧ facebook.com/yenpress
twitter.com/yenpress ❧ yenpress.tumblr.com
instagram.com/yenpress

First Yen Press Edition: August 2020

Yen Press is an imprint of Yen Press, LLC.
The Yen Press name and logo are trademarks of Yen Press, LLC.

Library of Congress Control Number: 2020937472

ISBNs: 978-1-9753-1491-0 (paperback)
978-1-9753-1492-7 (ebook)

10 9 8 7 6 5 4 3 2 1

BVG

Printed in the United States of America

SUFFERING A TRAGIC ACCIDENT AND FINDING ONESELF REBORN IN A FANTASY WORLD—

WOULD THIS LIFE BE ONE OF A HERO? A PRINCESS? IT FEELS LIKE YOU HAVE THE CHEAT KEY TO BECOMING THE CHOSEN ONE.

A CHANCE EVERYONE DREAMS OF.

CHAPTER 1

TRACES OF MEMORY

BUT THAT ROLE WASN'T FOR THIS NEW ME...

BY SOME TRICK OF FATE, IT INSTEAD FELL TO THE MAN WHO WOULD (SUPPOSEDLY) STAND BY MY SIDE.

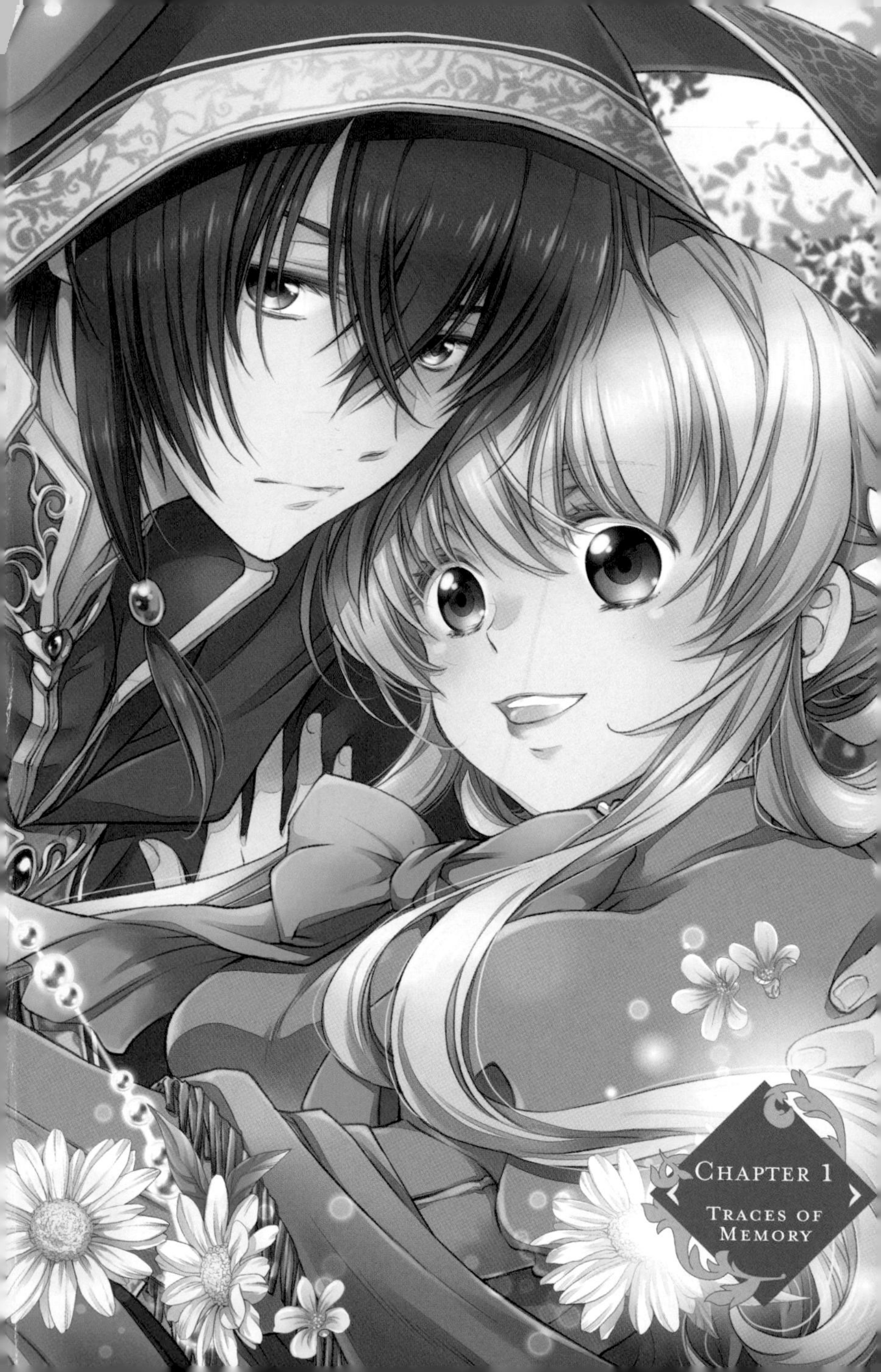
Chapter 1
Traces of Memory